Development AND Underdevelopment

FOURTH EDITION

Development AND Underdevelopment

The Political Economy of Global Inequality

EDITED BY
Mitchell A. Seligson and
John T Passé-Smith

LYNNE
RIENNER
PUBLISHERS

BOULDER
LONDON

Published in the United States of America in 2008 by
Lynne Rienner Publishers, Inc.
1800 30th Street, Boulder, Colorado 80301
www.rienner.com

and in the United Kingdom by
Lynne Rienner Publishers, Inc.
3 Henrietta Street, Covent Garden, London WC2E 8LU

Library of Congress Cataloging-in-Publication Data
Development and underdevelopment : the political economy of global inequality /
edited by Mitchell A. Seligson and John T Passé-Smith. — 4th ed.
    p. cm.
  Includes bibliographical references and index.
  ISBN 978-1-58826-584-5 (pbk. : alk. paper)
  1. Developing countries—Economic conditions. 2. Economic development.
3. Income distribution. 4. Capitalism. 5. Economic history—1945– .
6. Social history—1945– . I. Seligson, Mitchell A. II. Passé-Smith, John T.
  HC59.7.D4453   2008
  338.9—dc22

                                                        2008004522

British Cataloguing in Publication Data
A Cataloguing in Publication record for this book
is available from the British Library.

Printed and bound in the United States of America

♻   Printed on 30% postconsumer recycled paper

∞   The paper used in this publication meets the requirements
    of the American National Standard for Permanence of
    Paper for Printed Library Materials Z39.48-1992.

    5 4 3 2 1

For Amber Levanon Seligson,
with love and admiration

and

For Shirley Elizabeth Smith,
with love and respect

CONTENTS

PREFACE

THE WORLD IS NOT AT PEACE. INVASIONS, CIVIL WARS, AND BORDER CONFLICTS ARE in the news every day. Horrific photos of mutilation and death greet us at the breakfast table along with our morning newspaper. Many have thought that the ending of the East-West conflict would eliminate world conflicts generally. Some saw the end of the Cold War as "the end of history." Sadly, our experiences in the post–Cold War period have not met that expectation. Indeed, it seems as if the world is more unstable and conflict-prone than ever. Many of those conflicts revolve around issues of ethnic or religious difference, but a constant theme in armed conflicts worldwide is the struggle over resources and the wealth that goes with them. The yawning gaps in wealth that so sharply demarcate rich nations from poor, and rich people from poor people, seem to be a relentless promoter of conflict.

This book delves into the international gap in wealth between rich and poor nations and the domestic gap in wealth between rich and poor people. When did those gaps begin? What is their cause? How can they be narrowed? The answers to all of these vital questions can be found in this reader. It is a substantially revised version of its four predecessors, *The Gap Between Rich and Poor* (1984) and *Development and Underdevelopment: The Political Economy of Inequality* (1993; second edition, 1998; third edition, 2003).

Lynne Rienner was an editor when the idea for the first version emerged. She liked the concept and nursed it through the various stages of production. By the time the book had sold out, however, Lynne was the owner of her own academic press. She expressed interest in producing a revised version. We are deeply grateful for her faith in the enterprise, since with this new version we have now gone through five separate editions of this reader.

The original volume grew out of a seminar taught by Mitchell Seligson at the University of Arizona. In preparing for the seminar while on sabbatical at the University of Essex in England, he recognized that there was a great deal of research addressing the three questions posed above, and he attempted to organize that material for his students. Although there were a number of collections at the time that examined political and economic development, none directly addressed the questions he sought to answer. In addition, the then most recent theoretical and empirical research was absent from those volumes.

When the seminar was taught for the first time, the students attending helped refine the thinking that went into its separation. One of those students, John Passé-Smith, was so stimulated by the subject matter presented in the seminar that he wrote his doctoral dissertation on it. When Seligson was about to begin a sabbatical, Passé-Smith suggested that a new edition of the volume be produced, incorporating the latest scholarship on the problem of the dual gaps between rich and poor. Hence this collaborative effort emerged, with Seligson and Passé-Smith serving as coeditors for every edition after the first one.

In this revision we have sought to retain the classics included in the earlier editions of this book, but the field is so rapidly evolving that we felt we needed to update the book with more of the recent contributions to the literature. We also reorganized the volume so as to make its presentation more logical and easier for the student to grasp. As a result, of the thirty-three contributions to this edition, twenty appeared in one or more of the prior editions, and thirteen are new.

The present edition begins with a reorganized Part 1 that provides strong evidence of the international and domestic gaps between rich and poor. A new Part 2 has been added on the emergence of the international gap in wealth over the long term. These studies trace the gap back over centuries, even thousands of years, and attempt to explain when, where, and why it emerged.

Part 3, which focuses on the domestic gap between rich and poor, is similar to the prior edition. Part 4 focuses on the convergence thesis. It begins with W. W. Rostow's classic work on the stages of economic growth, which implies that eventually all countries will pass through these stages and become rich. It is then partially supported but partially refuted by William Baumol.

Part 5, on the impact of culture on development, which underwent a major revision in the previous edition, is presented here in largely the same form. The classic contributions of David McClelland, Lawrence Harrison, and Herman Kahn are retained, along with the recent empirical test of Jim Granato, Ronald Inglehart, and David Leblang.

Dependency and world systems theory is covered in Part 6. The classic piece by Andre Gunder Frank has been added, but the study of the Irish case and the Canadian case are retained from the previous edition. A study of transnational corporations has been added.

Part 7 focuses squarely on institutions, and opens with the fascinating "Big Bills Left on the Sidewalk," by Mancur Olson, which makes a strong case to the effect that poor countries are poor because they have bad institutions and policies. This argument is strengthened by a study of Mauritius. Part 7 also includes the classic work by Michael Lipton on urban bias and a newer work on the impact of democracy on growth by Adam Przeworski and Fernando Limongi. The section ends with a comparison of Latin America and Asia by Nancy Birdsall and Richard Sabot, retained from the third edition.

An entirely new section (Part 8) has been added on the impact of globalization. Here research by Anthony Giddens, Branko Milanovic, and the World Bank explains what globalization has meant for inequality. The book once again concludes with a summary chapter on directions for further research.

We have organized the volume so that it will be of maximum utility in the classroom. The parts of the book are ordered so as to enable the instructor to assign any one section as a self-contained unit. We find, however, that the order in which the parts are presented here makes a logical path that the student can easily follow. Parts 1–3 provide the basic "facts" of the gap: the size of the gap between rich and poor countries and the size of the gap between rich and poor people, and its origins. Parts 4–8 provide varied explanations of the gaps and their future trends.

We are indebted to numerous individuals for helping us prepare the revised manuscript for the publisher. Mary Sue Passé-Smith worked relentlessly and offered invaluable advice. This book would not have been completed without her help. Also, Brindon Mangiapane, a student at the University of Central Arkansas, worked many hours on the book, and his labor and advice are very much appreciated. Seligson's graduate assistant at Vanderbilt, Abby Córdova, made many helpful suggestions, as did students in his graduate seminars on "The Politics of Global Inequality." Finally, we would like to thank the many authors and publishers who so kindly granted permission for their works to appear here.

—*Mitchell A. Seligson and*
John T Passé-Smith

1

The Dual Gaps: An Overview of Theory and Research

MITCHELL A. SELIGSON

THERE IS THE OLD STORY ABOUT ECONOMISTS: PUT TWO OF THEM IN A ROOM AND ask for a prediction, and you will get three answers. So, too, it seems in the field of economic growth, and the problem is not just limited to economists, since political scientists, sociologists, anthropologists, geographers, and other social scientists have all expressed strikingly different explanations for the great gap between rich and poor, the subject of this volume. Fortunately, in this field at least, all is not chaos; there has been a growing consensus over the years about the nature of the gap, its causes, and consequences. In this volume, the reader will be able to detect this movement toward consensus, even though key issues remain unresolved.

One thing that has become very clear is that classical economic theory was wrong about the gap between rich nations and poor. As John Passé-Smith puts it so nicely, that theory suggested that "we will all be rich." This volume contains a great deal of evidence that contradicts that theory. According to W. W. Rostow's thesis (see Chapter 14 of this volume), underdevelopment is only a stage that nations pass through on their way to becoming developed. But the data we have at hand tell a different story. The income gap between rich and poor countries has grown dramatically since World War II. In 1950 the average per capita income (in 1980 US dollars) of low-income countries was $164, whereas the per capita income of the industrialized countries averaged $3,841, yielding an absolute income gap of $3,677. Thirty years later, in 1980, incomes in the poor countries had risen to an average of only $245, whereas those in the industrialized countries had soared to $9,648; the absolute gap in 1980 stood at $9,403.[1] For this period, then, there is clear evidence to support the old adage that "the rich get richer." It is not true, however, that the poor get poorer, not literally anyway, but that would be a perverse way of looking at these data. A more realistic view of the increases in "wealth" in the poor countries would show that in this thirty-year period their citizens increased their incomes by an

1

average of only $2.70 a year, less than what a North American might spend for lunch at a neighborhood fast-food restaurant. And in terms of relative wealth, the poor countries certainly did get poorer; the total income (gross national product, or GNP) of the high-income countries declined from 4.3 percent of the income earned by the industrialized countries in 1950 to a mere 2.5 percent by 1980.

The growth in the gap has continued on into the new century. By 2001 the gap was wider than ever, according to the World Bank. In that year the low-income countries averaged only $430 in gross national income in current dollars (GNI, the revised term for gross national product) while the high-income countries averaged $26,710, or a gap of $26,280! The relative gap had become even greater by 2001 than it was in 1980, with the income of the low-income countries equal to only 1.8 percent of that of the industrialized countries. In other words, since 1950 the relative gap between rich and poor countries had widened by 60 percent.[2] In the appendix of this book we provide the 2005 GNI per capita data, showing how the trend continues. The low-income countries have incomes that average $580 compared to the high-income country average of $35,131; by 2005, the poor were earning only 1.7 percent of the incomes of the rich.

One might suspect that these data do not reflect the general pattern of growth found throughout the world but may be excessively influenced by the disappointing performance of a few "basket case" nations. That suspicion is unfounded. The low-income countries comprise two-fifths of the world's population; 2.2 billion out of the world's 6.4 billion people live in countries with per capita incomes that average less than $600 a year.[3] It is also incorrect to speculate that because the growth rates of some poor countries have recently outperformed those of the industrialized countries, the gap will soon be narrowed. In Chapter 2, John Passé-Smith tells us that it could take Pakistan's 152 million people 1,152 years to close the gap. Even in the "miracle countries" such as China, where growth rates have been far higher than in the industrialized countries, the gap will take 64 years to close on the unrealistic assumption that China could maintain its present level of growth for many decades to come.

There is another gap separating rich from poor: many developing nations have long experienced a growing gap between their own rich and poor citizens, as the articles in Part 3 of this volume demonstrate. Many poor people who live in poor countries, therefore, are falling further behind not only the world's rich but also their more affluent countrymen. Moreover, precisely the opposite phenomenon has taken place within many (but not all) of the richer countries, where the gap between rich and poor is far narrower today than it was a century ago.[4] The world's poor, therefore, find themselves in double jeopardy.

The consequences of these yawning gaps can be witnessed every day. In the international arena, tensions between the "haves" and "have nots" dominate debate in the United Nations and other international fora. The poor countries demand a "New International Economic Order" (NIEO), which they hope will result in the transfer of wealth away from the rich countries, or at least stem the hemorrhage of the loss of their own wealth. The industrialized countries have responded with foreign aid programs that, by all accounts, have at best only made a small dent in the problem. Within the developing countries, domestic stability is frequently tenuous at best, as victims of the gap between rich and poor (along with their sympathizers) seek redress through violent means. The guerrilla fighting that spotted the globe during the Cold War may have been fueled by international conflict, but, as shown by Edward N. Muller and Mitchell A. Seligson in Chapter 13 of this volume, its root cause invariably can be traced to domestic inequality and deprivation, whether relative or absolute. This remains true in the post–Cold War era, and may well be, in the final analysis, the key cause of the rise of global terrorism.

Thinking and research on the international and domestic gaps between rich and poor have been going through a protracted period of debate that can be traced back to the end of World War II. The war elevated the United States to the position of world leader, and in that position the nation found itself confronted with a Western Europe in ruins. The motivations behind the Marshall Plan for rebuilding Europe are debated to this day, but two things remain evident: unprecedented amounts of aid were given, and the expected results were rapidly achieved. War-torn industries were rebuilt, new ones were begun, and economic growth quickly resumed. Similarly, Japan, devastated by conventional and nuclear attack, was able to rebuild its economy and become a world leader in high-technology industrial production.

The successful rebuilding of Europe and Japan encouraged many to believe that similar success would meet efforts to stimulate growth in the developing world. More often than not, however, such efforts have failed or fallen far below expectations. Even when programs have been effective and nations have seemed well on their way toward rapid growth, many of them nonetheless continued to fall farther and farther behind the wealthy countries. Moreover, growth almost inevitably seemed to be accompanied by a widening income gap within the developing countries. Only in Asia have we seen some reversal of this worldwide trend, where poor nations have grown rapidly while income inequality has not worsened and in some cases even improved. The lessons of Asia, therefore, are important ones. Thus, even well into the new century, the world is still confronted by what Paul Collier refers to as "The Bottom Billion."[5]

Over the years an impressive volume of research on explaining the "gap" question has been generated, and we have attempted to include some of the very best of it in this collection. The authors represented here present a wide-ranging treatment of the thinking that is evolving on the subject of the international and domestic gaps between rich and poor. Their studies are not confined to a single academic discipline or geographic area. Rather, their work reflects a variety of fields, including anthropology, economics, political science, psychology, and sociology, and they have examined the problems from the viewpoint of a single country or region as well as with a microanalytic approach.

The volume is organized to first present to the reader a broad picture defining the international and domestic gaps between the rich and the poor. This picture is contained in Part 1. Part 2 takes the long-term view, going back in some cases thousands of years to attempt to locate the point in time when the gap between rich and poor began. Part 3 looks at the domestic income inequality gap. Part 4 explores the classic explanation for closing the gap and the convergence/divergence thesis. The remaining parts of the volume, Parts 5 through 8, attempt to explain the existence of the gaps, with Part 5 looking at culture, Part 6 looking at dependency and world systems, Part 7 focusing on institutions, and Part 8 exploring the impact of globalization on the gap.

In Part 1, "Is There a Gap Between Rich and Poor Countries?" we present a broad overview of the facts of the international gap. The chapters in that section show that the gap between rich and poor countries is wide and growing. John Passé-Smith (Chapter 2) and Robert Hunter Wade (Chapter 3) show that even though some countries manage to narrow the gap, most do not. Glenn Firebaugh (Chapter 4) finds that in recent years the gap has neither grown nor shrunk but is remaining stable. These findings are robust even when the newer way of calculating per capita incomes, called purchasing power parity, is used as Passé-Smith shows in Chapter 5.

Part 2, "The Historical Origins of the Gap," takes the long-term view. Angus Maddison has collected the longest time series of world wealth of any scholar. He shows that the gap is anything but a recent phenomenon, but that it has widened a great deal since the 1800s. Jared Diamond (Chapter 7) takes even a longer-range view, looking back to the first *Homo sapiens*. Diamond's emphasis on geography, climate, and other natural conditions is disputed by two teams of scholars, whose studies are found in Chapters 8 and 9. The emphasis in this work is that institutions are what matter. The age of imperialism established different kinds of institutions among the colonized parts of the world; some focused on extraction of resources and others on building a more equitable community. According to the institutions arguments, conditions confronted by colonial settlers strongly determined the kinds of institutions that were put in place, and those institutions determined, over the centuries, the rate of economic growth.

Part 3, "The Other Gap: Domestic Income Inequality," examines domestic inequality. Simon Kuznets (Chapter 11) sees widening domestic income inequality as an almost inevitable by-product of development. He traces a path that seems to have been followed quite closely by nations that have become industrialized. The process begins with relative domestic equality in the distribution of income. The onset of industrialization produces a significant shift in the direction of inequality and creates a widening gap. Once the industrialization process matures, however, the gap is again reduced. This view was certainly held by those who still regard the Marshall Plan as the model for the resolution of world poverty. In Chapter 12 the policy implications of attempting to alter the "natural" distribution of income are discussed. In Chapter 13, Edward N. Muller and Mitchell A. Seligson show that domestic income inequality is linked to violence in the form of insurgency and therefore that there are real societal costs to pay beyond any ethical ones.

Whereas Parts 1, 2, and 3 of the book presents the basic argument on the extent and duration of the international and domestic gap, Part 4 examines the evidence for the so-called convergence thesis. This thesis argues that even though Kuznets may have been right, in the long run, rich and poor countries all will follow the same stages of growth. W. W. Rostow's classic work on the stages of economic growth (Chapter 14) leads to the conclusion that all countries will eventually converge. William Baumol reports on a study of countries over a 110-year period and finds that economies do converge. However, he notes that there is a "convergence club" and not all countries are "members." For those countries, convergence between rich and poor becomes an ever-receding dream. In the following chapter, J. Bradford De Long, however, criticizes the piece by Baumol, arguing that it is flawed by sample selection bias. When De Long corrects for the sample selection bias, convergence disappears.

Explanations for the gaps have often focused on different aspects of national culture. We have all heard the expression "Germans are so industrious, that is why they are rich," or "the Japanese work so hard, it is no wonder that they are so wealthy." Part 5 of this volume, "Culture and Development," presents evidence pro and con on the role of culture. Specifically, the cultural values associated with industrialization are seen as foreign to many developing nations, which apparently are deeply attached to more traditional cultural values. According to the cultural thesis, punctuality, hard work, achievement, and other "industrial" values are the keys to unlocking the economic potential of poor countries. Most adherents of this perspective believe that such values can be inculcated through deliberate effort. For example, this is the thesis of David McClelland in Chapter 17, who writes about the importance of high "N-Achievement" for growth. Lawrence E. Harrison has written extensively on this thesis, and in Chapter 18 he makes a broad case that values matter most in development. Others argue that the values will emerge naturally as the result of a worldwide process of diffusion of values functional for development. This perspective has been incorporated into a more general school of thought focusing on the process called "modernization." Development occurs and the international gap is narrowed when a broad set of modern values *and* institutions is present. The success of the Asian economies in recent years has led some to speculate that there are cultural values found there that foster growth. This view, a variant on Max Weber's classic notion of the value of the Protestant ethic, is termed the "Confucian ethic," as is shown in Herman Kahn's study (Chapter 19). Quantitative evidence for the importance of culture is presented in Chapter 20.

In marked contrast to the convergence theory and the cultural perspectives on the gap, which suggest that the phenomenon of rich and poor disparity can be transitory, a third school of thought comes to rather different conclusions. Part 6, "Dependency and World Systems Theory: Still Relevant?" looks at these two very important schools of thought. The scholars supporting this approach—known as *dependentistas*—observe that the economies of the developing nations have been shaped in response to forces and conditions established by the industrialized nations and that their development has been both delayed and dependent as a result. The *dependentistas* conclude that the failure of poor countries is a product of the distorted development brought on by dependency relations. In Part 6 the dependency and world-system perspectives are presented by the major writers in the field and refuted by others based on careful studies of large data sets. The classic article in the field by Andre Gunder Frank begins this section (Chapter 21). The case studies of Canada (Chapter 22) and Ireland (Chapter 23) suggest that dependency is a problem not only for the developing world but for some parts of the industrialized world as well. The section concludes with a look at transnational corporations and the claim that they slow the growth of developing countries (Chapter 24).

Part 7, "The Role of Institutions," presents the final and most recent explanation of the gaps, focusing attention on the role of states within the Third World. As socialist economies throughout the world proved incapable of keeping up with the capitalist industrialized countries, international development agencies focused their attention on the need for institutional and policy reforms within the Third World. This attention brought with it a host of neoliberal policy prescriptions, including privatization, trade liberalization, and the ending of import substitution industrialization (ISI) policies. The collapse of the Soviet Union and the socialist states of Eastern Europe, along with increasing capitalist economics in China, has reinforced this tendency. According to the perspective that focuses on institutions, errors of state policy are largely responsible for the gaps. This is the thesis argued by Mancur Olson Jr., whose "Big Bills Left on the Sidewalk (Chapter 25) has become a classic in the field. The role of good institutions and policies is nicely illustrated for the case of Mauritius by Arvind Subramanian in Chapter 26. One way these policies get distorted is as a result of "urban bias" (Chapter 27). From this perspective, there are numerous policies in the Third World that favor the cities over the countryside, with the result that growth is slowed and the gap between rich and poor nations widens.

Because of the dramatic increase in the number of democratic governments in recent years, the focus on states has raised concerns over the connection between democracy on the one hand and growth and inequality on the other. Some have argued that democratic political systems are less capable than their authoritarian counterparts of setting a clear economic agenda, whereas others have argued that democracies not only are good for growth but also are inherently egalitarian in nature and hence help reduce the domestic gap between rich and poor. The chapter by Adam Przeworski and Fernando Limongi (Chapter 28) presents the evidence in this debate. In contrast, Nancy Birdsall and Richard Sabot (Chapter 29) focus less on institutions and more on human capital, specifically education, as the key to growth.

Part 8, "The Impact of Globalization," is a new section of the book that presents three chapters on the impact of globalization on the two gaps. Anthony Giddens (Chapter 30) offers a definition of globalization and concludes that on balance, globalization reduces inequality. He asserts that while some members of the developing world have been left behind, others have participated in "reverse colonization" of the wealthier countries. Branko Milanovic (Chapter 31), in comparison, finds growing inequality but questions whether we should be concerned with levels of inequality or levels of actual poverty and consumption. He argues that globalization means that more people have access to cheap forms of communication and transportation and this could mean that poor people in poor countries are less satisfied with what they have because they are able to see what wealthier people possess. Finally, the World Bank's assessment of globalization (Chapter 32) is that the developing countries that have joined in globalization have experienced rapid economic growth with no systematic change in domestic inequality, resulting in a reduction in absolute poverty in these countries. Although the World Bank reports an overall decline in inequality, it notes that where divergence appears to be occurring, it is not the fault of globalization but the nonglobalizing developing countries that are experiencing the divergence.

The readers of this volume will come away from it with a clear sense of the causes of the gaps between the rich and poor. It is to be hoped that some of those readers might someday help in implementing the "cure."

Notes

1. These figures are based on the World Bank's *World Development Report 1980* (New York: Oxford University Press, 1980), 34.

2. Data from World Bank, *World Development Report 2003* (New York: Oxford University Press, 2003), 234–235.

3. Data taken from the World Bank, "2006 World Development Indicators," online at http://www.devdata.worldbank.org.

4. Although in some industrial countries, such as the United States, income inequality seems to have been increasing in recent decades.

5. Paul Collier, *The Bottom Billion: Why the Poorest Countries Are Falling Behind and What Can Be Done About It?* (Oxford: Oxford University Press, 2007).

PART 1

Is There a Gap Between Rich and Poor Countries?

2

Characteristics of
the Income Gap
Between Countries

John T Passé-Smith

The purpose of this chapter is to set out the long-term characteristics of the gap between rich and poor countries. Much of the rest of the book then presents the various arguments for why the gap exists and the policies that governments could follow in hopes of reducing the gap. That task has been made more complex by the fact that the debate over the gap has increasingly focused on its very existence and whether or not it is constant or expanding. Robert Hunter Wade and Glenn Firebaugh address the measurement of the gap in Chapters 3 and 4, and Branko Milanovic returns to the topic in Chapter 31. The present chapter retains its original purpose of examining global inequality between countries in the post–World War II era using the World Bank's income categories. This will give the reader an understanding of the characteristics of the gap between rich and poor countries and a starting point for understanding the impact of using different measures of the gap as presented in the aforementioned chapters. World economic trends are presented in four sections that review global rates of growth, the absolute gap, the relative gap, and country mobility. ■

Rates of Economic Growth, 1960–2005

Following Western Europe's rapid recovery after World War II, the governments of the industrialized countries turned their attention to aiding Third World nations in their development efforts. In the 1950s and early 1960s, economic growth became the centerpiece of economists' development plans. To that end the United Nations declared the 1960s the "Development Decade" and set a goal of 6 percent annual growth as necessary to raise the poverty-stricken to a decent standard of living within a reasonable time frame (Dube 1988, 2–3). Early analysis of economic trends by David Morawetz (1977) indicated that although the whole world had experienced relatively rapid growth, the gap between the high-income and poor countries had widened. This chapter extends the analysis of Morawetz.

For the current study, data were obtained from the World Bank's *World Development Indicators, 2007* (online). Growth rates were computed using the regression method described by the World Bank in the *World Development Report* (1988, 288–289).[1] The income groupings and regional designations were borrowed from the World Bank's *World Development Indicators, 2007* (see the Tables, Quick Reference section wherein the technical notes offer the "Classification of economies by income and region").[2] All gross domestic products per capita (GDP/pc) are in constant US dollars with a base year of 2000. The cut-offs for the income groups were computed from those created by the World Bank. In the analysis offered here, high-income countries are those with a GDP/pc of $9,401 and higher; upper-middle-income countries have a GDP/pc between $3,051 and $9,400; lower-middle-income countries have a GDP/pc of $766 to $3,050; and the poor countries are those with a GDP/pc of less than $765.[3]

Over the forty-six-year period 1960–2005, the annual average rate of GDP/pc growth for the world has been about 1.61 percent (see Table 2.1). To put this achievement in perspective, it should be understood that the modern era of economic growth that catapulted Western Europe, the United States, and several other countries into a position of global economic dominance by the 1950s was triggered by the Industrial Revolution and reached an annual average of 1.6 percent. Simon Kuznets referred to this "long century of growth" (about 1820 to 1950) as unprecedented (Kuznets 1972, 19). What is so remarkable about the current global rate of 1.61 percent per annum is that it is calculated from all countries (those for which data exist) rather than just the fastest-growing countries. Although this rate of growth has not been sustained for over a century, it is now approaching fifty years. Given the current *levels* of growth, it is clear the entire world did not come close to this *rate* of economic growth during Kuznets's long century, but it was almost certainly an era during which only a few countries achieved fantastic economic success while the rest of the world grew only slowly or not at all.

Breaking the forty-six-year period down into decadal units, it is also easy to see that economic growth at the outset was quite strong, rising to 2.94 percent per annum in the 1960s. Growth in the 1970s, although weaker, still averaged 2.3 percent. The debt crisis of the 1980s and the financial crisis of the 1990s held global growth to less than 1 percent. However, the new century has witnessed a period of economic recovery and expansion, with the global average annual rate of economic growth rising to 2.61 percent. Again, it is important to point out that this is not just the successful countries that are being discussed, as in the case of the long century, but rather the average annual rate of economic expansion for 168 countries.

Table 2.1   Annual Average Percentage Growth Rates by Income Grouping

	1960–2005	1960–1969	1970–1979	1980–1989	1990–1999	2000–2005
High-income	2.25	3.34	1.66	1.29	1.72	2.12
	(8)	(9)	(21)	(30)	(33)	(33)
Upper-middle-income	2.25	4.14	2.88	1.49	1.83	3.12
	(18)	(19)	(18)	(24)	(32)	(27)
Lower-middle-income	2.20	4.14	3.31	0.78	−0.23	2.77
	(25)	(28)	(34)	(45)	(52)	(49)
Poor	0.89	1.55	1.57	0.53	0.70	2.49
	(43)	(43)	(43)	(40)	(54)	(58)
World	1.61	2.94	2.30	0.94	0.82	2.61
	(94)	(99)	(116)	(139)	(172)	(168)

Source: World Bank, *World Development Indicators, 2007* (Washington, DC: World Bank, 2007).

Note: Number of countries in parentheses.

For the period as a whole, the high-income and the upper-middle-income countries had the highest growth rates. The annual average mean growth rate of both groups from 1960 to 2005 was 2.25 percent; the lower-middle-income countries grew at an average annual rate of 2.20 percent. Only the poor countries averaged less than 1 percent growth per year (0.89 percent). The pattern of growth found in Table 2.1 contradicts the predictions offered by convergence theorists such as William Baumol (see Chapter 15), who assert that the gap between rich and poor will disappear over the long run. They argue that the poorer countries have the highest growth potential and that as this potential is realized, the gap will dissolve. Of course, if convergence in its purest form were occurring today, the growth rates of the poorest countries would be the highest, followed by the middle-income countries, with the high-income countries exhibiting the lowest growth rates.

In his 1982 study of world growth, Robert Jackman discovered what he termed the "modified Matthew effect" (1982, 175). In the Bible, the Book of Matthew contains a reference to the continued accumulation of wealth by the rich and the further impoverishment of the poor; by the "modified Matthew effect," Jackman meant that both the high-income and middle-income countries were growing richer. In fact, he discovered that the middle-income countries were growing faster than the high-income ones (i.e., converging) while the poor fell further behind. Convergence theorists later made reference to such a pattern, which they referred to as "modified convergence." Here the countries predicted to converge—the so-called convergence club—did not include the poorest countries, which lacked the human capital to take advantage of their high-growth potential (see Abramovitz 1986).

Referring back to Table 2.1, the annual average rates of growth for the high-income, upper-middle-income, lower-middle-income, and poor countries are broken down by decades. I first analyzed global growth for this volume in 1993, and for the first time, the modified version of the "Matthew effect" is found to be at work in every single decade. The upper-middle-income countries in every decadal period have a higher growth rate than the upper-income countries, and the lower-middle-income countries only fail to surpass the growth rate of the high-income countries during the 1980s and 1990s. There is also brighter news concerning the poorest countries. For the first time I can report that if the pattern held over time, there would be evidence for the pure convergence theory. Between 2000 and 2005 the slowest-growing income group is the upper-income group. Even the poor are participating in a brief period of convergence. Although this is very positive news, sober analysis suggests that it would take decades if not centuries for the poor to actually converge with the upper-income group, and given past performance it is unlikely that they will be able to sustain this short-term success.

The 1960s was a period of rapid economic expansion. Both middle-income groups grew in excess of 4 percent, and even the poor countries were able to top 1.5 percent. Upper-income countries experienced strong economic growth averaging 3.34 percent. Although the 1970s witnessed slower growth than that of the 1960s, it was still quite impressive. Awash in petrodollars reinvested in the high-income countries by the oil-exporting nations, bankers in the First World hoped to avoid inflation by making more money available to developing countries. During the 1970s the upper-middle-income countries grew at a healthy 2.88 percent per year while the lower-middle-income countries' economies expanded at a 3.31 percent rate. The poor continued growing through the 1970s, averaging 1.57 percent per annum. Though the 1970s were a time of relatively easy money and economic growth for the middle-income and poor countries, the debt came due and growth rates dissipated. The 1980s are now referred to as "the lost decade." The economic hope for the future that characterized the 1970s gave way to the debt crisis and despair of the 1980s.

It is interesting to note that hard economic times, such as those experienced in the 1980s and 1990s, hit the poorest countries the hardest. This could go a long way in explaining the persistence of the gap between rich and poor countries throughout time. In the 1980s, global growth fell below 1 percent—to 0.94 percent—from the previous decade's 2.30 percent. During this period the upper-income countries' growth rate declined from 1.66 percent to 1.29 percent, and the upper-middle-income countries registered a larger decline, from 2.88 percent to 1.49 percent. The other two income categories, however, fell below 1 percent growth. Lower-middle-income countries grew at a 0.78 percent pace while the poor grew at only 0.53 percent. Hard economic times continued into the 1990s, and as the period wore on, the lower-middle-income countries were hit the hardest. During the 1990s, the economies of those countries actually began to shrink at a rate of –0.23 percent per year. Although poor countries continued to grow at less than 1 percent, they actually improved slightly, to 0.70 percent. The upper-income and upper-middle-income countries, however, were rebounding. The upper-income countries' economies achieved 1.72 percent growth in the 1990s while the upper-middle-income countries grew at a 1.83 percent pace.

To gain an understanding of the human dimension of the gap, Table 2.2 provides information on the percentage of the world's population living in high-income, upper-middle-income, lower-middle-income, and poor countries. The table shows that the percentage of people living in the wealthiest countries in the world is relatively small and remarkably stable. The percentage of the world population living in upper-income countries was 10.69 percent in 1960. That percentage climbs to 18.68 by 1980 and then declines and remains relatively constant at 15.7 percent between 1990 and 2005. At the other end of the spectrum, those living in the poor countries constituted 65.53 percent of the world's population in 1960, declining slightly to 58.82 percent thirty years later in 1990. Interestingly, the percentage of people living in the poor countries drops dramatically to 36.41 percent in 2000 and remains relatively constant through 2005. Examining the percentage of population in the lower-middle-income countries reveals that the lower-middle-income group experienced a dramatic increase in population at the same time the poor countries' population diminished. The poor countries' decline and the lower-middle-income groups' increase are signaling the economic expansion in China. Other than China's obvious impact on the percentages, it is remarkable how stable the income groups are in terms of global percentage of population.

Table 2.2 Percentage of World Population by World Bank Income Grouping

	1960	1970	1980	1990	2000	2005
High-income	10.69 (9)	18.63 (21)	18.68 (30)	15.70 (33)	15.78 (40)	15.70 (34)
Upper-middle-income	13.24 (19)	6.13 (18)	10.14 (25)	9.94 (32)	8.45 (33)	9.93 (29)
Lower-middle-income	10.54 (28)	10.84 (34)	11.95 (45)	15.54 (52)	39.36 (50)	38.17 (52)
Poor	65.53 (43)	64.40 (43)	59.23 (40)	58.82 (54)	36.41 (59)	36.20 (53)
World population in billions	2.38 (99)	3.04 (116)	3.84 (140)	5.08 (171)	5.90 (182)	6.24 (168)

Source: World Bank, *World Development Indicators, 2007* (Washington, DC: World Bank, 2007).
Note: Number of countries in parentheses.

Level of development measures production and not standards of living or income. One way to overcome this issue is to use a purchasing power parity conversion factor to convert national accounts statistics, producing a statistic that is more sensitive to standards of living within a country. Issues surrounding the decision to use exchange-rate-converted versus purchasing-power-parity converted national accounts statistics is discussed in this volume by Robert Hunter Wade in Chapter 3, Glenn Firebaugh in Chapter 4, Angus Maddison in Chapter 6, and Branko Milanovic in Chapter 31. Another way to get at standards of living is to see if increasing levels of growth correlate with improved standards of living. Table 2.3 presents the standard of living of the four income groups as measured by the human development index (HDI), a composite index of the standard of living of a country as measured by three different aspects of human development: health, knowledge, and wealth. Health is measured by the life expectancy of a country; knowledge is measured by the levels of literacy and school enrollment in a society; and wealth is measured by a purchasing-power-parity-converted GDP.

Table 2.3 shows without fail that each income group measures higher on the HDI scale than the next lower income grouping. This means that as a country increases its level of growth, it also experiences an increased standard of living. The table also makes clear that every income group is experiencing an improved standard of living over time. This means that the entire world's standard of living is improving. Searing pictures of poverty and starvation in poor countries should be cause for cautious interpretation of these measures, but it is a rather hopeful sign that even the poor countries' HDI measure has improved from 0.387 in 1975 to 0.498 in 2004. Even upper-income countries, which one may assume would be as high as they could be in HDI, have improved from 0.834 in 1975 to 0.92 in 2004. One very interesting conclusion to be drawn

Table 2.3   Average Human Development Index by Income Grouping

	1975	1980	1985	1990	1995	2000	2004
High-income	0.834 (22)	0.845 (27)	0.859 (27)	0.884 (28)	0.901 (29)	0.915 (31)	0.920 (36)
Upper-middle-income	0.744 (14)	0.760 (19)	0.781 (18)	0.787 (22)	0.801 (24)	0.799 (24)	0.794 (35)
Lower-middle-income	0.599 (31)	0.614 (33)	0.652 (34)	0.693 (38)	0.694 (41)	0.704 (38)	0.721 (49)
Poor	0.387 (33)	0.411 (32)	0.443 (39)	0.464 (44)	0.484 (48)	0.490 (42)	0.498 (49)
World	0.601 (100)	0.636 (111)	0.650 (119)	0.672 (133)	0.683 (143)	0.702 (136)	0.714 (169)

Source: World Bank, *World Development Indicators, 2007* (Washington, DC: World Bank, 2007).

Note: Number of countries in parentheses.

from the HDI is that the twenty years of economic turmoil and decline for lower-middle-income and poor countries are invisible in Table 2.3. For all four income groups the HDI improves every single period without one reversal. Whether this points to an ever-increasing standard of living in the world or a fundamental flaw in this measure is beyond the scope of this chapter.

The economic growth rates of the World Bank's geographic regions are presented in Table 2.4. The World Bank separates out two groupings of rich (those belonging to the Organization for Economic Cooperation and Development [OECD] and non-OECD) and then places the remaining countries in geographic regions. Table 2.4 shows that global growth was reasonably spread throughout the world. Each region except for Latin America and sub-Saharan Africa has achieved economic growth in excess of 2 percent. East Asia and the Pacific, containing China and some of the so-called Asian NICs (newly industrializing countries), is the fastest-growing region, with an annual average growth rate of 3.41 percent between 1960 and 2005. This region maintained the most stable and strong growth rate throughout the entire period even though it was not necessarily the fastest-growing region each decade. During the 1960s the Middle East and North Africa achieved the highest rate of growth (8.61 percent) and maintained a relatively high 3.25 percent rate through the 1970s, but the 1980s witnessed a collapse of economic growth in

Table 2.4 **Annual Average Gross Domestic Product per Capita Growth Rates by World Bank Geographic Region Grouping**

	1960–2005	1960–1969	1970–1979	1980–1989	1990–1999	2000–2005
High-income (OECD)	2.64 (22)	4.16 (22)	2.72 (23)	2.50 (24)	2.10 (25)	1.70 (25)
High-income (Non-OECD)	4.07 (5)	5.14 (7)	3.08 (11)	0.72 (17)	1.32 (19)	4.08 (13)
East Asia and Pacific	3.41 (7)	2.59 (8)	3.23 (10)	2.03 (11)	2.49 (16)	2.00 (19)
Europe and Central Asia	2.53 (1)	5.99 (1)	4.40 (4)	1.97 (8)	−3.43 (23)	6.52 (24)
Latin America and Caribbean	1.11 (22)	1.85 (22)	2.11 (23)	0.18 (28)	1.89 (28)	1.43 (24)
Middle East and North Africa	2.13 (3)	8.61 (5)	3.25 (7)	0.37 (7)	1.34 (10)	1.84 (11)
South Asia	2.09 (5)	1.89 (5)	1.03 (5)	3.26 (6)	3.19 (6)	3.54 (7)
Sub-Saharan Africa	0.18 (29)	1.52 (29)	1.34 (33)	−0.18 (38)	0.40 (45)	1.53 (45)

Source: World Bank, *World Development Indicators, 2007* (Washington, DC: World Bank, 2007).

Note: Number of countries in parentheses.

this region, as well as in most other regions of the world. In the Middle East and North Africa the rate of economic growth fell to 0.37 percent, recovering to 1.34 percent in the 1990s. The worst economic performance was experienced by Europe and Central Asia in the 1990s, when the average annual rate of economic growth was –3.43 percent. Once again, the decade of slowest economic growth was the 1980s, with every region of the world experiencing economic contraction except South Asia—which actually tripled the growth rate that it had achieved in the previous decade. South Asian growth climbed from 1.03 percent in the 1970s to 3.26 percent in the 1980s.

Turning from income groups and regions to individual countries, Table 2.5 highlights the ten fastest- and slowest-growing countries. As mentioned previously, the rate of economic growth between 1960 and 2005 has been remarkable. This is apparent in the list of the ten fastest-growing countries. Four of the top ten fastest-growing countries (Botswana, China, Thailand, and Indonesia) are from the poor income group, and another four are from the lower-middle-income group (the Republic of Korea, Singapore, Malta, and Malaysia). Only

Table 2.5   The Fastest- and Slowest-Growing Countries, 1960–2005

The Ten Fastest-Growing Countries

Rank	Country	Economic Growth Rate, 1960–2005	Income Group, 1960
1	Botswana	7.36	Poor
2	China	6.88	Poor
3	Republic of Korea	6.11	Lower-middle-income
4	Singapore	5.81	Lower-middle-income
5	Malta	5.73	Lower-middle-income
6	Hong Kong	5.11	Upper-middle-income
7	Thailand	4.87	Poor
8	Indonesia	4.17	Poor
9	Malaysia	4.12	Lower-middle-income
10	Ireland	3.90	Upper-middle-income

The Ten Slowest-Growing Countries

Rank	Country	Economic Growth Rate, 1960–2005	Income Group, 1960
1	Liberia	–5.23	Poor
2	Dem. Rep. of Congo	–3.41	Poor
3	Niger	–1.98	Poor
4	Nicaragua	–1.64	Lower-middle-income
5	Zambia	–1.60	Poor
6	Madagascar	–1.52	Poor
7	Haiti	–1.19	Poor
8	Central African Republic	–1.04	Poor
9	Sierra Leone	–0.82	Poor
10	Venezuela	–0.66	Upper-middle-income

Source: World Bank, *World Development Indicators, 2007* (Washington, DC: World Bank, 2007).

two of the fastest-growing countries are from the upper-middle-income group (Hong Kong and Ireland), and none are from the upper-income group. The fastest-growing countries in the world between 1960 and 2005 grew at an annual average rate of from 3.90 percent (Ireland) to 7.36 percent (Botswana). As may be expected, Asia is well represented in the list of fastest-growing.

Unfortunately one region of the world dominates the list of the slowest-growing countries. Of the ten slowest-growing countries in the world between 1960 and 2005, only three are *not* from Africa (Nicaragua, Haiti, and Venezuela). The seven African countries on the list of the slowest-growing countries are Liberia, the Democratic Republic of Congo, Niger, Zambia, Madagascar, the Central African Republic, and Sierra Leone. The slowest-growing countries in the world all experienced negative growth, ranging from –0.66 percent per year in Venezuela to –5.23 percent in Liberia. Only two of the slowest-growing countries in the world came from income groups other than the poor: Nicaragua (lower-middle-income) and Venezuela (upper-middle-income).

The Absolute Gap

The absolute gap is the difference between the mean GDP/pc of a set of high-income countries and that of poorer countries or groups of countries. Simon Kuznets (1972) reported that in 1965 the mean GNP per capita of the high-income countries was $1,900, whereas that of the poor was $120.[4] One of the major trends over the previous 100 to 125 years, Kuznets argued, was that the absolute gap widened very slowly up until World War II and then began to accelerate. Kuznets stated, "[A] reasonable conjecture is that, in comparison with the quintupling of the per capita product of developed countries over the last century, the per capita product of the 'poor' LDCs rose two-thirds at most" (Kuznets 1972, 19). In his study of the gap, David Morawetz (1977) found that the absolute gap between the OECD and developing countries between 1950 and 1975 had more than doubled (from $2,191 to $4,839 in 1975 US dollars). Neither the developing countries as a group nor any of the geographic regions reported by Morawetz were able to achieve a narrowing of the absolute gap.

The data presented in Table 2.6 show that between 1960 and 2005 the absolute gap between the upper-income and the upper-middle-income countries grew at an annual average rate of $276. The absolute gap between the upper-income and the lower-middle-income group expanded at a rate of $256 per year. In terms of the size of the absolute gap, in 1960 the absolute gap between the upper-income and upper-middle-income countries was $6,404. By 2005 that gap had widened 2.9 times, to $19,090. The gap separating the upper-income countries from the lower-middle-income countries grew from $10,864 to $22,653 (in 2000 US dollars) and from $11,924 to $23,901 between the high-income and poor countries for the 1960–2005 period.

Table 2.6   The Absolute Gap, 1960–2005

Income Group	1960	1970	1980	1990	2000	2005	Average Annual Increase
Upper-middle-income	$6,404	$9,463	$12,364	$14,065	$16,128	$19,090	$276
Lower-middle-income	$10,864	$13,806	$16,156	$17,508	$19,587	$22,653	$256
Poor	$11,924	$14,981	$17,329	$18,719	$20,806	$23,901	$260
Absolute Gap by Region							
East Asia and Pacific	$5,895	$13,823	$15,504	$16,598	$18,495	$21,356	$336
Europe and Central Asia	$5,105	$12,732	$14,478	$15,641	$17,976	$20,584	$337
Latin America and Caribbean	$4,702	$12,373	$13,903	$15,105	$16,546	$19,853	$329
Middle East and North Africa	$5,546	$12,338	$14,170	$15,694	$17,059	$20,518	$325
South Asia	$6,201	$14,244	$16,114	$17,301	$18,969	$22,079	$345
Sub-Saharan Africa	$5,897	$13,891	$15,584	$16,915	$18,839	$22,067	$352

Source: World Bank, *World Development Indicators, 2007* (Washington, DC: World Bank, 2007).

The data here confirm what Kuznets (1972) and Morawetz (1977) found in earlier studies—that the absolute gap is growing wider—but does this really prove the old adage that "the rich get richer while the poor get poorer"? It should be obvious by now that the two middle-income groups and the poor, while falling farther behind in the absolute gap, are growing economically. Additionally, the human development index reported earlier also attests that they are somewhat better off than in the past. Figure 2.1, however, shows that between 1960 and 2005, the average GDP/pc of the upper-middle-income countries declined slightly, from $5,878 in 1960 to $5,176 in 2005, while the lower-middle-income countries' average GDP/pc climbed slightly, from $1,417 in 1960 to $1,613 in 2005. The economies of the poor countries remained listless throughout the period, starting out at $357 in 1960 and climbing to only $365 in 2005. The behavior of the gap shown in Figure 2.1 is in part explained by the fact that as countries succeed economically, they move to the next highest income group, which lowers the average income of the group they are entering, because they are poorer than the others in that group, as well as that of the group they are leaving, because they were the richest in that group.

The absolute gap as reported in Table 2.6 and Figure 2.1 seems to suggest that no matter how well countries perform economically, they can never catch

Figure 2.1   GDP/pc of High-Income, Upper-Middle-Income, Lower-Middle-Income, and Poor Countries (US$ 2000)

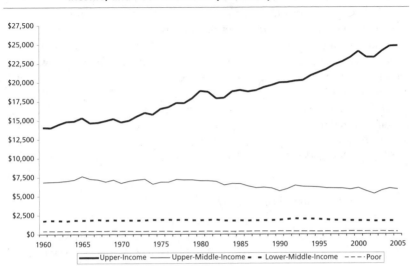

up to the rich. Unfortunately, for most countries this may be the case. However, for nonrich countries to catch up with the high-income countries at some time in the future, nonrich countries only need to grow faster than the upper-income countries. That said, the growth rates reported in Table 2.1 show that many countries are growing faster than rich countries but the gap is not apparently closing. As difficult as it is, the easy part is growing faster than the rich countries; the hard part is continuing to grow faster for as long as it takes to catch up. Alas, catching up could take hundreds if not thousands of years if the nonrich countries are relatively poor and their growth rates are only slightly faster than those of the high-income countries.

Further complicating the issue is the fact that even countries that are en route to closing the absolute gap appear to fall further behind before their progress becomes apparent. This is due to what Morawetz called the "simple algebra of the gap." The gap between high-income and poor countries will not actually close until the ratio of their GDP/pcs is equal to the inverse ratio of their growth rates. A relatively simple way to determine if a non-upper-income country can close the absolute gap is to divide the growth rate of the high-income country by the ratio of the non-upper-income country's GDP/pc to the high-income country's GNP/pc. This equation yields the growth rate the non-upper-income country must exceed in order to begin closing the absolute gap immediately. If, for example, the high-income countries have a mean GDP/pc of $8,000 and a growth rate of 2 percent, a nonrich country with a GDP/pc of $1,000 must exceed a growth rate of 16 percent in order to begin closing the absolute gap that year. Very few countries are able to achieve or maintain such a rate of economic expansion for very long.

Table 2.7 identifies the countries that are able to catch up to the upper-income countries. In 2005 the upper-income countries had a mean GDP/pc of $24,266 and an average annual growth rate of 2.25 percent. I separated out all of the non-upper-income countries that had an annual average growth rate greater than 2.25 percent. This constituted the group that could potentially catch up to the rich. I then projected their GDP/pc into the future by assuming that they would be able to sustain the growth rate that they had during the 1960 to 2005 period. Given this assumption, only twenty countries can hope to catch up to the high-income countries. Only seven countries—the Republic of Korea, Malta, Botswana, China, Portugal, Thailand, and Malaysia—have the opportunity to

Table 2.7   Closing the Absolute Gap

Country	GNP/pc (2000 $US)	Annual Average Growth Rate, 1960– 2005 (in percentage)	Number of Years Until the Gap Is Closed
Rich[a]	$24,266	2.25	—
Republic of Korea	13,210	6.11	17
Malta	9,618	5.73	28
Botswana	4,649	7.36	34
China	1,449	6.88	64
Portugal	11,023	3.42	70
Thailand	2,441	4.87	91
Malaysia	4,437	4.12	94
Indonesia	942	4.17	175
Belize	3,708	3.29	186
Seychelles	6,468	2.95	194
Egypt	1,624	3.13	316
Greece	12,799	2.41	410
Sri Lanka	1,002	3.03	420
Lesotho	550	3.03	499
Chile	5,721	2.54	511
Hungary	5,720	2.53	530
Dominican Republic	2,630	2.67	543
St. Vincent and the Grenadines	3,227	2.55	690
Pakistan	596	2.58	1,152
India	588	2.55	1,272

Source: World Bank, *World Development Indicators, 2007* (Washington, DC: World Bank, 2007).
Note: a. Those countries with a GNP/pc of more than $9,401 in 2000.

catch up to the high-income group within a century. Three more countries (Indonesia, Belize, and Seychelles) would catch up in the following century.

Returning to the algebra of the gap, it is instructive to see how the absolute gap behaves as a country catches up to the rich. Table 2.8 and Figure 2.2 isolate Indonesia's projected growth and the resulting absolute gap into the

Table 2.8   Indonesia's Path to Closing the Absolute Gap with the Rich

Year	Absolute Gap	Number of Years	Indonesia's GDP/pc/ Upper-Income GDP/pc	Upper-Income Growth Rate/ Indonesia's Growth Rate
2005	23,324	0	0.0388	0.5396
2025	35,737	20	0.0563	0.5396
2045	54,271	40	0.0817	0.5396
2065	81,301	60	0.1185	0.5396
2085	119,191	80	0.1719	0.5396
2105	168,608	100	0.2494	0.5396
2125	223,734	120	0.3618	0.5396
2145	259,974	140	0.5248	0.5396
2165	203,808	160	0.7613	0.5396
2185	−139,030	180	1.1043	0.5396
2186	−170,405	181	1.1251	0.5396

Source: World Bank, *World Development Indicators, 2007* (Washington, DC: World Bank, 2007).

Figure 2.2   The Absolute Gap Between the Upper-Income Countries and Indonesia

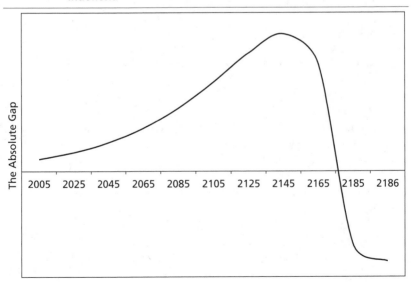

future. Notice that as the ratio of the GDP/pc and growth rate presented in columns 4 and 5 and discussed earlier approaches parity, the opening of the absolute gap slows. In the year 2145, the ratio approaches 1 and the following increment of time it exceeds 1 and the gap actually closes. Figure 2.2 graphically shows the same data, illustrating how the absolute gap continues to grow even though a country is in the process of catching up to the rich.

The Relative Gap

The relative gap measures the GDP/pc of the poor or middle-income groups as a percentage of that of the developed countries. Morawetz (1977) reported that the developing countries had narrowed the relative gap by about one-half of a percentage point between 1950 and 1975. He added that it might be easier for nonrich-income countries to narrow the relative gap than the absolute gap, thereby making it a more accessible development goal.

However, the results presented in Table 2.9 indicate that the upper- and lower-middle-income countries' GDP/pc expressed as a percentage of the GDP/pc of the high-income group has not improved once over the forty-six-year period under examination. In fact, the upper-middle-income group's GDP/pc expressed as a percentage of the GDP/pc of the rich shrank from 47.86 percent in 1960 to 21.33 percent in 2005. The relative gap for the lower-middle-income group declined from 11.54 percent in 1960 to 6.65 percent in 2005. The poor countries' experience was similar to that of the middle-income

Table 2.9   The Relative Gap (in percentage), 1960–2005

Income Group	1960	1970	1980	1990	2000	2005
Upper-middle-income	47.86	38.38	30.05	26.30	23.85	21.33
Lower-middle-income	11.54	10.09	8.60	8.26	7.52	6.65
Poor	2.91	2.44	1.97	1.91	1.76	1.51
Absolute Gap by Region						
East Asia and Pacific	7.95	4.64	5.38	6.13	6.24	7.01
Europe and Central Asia	20.28	12.18	11.65	11.53	8.88	10.37
Latin America and Caribbean	26.58	14.65	15.16	14.57	16.13	13.56
Middle East and North Africa	13.39	14.89	13.53	11.23	13.52	10.66
South Asia	3.17	1.74	1.67	2.15	3.84	3.86
Sub-Saharan Africa	7.92	4.18	4.90	4.33	4.50	3.91

Source: World Bank, *World Development Indicators, 2007* (Washington, DC: World Bank, 2007).

groups. Their relative gap score fell from 2.91 percent to 1.51 percent over the forty-six-year period. In other words, the relative gap between high-income and middle-income countries and high-income and poor countries widened between 1960 and 2005.

Mobility

Can countries move from one income group to another or substantially improve their ranking within a grouping? In terms of upward mobility across income groups, the record between 1970 and 2005 has been mixed. I selected the year 1970 to increase the number of countries included in the sample. Table 2.10 summarizes the movement of countries. Of the 100 countries in the sample, fifty-two remained in the same category in 2005 that they occupied in 1960. Unfortunately, thirty of the countries that occupied the poor income

Table 2.10   Mobility Across Income Groups, 1970 and 2005

Rich
Upper-income in 1970 and 2005 (N = 8): Denmark, Iceland, Luxembourg, Norway, Sweden, Switzerland, United Kingdom, United States
Joined upper-income from the upper-middle-income category (N = 18): Australia, Austria, Belgium, Finland, France, Greece, Hong Kong, Ireland, Israel, Italy, Japan, Netherlands, New Zealand, Spain
Joined upper-income from the lower-middle-income category (N = 4): Republic of Korea, Malta, Portugal, Singapore

---

Upper-Middle-Income
Upper-middle-income in 1970 and 2005 (N = 4): Argentina, Trinidad & Tobago, Uruguay, Venezuela
Joined upper-middle-income from the lower-middle-income category (N = 13): Belize, Brazil, Chile, Costa Rica, Gabon, Hungary, Libya, Malaysia, Mexico, Panama, Seychelles, South Africa, St. Vincent and the Grenadines
Joined upper-middle-income from the poor category (N = 1): Botswana

---

Lower-Middle-Income
Lower-middle-income in 1970 and 2005 (N = 10): Algeria, Bolivia, Colombia, Dominican Republic, Ecuador, El Salvador, Fiji, Guatemala, Nicaragua, Peru
Joined lower-middle-income from the poor category (N = 12): China, Republic of Congo, Arab Republic of Egypt, Guyana, Honduras, Indonesia, Morocco, Paraguay, Philippines, Sri Lanka, Syrian Arab Republic, Thailand

---

Poor
Poor in 1970 and 2005 (N = 30): Bangladesh, Benin, Burkina Faso, Burundi, Cameroon, Central African Republic, Chad, Democratic Republic of Congo, Côte d'Ivoire, Ghana, Haiti, India, Kenya, Lesotho, Liberia, Madagascar, Malawi, Mauritania, Nepal, Niger, Nigeria, Pakistan, Papua New Guinea, Rwanda, Senegal, Sierra Leone, Sudan, Togo, Zambia, Zimbabwe

---

Source: World Bank, *World Development Indicators, 2007* (Washington, DC: World Bank, 2007).

group in 1970 remained there in 2005. However, twenty-two countries joined the upper-income group that were not there in 1970, and fourteen countries joined the upper-income group that were not there in the earlier period. It is also important to note that not one country moved down from one income group to the next.

Another way to examine improvement in a country's position in the world economy is to look at the country's ranking. Table 2.11 shows that there was quite a bit of movement in country rankings between 1960 and 2005. This table offers the ten countries that moved up and down in the rankings of GDP/pc the most between 1960 and 2005. The country achieving the highest jump in the rankings was China, which moved up from a ranking of 110 in 1960 to 63 in 2005, an increase of 47. China's jump in the rankings is even more impressive when consideration is taken of the fact that of the top ten countries in terms of upward movement in the rankings of GDP/pc, China was originally ranked the lowest. In fact, it was ranked as one of the poorest in the world. Botswana was close behind China, with an upward movement in the rankings of GDP/pc of 45 places. Dominating the group of ten upward movers are some of the countries referred to as Asian NICs. On the other side of the ledger, six of the ten countries that plummeted downward through the rankings were African. In 1960, Liberia had the sixty-third largest GDP/pc in the world, but by 2005 its ranking had fallen to 108, a drop of 45 places in the rankings. Nicaragua fell 25 places in the rankings and was the only Latin American country on the list.

Conclusion

If scholars such as Kuznets and Morawetz are correct, the worldwide economic growth experienced since World War II is unprecedented. Between 1850 and 1950, the countries considered high-income in 1950 experienced economic expansion averaging 1.6 percent. Between 1960 and 2005 the entire world grew at an annual average rate of 1.61 percent. Between 1960 and 1980 or thereabouts, the countries of the world averaged about 2.5 percent economic growth. This extended period of rapid growth caused post–World War II generations to become accustomed to rapid economic growth, leading many people to believe that it was inevitable. The 1980s, with the debt crisis, and the 1990s, with the global financial crisis, drove growth rates down and dampened expectations, but the new century witnessed the return of rapid growth. Between 2000 and 2005 the world grew at an impressive rate of 2.61 percent, and—perhaps even more striking and hopeful—the poor countries, with growth rates averaging 2.49 percent annually, exceeded the growth rate of the rich. However, historical examination of growth rates instructs us that economic growth is not inevitable. Kuznets (1972) and Morawetz (1977) both

Table 2.11 Mobility in Rankings of GNP/pc (differences in rankings, 1970–2005)

| | The Upwardly Mobile | | | | The Downwardly Mobile | | |
| | GNP/pc Rank | | | | GNP/pc Rank | | |
Country	1970	2005	Difference	Country	1970	2005	Difference
China	110	63	47	Liberia	63	108	-45
Botswana	85	40	45	Nicaragua	51	76	-25
Thailand	80	52	28	Democratic Republic of Congo	89	111	-22
Indonesia	100	75	25	Côte d'Ivoire	62	82	-20
India	103	81	22	Kuwait	1	20	-19
Lesotho	105	83	22	Madagascar	84	103	-19
Republic of Korea	45	25	20	Zimbabwe	74	92	-18
Hong Kong	28	10	18	Kiribati	67	84	-17
Singapore	30	12	18	Central African Republic	87	104	-17
Sri Lanka	88	70	18	Georgia	58	74	-16

Source: World Development Indicators, 2007 (Washington, DC: World Bank, 2007).

concluded that, over time, countries have likely experienced periods of expansion followed by long periods of stagnation or contraction.

Second, the aforementioned data indicate that the gap between the rich and the nonrich has not closed. The absolute gap between the high-income and non-high-income countries has grown steadily since 1960. For the upper-middle-income countries, the absolute gap grew from $6,404 to $19,090. The gap between the rich and lower-middle-income countries expanded from $10,864 in 1960 to $22,653 in 2005, and the gap for the poor widened from a deficit of $11,924 to $23,901. On average, the absolute gap widened $276 for the upper-middle-income countries, $256 for the lower-middle-income countries, and $260 for the poor countries every year. In addition, none of the income groups were able to improve the relative gap.

Third, this analysis of income groups would have proven irrelevant if the percentage of the world's population in the lowest-income group was small or had fallen significantly. Unfortunately, such was not the case. Overall, the income groups remained remarkably stable as a percentage of the world's population. The only departure from this conclusion revolves around the movement of one country—China—from the poor group to the lower-middle-income group, which substantially changed the percentage. Between 1960 and 1990 the lower-middle-income group held about 10 to 15 percent of the world's population, but the percentage jumped to 39.36 percent in 2000 with the entry of China. Likewise, the poor group constituted about 60 percent of the world's population between 1960 and 1990, but that percentage dropped to 35.41 percent in 2000 after China moved from the poor to the lower-middle-income group. Although these measures do not represent income inequality within countries, it is still a very positive sign that the percentage of the world's population living in countries with a GDP/pc of less than $765 dropped from 65.53 percent in 1960 to 36.2 percent in 2005. Further, although these data do not show standard of living, Table 2.3, which reports the human development index by income group, shows that movement from one income group to the next does mean an improvement in the standard of living.

Fourth, the number of high-income countries increased from eight in 1970 to thirty in 2005. Twenty-two countries joined the high-income group during the forty-six-year period under investigation, and fourteen moved into the upper-middle-income category. Thirteen countries escaped the poor category between 1970 and 2000 even though thirty remain, and these thirty constitute over one-third of the world's population.

Finally, it appears that only twenty countries can close the gap with the high-income countries and only seven of those can do so within the next century: the Republic of Korea (17 years), Malta (28), Botswana (34), China (64), Portugal (70), Thailand (91), and Malaysia (94). If growth rates remain similar to those of the entire forty-six-year period, Botswana will be the first African country to join the high-income countries, in the year 2039.

Notes

1. The World Bank's income groups were offered in current gross national incomes per capita (2006). According to the World Bank, those countries with a current 2006 GNI/pc of $11,116 or greater are considered high-income; upper-middle-income countries have a GNI/pc of $3,596 to $11,115; lower-middle-income countries have a GNI/pc of $906 to $3,595; and the poor countries are those with a GNI/pc of less than $906. These categories were converted into constant 2000 US dollars. To convert these income breaks to constant 2000 GDP per capita figures, I calculated each income break as a percentage of the US GNI/pc. I then used that percentage to establish the income categories in the GDP/pc data set.

2. The growth rates are calculated by the regression method described in the *World Development Report 1988*. The least squares method finds the growth rate by fitting a least-squares trend line to the log of the gross national product per capita. This takes the equation form of $X_t = a + bt + e_t$, where X equals the log of the GNP/pc, *a* is the intercept, *b* is the parameter to be estimated, *t* is time, and *e* is the error term. The growth rate, *r*, is the [antilog (b)]–1. For further information, see *World Development Report 1988*, pp. 288–289. For a discussion of different methods of computing growth rates see Robert Jackman (1980), "A Note on the Measurement of Growth Rates in Cross-National Research," *American Journal of Sociology* 86: 604–610.

3. The regional categories were drawn from the World Bank's *World Development Indicators, 2007* online data set. The income categories were based on the 2006 GNI per capita. Since the World Bank offers its constant year GDP/pc data in 2000 US dollars, I determined the income breaks in GNI/pc as a percentage of US GNI/pc and then used these percentages to establish the breaks in the GDP/pc data set. The resulting income categories were: upper-income countries, with a GDP/pc of $9,401 or greater; upper-middle-income countries, with GDP/pc of $3,051 to $9,400; lower-middle-income countries, with a GDP/pc between $766 and $3,050; and poor countries, with a GDP/pc of $765 or less.

4. Kuznets defined high-income countries as those with a GNP/pc greater than $1,000 (1965 US dollars). A "narrow" definition of the poor countries set the GNP/pc cutoff point at $120 or less. For his more broadly defined poor category, Kuznets raised the cutoff point to $300. The middle-income group varied according to Kuznets's choice of the narrowly or broadly defined poor group in any particular example. Kuwait and Qatar were excluded because of the fact that their growth had been dependent upon a single commodity and did not reflect diversified growth. Puerto Rico was excluded because its GNP/pc was so tightly connected to the United States. Japan was included in the high-income group even though its GNP/pc was below the cutoff point because it had managed tremendous growth with very few natural resources. Thus its growth was achieved through diversified development of the economy. For further information on how Kuznets defined his income groups, see Ranis 1972.

References

Abramovitz, M. 1986. "Catching Up, Forging Ahead, and Falling Behind." *Journal of Economic History* 46: 385–406.

Dube, S. C. 1988. *Modernization and Development: The Search for Alternative Paradigms*. London: Zed.

Durning, A. B. 1990. "Ending Poverty." In L. Starke, ed., *State of The World, 1990*. New York: W. W. Norton.

International Monetary Fund. 1984. *International Financial Statistics: Supplement on Output Statistics*, 8. Washington, DC: International Monetary Fund.

Jackman, R. W. 1982. "Dependence on Foreign Investment and Economic Growth in the Third World." *World Politics* 34: 175–197.

——. 1980. "A Note on the Measurement of Growth Rates in Cross-National Research." *American Journal of Sociology* 86: 604–610.

Kahn, H. 1979. *World Economic Development: 1979 and Beyond.* Boulder, CO: Westview.

Kuznets, S. 1984. "Economic Growth and Income Inequality." In M. A. Seligson, ed., *The Gap Between Rich and Poor.* Boulder, CO: Westview.

——. 1979. *Growth, Population, and Income Distribution.* New York: W. W. Norton.

——. 1972. "The Gap: Concept, Measurement, Trends." In G. Ranis, ed., *The Gap Between Rich and Poor Nations.* London: Macmillan.

Lipton, M. 1989. *New Seeds and Poor People.* London: Unwin Hyman.

——. 1977. *Why the Poor People Stay Poor: A Study of Urban Bias in World Development.* London: Temple Smith.

Morawetz, D. 1977. *Twenty-Five Years of Economic Development: 1950–1975.* Washington, DC: World Bank.

World Bank. 2000. *World Development Indicators, 2000.* Washington, DC: International Bank for Reconstruction and Development/World Bank Group.

——. 1992. *The World Tables 1992.* Washington, DC: World Bank.

——. 1988, 1990. *World Development Report.* Oxford: Oxford University Press.

3

The Rising Inequality of World Income Distribution

ROBERT HUNTER WADE

One of the important debates surrounding the gap between rich and poor countries is what, if anything, a government should do. Robert Hunter Wade argues that conflicting conclusions about the gap have arisen in part due to the measure of inequality used, whether and how the measure is weighted, and the method of converting to a common currency. The varying recipes produce eight different measures of income inequality. Wade concludes that seven of the eight measures of inequality clearly show that the gap is worsening and the last suggests that the gap is stable. His warnings about the consequences of ignoring a worsening gap are amplified in Chapter 13 by Edward N. Muller and Mitchell A. Seligson, who tie income inequality to domestic political violence. ∎

DOES IT MATTER WHAT IS HAPPENING TO WORLD INCOME DISTRIBUTION (among all 6.2 billion people, regardless of where they live)? Amartya Sen, the recent Nobel laureate in economics, warns that arguing about the trend deflects attention from the central issue, which is the sheer magnitude of inequality and poverty on a world scale. Regardless of the trend, the magnitude is unacceptable (Sen, 2001). He is right, up to a point. The concentration of world income in the wealthiest quintile (fifth) of the world's population is indeed shocking and cannot meet any plausible test of legitimacy. The chart [Figure 3.1] shows the distribution of world income by population quintiles. Ironically,

Figure 3.1   Distribution of World GDP, 1989 (percent of total with quantities of population ranked by income)

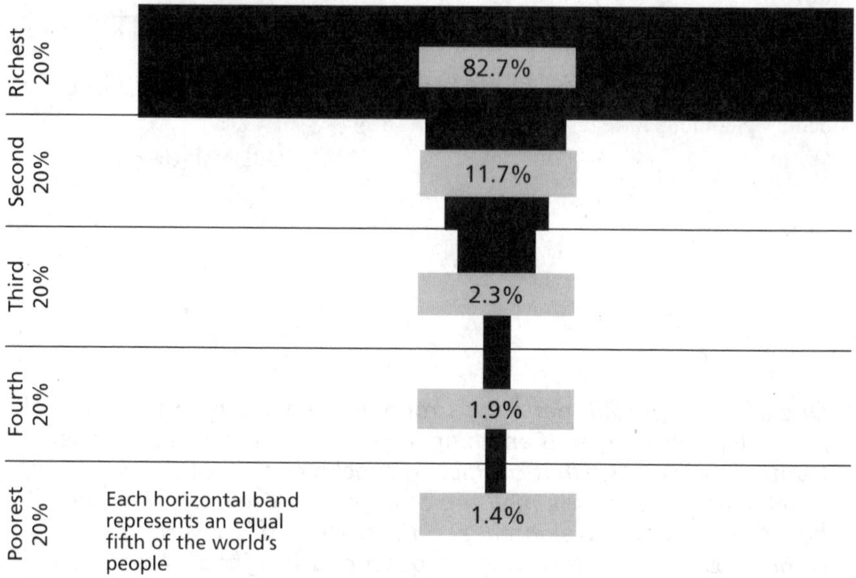

Richest 20%	82.7%
Second 20%	11.7%
Third 20%	2.3%
Fourth 20%	1.9%
Poorest 20% — Each horizontal band represents an equal fifth of the world's people	1.4%

Source: United Nations Development Programme, *Human Development Report 1992* (New York: Oxford University Press for the UNDP, 1992).

it resembles a champagne glass, with a wide, shallow bowl at the top and the slenderest of stems below.

But still, the trend does matter. Many champions of free trade and free capital movements say that world income distribution is becoming more equal as globalization proceeds, and on these grounds they resist the idea that reducing world income inequality should be an objective of international public policy. Moreover, many theories of growth and development generate predictions about *changes* in world income distribution; testing them requires information about trends. Indeed, the neoliberal paradigm—which has supplied the prescriptions known as the Washington Consensus that have dominated international public policy about development over the past twenty years—generates a strong expectation that as national economies become more densely interconnected through trade and investment, world income distribution tends to become more equal. And it is a fair bet that if presented with the statement, "World income distribution has become more equal over the past twenty years" and asked to agree, agree with qualifications, or disagree, a majority of Western economists would say, "agree" or "agree with qualifications."

If they are right, this would be powerful evidence in favor of the "law of *even* development," which says that all national economies gain from more integration into international markets (relative to less integration), and lower-cost, capital-scarce economies (developing countries) are likely to gain *more* from fuller integration than higher-cost, capital-abundant economies (developed countries). Developing countries wishing to catch up with standards of living in the West should therefore integrate fully into international markets (by lowering tariffs, removing trade restrictions, granting privileges to *foreign* direct investment, welcoming foreign banks, enforcing intellectual property rights, and so on) and let the decisions of private economic agents operating in free markets determine the composition and volume of economic activities carried out within the national territory. This "integrationist" strategy will maximize their rate of development; put the other way around, their development strategy should amount to an integrationist strategy—the two things are really one and the same.

Fortunately, the self-interest of the wealthy Western democracies coincides with this integrationist strategy for developing countries, because as developing countries grow richer, their demand for Western products expands and their capacity to absorb their population growth at home also expands, reducing the pressure on the West created by surging immigration. The World Bank, the IMF [International Monetary Fund], the World Trade Organization (WTO), and the other global supervisory organizations are therefore well justified in seeking to enforce maximum integration on developing countries for the good of all.

What Does the Evidence Show?

Therefore, a lot is at stake in the question of whether world income distribution has become more, or less, equal over the past twenty years or so. It turns out that there is no single correct answer, because the answer depends on which combination of measures one adopts. It depends on (1) the measure of inequality (a coefficient like the Gini, or quintile or decile [tenth] ratios), (2) the unit of inequality (countries weighted equally, or individuals weighted equally and countries weighted by population), and (3) the method of converting incomes in different countries to a common numeraire (current market exchange rates or purchasing power parity exchange rates). Treating these as either/or choices yields eight possible measures, each with some plausibility for certain purposes. Then there is the further question of what kind of data is used—the national income accounts or household income and expenditure surveys.

My reading of the evidence suggests that none of the eight alternative measures clearly shows that world income distribution has become more equal over the past twenty years. Seven of the eight show varying degrees of *increasing inequality*. The eighth—the one that uses the Gini coefficient, countries weighted by population, and purchasing power parity—shows no significant change in world income distribution. This is because the Gini coefficient gives excessive weight to changes around the middle of the distribution and insufficient weight to changes at the extremes and therefore, in this case, gives more weight (than a decile ratio) to fast-growing China; the use of countries weighted by population has the same effect; and the use of purchasing power parity tends to raise low incomes more than high incomes, compared with market exchange rates. Hence this combination generates the least rise in inequality. But a recent paper by Dowrick and Akmal (2001) suggests that the Penn World Tables, on which most calculations of purchasing power parity are based (see Heston and Summers, 1991), contain a bias that makes incomes of developing countries appear higher than they are. The tables consequently *understate* the degree and trend of inequality. When the bias is corrected, even the most favorable combination of measures shows rising inequality of world income distribution over the past twenty years, although the trend is less strong than the trend based on any of the other possible combinations.

It is often said that purchasing power parity measures should always be preferred to market exchange rates and that countries should always be weighted by population rather than treated as equal units of observation. Certainly, purchasing power parity measures are better for measuring relative purchasing power, or relative material welfare, though the available data are not good enough for them to be more than rough-and-ready approximations, especially for China and, before the early 1990s, the countries of the former Soviet Union. But data problems aside, we may also be interested in income for other purposes. Indeed, for most of the issues that concern the world at large—such as migration flows; the capacity of developing countries to repay foreign debts and import capital goods; the extent of marginalization of developing countries in the world polity; and, more broadly, the economic and geopolitical impact of a country (or region) on the rest of the world—then we should use market exchange rates to convert incomes in different countries into a common numeraire. After all, the reason why many poor countries are hardly represented in international negotiations whose outcomes profoundly affect them is that the cost of hotels, offices, and salaries in places like New York, Washington, and Geneva must be paid in U.S. dollars, not in purchasing power parity–adjusted dollars. Using market exchange rates, the conclusion is clear: all four combinations of measures using market exchange rates show that world income distribution has become *much more unequal.*

Causes of Increasing Inequality

What are the causes of the rise in world income inequality? The theory is not exactly what one might call watertight; the causality is very difficult to establish. Differential population growth between poorer and richer countries is one cause. The fall in non-oil commodity prices—by more than half in real terms between 1980 and the early 1990s—is another, affecting especially the poorest countries.

The debt trap is a third. Fast-growing middle-income developing countries, seeking to invest and consume more than can be covered by domestic incomes, tend to borrow abroad; and they borrow on terms that are more favorable when their capacity to repay is high and less favorable when—as in a financial crisis— their capacity to repay is low. We saw repeatedly during the 1980s and 1990s that countries that liberalized and opened their financial systems and then borrowed heavily—even if to raise investment rather than consumption—ran a significant risk of costly financial crisis. A crisis pulls them back down the world income hierarchy. Hence the debt trap might be thought of as a force in the world economy that is somewhat analogous to gravity.

Another basic cause is technological change. Technological change of the kind we have seen in the past two decades tends to reinforce the tendency for high-value-added activities (including innovation) to cluster in the (high-cost) Western economies rather than disperse to lower-cost developing countries. Silicon Valley is the paradigm: the firms that are pioneering the collapse of distance themselves congregate tightly in one small space. Part of the reason is the continuing economic value of tacit knowledge and "handshake" relationships in high-value-added activities. Technological change might be thought of as distantly analogous to electromagnetic levitation—a force in the world economy that keeps the 20 percent of the world's population living in the member countries of the Organization for Economic Cooperation and Development (OECD) comfortably floating above the rest of the world in the world income hierarchy. If we have world economy analogues of gravity and electromagnetism, can the world economy analogue of relativity theory be far behind?

Consequences

Income divergence helps to explain another kind of polarization taking place in the world system, between a zone of peace and a zone of turmoil. On the one hand, the regions of the wealthy pole show a strengthening republican order of economic growth and liberal tolerance (except toward immigrants), with technological innovation able to substitute for depleting natural capital. On the other hand, the regions of the lower- and middle-income poles contain many states whose capacity to govern is stagnant or eroding, mainly in Africa, the Middle East, Central Asia, the former Soviet Union, and parts of East Asia. Here, a rising proportion of the people find their access to basic necessities restricted at the same time as they see others driving Mercedes.

The result is a large mass of unemployed and angry young people, mostly males, to whom the new information technologies have given the means to threaten the stability of the societies they live in and even threaten social stability in countries of the wealthy zone. Economic growth in these countries often depletes natural capital and therefore future growth potential. More and more people see migration to the wealthy zone as their only salvation, and a few are driven to redemptive terrorism directed at the symbolic centers of the powerful.

Reorienting International Organizations

The World Bank and the IMF have paid remarkably little attention to global inequality. The Bank's *World Development Report 2000: Attacking Poverty* says explicitly that rising income inequality "should not be seen as negative," provided the incomes at the bottom do not fall and the number of people in poverty falls or does not rise. But incomes in the lower deciles of world income distribution have probably fallen absolutely since the 1980s; and one should not accept the Bank's claim that the number of people living on less than $1 a day remained constant at 1.2 billion between 1987 and 1998, because the method used to compute the figure for 1998 contains a downward bias relative to that used to compute the figure for 1987. Suppose, though, that the incomes of the lower deciles had risen absolutely and the number of people in absolute poverty had fallen, while inequality increased. The Bank's view that the rise in inequality should not be seen as a negative ignores the associated political instabilities and flows of migrants that—all notions of justice and fairness and common humanity aside—can harm the lives of the citizens of the rich world and the democratic character of their states.

The global supervisory organizations like the Bank, the IMF, the WTO, and the United Nations system should be giving the issue of global income inequality much more attention. If we can act on global warming—whose effects are similarly diffuse and long term—can we not act on global inequality? We should start by rejecting the neoliberal assumption of the Bretton Woods institutions over the past two decades, now powerfully reinforced by the emergent WTO, that development strategy boils down to a strategy for maximum integration of each economy into the world economy, complemented by domestic reforms to make full integration viable. The evidence on world income distribution throws this assumption into question—as does a lot of evidence of other kinds. International public policy to reduce world income inequality must include a basic change in the policy orientation of the World Bank, the IMF, and the WTO so as to allow them to sanction government efforts to impart directional thrust and nourish homegrown institutional innovations.

References

Dowrick, Steve, and Muhammad Akmal. 2001. "Explaining Contradictory Trends in Global Income Inequality: A Tale of Two Biases," *Faculty of Economic and Commerce.* Australian National University.

Heston, Alan, and Robert Summers. 1991. "The Penn World Tables (Mark 5): An Expanded Set of International Comparisons, 1950–1988," *Quarterly Journal of Economics* (May), pp. 327–68.

Rodrik, Dani, 2001. "The Global Governance of Trade as If Development Really Mattered" (unpublished).

Sen, Amartya. 2001. "If It's Fair, It's Good: 10 Truths About Globalization," *International Herald Tribune,* July 14–15.

Wade, Robert Hunter. 1990. *Governing the Market: Economic Theory and the Role of Government in East Asia's Industrialization.* Princeton: Princeton University Press.

———. 2001a. "Winners and Losers," *Economist,* April 28.

———. 2001b. "Globalization and World Income Distribution: Trends, Causes, Consequences, and Public Policy" (unpublished, July).

4

Empirics of World
Income Inequality

GLENN FIREBAUGH

*In this chapter, Glen Firebaugh disputes the findings of those who
argue that the world continues to experience a widening of the gap
between rich and poor countries. Firebaugh asserts that there are
two ways of looking at world income distribution. The standard approach is to use the country as the unit of analysis, so that each country represents one unit in the comparisons. The second way, the one
that Firebaugh argues is more persuasive, treats each person as the
unit of analysis. He accomplishes this by weighting the country data
by population size. When this is done, large countries, especially
China, play a great role. Since China's income grew at breakneck
speed in recent years, and China's total population size has also
grown enormously, the trends found in other studies are reversed.
Firebaugh also uses PPP (i.e., purchasing power–based income) data
rather than the exchange rate–based income data. The reader needs
to determine which method of measuring inequality is the more persuasive. Should we calculate the gap between nations as a function
of their total population size or limit ourselves to comparing each nation against all others irrespective of population size? The reader is
also directed to Chapter 31 where World Bank economist Branko Milanovic compares different methods of assessing the gap. As you will
see, good arguments can be made for each method, and Firebaugh is*

Reprinted with permission of the University of Chicago Press and the author from
the *American Journal of Sociology* 104, no. 6 (1999): 1597–1630.

persuasive in arguing for the former. Yet, since we already know that income inequality is a major cause of insurgency (see Chapter 13), if two nations have widely different levels of income, it may not be too important what their respective population sizes are. Consider conflicts between Pakistan and India, or tensions between China and North Korea. What seems to count in those cases is not the size of populations but many differences in culture, religion, income, and policy. In any event, even Firebaugh does not find evidence of convergence. ■

THE INDUSTRIAL REVOLUTION PRODUCED A STUNNING INCREASE IN THE INCOME DISparity between nations. At the beginning of the 19th century, average incomes in the richest nations were perhaps four times greater than those in the poorest nations. At the end of the 20th century, average incomes in the richest nations are 30 times larger—annual incomes of about $18,000 versus $600 (Summers, Heston, Aten, and Nuxoll 1994).

Is the income disparity between nations still increasing? The answer to that question is critical. Because of the great disparity in average income from nation to nation, it is intercountry inequality—not inequality within nations—that is the major component of total income inequality in the world today. A recent sociological study estimates that inequality across countries accounts for over 90% of current world income inequality as measured by the Gini index. Other studies give lower estimates, but all agree with Berry, Bourguignon, and Morrisson (1983b, p. 217) that "it is clear that the level of world inequality is . . . primarily due to differences in average incomes across countries rather than to intra-country inequality."

Although I begin with the question of whether intercountry inequality is still rising, the analysis does not end there. My aim is to provide the foundation for a general sociological literature on intercountry income inequality by getting the facts right about its key dimensions: Whether increasing or declining, is the trend in intercountry inequality due to differential economic growth across nations or to differential population growth across nations? Which countries contribute most to change in intercountry inequality? Are results robust over different inequality measures and income series? Although sociological studies of these important issues are rare, there is no good reason for sociologists to continue to shy away from studying intercountry inequality. Careful income estimates are available for over 100 nations, which constitutes a near-universe of the world's population (Summers et al. 1994), and convenient methods have been developed for analyzing income inequality for aggregates (Firebaugh 1998). The time is ripe for systematic sociological research on intercountry inequality. . . .

Cross-National Evidence

Cross-national studies of convergence appear at first glance to present a mish-mash of conflicting results. In this section I show that consistent findings do emerge when the studies are sorted carefully. I will also show that sociologists should not be too hasty to use the findings from economics to reach conclusions about trends in world income inequality because economists and sociologists are asking different questions.

It is useful first to place the convergence studies in historical perspective. At the outset of the Industrial Revolution average income in the richest nations was perhaps four times the average income in the poorest nations (Maddison 1995, chap. 2). Average income in the richest nations and poorest nations now differs by a factor of about 30. Over the long haul, then—from the late 18th century through much of the 20th—national incomes diverged. No one disputes that.

The more vexing question is what has happened since about 1960. Some studies conclude that there has been little or no change in intercountry inequality in recent decades (Berry et al. 1983a; Peacock et al. 1988; Schultz 1998) whereas other studies conclude that national incomes have continued to diverge (Jackman 1982; Sheehey 1996; Jones 1997; Korzeniewicz and Moran 1997).

There are three keys to making sense of these findings. The first key is weighting. Studies that do not weight generally find divergence, whereas studies that weight generally find very little change in intercountry inequality over recent decades. The second key is whether or not the national income data have been adjusted for "purchasing power parity" (PPP—elaborated in a subsequent section). The use of unadjusted data results in spurious divergence (Schultz 1998). The third key is China. Weighted studies that exclude China are suspect.

Studies of Unweighted Convergence

Table 4.1 summarizes key convergence studies from economics, sociology, and political science. In each of these studies the dependent variable is per capita income. Note that the income measure of choice is based on purchasing power parity; among recent studies only Korzeniewicz and Moran (1997) rely exclusively on income estimates that are based on the foreign exchange method.

The top panel of Table 4.1 summarizes studies that do not weight nations by size and the bottom panel summarizes studies that do. I begin with the studies in the top panel. One of the earliest reliable studies of cross-national convergence is Jackman's (1982) study of the relative income growth rates of 98 nations from 1960 to 1978. Jackman found an inverted-U pattern for the relationship between income growth rate and initial income—a pattern that was

Table 4.1 Summary of Major Studies of National Income Convergence*

Study	Data and Method	Conclusion
Unweighted by population:		
Jackman (1982; table 1, fig. 1)	Income growth rate, † 1960 (N=98); regression of rate on initial level	Divergence with inverted-U pattern
Abramovitz (1986)	1870–1979 income; ‡ coefficient of variation; 16 industrial nations (from Maddison 1982)	Long-run convergence among rich nations
Baumol (1986).	Same historical data as Abramovitz (1986), but uses regression	Long-run convergence among rich nations
Barro and Sala-i-Martin (1992; table 3, fig. 4)	Income growth rate, ‡ 1960–85 (N=98); regression of rate on initial level	Divergence
Sheehey (1996, table 2)	Income growth rate, ‡ 1960–88 (N=107 non-OPEC nations)	Divergence with inverted-U pattern
Jones (1997, tables 2, 3)	1960 and 1990 income (N=74); ‡ SD of logged income	Divergence for world but rich converge
Weighted by population:		
Berry et al. (1983a)	1950–77 income (N=124); ‡ Gini, Theil, mean log deviation, Atkinson	No overall trend
Peacock, Hoover, and Killian (1988, figs. 1, 2)	1950–80 income (N=53); ‡Theil	No overall trend, with convergence within world system strata and divergence between strata
Ram (1989)		
Table 1	1960–80 income (N=115; excludes China); ‡ Theil §	Divergence
Table 2	1960–80 inequality (N=21; regression of overall Theil on mean world income, 1960–80); excludes China in the Theil§	Inverted-U pattern
Korzeniewicz and Moran (1997)	1965–90 income (N=121); ‡ Gini, Theil	Divergence, especially in 1980s
Schulz (1998)	1960–89 income (N=120); ‖ Gini, variance of logged income, Theil	No trend for purchasing power parity income; divergence for foreign exchange (FX) rate income

Notes: *Because the object of this study is change in intercountry inequality, the table is restricted to studies of *unconditional* convergence, a term that refers to the absence of control variables. In regression analysis, unconditional convergence is examined by regressing growth rate of income per capita on intial level of income per capita. Conditional convergence is examined by adding control variables.

†Income estimates are based on foreign exchange rates.

‡Income estimates are based on purchasing power parity (PPP).

§The significance of excluding China in weighted analyses is addressed in the text. I do not note the unweighted analyses (top panel) that omit China because the omission of China hardly matters in those studies.

‖Income estimates are based both on foreign exchange rates and on purchasing power parity.

subsequently replicated in studies using different income measures and longer time periods (e.g., Summers and Heston 1991, table 4; Sheehey 1996). Despite this faster growth in the middle of the distribution, there is overall divergence because growth rates tend to be higher for the richest nations than for the poorest nations. Subsequent research has replicated the divergence finding as well (Barro and Sala-i-Martin 1992, table 3 and fig. 4; Sheehey 1996, table 2; Jones 1997, tables 2 and 3).

In short, when each national economy is given the same weight—the sort of convergence that interests economists because it bears on endogenous growth theory—there is an inverted-U pattern in which nations in the upper middle of the distribution tend to exhibit the fastest rates of income growth and those at the lower end of the distribution tend to exhibit the slowest rates of growth. The upshot is that national economies are diverging for the world as a whole even though there are convergence "clubs" (e.g., there is evidence of income convergence among Western European nations; see Abramovitz 1986; Baumol 1986; Jones 1997).

Studies of Weighted Convergence

Although it is weighted national convergence that bears most directly on sociologists' interest in world inequality, evidence on weighted national convergence is relatively scarce. In sharp contrast to the large and growing literature on unweighted convergence, the empirical literature on weighted convergence across nations consists of just a handful of studies.

The early study by Berry et al. (1983a) remains one of the best of these studies. Based on a large sample of nations containing most of the world's population, Berry et al. conclude, first, that economic growth in China was the most potent force equalizing world incomes from 1950 to 1977 and, second, that there was no clear-cut trend in intercountry income inequality from 1950 to 1977.

Remove China, then, and the data will show weighted divergence—precisely what Ram (1989) found for 1960–80 with China removed. Include China and the data will show no overall trend in intercountry income inequality in recent decades—precisely what Peacock et al. (1988) and Schultz (1998) found, replicating the main conclusion of Berry et al. (1983a). So the studies are quite consistent: Weighted by population, the data show no underlying trend in intercountry income inequality over recent decades; remove China, and the data show rising inequality.

Only one key finding remains to be explained: Korzeniewicz and Moran's (1997) anomalous finding of rising intercountry inequality despite their inclusion of China. Schultz (1998) provides the key to the puzzle. Schultz presents two sets of findings, one for income data based on purchasing power parity

(PPP) and one for income data based on foreign exchange (FX) rates (the type of income data used by Korzeniewicz and Moran). Intercountry income inequality rises for the FX income series but not for the PPP income series.

The important lesson to be learned from Schultz's (1998) two sets of findings is that researchers should not rely on official exchange rates when studying trends in relative national incomes. Though early studies in economics used FX estimates because PPP estimates were unavailable, PPP-based income is now the industry standard (in addition to the studies listed in Table 4.1 above, see Barro 1991; Mankiw et al. 1992; Levine and Renelt 1992; Quah 1996). The rationale for the switch to PPP income measures will be elaborated later.

To summarize: When each national economy is given the same weight, the data indicate national divergence. Yet weighted studies find stability (the weighted studies that find divergence do so because they exclude China or use dubious income data). So the issue turns on weighting: Do we want to give nations or individuals equal weight?

Weighted Versus Unweighted Convergence

Sociologists and economists are interested in intercountry convergence for different reasons. The stimulus for many economists is theoretical, to test theories of macroeconomic growth. Very often for economists, then, each nation represents one unit (one economy) and, in typical analyses, economic trends in Luxembourg count just as much as economic trends in China, even though China has nearly 3,000 times more people. By contrast, sociologists generally study intercountry income inequality because of what it can reveal about income inequality for the world as a whole (Korzeniewicz and Moran 1997), so sociologists are interested in whether there is intercountry convergence in the case where individuals, not nations, are given equal weight. Thus most sociologists are interested in weighted convergence. . . .

Weighting is likely to matter a lot in the case of intercountry inequality because nations vary so much in population size. Large nations such as China and India affect the weighted measure but have little effect on the unweighted measure, and the reverse is true for small, rich nations such as Luxembourg and Norway.

To verify the importance of weighting, Table 4.2 presents the weighted and unweighted trends in intercountry inequality from 1960 to 1989 (I use 1989 as the endpoint because the dissolution of the Soviet Union interrupts the income series at that point). I use variance of logged income (VarLog) because it is the inequality measure most often used in economic studies. Table 4.2 reports the results for five-year intervals.

The difference between the weighted and unweighted results is striking. The unweighted results confirm economists' findings of divergence. But when

Table 4.2   The 1960–89 Trends in Intercountry Income Inequality: Weighted Versus Unweighted Results

Year	Average World Income*		Inequality (VarLog)	
	Weighted	Unweighted	Weighted	Unweighted (Varlog)
1960	2,277	2,294	.91	.74
1965	2,660	2,729	1.04	.84
1970	3,118	3,266	1.08	.90
1975	3,426	3,761	1.11	.96
1980	3,835	4,303	1.07	1.02
1985	4,059	4,421	.96	1.08
1989	4,367	4,826	.96	1.18
1960–89 change (%)	+92	+110	+5	+59

Source: Summers et al. (1994).

Note: Real gross domestic product per capita is given in constant U.S. dollars (variable RGDPPC in the Penn income series, ver. 5.6); N=120 nations containing 92%–93% of the world population.

*Average per capita income for the 120 nations, in constant U.S. dollars. "Weighted average" indicates that the national means are weighted by population size.

nations are weighted by size, intercountry inequality increases monotonically until 1975 and declines thereafter; as a result, there is little net change in inequality from 1960 to 1989. . . .

Trend in Intercountry Income Inequality

The Korzeniewicz-Moran (1997) study provides a convenient point of departure for studying the trend in intercountry income inequality. As noted earlier, Korzeniewicz and Moran conclude that intercountry income inequality is rising. Because that conclusion fits nicely with a large body of sociological literature on world polarization, the study is likely to attract a good deal of attention among sociologists. Moreover, the finding seems plausible, given the growth spurt in world income in recent decades (Easterlin 1998): careful estimates (Summers et al. 1994) indicate that the world's per capita income, stated in constant U.S. dollars, almost doubled from 1960 to 1989 (from $2,277 in 1960 to $4,367 in 1989), and an increase of this magnitude certainly has enormous potential for destabilizing the distribution of income across nations. Have Korzeniewicz and Moran uncovered an important trend that other weighted studies have missed?

The answer is no. The Korzeniewicz-Moran findings are based on the FX rate method, which is an unreliable method for comparing national incomes (e.g., Summers and Heston 1991; Horioka 1994). It is well documented that the use of official exchange rates exaggerates intercountry inequality (Ram

1979) and produces spurious divergence in intercountry inequality (Summers and Heston 1991, table 4; Schultz 1998). When industry-standard income data are substituted for the data used by Korzeniewicz and Moran, the rise in intercountry inequality disappears. What Korzeniewicz and Moran have demonstrated is not world polarization but the "dangers of using market exchange rates when making international comparisons" (Horioka 1994, p. 298).

To demonstrate these points, it is necessary first to summarize central issues regarding the comparison of income across nations.

Income Data. International comparisons of economic activity traditionally were obtained by using the FX rate to convert each country's national account data to a common currency, usually the U.S. dollar. But FX rates are highly flawed calibrators of currencies for two reasons. First, many goods and services are not traded on the international market, so exchange rates are based on a restricted bundle of goods and services (Grosh and Nafziger 1986, p. 351). Because this failure to capture economic activity is especially acute for non-monetized exchange in nonindustrial nations, FX measures of national income tend to miss significant economic activity in poorer nations. Second, FX markets are not totally "free" but are routinely distorted by government policy and speculative capital movement. As a result, exchange rates fail to reflect accurately the actual purchasing power parities (PPPs) of currencies.

To alleviate the deficiencies of FX-based income measures, several economists at the University of Pennsylvania spearheaded an ambitious effort to estimate national incomes using PPP to calibrate local currencies. Cross-nation parity for goods and services was determined through detailed studies of national price structures. As a result of those efforts, there is now an income series—the Penn series (Summers, Kravis, and Heston 1980; Kravis, Heston, and Summers 1982; Summers and Heston 1991; Summers et al. 1994)—that does not rely on FX rate. Even critics of the PPP measure concede that it represents a big improvement over the old FX measure (Dowrick and Quiggin 1997).

To appreciate the severity of the problem with using foreign exchange rates to compare national incomes, consider the FX income estimates for China and Japan. The remarkable economic growth of China since 1978 (Nee 1991, fig. 1; Chow 1994; Mastel 1997) is reflected in the PPP income series, where China's income ratio jumps roughly 40% between 1975 and 1989. Incredibly, though, the FX-based World Bank income series used by Korzeniewicz and Moran fails to capture that growth; instead it indicates that China's growth rate lagged so far behind the rest of the world that the FX income ratio for China declined by a whopping one-third from 1970 to 1989 (from .139 to .090).

The FX estimates for Japan are just as misleading. Though Japan experienced brisk economic growth through the 1970s and 1980s (Tachi 1993; Argy and Stein 1997), per capita income in Japan at the end of the 1980s still fell well short of incomes in the richest nations in the West (Horioka 1994). Yet FX-based income estimates place Japan's 1989 per capita income above per capita incomes in many rich Western nations (12% higher than Sweden and 16% higher than the United States; see World Bank 1993).

How do FX income estimates become so distorted? The Japanese case is illustrative. The use of foreign exchange rates to compare incomes leads one to conclude that Japanese per capita income as a percentage of U.S. per capita income rose from 67% in 1985 to 121% in 1988 (Horioka 1994, table 1). Obviously an increase of this magnitude in just three years would have been nothing short of miraculous. In fact this stupendous increase is "nothing more than a statistical illusion" (Horioka 1994, p. 297) caused by the too-rapid appreciation of the yen from 238 yen to the dollar in 1985 to 128 yen to the dollar in 1988. As Horioka (1994, table 1) demonstrates, more realistic measurement indicates that the Japan/U.S. income ratio rose only marginally over those three years, from 0.74 in 1985 to 0.76 in 1988.

In addition to the evidence that official exchange rates yield implausible income estimates for specific nations such as Japan and China, there are critical theoretical reasons for using PPP-based estimates when comparing incomes across nations (Summers and Heston 1980, 1991; Grosh and Nafziger 1986). Though Korzeniewicz and Moran (1997, p. 1011) state that the FX rate method "provides a better relational indicator of *command over income*" (emphasis in original), to the extent that exchange rates bear on command over income, they do so in the *world marketplace*—a largely hypothetical concept in the workaday world of the vast majority of the world's population. For the vast majority of the world's population, foreign-exchange-rate income is largely moot, since most of what is produced is not traded internationally. People face local prices, not international prices. This is not to deny that foreign-exchange-rate price can affect local price, but it is to say that an ox does not become half-an-ox when a nation decides to devalue its currency by half relative to the U.S. dollar.

Trends for FX Versus PPP Income Estimates

Table 4.3 reports the 1965–89 trend in intercountry inequality based on both PPP and FX income. I try to replicate the Korzeniewicz and Moran (1997) study as closely as possible. First, I rely on the same source for FX income estimates—the World Bank (1993)—and I use the same population data. Second, I use 1965 as the starting point. Third, I use the inequality indexes they used, the Theil and the Gini (results for V^2 and VarLog are similar). Finally, to ensure that results do not vary because of sampling differences, both "samples" here represent a near-universe of the world's people.

Table 4.3   Results for PPP-Based Versus FX-Based Income Estimates

| Year | PPP | | FX | | | |
| | | | Theil | | Gini | |
	Theil	Gini	Nominal	Adjusted	Nominal	Adjusted
1965	.552	.560	.816	.762	.661	.643
1970	.548	.558	.826	.771	.666	.647
1975	.540	.555	.847	.775	.674	.650
1980	.531	.550	.878	.782	.681	.650
1985	.512	.539	.963	.835	.706	.663
1989	.526	.543	1.079	.900	.733	.683
1965–89 Change (%)	–4.7	–3.0	+32.2	+18.1	+10.9	+6.2

Source: Summers et al. (1994) for the PPP income data and World Bank (1993) for the FX income data.

Note: There are 120 nations in the PPP data set and 112 nations in the FX data set. The data sets contain both capitalist and socialist nations and all populous nations and cover over 90% of the world's population. Theil and Gini results are reported to allow comparison with results offered by Korzeniewicz and Moran (1997). Results for V^2 and VarLog lead to the same conclusions. Under FX, "nominal" uses exchange-rate income estimates as given and "adjusted" uses more realistic estimates of income trends in China and Japan.

The results vividly demonstrate the difference in the two income series. According to the PPP-based income estimates, intercountry inequality declined modestly from 1965 to 1989. Yet according to the FX-based estimates, intercountry income inequality shot up 32.2% based on the Theil and 10.9% based on the Gini. Korzeniewicz and Moran (1997, table 3) report similar results (increases of 38.2% based on the Theil and 12.5% based on the Gini). These results reinforce the warning of, among others, Summers and Heston (1991, p. 355) that "it really makes a difference if exchange rates are used rather than PPPs" so "the practice of using exchange rates as quick, easily obtained estimates of PPPs is invalidated" (p. 335).

To see if the misleading FX income estimates for China and Japan matter much, I estimated a second, adjusted set of FX-based trends in intercountry income inequality [table not included here]. These results are based on the same FX income data as before, except that I use better income ratio estimates for China and Japan. Using more defensible income ratios (based on PPP) for just those two nations reduces the observed increase in the Theil and the Gini by over 40%.

In short, Korzeniewicz and Moran found divergence because they used a dubious income measure. Lest there be any doubt that the FX data yield a specious increase in intercountry inequality, it should be noted that a recent technical analysis of the PPP data used here (Dowrick and Quiggen 1997) concludes that the PPP data are, if anything, biased in favor of polarization. If so, then my failure to replicate the Korzeniewicz-Moran polarization result using

PPP income cannot be dismissed on the ground that the use of PPP income as the yardstick stacks the deck against the polarization thesis.

If the FX income estimates tell the wrong story about recent trends in intercountry inequality, what is the right story? I now use PPP income estimates to answer that question. . . .

The Intercountry Income Inequality Plateau of 1960–89

It is well documented that, since about the mid-1970s, income inequality within the United States has risen after a long period of decline (Fischer et al. 1996; Nielsen and Alderson 1997). This phenomenon has been dubbed "the great U-turn" (Harrison and Bluestone 1988). Less appreciated is the pause in the long-run trend of rising intercountry inequality. This pause spans at least the 1960s, 1970s, and 1980s.

The discovery of a "great plateau" in the historical trend has important implications for our understanding of trends in world income inequality. One implication is that if income inequality across individuals has been increasing sharply for the world as a whole, as Korzeniewicz and Moran (1997) conclude, then the increase must be due to increases within nations. To cause the sort of increase in total world inequality that Korzeniewicz and Moran describe, the within-nation increase would need to be of colossal proportions because most of the total world income inequality is between, not within, nations.

A second implication of the plateau is that intercountry income inequality does not inevitably rise (or fall) with rising world income. Intercountry inequality was about the same in 1989 as it was 30 years earlier, and an important challenge for future studies is to determine why intercountry inequality remained so stable in a period when the world's average income shot up so rapidly. During a period of such great potential for destabilizing the distribution of income across nations, why did the variance neither increase nor decline? This study provides one part of the answer: offsetting trends in the most populous nations. The inequality-enhancing effects of rapid economic growth in Japan and sluggish economic growth in India were blunted by the inequality-reducing effects of rapid economic growth in China and slower-than-world-average population and economic growth in the United States over this period.

Finally, the discovery of the great plateau in weighted intercountry income inequality adds to the clamor for new sociological theories of national development (Gereffi 1989; Firebaugh 1992; Firebaugh and Beck 1994). Stable variance in the distribution of logged income across nations in a period of active core-periphery exchange calls into question fundamental assumptions sociologists have made about the impact of international exchange on national development. If the benefits of core-periphery movement of goods and capital in fact accrue primarily to rich nations and if this differential benefit is in fact the principal cause of intercountry income divergence (as dependency theory appears to claim), then it is hard to explain why the long-standing trend toward intercountry divergence was interrupted during an era of active core-periphery exchange.

References

Abramovitz, Moses. 1986. "Catching Up, Forging Ahead, and Falling Behind." *Journal of Economic History* 46:385–406.

Argy, Victor, and Leslie Stein. 1997. *The Japanese Economy*. New York: New York University Press.

Barro, Robert J. 1991. "Economic Growth in a Cross-Section of Countries." *Quarterly Journal of Economics* 106:407–43.

Barro, Robert J., and Xavier Sala-i-Martin. 1992. "Convergence." *Journal of Political Economy* 100:223–51.

Baumol, William J. 1986. "Productivity Growth, Convergence, and Welfare: What the Long-Run Data Show." *American Economic Review* 76:1072–85.

Berry, Albert, Francois Bourguignon, and Christian Morrisson. 1983a. "Changes in the World Distribution of Income between 1950 and 1977." *Economic Journal* 93:331–50.

———. 1983b. "The Level of World Inequality: How Much Can One Say?" *Review of Income and Wealth* 29:217–41.

Chow, Gregory C. 1994. *Understanding China's Economy*. Singapore: World Scientific.

Dowrick, Steve, and John Quiggin. 1997. "True Measures of GDP and Convergence." *American Economic Review* 87:41–64.

Easterlin, Richard A. 1998. *Growth Triumphant*. Ann Arbor: University of Michigan.

Firebaugh, Glenn. 1998. "Measuring Inequality: A Convenient Unifying Framework." Paper presented at the annual meeting of the Population Association of America, Chicago.

———. 1992. "Growth Effects of Foreign and Domestic Investment." *American Journal of Sociology* 98:105–30.

Firebaugh, Glenn, and Frank D. Beck. 1994. "Does Economic Growth Benefit the Masses? Growth, Dependence, and Welfare in the Third World." *American Sociological Review* 59:631–53.

Fischer, Claude S., Michael Hout, Martin Sanchez Jankowski, Samuel R. Lucas, Ann Swidler, and Kim Voss. 1996. *Inequality by Design*. Princeton, N.J.: Princeton University Press.

Gereffi, Gary. 1989. "Rethinking Development Theory: Insights from East Asia and Latin America." *Sociological Forum* 4:505–33.

Grosh, Margaret E., and E. Wayne Nafziger. 1986. "The Computation of World Income Distribution." *Economic Development and Cultural Change* 34:347–59.

Harrison, Bennett, and Barry Bluestone. 1988. *The Great U-Turn: Corporate Restructuring and the Polarizing of America*. New York: Basic Books.

Horioka, Charles Yuji. 1994. "Japan's Consumption and Saving in International Perspective." *Economic Development and Cultural Change* 42:293–316.

Jackman, Robert W. 1982. "Dependence on Foreign Investment and Economic Growth in the Third World." *World Politics* 34:175–96.

Jones, Charles I. 1997. "Convergence Revisited." *Journal of Economic Growth* 2:131–53.

Korzeniewicz, Roberto P., and Timothy P. Moran. 1997. "World-Economic Trends in the Distribution of Income, 1965–1992." *American Journal of Sociology* 102:1000–39.

Kravis, Irving B., Alan Heston, and Robert Summers. 1982. *World Product and Income.* Baltimore: Johns Hopkins University Press.

Levine, Ross, and David Renelt. 1992. "A Sensitivity Analysis of Cross-Country Growth Regressions." *American Economic Review* 82:942–63.

Maddison, Angus. 1995. *Explaining the Economic Performance of Nations.* Brookfield, Vt.: Edward Elgar.

Mankiw, N. Gregory, David Romer, and David N. Weil. 1992. "A Contribution to the Empirics of Economic Growth." *Quarterly Journal of Economics* 107:407–37.

Mastel, Greg. 1997. *The Rise of the Chinese Economy.* London: M. E. Sharpe.

Nee, Victor. 1991. "Social Inequalities in Reforming State Socialism: Between Redistribution and Markets in China." *American Sociological Review* 56:267–82.

Nielsen, Francois, and Arthur S. Alderson. 1997. "The Kuznets Curve and the Great U-Turn: Income Inequality in U.S. Counties, 1970 to 1990." *American Sociological Review* 62:12–33.

Peacock, Walter Gillis, Greg A. Hoover, and Charles D. Killian. 1988. "Divergence and Convergence in International Development: A Decomposition Analysis of Inequality in the World System." *American Sociological Review* 53:838–52.

Quah, Danny T. 1996. "Convergence Empirics across Economies with (Some) Capital Mobility." *Journal of Economic Growth* 1:95–124.

Ram, Rati. 1979. "International Income Inequality: 1970 and 1978." *Economics Letters* 4:187–90.

Schultz, T. Paul. 1998. "Inequality in the Distribution of Personal Income in the World: How It Is Changing and Why." *Journal of Economics* 11:307–44.

Sheehey, Edmund J. 1996. "The Growing Gap between Rich and Poor Countries: A Proposed Explanation." *World Development* 24:1379–84.

Summers, Robert, and Alan Heston. 1991. "The Penn World Table (Mark 5): An Expanded Set of International Comparisons, 1950–1988." *Quarterly Journal of Economics* 106:327–68.

Summers, Robert, Alan Heston, Bettina Aten, and Daniel Nuxoll. 1994. *Penn World Table* (PWT) Mark 5.6a Data (MRDF). Center for International Comparisons, University of Pennsylvania.

Summers, Robert, Irving B. Kravis, and Alan Heston. 1980. "International Comparisons of Real Product and Its Composition, 1950–1977." *Review of Income and Wealth* 26:19–66.

Tachi, Ryuichiro. 1993. *The Contemporary Japanese Economy*, translated by Richard Walker. Tokyo: University of Tokyo Press.

World Bank. 1993. *World Tables of Economic and Social Indicators, 1950–1992* (MRDF). Washington, D.C.: World Bank, International Economics Department. Distributed by Inter-University Consortium for Political and Social Research, Ann Arbor. Michigan.

5

Assessing Contending
Measures of the Income Gap

JOHN T PASSÉ-SMITH

AMARTYA SEN, NOBEL LAUREATE IN ECONOMICS, WARNED THAT DEBATING THE trends in global inequality is counterproductive because it diverts attention away from the sheer magnitude of the gap between rich and poor countries and thus away from global poverty (Sen 2001). Indeed, global poverty and the extent of the gap between rich and poor countries are immensely important, and we should not be distracted from their impact on people. One measure of this gap, the relative gap, shows that in 2005 poor countries' mean GDP/pc was 1.51 percent of the GDP/pc of the rich (see Chapter 2). However, once one fills in the specifics of the degree of human suffering resulting from such conditions, the question arises: Is it getting better or worse? This question is really no less important than understanding the extent of the problem because it allows policymakers and scholars to assess policy prescriptions. In other words, it is important to know if the liberal austerity policies required by the International Monetary Fund when loaning money to developing countries improves their conditions or makes them worse.

For many years the bulk of the evidence pointed to a widening gap. Most scholars seemed satisfied with the evidence and conclusion that the gap was expanding. Even staff writers at the International Monetary Fund and studies commissioned by the World Bank concluded that the gap between rich and poor was growing (see Chapter 3 by Robert Hunter Wade and Chapter 12 by IMF staff writers). However, in the 1980s, economics journals began giving more column space to the proponents of convergence theory. In its purest form, convergence theory proposes that the poorer the country, the higher its economic growth potential. Theorists such as Moses Abramovitz (1986), Paul Romer (1994), and William Baumol (1986) argued that productive technology invented and used in the very competitive markets of the First World relatively quickly lost its competitive advantage as innovation replaced innovation. This forced companies to adopt newer innovations and transfer antiquated productive technologies to the developing world, where they remained competitive. The poorer a country, the more generations of technology had yet to be absorbed; thus, they would have a higher potential to grow.

Although it would appear that most studies continue to find that that the gap is growing (Korzeniewicz and Moran 2005, 1997; Babones 2002; Wade 2001; IMF Staff 1998; Pritchett 1996; Maddison 1995; Peacock et al. 1988; Breedlove and Nolan 1988; De Long 1988; Morawetz 1977; Kirman and Tomasini 1969), a number of studies began to challenge the conventional wisdom and suggest that the gap was either stable or shrinking (Firebaugh 2003, 1999; Goesling 2001; Williamson 1996; Mankiw, Romer, and Weil 1992; Ram 1989; Baumol 1986; Abramovitz 1986). While this listing of studies blurs the nuances in the methodologies and conclusions drawn, it does amply demonstrate that there is now some degree of controversy concerning the behavior of the gap. Beyond the contradictory conclusions, the most striking factor differentiating the studies is that most of the studies concluding that the gap is growing utilize exchange-rate-converted *(fx)* national accounts statistics and those finding that the gap is stable or shrinking use purchasing-power-parity (PPP) converted data. Since this choice of data sets appears to have such a profound impact on the conclusions drawn, it is important to pause and reexamine the reasons for choosing one data set over the other.

The Problems with Exchange-Rate-Converted Data

Over time three major criticisms of *fx* national accounts statistics have been raised. The first is sometimes referred to as the "traveler's dilemma." As a person travels from one country to the next, the money it takes to buy a common provision, such as bread (or its equivalent), can be drastically different from one country to the next. In other words, the currency it takes to purchase one bagel in Little Rock, Arkansas, when converted to Mexican pesos may buy a bag full of tortillas in Guadalajara; yet that same currency converted to yen may not be sufficient to purchase much of anything at all in Tokyo. Thus a straightforward conversion of currency using an exchange rate does not measure the difference in purchasing power from one country to the next. Therefore, a country that appears to be poor due to a low GDP/pc may not be so poor if its currency purchases a relatively high volume of goods in comparison to other currencies. According to proponents of PPP conversions, GDPs converted to a common currency utilizing official exchange rates *overstate* the poverty of poor countries in a systematic way (Summers and Heston 1984; Morris 1979; Kravis et al. 1975; Heston 1973; and Kuznets 1972). At the intuitive level, they point out, humans simply could not survive at the apparent level of development as stated in *fx*-converted GDP/pc.

Second, even the most cursory examination of *fx* over time makes it manifestly clear that exchange rates fluctuate and, at times, do so rapidly and violently. A number of issues arise from these fluctuations that could inject significant error in the comparison of countries. For example, when attempting to compare a country's relative level of development, the simple act of selecting between the World Bank's beginning-of-year, midyear average, or end-of-year exchange rate for purposes of conversion can have a profound impact on a given country's apparent wealth. Indeed, Morris (1979, 10) illustrates this point when he highlighted the exchange rate behavior and its consequences for Brazil. Brazil's official exchange rate during the first quarter of 1981 was 70.8 cruzeiros per US dollar; by midyear the exchange rate had climbed to 91.8, and by year's end the official rate stood at 118.[1] A scholar's choice of which exchange rate to use to convert Brazil's national account statistics into a common currency would drastically change the apparent wealth of Brazil by up to 60 percent.

Further complicating the picture, economists suggest that when two countries enter into trade and neither government interferes in its respective economy in such a way as to distort prices, their exchange rates settle into "equilibrium." The equilibrium exchange rate is the perfect, or ideal, exchange rate for the countries at their current levels of development and interaction. Louka Katseli-Papaefstratiou (1979) asserts that if exchange rates were stable at the hypothesized equilibrium value, then exchange-rate-converted GDP/pc would be a more accurate reflection of a country's level of development; but, as was pointed out earlier, exchange rates are not stable. As noted, exchange rates fluctuate rather quickly, and for a variety of reasons, including inflation, changes in production techniques, government intervention in exchange markets, import and export barriers, and price shocks originating domestically or internationally. The restoration of equilibrium, however, occurs very slowly (for further discussion, see Katseli-Papaefstratiou 1979, 4). The rapid fluctuations away from equilibrium and the ponderous return to it are not synchronized with the World Bank's reporting of *fx*s, thereby rendering any systematic decision (to always use midyear averages or end-of-year data) potentially flawed. Katseli-Papaefstratiou further complicates the point by explaining that the equilibrium exchange rate itself is a hypothetical construct (1979, 4).

The third major criticism of *fx* data was described by Simon Kuznets (1972, 8), who asserted that because many low-income countries retain sizeable elements of precapitalistic production and noncash trade that go unreported in national accounts statistics, their national accounts overstated poverty. For example, a farmer may have a number of pigs that can be traded for other foodstuffs, clothing, services, and the like, but none of this economic activity is captured by national accounts statistics because barter transactions never become part of the moneyed economy. Even monetary transactions in the informal sector, however, are not included in national accounts statistics. For instance, the schoolteacher in Mexico City who earns extra cash by taping a "Taxi" sign on his or her automobile without an official permit will not report those earnings and thus will not be counted in the formal economy. As countries develop, Kuznets explains, these informal sectors gradually give way to the formal, moneyed economy that is measured with national accounts statistics.

Critics who adopt any or all of these three criticisms tend to support the same solution: the replacement of the exchange rate with a purchasing-power-parity conversion factor. Beginning in 1968 and continuing today, the International Comparisons Project (ICP) produces one such conversion factor. In 1984 Robert Summers and Alan Heston reported that the ICP had "develop[ed] a structural relationship between purchasing power parities and exchange rates . . . [that took] account of the variability of exchange rates" (1984, 207–208). The ICP conducts extensive research in thirty-four benchmark countries, and that information is used to extrapolate the data for the remaining nonbenchmark countries. In 1988 the sample was expanded to 130 countries covering the period 1950 to 1985. This data set has been regularly updated, and the current data set, the Penn World Tables 6.2, offers data for 188 countries between 1950 and 2004 (http://pwt.econ.upenn.edu/). The data set, according to PPP proponents, corrects for all three of the major problems of the *fx* conversion factor. It overcomes the traveler's dilemma by producing a real GDP/pc (PPP-converted GDP/pc) that can be trusted to convey the ability of an individual to purchase a set basket of goods from one country to the next. It also overcomes or adjusts for the vicissitudinous nature of the exchange rates. Finally, the PPP conversion factor is able to capture informal transactions by including variables measuring the structure of the economy.

Although economists have been quick to adopt PPP-converted national accounts statistics, sociologists and political scientists have only gradually migrated to PPP data. Although it has been slow, there does *seem* to be a trend toward the acceptance of the so-called real GDP/pc (hereafter called rGDP/pc). In fact, two of the studies cited earlier used PPP data from the Penn World Tables (version 5.6a) to show that global inequality is either stable (Firebaugh 1999) or converging (Goesling 2001). While both of these studies were published in a prestigious sociological journal (the *American Journal of Sociology*), the *fx*/PPP debate is far from settled. In 1997 Roberto Korzeniewicz and Timothy Moran specifically selected the more traditional World Bank *fx* data and concluded that divergence, not convergence, characterized international development (Korzeniewicz and Moran 1997). Salvatore Babones (2002) disputes the findings of Firebaugh, arguing that whether one uses PPP conversion factors or exchange rates, the gap is growing.

In the following section I will attempt to determine if the purchasing-power-parity conversion factor corrects for the problems identified here. In the final section I will examine the gap and its behavior across the two data sets.

GDP/pc and Real GDP/pcs Compared

Turning to the data, this section compares exchange rate with PPP-converted GDP/pc to determine if the rGDP/pc corrects for the weaknesses of the *fx* converted data. The exchange-rate-converted GDP/pc data were obtained from the World Bank's *World Development Indicators, 2007* (online). Growth rates for both data sets were computed using the regression method described by the World Bank in the *World Development Report* (World Bank 1988, 288–289).[2] The income groupings were borrowed from the World Bank's *World Development Indicators, 2007* (see the Tables, Quick Reference section where the technical notes offer the "Classification of economies by income and region").[3] All gross domestic products per capita, both *fx* and PPP, are in constant US dollars with a base year of 2000.

Criticism 1: The fx-*converted data do not take into account purchasing power. Poverty in poor countries is overstated because any traveler can tell you that money seems to go much further in poor countries.* A comprehensive test of this criticism of exchange-rate-converted data would have the researcher traveling from country to country purchasing a common basket of goods in order to see if the basket cost less in poorer countries, thus overstating the poverty of the poor. Since the money for that venture is unlikely to appear, a minimal test would be to see if the PPP data set makes countries appear to be richer than the *fx* data set. Whether this increased wealth for the poor actually reflects increased purchasing power will be left for others to determine. It should be mentioned, however, that the PPP conversion factor is one factor for the entire country. This means that the United States has one conversion factor that is supposed to identify the price at which a common basket of goods can be purchased, whether that person happens to be in Conway, Arkansas; Nashville, Tennessee; or New York, New York.

To determine if the ICP data make poor countries appear richer, Table 5.1 offers a comparison of the ICP and *fx*-converted GDP/pcs for 2003. The first column in Table 5.1 lists all of the countries identified in the *fx* data set as belonging to the lower-middle-income and poor groups in 2003. The overwhelming conclusion to be drawn from the data presented in Table 5.1 is that the ICP data set does indeed make poor countries appear to be richer. The GDP/pc of lower-middle-income countries when converted by the PPP is 295 percent higher than the exchange-rate-converted data. As should occur if the purchasing power parity is working appropriately, the average GDP/pc for the poor countries shows an even greater variation, with the poorest countries looking 419.9 percent richer than under the exchange-rate-converted data. Without exception, every single country's rGDP/pc in the lower-middle-income and poor categories is higher than the GDP/pc.

The column on the far right side of the table reports the human development index (HDI) for each country. The HDI is an attempt to measure coun-

Table 5.1 GDP/pc and rGDP/pc for Lower-Middle-Income and Poor Countries

	GDP/pc 2003	rGDP/pc 2003	rGDP/pc – GDP/pc (difference)	rGDP/pc as a Percentage of GDP/pc	HDI 2003
Lower-Middle-Income					
Thailand	$2,238	$7,275	$5,037	325.0	0.78
Dominican Republic	$2,430	$6,899	$4,469	283.9	0.75
Colombia	$2,035	$6,095	$4,060	299.5	0.79
Algeria	$1,974	$5,993	$4,019	303.5	0.73
China	$1,209	$4,970	$3,761	411.1	0.77
Paraguay	$1,319	$4,718	$3,399	357.6	0.76
Sri Lanka	$921	$4,274	$3,354	464.3	0.76
Indonesia	$872	$4,121	$3,249	472.4	0.71
Egypt, Arab Republic	$1,543	$4,759	$3,216	308.4	0.70
Ecuador	$1,411	$4,330	$2,919	306.9	0.77
Morocco	$1,339	$4,060	$2,721	303.2	0.64
El Salvador	$2,105	$4,752	$2,646	225.7	0.73
Nicaragua	$821	$3,410	$2,589	415.2	0.70
Philippines	$1,049	$3,576	$2,527	340.9	0.76
Peru	$2,148	$4,351	$2,203	202.5	0.77
Guatemala	$1,718	$3,805	$2,087	221.5	0.67
Bolivia	$1,020	$3,006	$1,986	294.8	0.69
Honduras	$942	$2,292	$1,349	243.2	0.68
Syrian Arab Republic	$1,130	$2,016	$886	178.4	0.72
Congo, Republic of	$935	$1,421	$486	152.0	0.52
Mean	*$1,458*	*$4,306*	*$2,848*	*295.3*	*0.72*
Poor					
India	$511	$2,990	$2,478	584.6	0.61
Pakistan	$545	$2,592	$2,047	475.6	0.54
Cameroon	$723	$2,713	$1,989	375.0	0.51
Zimbabwe	$479	$2,438	$1,958	508.5	0.49
Lesotho	$526	$2,005	$1,479	381.3	0.49
Côte d'Ivoire	$574	$2,019	$1,445	351.7	0.42
Nepal	$229	$1,441	$1,212	630.1	0.53
Ghana	$268	$1,440	$1,172	537.4	0.53
Rwanda	$244	$1,297	$1,054	532.4	0.45
Benin	$325	$1,345	$1,021	414.5	0.43
Senegal	$445	$1,407	$962	316.2	0.46
Burkina Faso	$247	$1,073	$827	435.2	0.34
Kenya	$417	$1,218	$801	291.9	0.49
Nigeria	$423	$1,223	$800	289.0	0.45
Chad	$208	$884	$675	424.3	0.37
Niger	$160	$835	$675	521.5	???
Burundi	$106	$764	$658	719.8	0.38
Malawi	$146	$770	$624	525.9	0.40
Zambia	$327	$946	$619	289.6	0.41
Togo	$243	$789	$545	324.3	0.50
Madagascar	$224	$759	$535	339.2	0.51
Mean	*$351*	*$1,474*	*$1,123*	*419.9*	*0.47*

Source: World Bank, *World Development Indicators, 2007* (Washington, DC: World Bank, 2007).

tries' standard of living by creating a composite index of health, education, and income. Even though the poorest countries appear to be richer, the HDI scores still make intuitive sense. The average HDI score of the lower-middle-income countries is 0.72 while the poor countries only average 0.47, as one would expect. A bivariate correlation of the HDI, GDP/pc, and rGDP/pc for the year 2003 indicates that the HDI is slightly more in tune with the rGDP/pc (r = 0.82) than the GDP/pc (r = 0.75).

Criticism 2: Exchange-rate-converted data are susceptible to fluctuations that are smoothed by the PPP conversion. As mentioned earlier, the criticism of *fx* data is that exchange rates are susceptible to wild and sometimes exaggerated fluctuations for a variety of reasons. One way to determine if the PPP converters are smoothing these fluctuations in exchange rates would be to examine correlation coefficients of GDP/pc and rGDP/pc of a select group of countries. Certainly this is not the most sophisticated test, but if one of two variables being correlated is fluctuating and the other corrects and smooths, then it should be detectable in a correlation coefficient. A low correlation coefficient between a country's GDP/pc and rGDP/pc would likely indicate that the PPP conversion factor was smoothing the more active exchange rate, while a very robust coefficient would suggest that the measures are either both smoothing or both moving together.

The data set was sorted by the GDP/pc in 1960, and the richest and poorest countries in each income group were selected. Each country's GDP/pc and rGDP/pc from 1960 to 2003 was correlated; the correlation coefficients are reported in Table 5.2. Admittedly, the correlation between GDP/pc and rGDP/pc should be high, but if the PPP conversion smooths fluctuations in exchange rate conversions, then it seems the coefficient should be somewhat lower than r = 0.99. The overall conclusion to be drawn from the table is that the correlation coefficients are very strong. One is not able to detect that the PPP-converted data are smoothing out wildly fluctuating *fx* data. The correlation coefficient for

Table 5.2   Correlation Coefficients of GDP/pc and rGDP/pc for Selected Countries

Country	Income Group	Correlation Coefficient
Switzerland	Upper-income	0.998
Iceland	Upper-income	0.999
Netherlands	Upper-middle-income	0.999
Hong Kong	Upper-middle-income	0.996
Mexico	Lower-middle-income	0.997
Dominican Republic	Lower-middle-income	0.988
Paraguay	Poor	0.993
Burundi	Poor	0.961

Sources: Computed from World Bank, *World Development Indicators, 2007* (Washington, DC: World Bank, 2007) and the Penn World Tables 6.2 (http://pwt.econ.upenn.edu/icp.html).

all of the countries except Burundi is in excess of r = .099; Burundi had a correlation coefficient of 0.96.

Criticism 3: Poor countries have active informal sectors that are not captured in the standard exchange rate conversion. This makes poor countries look poorer than they actually are. According to proponents of PPP, *fx* conversions exaggerate the poverty of the poor because transactions in the informal sector are not measured by the *fx* conversion factor. Thus, a pig traded for clothes or some other good or service is not measured as a part of the formal economy, and therefore when the data are aggregated, the country looks poorer than it actually is. As a country develops, the bartering and informal sector transactions disappear, so a much larger percentage of the actual economy is measured. Thus, it is thought that the *fx* conversion produces a much more accurate measure of wealth for rich countries than for the poor. Not only do the PPP-converted national accounts statistics make the poor countries look richer, but the countries that were rich in the 1950s and 1960s appear to be slightly less rich than the *fx* conversion makes them appear. If the expectations for the PPP conversion factor are met, it should be expected that the rGDP/pc for poor countries will be substantially higher than the GDP/pc, and the rGDP/pc for rich countries should be slightly lower than the GDP/pc. For countries moving from poverty to wealth, the rGDP/pc should at first be substantially higher than the GDP/pc, but if past patterns persist, somewhere in the development process the two measures (*fx* and PPP) should cross such that when the formerly poor country becomes wealthy, its rGDP/pc should be slightly lower than the GDP/pc.

Figures 5.1a through 5.1d graph both the GDP/pc and the rGDP/pc between 1960 and 2003 for Switzerland, Burkina Faso, the Republic of Korea, and Singapore. Switzerland was selected because it is one of the few countries that has been in the upper-income category for all forty-six years. Burkina Faso was selected because it remained in the poor category for the entire period under examination. Both the Republic of Korea and Singapore were selected because they climbed across the most income categories, rising from the lower-middle-income to the upper-income category. Here we should expect to see that the rGDP/pc of richer countries, such as Switzerland, makes them look somewhat less rich than does its GDP/pc. Burkina Faso is one of the poorest countries in the world; its rGDP/pc measure should make it look substantially richer than does its GDP/pc. With the Republic of Korea and Singapore, the rGDP/pc should initially make them look richer than their GDP/pc measurements, but then the lines should cross and, as they become upper-income countries, the rGDP/pc should make them look slightly poorer than their GDP/pc.

Figures 5.1a and 5.1b, depicting the economic growth of Switzerland and Burkina Faso, behave as expected. The rGDP/pc makes Burkina Faso appear to be substantially wealthier than the GDP/pc while making Switzerland ap-

Figure 5.1a   GDP/pc and rGDP/pc for Switzerland, 1960 to 2003

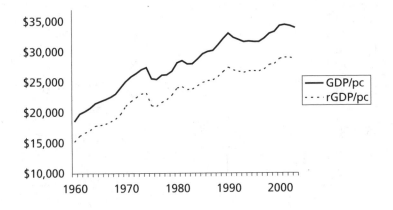

Figure 5.1b   GDP/pc and rGDP/pc for Burkina Faso, 1960 to 2003

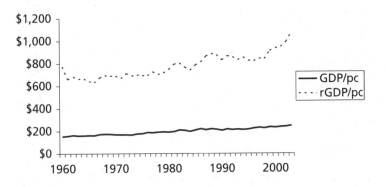

pear to be slightly less wealthy. Figures 5.1c and 5.1d, showing the Republic of Korea and Singapore's rapid and sustained economic growth, present a problem for proponents of PPP-converted figures. The exchange-rate-converted data are the heavy solid black line. At the outset all is well, as the figure confirms that the *fx* data overstate the poverty of the two developing countries when they were poorer. However, as they both continue to grow, the lines never reverse. The rGDP/pc continues to make both the Republic of Korea and Singapore look wealthier, even though Singapore's rGDP/pc surpasses that of the United Kingdom, Sweden, Belgium, and the Netherlands. In fact, it continues to do so throughout the entire time period. If the PPP conversion factor

Figure 5.1c   GDP/pc and rGDP/pc for the Republic of Korea, 1960 to 2003

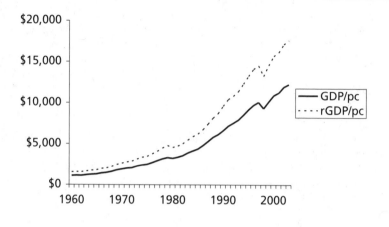

Figure 5.1d   GDP/pc and rGDP/pc for Singapore, 1960 to 2003

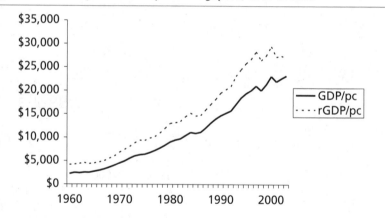

was going to work as it does for the old rich countries, we should expect that at some threshold the rGDP/pc will drop below the GDP/pc to make the Republic of Korea and Singapore look slightly poorer, as they do for the "old rich" countries such as Switzerland (see Figure 5.1a).

It could be, however, that the failure of the rGDP/pc to make these two newly rich countries (the Republic of Korea and Singapore) poorer is restricted to these two countries. Perhaps it is a quirk of their economies or the economic structure of the Asian NICs or just a fluke. Table 5.3 presents data

Table 5.3   Comparing GDP/pc and rGDP/pc for the Old Rich and the Newly Rich

	rGDP/pc 1960	GDP/pc 1960	rGDP/pc 2003	GDP/pc 2003	rGDP/pc Minus GDP/pc 1960	rGDP/pc Minus GDP/pc 2003
Old Rich[a]						
Switzerland	$15,254	$18,580	$28,792	$33,886	−$3,326	−$5,095
United States	$13,030	$14,134	$34,875	$35,313	−$1,104	−$437
Luxembourg	$12,888	$13,314	$49,261	$48,838	−$426	$424
Denmark	$11,354	$12,351	$27,970	$30,273	−$998	−$2,302
Sweden	$10,955	$11,242	$26,138	$28,327	−$287	−$2,189
Norway	$9,375	$10,650	$34,013	$38,404	−$1,274	−$4,391
United Kingdom	$10,353	$10,363	$26,044	$25,885	−$10	$159
Iceland	$8,252	$10,075	$26,352	$31,532	−$1,823	−$5,180
Mean	*$11,433*	*$12,589*	*$31,681*	*$34,057*	*−$1,156*	*−$2,377*
Newly Rich[b]						
Netherlands	$10,485	$9,268	$26,154	$24,148	$1,217	$2,006
Australia	$10,781	$8,978	$27,872	$22,405	$1,803	$5,467
New Zealand	$12,104	$8,185	$22,197	$14,802	$3,919	$7,395
France	$8,605	$7,703	$25,663	$22,963	$902	$2,700
Belgium	$8,051	$7,596	$25,262	$23,136	$456	$2,126
Austria	$8,495	$7,569	$27,567	$24,650	$926	$2,917
Finland	$7,674	$7,320	$23,786	$24,462	$354	−$676
Japan	$4,632	$7,099	$24,036	$37,244	−$2,467	−$13,207
Italy	$7,103	$5,818	$22,924	$19,465	$1,285	$3,459
Israel	$6,526	$5,533	$20,715	$17,307	$993	$3,409
Ireland	$5,380	$4,987	$28,247	$28,323	$392	−$76
Spain	$4,965	$3,716	$20,642	$15,138	$1,249	$5,504
Greece	$4,156	$3,120	$15,787	$11,882	$1,036	$3,904
Hong Kong, China	$3,264	$3,073	$27,656	$26,236	$191	$1,420
Portugal	$3,677	$2,337	$17,333	$10,966	$1,340	$6,367
Singapore	$4,211	$2,251	$27,004	$23,183	$1,960	$3,821
Korea, Rep.	$1,544	$1,110	$17,595	$12,245	$434	$5,350
Mean	*$6,568*	*$5,627*	*$23,555*	*$21,092*	*$941*	*$2,464*

Source: World Bank, *World Development Indicators, 2007* (Washington, DC: World Bank, 2007).
Notes: a. A country in the upper-income category all forty-six years (1960–2006).
   b. A country joining the upper-income category after 1960.

from all of the wealthy countries, both the "old rich" and the "new rich," and shows their GDP/pc and rGDP/pc for 1960 and 2003. The two columns on the far right side of the table show the difference between the rGDP/pc and the GDP/pc. The eight countries at the top of the table are the "old rich" upper-income countries that were upper-income in 1960 and in 2003. The countries at the bottom of the table are the "old rich" countries that joined the upper-income category after 1960. Note that in every single case the PPP-converted data made these original eight look slightly poorer than did the *fx*-converted data. However, all of the "new rich" countries except Japan experienced the opposite effect. The "new rich" all have rGDP/pc that continues to make them look richer than their GDP/pc.

The Gap Between Rich and Poor

A simple method of determining if the gap between rich and poor countries is opening or closing is to examine the standard deviation around the average GDP/pc of all countries over time. If the gap is closing, then the standard deviation should grow smaller, meaning that countries are moving closer to the world average GDP/pc. Figure 5.2 shows the mean rGDP/pc and GDP/pc for all countries (N = 78) and the standard deviations of both the rGDP/pc and the GDP/pc between 1960 and 2003. It is clear that global economic growth has been rather consistent over the entire period. The figure shows that both the real GDP/pc and the GDP/pc are growing larger over time. As should not be surprising by this point, the rGDP/pc for the world is larger than the GDP/pc, and a visual inspection of the means suggests that the gap between the rGDP/pc and the GDP/pc is opening very gradually over time.

The line representing standard deviations in Figure 5.2 rises as it moves from the bottom left toward the top right quadrant of the figure, meaning the standard deviations are getting larger and thus the gap between the richest and poorest countries in the world is opening wider. Also, the standard deviation of the rGDP/pc is smaller than the GDP/pc, which means that the gap between

Figure 5.2   Means of World GDP/pc and rGDP/pc and Standard Deviations

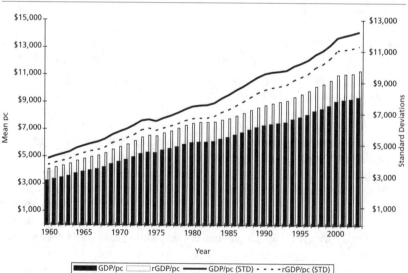

rich and poor is smaller when considering the rGDP/pc than the GDP/pc. In theory this is not too surprising in that the rGDP/pc is supposed to increase the apparent wealth of the poor and decrease the apparent wealth of the rich. If that were the case, then this pattern should be expected; however, the evidence suggests that the rGDP/pc is quite successful in making the poorer countries look richer but that it also makes most of the rich countries appear richer as well. That said, the rGDP/pc suggests that the gap between rich and poor is not as bad as that reported by the standard deviation of the mean GDP/pc. It is interesting to note that the means and standard deviations of the two move in such concert. It appears that both measures point to a very slight closing of— or at least slowing of the expansion of—the gap in 1974. This slight closing of the gap repeats again around 1982 and 1992.

The gap as illustrated in Figure 5.2, however, may be presenting a misleading picture. It would not be surprising that as the world grows richer, the increase in the standard deviation away from the mean would also grow larger as a reflection of that increase. The coefficient of variation standardizes the deviation score for changing means so that one can be relatively sure that an increase in the coefficient of variation is not a relic of an increasing mean value.[4] Figure 5.3 displays the coefficient of variation for the RGDP/pc and the GDP/pc and presents a slightly different picture of the world than appears in the previous figure.

The coefficient of variation (the standard deviation divided by the mean) grows larger as the gap grows wider and shrinks as the gap closes. When the

Figure 5.3 Coefficient of Variation, 1960 to 2003

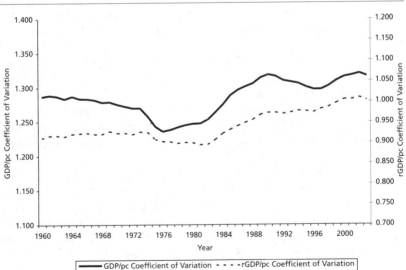

gap between rich and poor countries grows worse, the line representing the co-efficient of variation in the figure will move upward, and when countries are becoming more equal, the line representing the coefficient of variation will move downward. The coefficient of variation for the GDP/pc indicates that the gap between rich and poor lessened between 1960 (1.287) and 1976 (1.236) but then began to widen and did so steadily until 1990 (1.319). Although the rGDP/pc's coefficient of variation shows a similar trend over the entire time period, during the initial years the gap appeared to be unchanging; then, be-tween 1974 and 1982, it closed slightly (from 0.925 to 0.895). According to both the GDP/pc and rGDP/pc, global inequality between 1960 and 2003 worsened. The two straight dotted lines that rise steadily from the bottom left of the figure toward the top right of the figure are the trend lines for the GDP/pc and rGDP/pc. They display graphically that inequality is growing worse over time.

Growth Rates

The world grew at an average annual rate of 1.73 percent for the GDP/pc and 1.84 percent for the rGDP/pc for the seventy-eight countries in the sample (see Table 5.4). The *fx*-converted data shown in Table 5.4 indicate that the world grew impressively between 1960 and 1980; then, in the 1980s and 1990s, world growth declined from averages in excess of 2 percent to under 1 percent. The first five years of the new century witnessed a return of healthier growth rates as the world averaged 1.89 percent. The rGDP/pc shows an interesting difference. The 1960s and 1970s were strong growth decades with average rates at 2.8 percent and 2.44 percent, respectively; however, the 1980s and 1990s do not appear to be as bad when using the rGDP/pc growth rates. Nei-ther decade saw the global average drop below 1 percent. There was a global economic slowdown in the 1980s, with growth at only 1.06 percent; in the 1990s it climbed to 1.58 percent. However, between 2000 and 2003 the rGDP/pc growth rate plummeted to 0.82 percent.

Even though the purchasing-power-parity data set produces significantly different *levels* of development, with the major exception of the first few years after 2000, the rGDP/pc and GDP/pc growth rates are remarkably similar. Ranking the geographic regions by their growth rates results in identically or-dered data sets: East Asia and the Pacific (4.22 percent *fx*, 4.19 percent PPP), South Asia (2.38 percent and 2.73 percent), Middle East and North Africa (2.08 percent and 2.07 percent), Latin America and the Caribbean (1.06 percent and 1.18 percent), and sub-Saharan Africa (1.73 percent and 1.84 percent). Both data sets also have the Latin American countries the hardest hit by the debt cri-sis of the 1980s, showing them not only ranked last but with a negative growth rate in both (−.087 *fx*, −0.67 PPP).

Table 5.4   Annual Average Growth Rates (in percentage) by Geographic Region

	GDP/pc							rGDP/pc				
	1960–2005	1960–1969	1970–1979	1980–1989	1990–1999	2000–2005	1960–2003	1960–1969	1970–1979	1980–1989	1990–1999	2000–2003
Upper-income (N = 26)	2.80	4.30	3.02	2.43	2.30	1.96	2.80	4.35	3.00	2.27	2.35	1.20
East Asia and the Pacific (N = 5)	4.22	2.65	4.41	3.76	4.43	4.44	4.19	2.43	4.70	3.65	4.34	2.92
	1	1	2	1	1	1	1	3	1	1	1	1
Latin America and the Caribbean (N = 18)	1.06	2.22	2.41	-0.87	2.05	1.39	1.18	2.28	2.68	-0.67	1.71	-0.61
	4	2	3	5	3	4	4	4	3	5	4	5
Middle East and North Africa (N = 4)	2.08	2.03	4.53	0.64	1.42	2.24	2.07	3.30	3.21	0.93	1.71	1.53
	3	4	1	3	4	3	3	1	2	3	3	3
South Asia (N = 4)	2.38	2.05	1.52	2.93	2.93	2.98	2.73	2.66	1.98	3.30	2.88	1.94
	2	3	4	2	2	2	2	2	4	2	2	2
Sub-Saharan Africa (N = 21)	0.21	1.45	1.10	-0.54	-0.21	1.33	0.45	1.35	0.94	0.00	-0.40	0.72
	5	5	5	4	5	5	5	5	5	4	5	4
World (N = 78)	1.73	2.72	2.45	0.89	1.69	1.89	1.84	2.80	2.44	1.06	1.58	0.82

Source: World Bank, *World Development Indicators, 2007* (Washington, DC: World Bank, 2007).
Note: N = number of countries.

Conclusion

The first goal of this chapter was to explain the criticisms of the exchange-rate-converted national accounts statistics that have led to the increased usage of the purchasing-power-parity-converted data offered by the World Bank and the International Comparisons Project. Once the criticisms were enumerated I examined the ICP data set to see if it actually overcame the problems identified with the *fx* data. The second goal was to briefly examine the gap between rich and poor to compare the *fx* and PPP data set to determine if they came to different conclusions about the gap.

The first criticism of the *fx* data set was that it systematically overstates the poverty of the poor countries by not taking into account the fact that it takes less money to buy a common basket of goods in poor countries than in richer countries. Comparing the two data sets, I found that the purchasing-power-parity-converted data did in fact increase the apparent wealth of the poor countries. One issue noted was that the PPP-converted data provide one conversion factor for an entire country, so it assumes that the price of a basket of goods in Arkansas is the same you would pay for that same basket of goods in New York.

The second criticism of exchange-rate-converted data sets was that exchange rates fluctuate and that this fluctuation could potentially inflate or deflate the apparent wealth of a country. A very simple examination of correlation coefficients failed to detect any exchange-rate disturbances that the PPP conversion factor was correcting for.

The third criticism of the *fx*-converted data was that they do not measure the informal sector, meaning that once again the apparent poverty of the poor countries is overstated because the informal sector is so large and important in the developing world. The simple barter exchange of services for services or a pig for clothing is missed by the exchange-rate conversion. PPP proponents argue that the poorest countries have the most vibrant informal sectors, and as they develop, the informal sector fades and the exchange-rate-converted data more accurately reflect the level of development. An examination of the data showed that the rGDP/pc did increase the apparent wealth of the poorest countries. As for the rich countries, the rGDP/pc made them look slightly less wealthy, as the proponents of the PPP measure suggested it should. However, the data make clear that this is only true of the "old rich" countries, the ones that were rich over the entire period of investigation. The "new rich" countries—those countries that joined the rich after 1960—are always made to appear richer by the rGDP/pc even when their wealth surpasses that of the richest of the "old rich."

The criticisms of exchange-rate-converted data offered by the proponents of a purchasing-power-parity conversion factor are legitimate criticisms that should be taken seriously and addressed. However, effective criticism of the *fx*-converted GDP/pc does not mean that any alternative is better. Poverty may be overstated by the exchange-rate-converted data set, but any measure that makes the poor appear richer is not necessarily more accurate. That said, the rGDP/pc did boost the apparent wealth of the poorer countries. However, the "old rich" countries were made to look poorer by the rGDP/pc while the "new rich" countries continued to look richer even when their wealth per capita surpassed that of the "old rich." It is not clear why this occurred.

In terms of economic growth the two measures are remarkably similar. Analysis of standard deviations indicated that both PPP conversion factors and exchange rates lead to the conclusion that the gap between high-income and low-income countries is growing wider. Both showed that the long-term trend is toward greater inequality. However, they were slightly different when looking at shorter-term periods. In terms of growth rates the two measures were very similar. Both showed that the 1960s and 1970s were decades of rapid economic growth. They differed slightly when it came to the 1980s. The *fx* data showed this to be a decade of plummeting growth rates, while the PPP data showed some decline, but not as drastic. Also, the *fx* data showed the first few years of the new century as a time of renewed rapid growth, while the PPP data set reported very low growth rates. It is too soon to know if this discrepancy will continue into the future, but if previous trends hold, the differences shown will also dissipate.

Finally, the gap between rich and poor appears to be real and growing. The size of the gap looks to be a bit smaller when measured by the purchasing-power-parity data due to the conversion factor's propensity to make poor countries look substantially richer and some of the rich countries (the "old rich") look poorer. However, once this difference in the level of development is established, the growth rates produced by the data sets are remarkably similar. Figure 5.2 shows that the behavior of the gap between rich and poor as measured by the two data sets is very similar. This suggests that if one were examining the gap, it would be virtually irrelevant whether it was measured by the rGDP/pc or the GDP/pc because there is virtually no difference in the behavior of the gap. In terms of the level of growth, the gap as expressed by the rGDP/pc would be substantially smaller at first than that produced by the GDP/pc but would open wider no matter which data set is being used. The correlation coefficients in Table 5.2 reinforce Figure 5.2, showing that the rGDP/pc and GDP/pc are consistently highly correlated—meaning that they move together.

Notes

1. The example follows the logic of that used by Morris (1979, 10–11).

2. The growth rates for both the rGDP/pc and GDP/pc are calculated by the regression method described in the *World Development Report, 1988* (World Bank 1988,

288–289). The least squares method finds the growth rate by fitting a least squares trend line to the log of the gross domestic product per capita. This takes the equation form of $X_t = a + bt + e_t$. Where X equals the log of the GDP/pc, t is time, and b is the parameter to be estimated. The growth rate, r, is the [antilog (b)] – 1. For a discussion of different methods of computing growth rates see Jackman 1980.

3. The cutoffs for the income groups were computed from those created by the World Bank. In the following analysis, high-income countries are those with a GDP/pc of $9,401 and higher; upper-middle-income countries have a GDP/pc between $3,051 and $9,400; lower-middle-income countries have a GDP/pc of $766 to $3,050; and the poor countries are those with a GDP/pc of $765 or less.

4. The coefficient of variation is the standard deviation divided by the mean.

References

Abramovitz, Moses. 1986. "Catching Up, Forging Ahead, and Falling Behind." *Journal of Economic History* 46: 385–406.

Babones, Salvatore. 2002. "Population and Sample Selection Effects in Measuring International Income Inequality." *Journal of World-Systems Research* 8, 1 (Winter): 8–28.

Bairoch, P. 1981. "The Main Trends in National Economic Disparities Since the Industrial Revolution." In P. Bairoch and M. Lévy-Leboyer, eds. *Disparities in Economic Development Since the Industrial Revolution*. London: Macmillan.

Baumol, William J. 1986. "Productivity Growth, Convergence, and Welfare: What the Long-Run Data Show." *American Economic Review* 76 (December): 1072–1084.

Beckerman, W. 1966. *International Comparisons of Real Income*. Paris: OECD Development Center.

Berry, Albert, Francois Bourguignon, and Christian Morrisson. 1983a. "Changes in the World Distribution of Income Between 1950 and 1977." *Economic Journal* 93: 331–350.

———. 1983b. "The Level of World Inequality: How Much Can One Say?" *Review of Income and Wealth* 29: 217–241.

Breedlove, William J., and Patrick D. Nolan. 1988. "International Stratification and Inequality, 1960–1980." *International Journal of Sociology* 25: 105–123.

Chou, Yuan K. 2002. "Convergence: Do Poor Countries Tend to Catch Up with the Rich?" *Australian Economic Review* 35, 2: 221–226.

De Long, J. Bradford. 1988. "Productivity Growth, Convergence, and Welfare: Comment." *American Economic Review* 78, 5 (December): 1138–1154.

Dowrick, Steve, and Muhammad Akmal. 2003. "Contradictory Trends in Global Income Inequality: A Tale of Two Biases." Unpublished conference paper presented at the UNU/WIDER Conference in Helsinki, Finland, May 2003.

Dube, S. C. 1988. *Modernization and Development: The Search for Alternative Paradigms*. London: Zed.

Durning, A. B. 1990. "Ending Poverty." In L. Starke, ed. *State of the World, 1990*. New York: W. W. Norton.

Firebaugh, Glenn. 2003. *The New Geography of Global Income Inequality*. Cambridge, MA: Harvard University Press.

———. 1999. "Empirics of World Income Inequality." *American Journal of Sociology* 104, 6 (May): 1597–1630.

Gilbert, M., and I. Kravis. 1958. *An International Comparison of Comparative National Products and Price Levels: A Study of Western Europe and the United States.* Paris: Organization for European Economic Cooperation.

———. 1954. *An International Comparison of National Products and the Purchasing Power of Currencies.* Paris: Organization for European Economic Cooperation.

Goesling, Brian. 2001. "Changing Income Inequalities Within and Between Nations: New Evidence." *American Sociological Review* 66, 5: 745–761.

Heston, A. 1973. "A Comparison of Some Short-Cut Methods of Estimating Real Product per Capita." *Review of Income and Wealth* (March): 79–104.

International Monetary Fund. 1984. *International Financial Statistics: Supplement on Output Statistics,* 8. Washington, DC: International Monetary Fund.

———. 1980. *International Financial Statistics: Yearbook 1980.* Washington, DC: International Monetary Fund.

IMF Fiscal Affairs Department. 1998. *Economic Issues No. 16: Should Equity Be a Goal of Economic Policy?* International Monetary Fund.

Jackman, R. W. 1980. "A Note on the Measurement of Growth Rates in Cross-National Research." *American Journal of Sociology* 86: 604–610.

Katseli-Papaefstratiou, Louka T. 1979. *The Reemergence of the Purchasing Power Parity Doctrine in the 1970s.* Princeton, NJ: Princeton University Press.

Kirman, Alan P., and Luigi M. Tomasini. 1969. "A New Look at International Income Inequalities." *Economia Internazionale* 22: 437–461.

Korzeniewicz, Roberto Patricio, and Timothy Patrick Moran. 2005. "Theorizing the Relationship Between Inequality and Economic Growth." *Theory and Society* 34: 1000–1039.

———. 2000. "Measuring World Income Inequalities." *American Journal of Sociology* 106: 209–214.

———. 1997. "World-Economic Trends in the Distribution of Income, 1965–1992." *American Journal of Sociology* 102: 1000–1039.

Kravis, I. B., Z. Kenessey, A. Heston, and R. Summers. 1975. *A System of International Comparisons of Gross Product and Purchasing Power.* Baltimore: Johns Hopkins University Press.

Kuznets, S. 1972. "The Gap: Concept, Measurement, Trends." In G. Ranis, ed. *The Gap Between Rich and Poor Nations.* London: Macmillan.

Loungani, Prakash. 2003. "Inequality: Now You See It, Now You Don't." *Finance and Development* (September): 22–23.

Lucas, Robert E. 1988. "On the Mechanics of Economic Development." *Journal of Monetary Economics* 22: 2–42.

Maddison, Angus. 2001. *The World Economy: A Millennial Perspective.* Paris: OECD Press.

———. 1995. *Monitoring the World Economy, 1820–1992.* Washington, DC: Organization for Economic Cooperation and Development.

Mankiw, N. Gregory, David Romer, and David N. Weil. 1992. "A Contribution to the Empirics of Economic Growth." *Quarterly Journal of Economics* 107, 2 (May): 407–437.

Morawetz, David. 1977. *Twenty-Five Years of Economic Development, 1950 to 1975.* Washington, DC: World Bank.

Morris, M. D. 1979. *Measuring the Condition of the World's Poor: The Physical Quality of Life Index.* New York: Pergamon.

Peacock, Walter Gillis, Greg A. Hoover, and Charles D. Killian. 1988. "Divergence and Convergence in International Development: A Decomposition Analysis of Inequality in the World System." *American Sociological Review* 56, 6: 838–852.

Pritchett, Lant. 1996. "Forget Convergence: Divergence Past, Present, and Future." *Finance and Development* 33, 2: 40–43.

Ram, Rati. 1989. "Level of Development and Income Inequality: An Extension of Kuznets-Hypothesis to the World-Economy." *Kyklos* 42: 73–88.

Reuveny, Rafael, and William Thompson. 2004. "World Economic Growth, Systemic Leadership, and Southern Debt Crisis." *Journal of Peace Research* 41, 1: 5–24.

Romer, Paul. 1994. "The Origins of Endogenous Growth." *Journal of Economic Perspectives* 8: 3–22.

Sen, Amartya. 2001. "If It's Fair, It's Good: 10 Truths About Globalization." *International Herald Tribune,* July 15.

Summers, R., and A. Heston. 1988. "A New Set of International Comparisons of Real Product and Prices: Estimates for 130 Countries, 1950–1985." *Review of Income and Wealth* (March): 1–25.

———. 1984. "Improved International Comparisons of Real Product and Its Composition: 1950–1980." *Review of Income and Wealth* 3 (September): 207–259.

Sutcliffe, Bob. 2002. "A More or Less Unequal World? World Income Inequality in the 20th Century." Unpublished manuscript.

Wade, Robert Hunter. 2001. "The Rising Inequality of World Income Distribution." *Finance and Development* 38, 4.

Ward, M. 1985. *Purchasing Power Parities and Real Expenditures in the OECD*. Paris: OECD Press.

Whalley, John. 1979. "The Worldwide Income Distribution: Some Speculative Calculations." *Review of Income and Wealth* 25: 261–276.

Williamson, Jeffrey G. 1996. "Globalization, Convergence, and History." *Journal of Economic History* 56, 2: 277–306.

World Bank. 2000. *World Development Indicators, 2000*. Washington, DC: World Bank.

———. 1992. *The World Tables of Economic and Social Indicators, 1960–86*. Washington, DC: World Bank.

———. 1988. *World Development Report, 1998*. Oxford, UK: Oxford University Press.

PART 2

The Historical Origins of the Gap

6

The World Economy: A Millennial Perspective

ANGUS MADDISON

Angus Maddison has long been one of the most prominent economic historians, providing development scholars with some of the most reliable historical data with which to judge long-term economic growth patterns. In this chapter, Maddison discusses world economic growth since 1000 C.E. Maddison provides evidence that after reaching a low point around 1000, Western Europe began to grow such that it surpassed the production per capita of the rest of the world by the year 1500. After this point the gap between Western Europe and the rest of the world widened. By 1820 Western Europe produced about twice that produced by the rest of the world and from that point on, the gap grew very rapidly. In Part 4 of this book, we turn to convergence theory, which proposes that over the long run, per capita incomes will converge. Maddison's conclusions suggest that the long-term pattern is one marked by divergence rather than convergence. ◼

GDP Per Capita

Long-term estimates of world GDP are very recent. Research on real income growth by quantitative economic historians has been heavily concentrated on Europe, and generally confined to the past two centuries. Until recently what was known about earlier centuries was in large degree conjectural.

Maddison (1995) contained detailed estimates for different parts of the world economy for 1820 onwards, with a very crude provisional assessment

Reprinted with permission of the OECD from *The World Economy: A Millennial Perspective*, pp. 44–48. Copyright © 2001 by the OECD.

for 1500 to 1820. Here I have made a much more careful scrutiny of the evidence for centuries before 1820 and incorporated the results of Maddison (1998) on Chinese economic performance over two millennia.

The level and movement of per capita GDP is the primary general purpose indicator of changes in well-being and production potential, but one should keep in mind that per capita consumption has increased less over the long run because of the increased share of product allocated to investment and government. Labour productivity does not always move parallel to per capita income. The advances achieved in Sung China (960–1279) and in Japan in the seventeenth and eighteenth centuries required substantial increases in per capita labour effort. In the twentieth century we find the opposite phenomenon. Labour input per person fell substantially in Western Europe and Western Offshoots.

Table 6.1 summarises my findings for the past millennium. It shows clearly the exceptionalism of Western Europe's very lengthy ascension, and origins of the great divergence between the West (Group A) and the rest of the world (Group B).

The major conclusions I draw from the long term quantitative evidence are as follows:

(a) West European income was at a nadir around the year 1000. Its level was significantly lower than it had been in the first century. It was below that in China, India and other parts of East and West Asia;

(b) There was a turning point in the eleventh century when the economic ascension of Western Europe began. It proceeded at a slow pace, but by 1820 real income had tripled. The locus and characteristics of economic leadership changed. The North Italian city states and, in particular, Venice initiated the growth process and reopened Mediterranean trade. Portugal and Spain opened trade routes to the Americas and Asia, but were less dynamic than the Netherlands which became the economic leader around 1600, followed by the United Kingdom in the nineteenth century;

(c) Western Europe overtook China (the leading Asian economy) in per capita performance in the fourteenth century. Thereafter China and most of the rest of Asia were more or less stagnant in per capita terms until the second half of the twentieth century. The stagnation was initially due to indigenous institutions and policy, reinforced by colonial exploitation which derived from Western hegemony and was most marked from the eighteenth century onwards;

(d) West European appropriation of the natural resources of North America, introduction of European settlers, technology and organisation added a substantial new dimension to Western economic ascension from the eighteenth century onwards. Towards the end of the nineteenth century, the United States became the world economic leader;

(e) Japan was an exception to the Asian norm. In the course of the seventeenth, eighteenth and the first half of the nineteenth century, it caught up with and overtook China in per capita income. The Meiji takeover in 1868 involved

Table 6.1a   Growth of Per Capita GDP by Major Region, 1000–1998 (annual average compound growth rate)

	1000–1500	1500–1600	1600–1700	1700–1820	1820–1998
Western Europe	0.13	0.14	0.15	0.15	1.51
Western Offshoots	0.00	0.00	0.17	0.78	1.75
Japan	0.03	0.03	0.09	0.13	1.93
Average Group A	0.11	0.13	0.12	0.18	1.67
Latin America	0.01	0.09	0.19	0.19	1.22
Eastern Europe & Former USSR	0.04	0.10	0.10	0.10	1.06
Asia (excluding Japan)	0.05	0.01	–0.01	0.01	0.92
Africa	–0.01	0.00	0.00	0.04	0.67
Average Group B	0.04	0.02	0.00	0.03	0.95

Table 6.1b   Level of Per Capita GDP, Groups A and B, 1000–1998 (1990 international dollars)

	1000	1500	1600	1700	1820	1998
Average Group A	405	704	805	907	1,130	21,470
Average Group B	440	535	548	551	573	3,102

Table 6.1c   Popualation of Groups A and B, 1000–1998 (millions)

	1000	1500	1600	1700	1820	1998
Total Group A	35	76	95	110	175	838
Total Group B	233	362	461	493	866	5,069

Table 6.1d   GDP of Groups A and B, 1000–1998 (billions of 1990 international dollars)

	1000	1500	1600	1700	1820	1998
Total Group A	14.1	53.2	76.1	100.0	198.0	17,998
Total Group B	102.7	194.0	252.9	271.8	496.5	15,727

Source: Appendix B [of original text; not included here].

massive institutional change aimed at catching up with the West. This was achieved in income terms in the 1980s, but not yet in productivity;

(f) The colonial takeover in Latin America had some analogy to that in North America, but Iberian institutions were less propitious to capitalist development than those in North America. Latin America included a much larger indigenous population which was treated as an underclass without access to land or education. The social order was not greatly changed after independence. Over the long run the rise in per capita income was much smaller than in North America, but faster than in Asia or Africa;

(g) African per capita income was lower in 1820 than in the first century. Since then there has been slower advance than in all other regions. The income level in 1998 was little better than that of Western Europe in 1820. Population growth is now faster than in any other region—eight times as fast as in Western Europe;

(h) The most dynamic growth performance has been concentrated on the past two centuries. Since 1820 per capita income has risen 19-fold in Group A, and more than 5-fold in the rest of the world—dwarfing any earlier advance and compressing it into a very short time span.

One may ask what is new in these findings. In the first place there is the quantification which clarifies issues that qualitative analysis leaves fuzzy. It helps to separate stylised facts from the stylised fantasies which are sometimes perceived to be reality. It is more readily contestable and likely to be contested. It sharpens scholarly discussion, and contributes to the dynamics of the research process. It is also useful to have a world picture because it helps to identify what is normal and what is exceptional.

My findings differ in some respects from earlier interpretations of the length and pace of Western Europe's economic ascension. There has been a general tendency to date it from 1500 when Europeans encountered America and first made a direct entry into the trading world of Asia. Max Weber attributed Europe's advance to the rise of Protestantism, and this thesis attracted attention because it was congruent with the conventional wisdom about the beginning of the European ascension. I no longer believe that there was a sharp break in the pace of advance of per capita income around 1500.

Kuznets (1966, Chapter 1) suggested that "modern economic growth" is a distinctive economic epoch preceded by merchant capitalism in Western Europe "from the end of the fifteenth to the second half of the eighteenth century," and an "antecedent epoch of feudal organisation." In Kuznets (1973, pp. 139–41), he advanced what seemed to be a reasonable view about the rate of per capita GDP growth in Western Europe in the merchant capitalist period. In Maddison (1995), I accepted Kuznets' hypothesis for his merchant capitalist period, but I now believe that growth was slower then than Kuznets suggested, and that the pace of advance between the eleventh and the fifteenth centuries was not much different. For this reason, it does not seem valid to distinguish between epochs of "feudal organisation" and "merchant capitalism." Instead I would characterise the whole period 1000–1820 as "proto-capitalist."

I also differ from Kuznets on the timing of the transition to what he called "modern economic growth" (which I call "capitalist development"). The evidence now available suggests that the transition took place around 1820 rather than in 1760. The revisionist work of Crafts (1983 and 1992) and others has helped to break the old notion of a sudden take-off in the second half of the eighteenth century in England. Recent research on the Netherlands shows income to have been higher there than in the United Kingdom at the end of the eighteenth century. Work in the past twenty years on the quantitative history of other West European countries provides further reason for postdating the transition and modifying the old emphasis on British exceptionalism.

My analysis of US economic performance shows a rapid advance in the eighteenth century in contrast to the findings of Gallman (1972) and Mancall and Weiss (1999). The essential reason for the difference is that I include rough estimates of the indigenous population and its GDP as well as the activity of European settlers (I also did this for Australia, Canada and New Zealand).

My assessment of Japanese development differs from the conventional wisdom. I have quantified its economic performance in the Tokugawa period and compared it with China. Most analysts concentrate on comparisons between Japan and Western Europe in the Meiji period, and ignore the Asian context.

Gerschenkron (1965) and Rostow (1960 and 1963) both emphasised the idea that "take-offs" were staggered throughout the nineteenth century in West European countries. Kuznets (1979, p. 131) endorsed this view. In fact growth acceleration was more synchronous in Western Europe than they believed.

There are two schools of thought about the relative performance of Europe and Asia. The mainstream view was clearly expressed by Adam Smith in 1776. He was not a practitioner of political arithmetic but on the basis of the "price of labour" and other evidence, his ordinal ranking from the top downwards was as follows for the 1770s: Netherlands, England, France, British North American colonies, Scotland, Spain, Spanish colonies in America, China, Bengal (depressed by the East India Company's plundering).

This mainstream view is reflected in Landes (1969, pp. 13–14) whose overall assessment, like that of Smith, was similar to mine. "Western Europe was already rich before the Industrial Revolution—rich by comparison with other parts of the world of that day. This wealth was the product of centuries of slow accumulation, based in turn on investment, the appropriation of extra-European resources and labour, and substantial technological progress, not only in the production of material goods, but in the organisation and financing of their exchange and distribution . . . it seems clear that over the near-millennium from the year 1000 to the eighteenth century, income per head rose appreciably—perhaps tripled."

In Maddison (1983), I contrasted the Landes view with Bairoch's (1981) assessment of relative income per head. He suggested that China was well ahead of Western Europe in 1800, Japan and the rest of Asia only 5 per cent lower than Europe, Latin America well ahead of North America, and Africa about two thirds of the West European level. This highly improbable scenario was never documented in the case of Asia, Latin America or Africa. His figures for these areas were essentially guesstimates. Bairoch consistently took the position that the third world had been impoverished by the rich countries (see Bairoch, 1967), and he was, in fact, fabricating ammunition for this hypothesis (see the critique of Chesnais, 1987).

In spite of its shaky foundations, Bairoch's assessment has been influential. Braudel (1985, vol. 3 pp. 533–4) acknowledged "the great service Paul Bairoch has rendered to historians" and believed "it is virtually beyond question that Europe was less rich than the worlds it was exploiting, even after the fall of Napoleon." Andre Gunder Frank (1998, pp. 171 and 284) cites Bairoch and suggests that "around 1800 Europe and the United States, after long lagging behind, suddenly caught up and then overtook Asia economically and politically. Pomeranz (2000) cites Bairoch more cautiously (p. 16) but his sinophilia drives him to the same conclusion. He suggests (p. 111), there is "little reason to think that West Europeans were more productive than their contemporaries in various other densely populated regions of the Old World prior to 1750 or even 1800."

Maddison (1983) contrasted the assessments of Landes and Bairoch and commented: "These remarkably different quantitative conclusions have very different analytical implications. If Bairoch is right, then much of the backwardness of the third world presumably has to be explained by colonial exploitation, and much less of Europe's advantage can be due to scientific precocity, centuries of slow accumulation, and organisational and financial prosperity."

In view of the laborious efforts I have since made to accumulate quantitative evidence on this topic, I now conclude that Bairoch and his epigoni are quite wrong. To reject them is not to deny the role of colonial exploitation, but this can be better understood by taking a more realistic view of Western strength and Asian weakness around 1800.

The major problem in growth analysis is to explain why such a large divergence developed between the advanced capitalist group and the rest of the world. There are, of course, some examples of past convergence, e.g. Europe's rise from its nadir to overtake China, the Japanese catch-up with China in Tokugawa times, and subsequently with the advanced capitalist group. Western Europe achieved a very substantial degree of catch-up on the United States in the golden age after the second world war; resurgent Asia (China, India, the so-called tigers and others) have narrowed their degree of backwardness substantially over the past quarter century.

In attempting to understand the causes of divergence and the possibilities for catch-up in different parts of the world economy, there is no universal schema which covers the whole millennium. The operative forces have varied between place and period.

References

Bairoch, P. 1981. "The Main Trends in National Economic Disparities since the Industrial Revolution." Pp. 3–17 in *Disparities in Economic Development since the Industrial Revolution,* edited by P. Bairoch and M. Levy-Leboyer. London: Macmillan.

Bairoch, P. 1967. *Diagnostic de l'évolution économique du tiers-monde 1900–1966,* Gauthiers-Villars, Paris.

Braudel. F. 1985. *Civilisation and Capitalism, 15th–18th Century,* 3 vols., Fontana, London.

Chesnais, J.-C. 1987. *La Revanche du Tiers-Monde,* Laffont, Paris.

Crafts, N.F.R. 1983. "British Economic Growth, 1700–1831: A Review of the Evidence," *Economic History Review,* May, pp. 177–199.

Crafts, N.F.R., and C. K. Harley. 1992. "Output Growth and the British Industrial Revolution: A Restatment of the Crafts-Harley View," *Economic History Review,* November, pp. 703–730.

Frank. A.G. 1998. *Reorient: Global Economy in the Asian Age,* University of California Press, Berkeley.

Gallman, R.E. 1972. "The Pace and Pattern of American Economic Growth," in Davis and Associates.

Gerschenkron, A. 1965. *Economic Backwardness in Historical Perspective,* Praeger, New York.

Kuznets, S. 1979, *Growth, Population and Income Distribution,* Norton, New York.

Kuznets, S. 1973. *Population, Capital and Growth: Selected Essays,* Norton, New York.

Kuznets, S. 1966. *Modern Economic Growth,* Yale.

Landes, D.S. 1969. *The Unbound Prometheus,* Cambridge University Press, Cambridge.

Maddison, A. 1998. *Chinese Economic Performance in the Long Run,* OECD Development Centre, Paris.

Maddison, A. 1995. *Monitoring the World Economy 1820–1992,* OECD Development Centre, Paris.

Maddison, A. 1983. "A Comparison of Levels of GDP Per Capita in Developed and Developing Countries, 1700–1980," *Journal of Economic History,* March, pp. 27–41.

Mancall, Peter C., and Thomas Weiss. 1999. "Was Economic Growth Likely in Colonial British North America?" *Journal of Economic History,* Vol. 59, Issue 1, pp. 17–40.

Pomeranz, K. 2000. *The Great Divergence,* Princeton University Press, Princeton.

Rostow, W.W. 1963. *The Economics of Takeoff into Sustained Growth,* MacMillan, London.

Rostow, W.W. 1960. *The Stages of Economic Growth,* Cambridge University Press, Cambridge.

7

Why Did Human History Unfold Differently on Different Continents for the Last 13,000 Years?

JARED DIAMOND

This chapter reflects a new debate over how the gap came into existence and why certain countries are the ones that are now rich. In other words, why did development occur and wealth amass in Europe and not in sub-Saharan Africa? This is the question addressed by Jared Diamond in his tremendously influential book, Guns, Germs, and Steel. *Diamond's appeal went well beyond the academic world, landing the book on the* New York Times *bestseller list and winning him a Pulitzer Prize. The book opens with Diamond being asked by a villager in a developing country, why had Europeans developed so much material wealth while people in his region had developed so little? Diamond then begins to weave his geographic explanation for why development first began to occur in the West. The following excerpt is from a lecture by Diamond in which he offers a brief overview of the arguments offered in* Guns, Germs, and Steel. ■

I'VE SET MYSELF THE MODEST TASK OF TRYING TO EXPLAIN THE BROAD PATTERN OF human history, on all the continents, for the last 13,000 years. Why did history take such different evolutionary courses for peoples of different continents? This problem has fascinated me for a long time, but it's now ripe for a new synthesis because of recent advances in many fields seemingly remote from history, including molecular biology, plant and animal genetics and biogeography, archaeology, and linguistics.

Reprinted with permission of the author.

As we all know, Eurasians, especially peoples of Europe and eastern Asia, have spread around the globe, to dominate the modern world in wealth and power. Other peoples, including most Africans, survived, and have thrown off European domination but remain behind in wealth and power. Still other peoples, including the original inhabitants of Australia, the Americas, and southern Africa, are no longer even masters of their own lands but have been decimated, subjugated, or exterminated by European colonialists. Why did history turn out that way, instead of the opposite way? Why weren't Native Americans, Africans, and Aboriginal Australians the ones who conquered or exterminated Europeans and Asians?

This big question can easily be pushed back one step further. By the year A.D. 1500, the approximate year when Europe's overseas expansion was just beginning, peoples of the different continents already differed greatly in technology and political organization. Much of Eurasia and North Africa was occupied then by Iron Age states and empires, some of them on the verge of industrialization. Two Native American peoples, the Incas and Aztecs, ruled over empires with stone tools and were just starting to experiment with bronze. Parts of sub-Saharan Africa were divided among small indigenous Iron Age states or chiefdoms. But all peoples of Australia, New Guinea, and the Pacific islands, and many peoples of the Americas and sub-Saharan Africa, were still living as farmers or even still as hunter/gatherers with stone tools.

Obviously, those differences as of A.D. 1500 were the immediate cause of the modern world's inequalities. Empires with iron tools conquered or exterminated tribes with stone tools. But how did the world evolve to be the way that it was in the year A.D. 1500?

This question too can be easily pushed back a further step, with the help of written histories and archaeological discoveries. Until the end of the last Ice Age around 11,000 B.C., all humans on all continents were still living as Stone Age hunter/gatherers. Different rates of development on different continents, from 11,000 B.C. to A.D. 1500, were what produced the inequalities of A.D. 1500. While Aboriginal Australians and many Native American peoples remained Stone Age hunter/gatherers, most Eurasian peoples, and many peoples of the Americas and sub-Saharan Africa, gradually developed agriculture, herding, metallurgy, and complex political organization. Parts of Eurasia, and one small area of the Americas, developed indigenous writing as well. But each of these new developments appeared earlier in Eurasia than elsewhere.

So, we can finally rephrase our question about the evolution of the modern world's inequalities as follows. Why did human development proceed at such different rates on different continents for the last 13,000 years? Those differing rates constitute the broadest pattern of history, the biggest unsolved problem of history, and my subject today.

Historians tend to avoid this subject like the plague, because of its apparently racist overtones. Many people, or even most people, assume that the an-

swer involves biological differences in average IQ among the world's populations, despite the fact that there is no evidence for the existence of such IQ differences. Even to ask the question why different peoples had different histories strikes some of us as evil, because it appears to be justifying what
happened in history. In fact, we study the injustices of history for the same reason that we study genocide, and for the same reason that psychologists study
the minds of murderers and rapists: not in order to justify history, genocide,
murder, and rape, but instead to understand how those evil things came about,
and then to use that understanding so as to prevent their happening again. In
case the stink of racism still makes you feel uncomfortable about exploring
this subject, just reflect on the underlying reason why so many people accept
racist explanations of history's broad pattern: we don't have a convincing alternative explanation. Until we do, people will continue to gravitate by default
to racist theories. That leaves us with a huge moral gap, which constitutes the
strongest reason for tackling this uncomfortable subject.

Let's proceed continent-by-continent. As our first continental comparison,
let's consider the collision of the Old World and the New World that began
with Christopher Columbus's voyage in A.D. 1492, because the proximate factors involved in that outcome are well understood. I'll now give you a summary and interpretation of the histories of North America, South America, Europe, and Asia from my perspective as a biogeographer and evolutionary
biologist—all that in ten minutes; two minutes per continent. . . .

Most of us are familiar with the stories of how a few hundred Spaniards
under Cortés and Pizarro overthrew the Aztec and Inca Empires. The populations of each of those empires numbered tens of millions. We're also familiar
with the gruesome details of how other Europeans conquered other parts of the
New World. The result is that Europeans came to settle and dominate most of
the New World, while the Native American population declined drastically
from its level as of A.D. 1492. Why did it happen that way? Why didn't it instead happen that the Emperor Montezuma or Atahuallpa led the Aztecs or
Incas to conquer Europe?

The proximate reasons are obvious. Invading Europeans had steel swords,
guns, and horses, while Native Americans had only stone and wooden weapons
and no animals that could be ridden. Those military advantages repeatedly enabled troops of a few dozen mounted Spaniards to defeat Indian armies num-
bering in the thousands.

Nevertheless, steel swords, guns, and horses weren't the sole proximate
factors behind the European conquest of the New World. Infectious diseases
introduced with Europeans, like smallpox and measles, spread from one Indian tribe to another, far in advance of Europeans themselves, and killed an estimated 95% of the New World's Indian population. Those diseases were endemic in Europe, and Europeans had had time to develop both genetic and
immune resistance to them, but Indians initially had no such resistance. That

role played by infectious diseases in the European conquest of the New World was duplicated in many other parts of the world, including Aboriginal Australia, southern Africa, and many Pacific islands.

Finally, there is still another set of proximate factors to consider. How is it that Pizarro and Cortés reached the New World at all, before Aztec and Inca conquistadors could reach Europe? That outcome depended partly on technology in the form of oceangoing ships. Europeans had such ships, while the Aztecs and Incas did not. Also, those European ships were backed by the centralized political organization that enabled Spain and other European countries to build and staff the ships. Equally crucial was the role of European writing in permitting the quick spread of accurate detailed information, including maps, sailing directions, and accounts by earlier explorers, back to Europe, to motivate later explorers.

So far, we've identified a series of proximate factors behind European colonization of the New World: namely, ships, political organization, and writing that brought Europeans to the New World; European germs that killed most Indians before they could reach the battlefield; and guns, steel swords, and horses that gave Europeans a big advantage on the battlefield. Now, let's try to push the chain of causation back further. Why did these proximate advantages go to the Old World rather than to the New World? Theoretically, Native Americans might have been the ones to develop steel swords and guns first, to develop oceangoing ships and empires and writing first, to be mounted on domestic animals more terrifying than horses, and to bear germs worse than smallpox.

The part of that question that's easiest to answer concerns the reasons why Eurasia evolved the nastiest germs. It's striking that Native Americans evolved no devastating epidemic diseases to give to Europeans, in return for the many devastating epidemic diseases that Indians received from the Old World. There are two straightforward reasons for this gross imbalance. First, most of our familiar epidemic diseases can sustain themselves only in large dense human populations concentrated into villages and cities, which arose much earlier in the Old World than in the New World. Second, recent studies of microbes, by molecular biologists, have shown that most human epidemic diseases evolved from similar epidemic diseases of the dense populations of Old World domestic animals with which we came into close contact. For example, measles and TB evolved from diseases of our cattle, influenza from a disease of pigs, and smallpox possibly from a disease of camels. The Americas had very few native domesticated animal species from which humans could acquire such diseases.

Let's now push the chain of reasoning back one step further. Why were there far more species of domesticated animals in Eurasia than in the Americas? The Americas harbor over a thousand native wild mammal species, so you might initially suppose that the Americas offered plenty of starting material for domestication.

In fact, only a tiny fraction of wild mammal species has been successfully domesticated, because domestication requires that a wild animal fulfill many prerequisites: the animal has to have a diet that humans can supply; a rapid growth rate; a willingness to breed in captivity; a tractable disposition; a social structure involving submissive behavior towards dominant animals and humans; and lack of a tendency to panic when fenced in. Thousands of years ago, humans domesticated every possible large wild mammal species fulfilling all those criteria and worth domesticating, with the result that there have been no valuable additions of domestic animals in recent times, despite the efforts of modern science.

Eurasia ended up with the most domesticated animal species in part because it's the world's largest land mass and offered the most wild species to begin with. That preexisting difference was magnified 13,000 years ago at the end of the last Ice Age, when most of the large mammal species of North and South America became extinct, perhaps exterminated by the first arriving Indians. As a result, Native Americans inherited far fewer species of big wild mammals than did Eurasians, leaving them only with the llama and alpaca as a domesticate. Differences between the Old and New Worlds in domesticated plants, especially in large-seeded cereals, are qualitatively similar to these differences in domesticated mammals, though the difference is not so extreme.

Another reason for the higher local diversity of domesticated plants and animals in Eurasia than in the Americas is that Eurasia's main axis is east/west, whereas the main axis of the Americas is north/south. Eurasia's east/west axis meant that species domesticated in one part of Eurasia could easily spread thousands of miles at the same latitude, encountering the same day length and climate to which they were already adapted. As a result, chickens and citrus fruit domesticated in Southeast Asia quickly spread westward to Europe; horses domesticated in the Ukraine quickly spread eastward to China; and the sheep, goats, cattle, wheat, and barley of the Fertile Crescent quickly spread both west and east.

In contrast, the north/south axis of the Americas meant that species domesticated in one area couldn't spread far without encountering day lengths and climates to which they were not adapted. As a result, the turkey never spread from its site of domestication in Mexico to the Andes; llamas and alpacas never spread from the Andes to Mexico, so that the Indian civilizations of Central and North America remained entirely without pack animals; and it took thousands of years for the corn that evolved in Mexico's climate to become modified into a corn adapted to the short growing season and seasonally changing day length of North America.

Eurasia's domesticated plants and animals were important for several other reasons besides letting Europeans develop nasty germs. Domesticated plants and animals yield far more calories per acre than do wild habitats, in which most species are inedible to humans. As a result, population densities of farmers and herders are typically ten to a hundred times greater than those of hunter/gatherers. That fact alone explains why farmers and herders everywhere in the world have been able to push hunter/gatherers out of land suitable for farming and herding. Domestic animals revolutionized land transport. They also revolutionized agriculture, by letting one farmer plough and manure much more land than the farmer could till or manure by the farmer's own efforts. Also, hunter/gatherer societies tend to be egalitarian and to have no political organization beyond the level of the band or tribe, whereas the food surpluses and storage made possible by agriculture permitted the development of stratified, politically centralized societies with governing elites. Those food surpluses also accelerated the development of technology, by supporting craftspeople who didn't raise their own food and who could instead devote themselves to developing metallurgy, writing, swords, and guns.

Thus, we began by identifying a series of proximate explanations—guns, germs, and so on—for the conquest of the Americas by Europeans. Those proximate factors seem to me ultimately traceable in large part to the Old World's greater number of domesticated plants, much greater number of domesticated animals, and east/west axis. The chain of causation is most direct in explaining the Old World's advantages of horses and nasty germs. But domesticated plants and animals also led more indirectly to Eurasia's advantage in guns, swords, oceangoing ships, political organization, and writing, all of which were products of the large, dense, sedentary, stratified societies made possible by agriculture.

Let's next examine whether this scheme, derived from the collision of Europeans with Native Americans, helps us understand the broadest pattern of African history, which I'll summarize in five minutes. I'll concentrate on the history of sub-Saharan Africa, because it was much more isolated from Eurasia by distance and climate than was North Africa, whose history is closely linked to Eurasia's history. Here we go again:

Just as we asked why Cortés invaded Mexico before Montezuma could invade Europe, we can similarly ask why Europeans colonized sub-Saharan Africa before sub-Saharans could colonize Europe. The proximate factors were the same familiar ones of guns, steel, oceangoing ships, political organization, and writing. But again, we can ask why guns and ships and so on ended up being developed in Europe rather than in sub-Saharan Africa. To the student of human evolution, that question is particularly puzzling, because humans have been evolving for millions of years longer in Africa than in Europe, and even anatomically modern *Homo sapiens* may have reached Europe from Africa only within the last 50,000 years. If time were a critical factor in the development of human societies, Africa should have enjoyed an enormous head start and advantage over Europe.

Again, that outcome largely reflects biogeographic differences in the availability of domesticable wild animal and plant species. Taking first domestic animals, it's striking that the sole animal domesticated within sub-Saharan Africa was (you guessed) a bird, the Guinea fowl. All of Africa's mammalian domesticates—cattle, sheep, goats, horses, even dogs—entered sub-Saharan Africa from the north, from Eurasia or North Africa. At first that sounds astonishing, since we now think of Africa as the continent of big wild mammals. In fact, none of those famous big wild mammal species of Africa proved domesticable. They were all disqualified by one or another problem such as: unsuitable social organization, intractable behavior, slow growth rate, and so on. Just think what the course of world history might have been like if Africa's rhinos and hippos had lent themselves to domestication! If that had been possible, African cavalry mounted on rhinos or hippos would have made mincemeat of European cavalry mounted on horses. But it couldn't happen.

Instead, as I mentioned, the livestock adopted in Africa were Eurasian species that came in from the north. Africa's long axis, like that of the Americas, is north/south rather than east/west. Those Eurasian domestic mammals spread southward very slowly in Africa, because they had to adapt to different climate zones and different animal diseases.

The difficulties posed by a north/south axis to the spread of domesticated species are even more striking for African crops than they are for livestock. Remember that the food staples of ancient Egypt were Fertile Crescent and Mediterranean crops like wheat and barley, which require winter rains and seasonal variation in day length for their germination. Those crops couldn't spread south in Africa beyond Ethiopia, beyond which the rains come in the summer and there's little or no seasonal variation in day length. Instead, the development of agriculture in the sub-Sahara had to await the domestication of native African plant species like sorghum and millet, adapted to Central Africa's summer rains and relatively constant day length.

Ironically, those crops of Central Africa were for the same reason then unable to spread south to the Mediterranean zone of South Africa, where once again winter rains and big seasonal variations in day length prevailed. The southward advance of native African farmers with Central African crops halted in Natal, beyond which Central African crops couldn't grow—with enormous consequences for the recent history of South Africa.

In short, a north/south axis and a paucity of wild plant and animal species suitable for domestication were decisive in African history, just as they were in Native American history. Although native Africans domesticated some plants in the Sahel and in Ethiopia and in tropical West Africa, they acquired valuable domestic animals only later, from the north. The resulting advantages of Europeans in guns, ships, political organization, and writing permitted Europeans to colonize Africa, rather than Africans to colonize Europe.

8

Institutions Rule:
The Primacy of Institutions over Geography and Integration in Economic Development

DANI RODRIK, ARVIND SUBRAMANIAN,
AND FRANCESCO TREBBI

*In the previous chapter Jared Diamond proposed a geographic expla-
nation for the origins of the gap. In this chapter the authors identify
three contending explanations for the origins of the gap: (1) the geographic explanation, as represented by Diamond's work; (2) expansion
of and participation in international trade; and (3) the establishment
of effective government and the respect of private property. The authors conclude that "geography is not destiny." They then cautiously
describe the varied policies and institutions that promote economic
success.* ■

AVERAGE INCOME LEVELS IN THE WORLD'S RICHEST AND POOREST NATIONS DIFFER
by a factor of more than 100. Sierra Leone, the poorest economy for which we
have national income statistics, has a per-capita GDP of $490, compared to
Luxembourg's $50,061. What accounts for these differences, and what (if any-
thing) can we do to reduce them? It is hard to think of any question in economics that is of greater intellectual significance, or of greater relevance to the vast
majority of the word's population.

In the voluminous literature on this subject, three strands of thought
stand out. First, there is a long and distinguished line of theorizing that places

Excerpted from Dani Rodrik, Arvind Subramanian, and Francesco Trebbi, "Institutions Rule: The Primacy of Institutions over Geography and Integration in Economic Development," *Journal of Economic Growth* 9 (November 2004): 131–165.
Reprinted by permission.

geography at the center of the story. Geography is a key determinant of climate, endowment of natural resources, disease burden, transport costs, and diffusion of knowledge and technology from more advanced areas. It exerts therefore a strong influence on agricultural productivity and the quality of human resources. Recent writings by Jared Diamond and Jeffrey Sachs are among the more notable works in this tradition. . . .

A second camp emphasizes the role of international trade as a driver of productivity change. We call this the *integration* view, as it gives market integration, and impediments thereof, a starring role in fostering economic convergence between rich and poor regions of the world.

Finally, a third group of explanations centers on *institutions,* and in particular the role of property rights and the rule of law. In this view, what matters are the rules of the game in a society and their conduciveness to desirable economic behavior.

Growth theory has traditionally focused on physical and human capital accumulation, and, in its endogenous growth variant, on technological change. But accumulation and technological change are at best proximate causes of economic growth. No sooner have we ascertained the impact of these two on growth—and with some luck their respective roles also—that we want to ask: But why did some societies manage to accumulate and innovate more rapidly than others? The three-fold classification offered above—geography, integration, and institutions—allows us to organize our thoughts on the "deeper" determinants of economic growth. These three are the factors that determine which societies will innovate and accumulate, and therefore develop, and which will not.

Since long-term economic development is a complex phenomenon, the idea that any one (or even all) of the above deep determinants can provide an adequate accounting of centuries of economic history is, on the face of it, preposterous. Historians and many social scientists prefer nuanced, layered explanations where these factors interact with human choices and many other not-so-simple twists and turns of fate. But economists like parsimony. We want to know how well these simple stories do, not only on their own or collectively, but more importantly, vis-à-vis each other. How much of the astounding variation in cross-national incomes around the world can geography, integration, and institutions explain? . . .

Trade fundamentalists and institutionalists have a considerably more difficult job to do, since they have to demonstrate causality for their preferred determinant, as well as identify the effective channel(s) through which it works. For the former, the task consists of showing that arrows (4) and (5)—capturing the direct impact of integration on income and the indirect impact through institutions, respectively—are the relevant ones, while arrows (6) and (7)—reverse feedbacks from incomes and institutions, respectively—are relatively insignificant. Reverse causality cannot be ruled out easily, since expanded trade and integration can be mainly the result of increased productivity in the economy and/or improved domestic institutions, rather than a cause thereof.

Institutionalists, meanwhile, have to worry about different kinds of reverse causality. They need to show that improvements in property rights, the rule of law, and other aspects of the institutional environment are an independent determinant of incomes . . . and are not simply the consequence of higher incomes . . . or of greater integration. . . .

Acemoglu, Johnson, and Robinson (AJR, 2001) use mortality rates of colonial settlers as an instrument for institutional quality. They argue that settler mortality had an important effect on the type of institutions that were built in lands that were colonized by the main European powers. Where the colonizers encountered relatively few health hazards to European settlement, they erected solid institutions that protected property rights and established the rule of law. In other areas, their interests were limited to extracting as much resources as quickly as possible, and they showed little interest in building high-quality institutions. Under the added assumption that institutions change only gradually over time, AJR argue that settler mortality rates are therefore a good instrument for institutional quality.

Our approach in this paper consists of using the Frankel and Romer and Acemoglu instruments simultaneously. . . .

This exercise yields some sharp and striking results. Most importantly, we find that the quality of institutions trumps everything else. Once institutions are controlled for, integration has no direct effect on incomes, while geography has at best weak direct effects. Trade often enters the income regression with the "wrong" (i.e., negative) sign, as do many of the geographical indicators. By contrast, our measure of property rights and the rule of law always enters with the correct sign, and is statistically significant, often with t-statistics that are very large. . . .

Our estimates indicate that an increase in institutional quality of one standard deviation, corresponding roughly to the difference between measured institutional quality in Bolivia and South Korea, produces a 2 log-points rise in per-capita incomes, or a 6.4-fold difference—which, not coincidentally, is also roughly the income difference between the two countries. . . .

We also use a large number of alternative indicators of geography, integration, and institutions. To get a sense of the magnitude of the potential impacts, we can compare two countries, say Nigeria and Mauritius, both in Africa. If the OLS relationship is indeed causal, the coefficients . . . would suggest that Mauritius's per capita GDP should be 5.2 times that of Nigeria, of which 21 percent would be due to better institutions, 65 percent due to greater openness, and 14 percent due to better location. In practice, Mauritius's income ($11,400) is 14.8 times that of Nigeria ($770).

What Does It All Mean?

A. An instrument does not a theory make. One reading of the AJR paper, and the one strongly suggested by their title—"The Colonial Origins of Comparative Development"—is that they regard experience under the early period of colonization as a fundamental determinant of current income levels. While the AJR paper is certainly suggestive on this score, in our view this interpretation of the paper's central message would not be entirely correct. One problem is that AJR do not carry out a direct test of the impact of colonial policies and institutions. Furthermore, if colonial experience were the key determinant of income levels, how would we account for the variation in incomes among countries that had never been colonized by the Europeans? . . .

B. The primacy of institutional quality does not imply policy ineffectiveness. Easterly and Levine (2002) assert that (macroeconomic) policies do not have an effect on incomes, once institutions are controlled for. Our view on the effectiveness of policy is similar to that expressed in AJR (2001, 1395): there are "substantial economic gains from improving institutions, for example as in the case of Japan during the Meiji Restoration or South Korea during the 1960s" or, one may add, China since the late 1970s. The distinction between institutions and policies is murky, as these examples illustrate. The reforms that Japan, South Korea, and China undertook were policy innovations that eventually resulted in a fundamental change in the institutional underpinning of their economies. . . .

This suggests that it is inappropriate to regress income levels on institutional quality *and* policies, as Easterly and Levine (2002) do. The problem is not just that incomes move slowly while policies can take sudden turns. In principle this could be addressed by taking long-term averages of policies. (Easterly and Levine average their policy measures over a number of decades.) It is that measures of institutional quality already contain all the relevant information about the impact of policies. . . .

Moreover, a geography theory of institutions can understate the impact that policies can play in changing them over time. As an empirical matter, institutions have changed remarkably in the last three decades. . . .

A purely geographical theory of institutions would have difficulty in accounting for these changes. Indeed, if the first stage regressions reported in Panel C of Table 2 [of the original work] are run over the last three decades, the coefficient on settler mortality declines from 0.94 in the 1970s to 0.87 in the 1980s and 0.71 in the 1990s, illustrating the mutability of institutions, and the declining importance of history (on the AJR interpretation of settler mortality) or geography (on the EL interpretation of settler mortality) in explaining the cross-national variation in institutions.

C. The hard work is still ahead. How much guidance do our results provide to policymakers who want to improve the performance of their economies? Not much at all. Sure, it is helpful to know that geography is not

Table 8.1 Determinants of Development: Core Specifications, Ordinary Least Squares Estimates

					Log GDP per Capita				
	Acemoglu et al. Sample			Extended Acemoglu et al. Sample			Large Sample		
Dependent variable	(1)	(2)	(3)	(4)	(5)	(6)	(7)	(8)	(9)
Geography (DISTEQ)	0.74 (4.48)*	0.20 (1.34)	0.32 (1.85)**	0.80 (5.22)*	0.22 (1.63)	0.33 (2.11)**	0.76 (10.62)*	0.20 (2.48)**	0.23 (2.63)*
Institutions (RULE)		0.78 (7.56)*	0.69 (6.07)*		0.81 (9.35)*	0.72 (6.98)*		0.81 (12.12)*	0.78 (10.49)*
Integration (LCOPEN)			0.16 (1.48)			0.15 (1.53)			0.08 (1.24)
Observations	64	64	64	79	79	79	137	137	137
R-square	0.25	0.57	0.59	0.26	0.61	0.62	0.42	0.71	0.71

Notes: The dependent variable is per capita GDP in 1995, PPP basis. There are three samples for which the core regressions are run: (i) the first three columns correspond to the sample of 64 countries in Acemoglu et al. (2001); (ii) columns (4)–(6) use a sample of 79 countries for which data on settler mortality (LOGEM4) have been compiled by Acemoglu et al.; and (iii) columns (7)–(9) use a larger sample of 137 countries. The regressors are: (i) DISTEQ, the variable for geography, which is measured as the absolute value of latitude of a country; (ii) Rule of Law (RULE), which is the measure for institutions; and (iii) LCOPEN, the variable for integration, which is measured as the ratio of nominal trade to nominal GDP. All regressors, except DISTEQ and RULE, in the three panels are in logs. See the Appendix [in the original text] for more detailed variable definitions and sources. *T-statistics* are reported under coefficient estimates. Significance at the 1, 5, and 10 percent levels is denoted respectively by *, **, and ***.

destiny, or that focusing on increasing the economy's links with world markets is unlikely to yield convergence. But the operational guidance that our central result on the primacy of institutional quality yields is extremely meager.

We illustrate the difficulty of extracting policy-relevant information from our findings using the example of property rights. Obviously, the presence of clear property rights for investors is a key, if not the key, element in the institutional environment that shapes economic performance. Our findings indicate that when investors believe their property rights are protected, the economy ends up richer. But nothing is implied about the actual form that property rights should take. We cannot even necessarily deduce that enacting a *private* property-rights regime would produce superior results compared to alternative forms of property rights.

If this seems stretching things too far, consider the experiences of China and Russia. China still retains a socialist legal system, while Russia has a regime of private property rights in place. Despite the absence of formal private property rights, Chinese entrepreneurs have felt sufficiently secure to make large investments, making that country the world's fastest growing economy over the last two decades. In Russia, by contrast, investors have felt insecure, and private investment has remained low. . . . Credibly signaling that property rights will be protected is apparently more important than enacting them into law as a formal private property rights regime.

So our findings do not map into a determinate set of policy desiderata. Indeed, there is growing evidence that desirable institutional arrangements have a large element of context specificity, arising from differences in historical trajectories, geography, political economy, or other initial conditions. . . . [T]his could help explain why successful developing countries—China, South Korea, and Taiwan among others—have almost always combined unorthodox elements with orthodox policies. It could also account for why important institutional differences persist among the advanced countries of North America, Western Europe, and Japan—in the role of the public sector, the nature of the legal systems, corporate governance, financial markets, labor markets, and social insurance mechanisms, among others.

Consequently, there is much to be learned still about what improving institutional quality means on the ground. This, we would like to suggest, is a wide open area of research. Cross-national studies of the present type are just a beginning that point us in the right direction.

References

Acemoglu, Daron, Simon Johnson, and James A. Robinson. 2001. "The Colonial Origins of Comparative Development: An Empirical Investigation," *American Economic Review*, 91, 5, December, 1369–1401.

Diamond, Jared, 1997. *Guns, Germs, and Steel*. New York: W. W. Norton & Co.

Easterly, W., and R. Levine. 2002. "Tropics, Germs, and Crops: How Endowments Influence Economic Development," mimeo, Center for Global Development and Institute for International Economics.

Rodrik, Dani. 2003. "Institutions, Integration, and Geography: In Search of the Deep Determinants of Economic Growth," in Rodrik, ed., *In Search of Prosperity: Analytic Country Studies on Growth*. Princeton, NJ: Princeton University Press.

9

The Colonial Origins of Comparative Development: An Empirical Investigation

DARON ACEMOGLU, SIMON JOHNSON,
AND JAMES A. ROBINSON

This chapter provides strong evidence that the contemporary gap between rich and poor nations has its origins in the colonial period. According to the authors, two very different kinds of colonies were established by the European powers. One of these was the "extractive state," in which the main goal of the colonizing power was to transfer as much wealth as possible back home to the imperial power. In those states, the institutions that emerged did not protect private property or provide for checks on authority. In contrast, "neo-European" colonies emerged with an emphasis on local development, protection of private property, and strong checks on the power of authorities. According to the authors, the kind of state that formed determined its long-run development success. If this argument is supported by subsequent research, then it suggests that the gap between rich and poor nations was actually predetermined centuries ago. ■

WHAT ARE THE FUNDAMENTAL CAUSES OF THE LARGE DIFFERENCES IN INCOME PER capita across countries? Although there is still little consensus on the answer to this question, differences in institutions and property rights have received considerable attention in recent years. Countries with better "institutions," more secure property rights, and less distortionary policies will invest more in

Excerpted from Daron Acemoglu, Simon Johnson, and James A. Robinson, "The Colonial Origins of Comparative Development: An Empirical Investigation," *American Economic Review* 91, 5 (2001): 1369–1401. Reprinted with permission. The authors' notes have been deleted.

physical and human capital, and will use these factors more efficiently to achieve a greater level of income. . . .

At some level it is obvious that institutions matter. Witness, for example, the divergent paths of North and South Korea, or East and West Germany, where one part of the country stagnated under central planning and collective ownership, while the other prospered with private property and a market economy. Nevertheless, we lack reliable estimates of the effect of institutions on economic performance. It is quite likely that rich economies choose or can afford better institutions. Perhaps more important, economies that are different for a variety of reasons will differ both in their institutions and in their income per capita. To estimate the impact of institutions on economic performance, we need a source of exogenous variation in institutions. In this paper, we propose a theory of institutional differences among countries colonized by Europeans, and exploit this theory to derive a possible source of exogenous variation. Our theory rests on three premises:

1. There were different types of colonization policies which created different sets of institutions. At one extreme, European powers set up "extractive states," exemplified by the Belgian colonization of the Congo. These institutions did not introduce much protection for private property, nor did they provide checks and balances against government expropriation. In fact, the main purpose of the extractive state was to transfer as much of the resources of the colony to the colonizer. At the other extreme, many Europeans migrated and settled in a number of colonies, creating what the historian Alfred Crosby (1986) calls "Neo-Europes." The settlers tried to replicate European institutions, with strong emphasis on private property and checks against government power. Primary examples of this include Australia, New Zealand, Canada, and the United States.
2. The colonization strategy was influenced by the feasibility of settlements. In places where the disease environment was not favorable to European settlement, the cards were stacked against the creation of Neo-Europes, and the formation of the extractive state was more likely.
3. The colonial state and institutions persisted even after independence. Colonies where Europeans faced higher mortality rates are today substantially poorer than colonies that were healthy for Europeans. Our theory is that this relationship reflects the effect of settler mortality working through the institutions brought by Europeans. . . .

The Hypothesis and Historical Background

We hypothesize that settler mortality affected settlements; settlements affected early institutions; and early institutions persisted and formed the basis of current institutions. In this section, we discuss and substantiate this hypothesis. The next subsection discusses the link between mortality rates of settlers and settlement decisions, then we discuss differences in colonization policies, and finally, we turn to the causes of institutional persistence.

Mortality and Settlements

There is little doubt that mortality rates were a key determinant of European settlements. Curtin (1964, 1998) documents how both the British and French press informed the public of mortality rates in the colonies. Curtin (1964) also documents how early British expectations for settlement in West Africa were dashed by very high mortality among early settlers, about half of whom could be expected to die in the first year. In the "Province of Freedom" (Sierra Leone), European mortality in the first year was 46 percent, in Bulama (April 1792–April 1793) there was 61 percent mortality among Europeans. In the first year of the Sierra Leone Company (1792–1793), 72 percent of the European settlers died. On Mungo Park's Second Expedition (May–November 1805), 87 percent of Europeans died during the overland trip from Gambia to the Niger, and all the Europeans died before completing the expedition.

An interesting example of the awareness of the disease environment comes from the Pilgrim fathers. They decided to migrate to the United States rather than Guyana because of the high mortality rates in Guyana (see Crosby 1986, pp. 143–44). Another example comes from the Beauchamp Committee in 1795, set up to decide where to send British convicts who had previously been sent to the United States. One of the leading proposals was the island of Lemane, up the Gambia River. The committee rejected this possibility because they decided mortality rates would be too high even for the convicts. Southwest Africa was also rejected for health reasons. The final decision was to send convicts to Australia.

The eventual expansion of many of the colonies was also related to the living conditions there. In places where the early settlers faced high mortality rates, there would be less incentive for new settlers to come.

Types of Colonization and Settlements

The historical evidence supports both the notion that there was a wide range of different types of colonization and that the presence or absence of European settlers was a key determinant of the form colonialism took. Historians, including Robinson and Gallagher (1961), Gann and Duignan (1962), Denoon (1983), and Cain and Hopkins (1993), have documented the development of "settler colonies," where Europeans settled in large numbers, and life was modeled after the home country. Denoon (1983) emphasizes that settler colonies had representative institutions which promoted what the settlers wanted and that what they wanted was freedom and the ability to get rich by engaging in trade. He argues that "there was undeniably something capitalist in the structure of these colonies. Private ownership of land and livestock was well established very early . . ." (p. 35).

When the establishment of European-like institutions did not arise naturally, the settlers were ready to fight for them against the wishes of the home country. Australia is an interesting example here. Most of the early settlers in Australia were ex-convicts, but the land was owned largely by ex-jailors, and there was no legal protection against the arbitrary power of landowners. The settlers wanted institutions and political rights like those prevailing in England at the time. They demanded jury trials, freedom from arbitrary arrest, and electoral representation. Although the British government resisted at first, the settlers argued that they were British and deserved the same rights as in the home country (see Robert Hughes 1987). Cain and Hopkins write (1993, p. 237): "from the late 1840s the British bowed to local pressures and, in line with observed constitutional changes taking place in Britain herself, accepted the idea that, in mature colonies, governors should in future form ministries from the majority elements in elected legislatures." They also suggest that "the enormous boom in public investment after 1870 [in New Zealand] . . . was an attempt to build up an infrastructure . . . to maintain high living standards in a country where voters expected politicians actively to promote their economic welfare" (p. 225).

This is in sharp contrast to the colonial experience in Latin America during the seventeenth and eighteenth centuries, and in Asia and Africa during the nineteenth and early twentieth centuries. The main objective of the Spanish and the Portuguese colonization was to obtain gold and other valuables from America. Soon after the conquest, the Spanish crown granted rights to land and labor (the encomienda) and set up a complex mercantilist system of monopolies and trade regulations to extract resources from the colonies.

Europeans developed the slave trade in Africa for similar reasons. Before the mid-nineteenth century, colonial powers were mostly restricted to the African coast and concentrated on monopolizing trade in slaves, gold, and other valuable commodities—witness the names used to describe West African countries: the Gold Coast, the Ivory Coast. Thereafter, colonial policy was driven in part by an element of superpower rivalry, but mostly by economic motives. Michael Crowder (1968, p. 50), for example, notes: "it is significant that Britain's largest colony on the West Coast [Nigeria] should have been the one where her traders were most active and bears out the contention that, for Britain . . . flag followed trade." Lance E. Davis and Robert A. Huttenback (1987, p. 307) conclude that "the colonial Empire provides strong evidence for the belief that government was attuned to the interests of business and willing to divert resources to ends that the business community would have found profitable." They find that before 1885 investment in the British empire had a return 25 percent higher than that on domestic investment, though afterwards the two converged. Andrew

Roberts (1976, p. 193) writes: "[from] . . . 1930 to 1940 Britain had kept for it-self 2,400,000 pounds in taxes from the Copperbelt, while Northern Rhodesia received from Britain only 136,000 pounds in grants for development." Simi-larly, Patrick Manning (1982) estimates that between 1905 and 1914, 50 percent of GDP in Dahomey was extracted by the French, and Crawford Young (1994, p. 125) notes that tax rates in Tunisia were four times as high as in France.

Probably the most extreme case of extraction was that of King Leopold of Belgium in the Congo. Gann and Duignan (1979, p. 30) argue that following the example of the Dutch in Indonesia, Leopold's philosophy was that "the colonies should be exploited, not by the operation of a market economy, but by state in-tervention and compulsory cultivation of cash crops to be sold to and distributed by the state at controlled prices." Jean-Philippe Peemans (1975) calculates that tax rates on Africans in the Congo approached 60 percent of their income dur-ing the 1920s and 1930s. Bogumil Jewsiewicki (1983) writes that during the pe-riod when Leopold was directly in charge, policy was "based on the violent ex-ploitation of natural and human resources," with a consequent "destruction of economic and social life . . . [and] . . . dismemberment of political structures."

Overall, there were few constraints on state power in the nonsettler colonies. The colonial powers set up authoritarian and absolutist states with the purpose of solidifying their control and facilitating the extraction of re-sources. Young (1994, p. 101) quotes a French official in Africa: "the Euro-pean commandant is not posted to observe nature. . . . He has a mission . . . to impose regulations, to limit individual liberties . . . , to collect taxes." Manning (1988, p. 84) summarizes this as: "In Europe the theories of representative de-mocracy won out over the theorists of absolutism. . . . But in Africa, the Euro-pean conquerors set up absolutist governments, based on reasoning similar to that of Louis XIV."

Institutional Persistence

There is a variety of historical evidence, as well as our regressions, suggesting that the control structures set up in the nonsettler colonies during the colonial era persisted, while there is little doubt that the institutions of law and order and private property established during the early phases of colonialism in Aus-tralia, Canada, New Zealand, the United States, Hong Kong, and Singapore have formed the basis of the current-day institutions of these countries.

Young emphasizes that the extractive institutions set up by the colonial-ists persisted long after the colonial regime ended. He writes: "although we commonly described the independent polities as 'new states,' in reality they were successors to the colonial regime, inheriting its structures, its quotidian routines and practices, and its more hidden normative theories of governance" (1994, p. 283). An example of the persistence of extractive state institutions into the independence era is provided by the persistence of the most prominent extractive policies. In Latin America, the full panoply of monopolies and regulations, which had been created by Spain, remained intact after independence, for most of the nineteenth century. Forced labor policies persisted and were even intensified or reintroduced with the expansion of export agriculture in the latter part of the nineteenth century. Slavery persisted in Brazil until 1886, and during the sisal boom in Mexico, forced labor was reintroduced and persisted up to the start of the revolution in 1910. Forced labor was also reintroduced in Guatemala and El Salvador to provide labor for coffee growing. In the Guatemalan case, forced labor lasted until the creation of democracy in 1945. Similarly, forced labor was reinstated in many independent African countries, for example, by Mobutu in Zaire.

There are a number of economic mechanisms that will lead to institutional persistence of this type. Here, we discuss three possibilities.

1. Setting up institutions that place restrictions on government power and enforce property rights is costly (see, e.g., Acemoglu and Thierry Verdier 1998). If the costs of creating these institutions have been sunk by the colonial powers, then it may not pay the elites at independence to switch to extractive institutions. In contrast, when the new elites inherit extractive institutions, they may not want to incur the costs of introducing better institutions, and may instead prefer to exploit the existing extractive institutions for their own benefits.

2. The gains to an extractive strategy may depend on the size of the ruling elite. When this elite is small, each member would have a larger share of the revenues, so the elite may have a greater incentive to be extractive. In many cases where European powers set up authoritarian institutions, they delegated the day-to-day running of the state to a small domestic elite. This narrow group often was the one to control the state after independence and favored extractive institutions.

3. If agents make irreversible investments that are complementary to a particular set of institutions, they will be more willing to support them, making these institutions persist (see, e.g., Acemoglu, 1995). For example, agents who have invested in human and physical capital will be in favor of spending money to enforce property rights, while those who have less to lose may not be. . . .

Mortality of Early Settlers

Sources of European Mortality in the Colonies

In this subsection, we give a brief overview of the sources of mortality facing potential settlers. Malaria (particularly *Plasmodium falciporum*) and yellow fever were the major sources of European mortality in the colonies. In the tropics, these two diseases accounted for 80 percent of European deaths, while gastrointestinal diseases accounted for another 15 percent (Curtin 1989, p. 30). Throughout the nineteenth century, areas without malaria and yellow fever, such as New Zealand, were more healthy than Europe because the major causes of death in Europe—tuberculosis, pneumonia, and smallpox—were rare in these places (Curtin 1989, p. 13).

Both malaria and yellow fever are transmitted by mosquito vectors. In the case of malaria, the main transmitter is the *Anopheles gambiae* complex and the mosquito *Anopheles funestus*, while the main carrier of yellow fever is *Aedes aegypti*. Both malaria and yellow fever vectors tend to live close to human habitation.

In places where the malaria vector is present, such as the West African savanna or forest, an individual can get as many as several hundred infectious mosquito bites a year. For a person without immunity, malaria (particularly *Plasmodium falciporum*) is often fatal, so Europeans in Africa, India, or the Caribbean faced very high death rates. In contrast, death rates for the adult local population were much lower (see Curtin [1964] . . .). Curtin (1998, pp. 7–8) describes this as follows:

> Children in West Africa . . . would be infected with malaria parasites shortly after birth and were frequently reinfected afterwards; if they lived beyond the age of about five, they acquired an apparent immunity. The parasite remained with them, normally in the liver, but clinical symptoms were rare so long as they continued to be infected with the same species of *P. falciporum*.

The more recent books on malariology confirm this conclusion. For example, "In stable endemic areas a heavy toll of morbidity and mortality falls on young children but malaria is a relatively mild condition in adults" (Herbert M. Gilles and David A. Warren 1993, p. 64; see also the classic reference on this topic, Leonard J. Bruce-Chwatt 1980, Chapter 4; Roy Porter, 1996). Similarly, the World Health Organization (WHO) points out that in endemic malaria areas of Africa and the Western Pacific today ". . . the risk of malaria severity and death is almost exclusively limited to non-immunes, being most serious for young children over six months of age . . . surviving children develop their own immunity between the age of 3–5 years" (Jose A. Najera and Joahim Hempel 1996).

People in areas where malaria is endemic are also more likely to have genetic immunity against malaria. For example, they tend to have the sickle-cell trait, which discourages the multiplication of parasites in the blood, or deficiencies in glucose-6-phosphate dehydrogenase and thalassaemia traits, which also protect against malaria. Porter (1996, p. 34) writes: "In such a process, . . . close to 100 percent of Africans acquired a genetic trait that protects them against vivax malaria and probably against falciporum malaria as well." Overall, the WHO estimates that malaria kills about 1 million people per year, most of them children. It does not, however, generally kill adults who grew up in malaria endemic areas (see Najera and Hempel 1996).

Although yellow fever's epidemiology is quite different from malaria, it was also much more fatal to Europeans than to non-Europeans who grew up in areas where yellow fever commonly occurred. Yellow fever leaves its surviving victims with a lifelong immunity, which also explains its epidemic pattern, relying on a concentrated nonimmune population. Curtin (1998, p. 10) writes: "Because most Africans had passed through a light case early in life, yellow fever in West Africa was a strangers' disease, attacking those who grew up elsewhere." Similarly, Michael B.A. Oldstone (1998, p. 49) writes:

> Most Black Africans and their descendants respond to yellow fever infection with mild to moderate symptoms such as headache, fever, nausea, and vomiting, and then recover in a few days. This outcome reflects the long relationship between the virus and its indigenous hosts, who through generations of exposure to the virus have evolved resistance.

In contrast, fatality rates among nonimmune adults, such as Europeans, could be as high as 90 percent.

Advances in medical science have reduced the danger posed by malaria and yellow fever. Yellow fever is mostly eradicated (Oldstone 1998, Chapter 5), and malaria has been eradicated in many areas. Europeans developed methods of dealing with these diseases that gradually became more effective in the second half of the nineteenth century. For example, they came to understand that high doses of quinine, derived from the cinchona bark, acted as a prophylactic and prevented infection or reduced the severity of malaria. They also started to undertake serious mosquito eradication efforts and protect themselves against mosquito bites. Further, Europeans also learned that an often effective method of reducing mortality from yellow fever is flight from the area, since the transmitter mosquito, *Aedes aegypti,* has only a short range. Nevertheless, during much of the nineteenth century, there was almost a complete misunderstanding of the nature of both diseases. For example, the leading theory for malaria was that it was caused by "miasma" from swamps, and quinine was not used widely. The role of small collections of water to breed mosquitoes and transmit these diseases was not understood. It was only in the late nineteenth century that Europeans started to control these diseases.

These considerations, together with the data we have on the mortality of local people and population densities before the arrival of Europeans, make us believe that settler mortality is a plausible instrument for institutional development: these diseases affected European settlement patterns and the type of institutions they set up, but had little effect on the health and economy of indigenous people.

A final noteworthy feature, helpful in interpreting our results, is that malaria prevalence depends as much on the microclimate of an area as on its temperature and humidity, or on whether it is in the tropics; high altitudes reduce the risk of infection, so in areas of high altitude, where "hill stations" could be set up, such as Bogota in Colombia, mortality rates were typically lower than in wet coastal areas. However, malaria could sometimes be more serious in high-altitude areas. For example, Curtin (1989, p. 47) points out that in Ceylon mortality was lower in the coast than the highlands because rains in the coast washed away the larvae of the transmitter mosquitoes. Similarly, in Madras many coastal regions were free of malaria, while northern India had high rates of infection. Curtin (1998, Chapter 7) also illustrates how there were marked differences in the prevalence of malaria within small regions of Madagascar. This suggests that mortality rates faced by Europeans are unlikely to be a proxy for some simple geographic or climatic feature of the country.

Data on Potential Settle Mortality

Our data on the mortality of European settlers come largely from the work of Philip Curtin. Systematic military medical record keeping began only after 1815, as an attempt to understand why so many soldiers were dying in some places. The first detailed studies were retrospective and dealt with British forces between 1817 and 1836. The United States and French governments quickly adopted similar methods (Curtin 1989, pp. 3, 5). Some early data are also available for the Dutch East Indies. By the 1870s, most European countries published regular reports on the health of their soldiers.

The standard measure is annualized deaths per thousand mean strength. This measure reports the death rate among 1,000 soldiers where each death is replaced with a new soldier. Curtin (1989, 1998) reviews in detail the construction of these estimates for particular places and campaigns, and assesses which data should be considered reliable.

Curtin (1989), *Death by Migration,* deals primarily with the mortality of European troops from 1817 to 1848. At this time modern medicine was still in its infancy, and the European militaries did not yet understand how to control malaria and yellow fever. These mortality rates can therefore be interpreted as reasonable estimates of settler mortality. They are consistent with substantial evidence from other sources (see, for example, Curtin [1964, 1968]). Curtin (1998), *Disease and Empire,* adds similar data on the mortality of soldiers in the second half of the nineteenth century. In all cases, we use the earliest available number for each country, reasoning that this is the best estimate of the mortality rates that settlers would have faced, at least until the twentieth century.

The main gap in the Curtin data is for South America since the Spanish and Portuguese militaries did not keep good records of mortality. Hector Gutierrez (1986) used Vatican records to construct estimates for the mortality rates of bishops in Latin America from 1604 to 1876. Because these data overlap with the Curtin estimates for several countries, we are able to construct a data series for South America. Curtin (1964) also provides estimates of mortality in naval squadrons for different regions which we can use to generate alternative estimates of mortality in South America. . . .

Concluding Remarks

Many economists and social scientists believe that differences in institutions and state policies are at the root of large differences in income per capita across countries. There is little agreement, however, about what determines institutions' and government attitudes towards economic progress, making it difficult to isolate exogenous sources of variation in institutions to estimate their effect on performance. In this paper we argued that differences in colonial experience could be a source of exogenous differences in institutions.

Our argument rests on the following premises: (1) Europeans adopted very different colonization strategies, with different associated institutions. In one extreme, as in the case of the United States, Australia, and New Zealand, they went and settled in the colonies and set up institutions that enforced the rule of law and encouraged investment. In the other extreme, as in the Congo or the Gold Coast, they set up extractive states with the intention of transferring resources rapidly to the metropole. These institutions were detrimental to investment and economic progress. (2) The colonization strategy was in part determined by the feasibility of European settlement. In places where Europeans faced very high mortality rates, they could not go and settle, and they were more likely to set up extractive states. (3) Finally, we argue that these early institutions persisted to the present. Determinants of whether Europeans could go and settle in the colonies, therefore, have an important effect on institutions today. We exploit these differences as a source of exogenous variation to estimate the impact of institutions on economic performance.

There is a high correlation between mortality rates faced by soldiers, bishops, and sailors in the colonies and European settlements; between European settlements and early measures of institutions; and between early institutions and institutions today. We estimate large effects of institutions on income per capita using this source of variation. We also document that this relationship is not driven by outliers, and is robust to controlling for latitude, climate, current disease environment, religion, natural resources, soil quality, ethnolinguistic fragmentation, and current racial composition.

It is useful to point out that our findings do not imply that institutions today are predetermined by colonial policies and cannot be changed. We emphasize colonial experience as one of the many factors affecting institutions. Since mortality rates faced by settlers are arguably exogenous, they are useful as an instrument to isolate the effect of institutions on performance. In fact, our reading is that these results suggest substantial economic gains from improving institutions, for example as in the case of Japan during the Meiji Restoration or South Korea during the 1960s.

There are many questions that our analysis does not address. Institutions are treated largely as a "black box": The results indicate that reducing expropriation risk (or improving other aspects of the "cluster of institutions") would result in significant gains in income per capita, but do not point out what concrete steps would lead to an improvement in these institutions. Institutional features, such as expropriation risk, property rights enforcement, or rule of law, should probably be interpreted as an equilibrium outcome, related to some more fundamental "institutions," e.g., presidential versus parliamentary system, which can be changed directly. A more detailed analysis of the effect of more fundamental institutions on property rights and expropriation risk is an important area for future study.

References

Acemoglu, Daron. "Reward Structures and the Allocation of Talent." *European Economic Review*, January 1995, 39(1), pp. 17–33.

Acemoglu, Daron and Verdier, Thierry. "Property Rights, Corruption and the Allocation of Talent: A General Equilibrium Approach." *Economic Journal*, September 1998, 108(450), pp. 1381–403.

Bruce-Chwatt, Leonard J. *Essential malariology*. London: Wiley Medical Publications, 1980.

Cain, Philip J. and Hopkins, Antony G. *British imperialism: Innovation and expansion 1688–1914*. New York: Longman, 1993.

Crosby, Alfred. *Ecological imperialism: The biological expansion of Europe 900–1900*. New York: Cambridge University Press, 1986.

Crowder, Michael. *West Africa under colonial rule*. Chicago: Northwestern University Press, 1968.

Curtin, Philip D. *The image of Africa*. Madison, WI: University of Wisconsin Press, 1964.

———. "Epidemiology and the Slave Trade." *Political Science Quarterly*, June 1968, 83(2), pp. 181–216.

———. *Death by migration: Europe's encounter with the tropical world in the 19th century*. New York: Cambridge University Press, 1989.

———. *Disease and empire: The health of European troops in the conquest of Africa*. New York: Cambridge University Press, 1998.

Davis, Lance E. and Huttenback, Robert A. *Mammon and the pursuit of empire: The political economy of British imperialism, 1860–1912*. Cambridge: Cambridge University Press, 1987.

Denoon, Donald. *Settler capitalism: The dynamics of dependent development in the southern hemisphere.* Oxford: Clarendon Press, 1983.

Gann, Lewis H. and Duignan, Peter. *White settlers in tropical Africa.* Baltimore, MD: Penguin, 1962.

———. *The rulers of Belgian Africa.* Princeton, NJ: Princeton University Press, 1979.

Gilles, Herbert M. and Warren, David A. *Bruce-Chwatt's* Essential malariology, 3rd Ed. London: Arnold, 1993.

Gutierrez, Hector. "La Mortalité des Eveques Latino-Americains aux XVIIe et XVIII Siècles." *Annales de Demographie Historique,* 1986, pp. 29–39.

Hughes, Robert. *The fatal shore.* London: Collins Harvill, 1987.

Jewsiewicki, Bogumil. "Rural Society and the Belgian Colonial Economy," in D. Birmingham and P. M. Martin, eds., *The history of Central Africa,* volume II. New York: Longman, 1983, pp. 95–125.

Manning, Patrick. *Slavery, colonialism, and economic growth in Dahomey, 1640–1980.* New York: Cambridge University Press, 1982.

———. *Francophone sub-Saharan Africa, 1880–1995.* New York: Cambridge University Press, 1988.

Najera, Jose A. and Hempel, Joahim. "The Burden of Malaria." 1996, downloaded from the World Health Organization's Roll Back Malaria website, http://mosquito.who .int/docs/b.

Oldstone, Michael B. A. *Viruses, plagues, and history.* New York: Oxford University Press, 1998.

Peemans, Jean-Philippe. "Capital Accumulation in the Congo under Colonialism: The Role of the State," in Lewis H. Gann and Peter Duignan, eds., *Colonialism in Africa 1870–1960,* volume 4, *The economics of colonialism.* Stanford, CA: Hoover Institution Press, 1975, 165–212.

Porter, Roy, ed. *The Cambridge illustrated history of medicine.* Cambridge: Cambridge University Press, 1996.

Roberts, Andrew. *A history of Zambia.* London: Heinemann, 1976.

Robinson, Ronald E. and Gallagher, John. *Africa and the Victorians: The official mind of imperialism.* London: Macmillan, 1961.

Young, Crawford. *The African colonial state in comparative perspective.* New Haven, CT: Yale University Press, 1994.

10

The Great Escape:
The Industrial Revolution in
Theory and in History

GREGORY CLARK

Gregory Clark, the author of the pathbreaking book A Farewell to Alms *(2007) rejects the argument made in the previous three chapters that the gap between rich and poor is caused by geography (Chapter 7), institutions (Chapter 8), or colonial origins (Chapter 9). Clark argues instead that up until the Industrial Revolution, the entire world was caught in the "Malthusian Trap" and remained as poor if not poorer than it was in the Stone Age. In the nineteenth century, however, with the emergence of the Industrial Revolution in England, the great gap between rich and poor countries began. Clark points to a gradual culture shift as the cause of this great change.* ■

WORLD ECONOMIC HISTORY IS SURPRISINGLY SIMPLE, AND CAN BE PRESENTED IN one diagram as in Figure 10.1 below. Before 1800 income per capita for all societies we observe fluctuated, but there was no upward trend. The great span of human history—from the arrival of anatomically modern man to Confucius, Plato, Aristotle, Michelangelo, Shakespeare, Beethoven, and all the way to Jane Austen indeed—was lived in societies caught in the Malthusian trap. Jane Austen may write about refined conversation over tea served in china cups, but for the mass of people as late as 1813 material conditions were no better than their ancestors of the African savannah. The Darcys were few, the poor plentiful.[1]

Then came the Industrial Revolution. Incomes per capita began a sustained growth in a favored group of countries around 1820. In the last two hundred years in the most fortunate countries real incomes per capita rose 10–15 fold. But prosperity has not come to all societies. Living standards in some

---

Reprinted by permission of the author.

Figure 10.1   World Economic History in One Picture

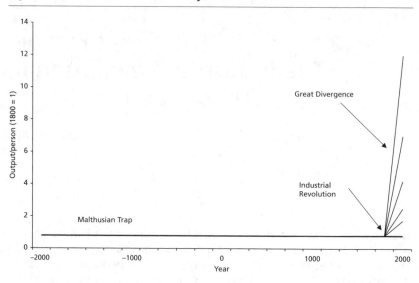

countries are as low as they were for the mass of humanity before 1800. Indeed there is good argument that living conditions for the poorest countries in the world are lower now than for the average person before 1800. This divergence in fortunes since the Industrial Revolution has recently been labeled "the Great Divergence."[2]

Thus world economic history poses three interconnected problems: the long persistence of the Malthusian trap, the escape from that trap in the Industrial Revolution, and the consequent Great Divergence. Explaining the Industrial Revolution also implicitly requires explaining the Malthusian Trap, and the Great Divergence.

Recently a distinguished group of economists—Gary Becker, Oded Galor, Gary Hanson, Chad Jones, Michael Kremer, Robert Lucas, Omar Moav, Douglass North, Edward Prescott, Nancy Stokey, David Weil—have turned once more to the eternal question of the Industrial Revolution. They have sought to build formal models that would explain the long delay in escaping from the Malthusian trap, and sustained growth once the escape occurred. Implicitly they also answer the question "Was the Industrial Revolution inevitable?" This article summarizes and reviews these theories, and asks whether the growth of knowledge about pre-industrial societies, which has been considerable in the last twenty years, offers any further constraints or suggestions for a theory of the Industrial Revolution.

Despite the enormous complexity of modern economies, the growth of income per person since the Industrial Revolution reduces to just two possible sources. The first is more capital per person. The second is improved efficiency in the use of capital, labor and land in producing output. But economists have concluded that two sources of growth is one too many, and that there can be only one source of the great boom in income per person, capital. Advances in the measured efficiency of economies don't just drop out of the sky, but result from search for better techniques. Thus the same *measured* amount of capital, labor and land may now produce more output than before. But that is because of time invested in learning more effective ways to build machines, and better ways to utilize machinery and workers. This search for improvement, involving resources, is just another form of investment.

This presumption of the centrality of capital accumulation in economic growth was not put to serious empirical test until the 1940s. But by the 1950s a number of economists, most famously Robert Solow, had conducted studies that showed at the industry and national levels the residual growth in efficiency of the economy explained almost all growth of output per person. This result has been confirmed in numerous studies since, including studies on the English Industrial Revolution itself. Physical capital accumulation explains only about one third of the growth of income per person over time, and about one third of the differences in income per person across countries. Economic growth since the Industrial Revolution thus seems to mock one of the truisms of elementary economics: "No free lunch." For the last 200 years the people of the advanced economies have fed on a rich diet of free lunches, and the affluence of modern life is founded on this manna from heaven. Further, we shall see below that the most plausible explanation of the growth of physical capital per person since the Industrial Revolution is the existence of the large efficiency residual.

The oddity of the substantial residual is a recent occurrence. As noted, there is no evidence of any long run gains in income per capita before 1800. In the Malthusian economy that preceded 1800 all productivity growth is absorbed by population increases. . . . We know that typically in pre-industrial societies the share of land in national income is much larger than since the Industrial Revolution. In England it was about 20–25% from 1300 to 1750 (Clark 2001). Thus we can calculate long run technological advance at a world scale before 1800 just by looking at long run population growth, as Kremer (1993) pointed out. . . . For the world as a whole there is no period before 1700 when the calculated world rate of efficiency advance exceeds 0.1% per year. . . . The conventional figures for income growth in England after 1800 suggest that by the nineteenth century the measured productivity growth rate was about 0.8%, close to modern levels for advanced economies. Figure 10.2 shows TFP [total factor productivity] growth rates as estimated by Nick Crafts and Knick Harley and others for England since the Industrial Revolution (Crafts and Harley 1992). Their estimates suggest a relatively abrupt transition to modern levels of productivity growth circa 1800–1830. In a matter of less than 50 years the English economy seemingly underwent a fundamental shift from pre-industrial productivity growth

Figure 10.2   Estimated Efficiency Growth Rates, England, 1700–2000

rates to those of the modern epoch. This focuses attention on the Industrial Revolution in 1770 in England as the epochal event of world history.

Explaining Modern Productivity Growth

How do we explain the appearance of an important residual in growth since the Industrial Revolution? There are only two ways this can happen. Either the capital stock grew much more rapidly than has been measured, and/or the weight accorded to capital, has to be larger.

The capital stock has three important components: tangible capital—buildings, machinery, inventories, intangible capital—research and development expenditures, and human capital—educational investments that increase labor productivity. Until the 1950s measures of the capital stock focused on tangible physical capital. Dennison and Kendrick noted that the labor supply in modern economies incorporates important human capital. But adding human capital did not eliminate the residual, or even reduce it radically. The size of the human capital stock, even in as highly educated a place as the modern USA, makes it still somewhat less than the physical capital stock. And the private rate of return to human capital, which probably exceeds the social return, is about the same as for physical capital. Thus in the USA in 2000 the capital cost of all schooling per member of the active labor force can be estimated as $182,700, based on the average years of education per worker and the cost of schooling per year (including foregone wages). But the stock of physical capital per worker in the US in 2000 was still greater at \$210,500. The share of income derived from this human capital investment per worker, assuming a 10% return on the investment in line with the estimates of George Psacharopoulos, was 26%, compared to 28% for physical capital.

But if we look at economic growth in the US from 1990 to 2000, the growth rate of physical capital at 1.27% per year was twice as fast as the growth of the human capital stock per worker at 0.67%. Thus of the overall growth rate of income per labor hour of 1.89% in this decade, physical capital accumulation per worker explained 0.36%, leaving a residual productivity growth of 1.53%. But including human capital accumulation only explained another 0.18% of the growth, leaving the residual at 1.36% per year, which was 72% of the growth of output per worker hour. And as noted education in modern economies is likely not capital formation but consumption, and costly signaling to employers of individuals likely workplace productivity.

In earlier decades the growth of human capital per worker was much faster (thus in the years 1940–1963 the growth rate estimated in the same way is 2.20% per year). But correspondingly the share of income attributed to human capital was smaller. Thus though including consideration of human capital always reduces the size of the residual attributed to productivity gains in the modern era, these effects were never strong enough to explain more than 30% of the residual.

Equally simply adding in human capital to growth accounting exercises in Industrial Revolution England will not explain the apparent sudden rise of the residual. Estimated literacy rates in England from the 1580s to the 1920s show that there was in fact little change in literacy rates for men, the bulk of the labor force in the Industrial Revolution period. The human capital stock grew little (and was still very small relative to the physical capital stock).

By the 1970s it was clear that while better measurement of capital might reduce the apparent contribution of the residual somewhat, the residual was still the major element in the story of modern growth of income per person.

Though the direct evidence is extremely thin, it is at least plausible to argue that modern economic growth has resulted largely from the investment in a particular type of capital, "knowledge capital" devoted to improving the production process. Further since the detailed history of the Industrial Revolution laid out by historians in the past 50 years has emphasized the key role of technological advance the task is seemingly one of showing why either the demand and/or the supply of innovation increased in England in the 1760s.

The Unimportance of Physical Capital

Acknowledging the importance of investment in a particular type of capital, knowledge, would seem to imply that there have been two important sources of growth since the Industrial Revolution: efficiency growth fueled by investment in "knowledge capital" which explains 50–70% of growth of income per person, and separately additions to the stock of physical and human capital which explain the other 30–50%. However if investments in "knowledge capital" explain modern efficiency growth, then these knowledge investments also explain the accumulation of physical and human capital. For if efficiency advances (generated by investments in knowledge) and physical and human capital were truly independent sources of income growth then there could be economies with rapid growth of physical capital per person, but no efficiency gains, and economies with rapid efficiency gains but little growth of physical capital per person. In practice both across time and across countries at any given time there is a close association between capital stock growth rates (whether physical or human) and efficiency growth.

Thus investments in knowledge capital that generated efficiency growth not only explain most of modern economic growth at a proximate level, they essentially explain all economic growth. Thus any satisfying account of the Industrial Revolution has to do just the following things. First explain why *no* society before 1800—not ancient Babylon, Pharaonic Egypt, China through countless centuries, Classical Greece, Imperial Rome, Renaissance Tuscany, medieval Flanders, the Aztecs, Mogul India, the Dutch Republic—expanded the stock of knowledge by more than 10% a century. Then explain why within 50 years of 1800 the rate of growth of knowledge rose to modern rates in one small country on the margins of Europe, Britain. And of course explain why economies around the world have benefited from this knowledge expansion to such different degrees. Then we will understand the history of man.

Theories of the Industrial Revolution

Theories of the Industrial Revolution offered by economists fall into three basic types, each of which faces characteristic difficulties. These three types are:

Exogenous growth theories. Some feature outside the economy, such as the institutions of the society, or the relative scarcities of different inputs in production, changed, inducing investment in expanding the production technique by potential innovators within economies. Such a change would include, for example, changes in the institutions governing the appropriability of knowledge, or the security of all property, as posited by Douglass North and others. Thus North and Weingast argue that the arrival of the constitutional monarchy in England in 1689 was the key political innovation that ushered in modern economic growth (North and Weingast 1989). Joel Mokyr argues that the Enlightenment, an intellectual movement among the elite of Western European society in the eighteenth century, but that had its roots much earlier, was the exogenous shock that changed the fundamental dynamic of the economy (Mokyr 2003). These theories would predict that we will find in England in 1760, or shortly before then, an institutional or other innovation not seen in *any* earlier society.

Multiple equilibrium theories. A shock—disease, war, conquest of new lands—lead the economy to jump from the bad, stagnant equilibrium of the Malthusian embrace to the good, dynamic equilibrium of the modern world. A particular class of theories that has recently attracted adherents in economics is one where families switch from having large numbers of children, each of whom they invest little time in, to one where families have small numbers of children whom they lavish much attention on.

Endogenous growth theories. A feature internal to the economic system, some state variable, evolved over time in the long pre-industrial era to eventually create the pre-conditions for modern economic growth. The Industrial Revolution was thus pre-determined from the time the first human appeared on the African Savannah. It was just a matter of time before the economic conditions for rapid technological progress were created. The question then is "what is different about the economy of England in 1760, compared to Florence in 1300, China in 500, Rome at the time of Christ or Athens at the time of Plato?" Posited internal drivers of the economic system that eventually created the Industrial Revolution have included the size of the population itself, and an evolution through natural selection of the characteristics of the population.

Exogenous Growth Theories

For economists the great exogenous force that is continually invoked as determining the lives of men and the fates of economies is the institutions that govern societies, determining who owns what, how secure property is, and how property gets transferred (see, for example, North and Thomas 1973, North and Weingast 1989, Jones 2002, Acemoglu, Johnson and Robinson 2001, 2002). The preferred assumption is that the desires and rationalities of people in all human societies are essentially the same. The medieval peasant in Europe, the Indian cooly, the bushman of the *veld* share a common set of aspirations, and a common ability to act to achieve those aspirations. What differs across societies, however, are the institutions that govern economic life. If sustained rapid productivity advance is not observed before 1800 in any society, it must be because all these societies' innovation got even less reward than in our own.

The picture many modern economists thus have of the world before the Industrial Revolution is thus composed of a mixture of all the bad movies ever made about early societies. Vikings pour out of long ships to loot and pillage defenseless peasants and burn the libraries of monasteries. Mongol hordes flow out of the steppe on horseback to sack Chinese cities. Clerical fanatics burn at the stake those who dare to question arcane religious doctrines. Peasants groan under the heel of rapacious lords whose only activity is feasting and fighting. Aztec priests cut out the hearts with obsidian knives from screaming, writhing victims. In this world who has the time, the energy, or the incentive to develop new technology?

This picture of the pre-industrial world is true for some societies, but to explain the long delay in the arrival of the Industrial Revolution it needs to be true for all. And some agrarian societies in the long Malthusian interval turn out to be orderly and peaceable places, even by the standards of the modern USA. While many hunter gatherer and subsistence agriculture societies have extraordinarily high numbers of deaths from violence by the standards of the modern US, others such as England as early as the thirteenth century are peaceable and ordered. Indeed medieval England was a lot more peaceable and ordered, judging by homicide statistics, than many modern societies such as Brazil or Colombia.

The advantage of a theory which relies on some exogenous shock to the economic system is that it can hopefully account for the seeming sudden change in the growth rate of measured efficiency around 1800. Institutions can change suddenly and dramatically—witness the French Revolution, the Russian Revolution, or the recent Iranian Revolution that overthrew the Shah.

These theories of an institutional shift in appropriability face two major difficulties, however, one conceptual, one empirical. The conceptual difficulty is that if modern economic growth can be produced by a simple institutional change, then why in all the varied and various societies that the world has seen since 10,000 BC and before was there none which stumbled upon the right set of institutions that made knowledge property? Societies varied markedly in what could be property and how property was transferred between owners. For example, in civil cases over possession of land in the legal system established by the Normans in medieval England after 1066, the party whose right to land was contested could elect to prove his or her title through armed combat with his opponent! This may seem to us a crazy way of settling property disputes, but the point is that societies have made all kinds of different choices about institutional forms. Why did some not stumble upon the right set of institutions? It seems that we cannot rely on chance here in institutional choice. There must be something that is keeping the institutions of the pre-industrial world in the "bad" state. But that requires us to switch either to a multiple equilibria theory, or to one of endogenous growth, which we will discuss below.

It is true that the early societies we know of in detail seem to have lacked the legal notion that you could own property in ideas or innovations. Thus in both the Roman and Greek worlds when an author published a book there was no legal or practical way to stop the pirating of the text. Copies could be freely made by anyone who acquired a version of the manuscript (on papyrus rolls), and the copier could amend and alter the text at will. It was not uncommon for a text to be reissued under the name of a new "author." It was common to condemn such pirating of works or ideas as immoral. But writings and inventions were just not viewed as commodities with a market value.

While the ancients may have lacked them, there were systems of intellectual property rights in place, however, long before the Industrial Revolution. The earliest established foundations of a modern patent system were found in the thirteenth century in Venice. By the fifteenth century in Venice true patents in the modern sense were regularly being awarded. Thus in 1416 the Council of Venice gave a 50 year patent to Franciscus Petri from Rhodes, who was thus a foreigner, for a new type of fulling mill. By 1474 the Venetian patent law had been codified. There is evidence for Florence also in the fifteenth century of the awarding of patents. The Venetian innovation granting property rights in knowledge, which was very important to the famous Venetian glass industry, spread to Belgium, the Netherlands, England, Germany, France and Austria in the sixteenth century as a consequence of the movement of Italian glass workers to these other countries. Thus by the sixteenth century all the major European countries, at least on an ad hoc basis, granted property rights in knowledge to innovators. They did this in order to attract skilled craftsmen with superior techniques to their lands. The spread of formal patent systems thus predates the Industrial Revolution by at least 350 years.

The claims of North and his associates for the superiority of the property rights protections afforded by the patent system in eighteenth century England thus stem from the way in which the system operated after the Glorious Revolution of 1688–1689 established the supremacy of Parliament over the King. Under the patent system introduced in the reign of Elizabeth I (1568–1603) the system was supervised by government ministers. Political interference led to the creation of spurious monopolies for techniques already developed, or the denial of legitimate claims. After the Glorious Revolution Parliament sought to avoid this by devolving the supervision of patents to the courts. Generally the courts would allow any patent to be registered as long as no other party objected. No other major European country had a formal patent system as in England before 1791. This still places the key institutional innovation a good 80 years before the Industrial Revolution.

There also existed other institutions in, for example, medieval European society, which we would think would promote innovation better than the modern patent system. Producers in many towns were organized into guilds which represented the interests of the trade. These guilds were in a position to tax members to facilitate lump sum payments to innovators to reveal productive new techniques to the members.

The empirical difficulty with the appropriability argument is the appallingly weak evidence that there was any great gain in the returns to innovators in England in the 1760s and later. The textile industry for example was in the vanguard of technological change in the Industrial Revolution period. . . . From 1770 to 1869 TFP rose about 22 fold. Perhaps two thirds of the productivity growth experienced by the English economy from 1760 to 1869 can be attributed directly to the innovations in textiles.

Yet the gains of the textile innovators were modest in the extreme. The value of the cotton textile innovations alone by the 1860s, for example, was about £115 million in extra output per year. But a trivially small share of this value of extra output ever flowed to the innovators. Patents mostly provided poor protection, the major gains to innovators coming through appeals post hoc to public beneficence through Parliament. Also the patent system shows none of the alleged separation from political interference. The reason for this is that Parliament could, on grounds of the public good, extend patents beyond the statutory 17 years to adequately reward those who made significant innovations. James Watt was the beneficiary of such a grant. But such grants depended on social and political protection just as much as in the old days.

The profit rates of major firms in the industry also provide good evidence that most of the innovation in the textile industry was quickly leaking from the innovators to other producers with no rewards to the innovators. Knick Harley (1997) has reconstructed the profit rates being made by some of the more successful cotton spinning and weaving firms in the early Industrial Revolution period. The cotton spinners Samuel Greg and Partners earned an average profit from 1796 to 1819 of 11.7% per year, just the normal commercial return for a risky venture such as manufacturing. Given the rapid improvements in cotton spinning productivity going on in the industry in these years it suggests that whatever innovations were being introduced were spreading from one firm to another very quickly. Otherwise leading firms such as Samuel Greg would have made large profits compared to their competitors. Similarly the firm of William Grey and Partners made less than 2% per year from 1801 to 1810, a negative economic profit rate. The innovations in the cotton spinning industry seem to have mainly caused prices to fall, leaving little excess profits for the firms that were innovating. Thus a third firm, Richard Hornby and partners, in the years 1777 to 1809 was in a sector of the industry, hand loom weaving, which had not yet been transformed by any technological advance. Yet its average profit rate was 11.4%, as high as Samuel Greg in the innovating part of the industry. The conclusion is that the host of innovations in cotton textiles do not seem to have particularly rewarded the innovators. Only a few such as Arkwright and the Peels became noticeably wealthy. Of the 379 people dying in 1860–1869 in Britain who left estates of £0.5 million or more, only 17 were in the textile industry, even though as noted from 1760–1769 to 1860–1869 this one sector generated the majority of productivity growth in the economy (Rubinstein, 1981). The Industrial Revolution economy was spectacularly bad at rewarding innovation. This is why Britain has few foundations to rival the great private philanthropies and universities of the USA. Its innovators captured little of the rewards.

Thus there is no evidence that it was institutional changes providing better rewards for innovators in the Industrial Revolution era that unleashed mankind's creative potential.

Multiple Equilibrium Theories

The theories discussed above in which a parameter shift external to the economic system provides the Industrial Revolution are clearly unsatisfactory. An alternative class of models posits that the Malthusian state was a low level equilibrium that was replaced, as a result of some exogenous shock, with the modern growth equilibrium.

"Bad" equilibrium theories have come in a number of forms. One set seeks to explain through the political economy of institutions why systematically early societies had institutions that discouraged economic growth. The common feature that North and others point to in early societies is that political power was not achieved by popular elections. Indeed there is a close association between democracy and economic growth. By the time England achieved its Industrial Revolution it was a constitutional democracy where the king was merely a figurehead. The USA, the leading nation in the world in economic terms since the 1870s, has always been a democracy also. In pre-industrial societies, as a generalization, the rulers ultimately rested their political position on the threat of violence.

For economic efficiency in any society property rules have to be chosen to create the maximum value of economic output. In such a case a disjuncture can arise between the property rules in the society that will maximize the total value of output, and the property rules that will maximize the output going to the ruling elite. Indeed North et al. have to argue that such a disjuncture systematically arises in all societies before 1800.

I will not deal at length with the idea of the bad political equilibrium, despite its continuing popularity, because political changes as occurred in England in 1688–1689 so spectacularly fail to explain the Industrial Revolution. They are too early, and economic actors at the time did not regard them as important (Clark 1996). Also we shall see below another disturbing development for proponents of the Glorious Revolution as the turning point in history—evidence is emerging that output per person and productivity were growing as rapidly in England in the bad old years 1600–1688 as in 1689–1860! Modern growth had begun under autocracy.

This argument that pre-industrial society was stuck in a bad equilibrium has taken other, potentially more defensible, forms. The one that has attracted most attention by economic theorists recently is that in the Malthusian world parents were induced to have large numbers of children, each of whom they provided little to in the way of training or education. One of the great social changes in the advanced industrial economies since the Industrial Revolution is a decline in the number of children the average woman gave birth to, from 5–6 to 2 or less. Proponents of this interpretation of the Industrial Revolution such as Gary Becker and Robert Lucas argue that this switch, induced by changing economic circumstances, has been accompanied by a great increase in the time and attention invested in each child. People are not the same in all societies. The continual efficiency growth of the modern world has thus been created by higher quality people. The supply of innovations was increased by more human capital.

The Industrial Revolution was associated with an increase in the education level. So increases in human capital that created knowledge externalities, at the gross level, would seemingly be a candidate source of the Industrial Revolution. We also know, though only through very indirect methods, that even quite sophisticated earlier societies, such as the Roman Empire or Renaissance Florence, seemed to have much lower levels of general literacy and numeracy.

We certainly can find interesting evidence that the average numeracy and literacy of even rich people in most Malthusian economies were surprisingly poor. A prosperous land owner in Roman Egypt, Isidorus Aurelius, for example, variously declared his age in legal documents in a less than two year span in 308–309 AD as 37, 40, 45 and 40. Clearly Isidorus had no clear idea of his age. Other sources show he was illiterate (Duncan-Jones 1990, p. 80). A lack of knowledge of their true age was widespread among the Roman upper classes as evidenced by age declarations made by their survivors on tombstones. In populations where ages are recorded accurately, 20% of the recorded ages will end in 5 or 10. We can thus construct a score variable Z, which measures the degree of "age heaping," where $Z = (X - 20)*1.25$, and X is the percentage of age declarations ending in 5 or 10, to measure the percentage of the population whose real age is unknown. This measure of the percentage of people who did not know their true age correlates moderately well in modern societies with the degree of literacy.

Among those wealthy enough to be commemorated by an inscribed tombstone in the Roman Empire, typically half had unknown ages. Age awareness did correlate with social class within the Roman Empire. More than 80% of office holders' ages seem to have been known by their relatives. When we compare this with death records for modern Europe we find that by the eve of the Industrial Revolution age awareness in the general population had increased markedly.

We can also look at the development of age awareness by looking at census of the living. Some of the earliest of these are for medieval Italy, including the famous Florentine Catasto of 1427. Even though Florence was then one of the richest cities of the world, and the center of the Renaissance, 32% of the city population did not know their age. In comparison a census of 1790 of the small English borough of Corfe Castle in Dorset, with a mere 1,239 inhabitants, most of them laborers, shows that all but 8% knew their age. In 1790 again awareness correlates with measures of social class, with universal knowledge among the higher status families, and lower age awareness among the poor. But the poor of Corfe Castle or Terling in Essex had as much age awareness as office holders in the Roman Empire.

Another feature of the Roman tombstone age declarations is that ages seem to be greatly overstated for many adults. Thus while we know that life expectancy in ancient Rome was probably on the order of 20–25 at birth, tombstones record people as dying at ages as high as 120. Thus for North African tombstones, 3% of the deceased are recorded as dying at age 100 or more. Almost all of these 3% must have been 20–50 years younger than was recorded. Yet their descendants did not detect any implausibility in recording these fabulous ages. In contrast the Corfe Castle census records a highest age of 90, well within the range of possibilities given life expectancy in rural England in these years.

But this picture of the Malthusian world bursting with ill-kempt, ill-cared-for children is based on a premise derived from a cross section of countries in the *modern* world, which is that the number of *surviving* children per family declines with income. It is certainly true that the number of children born per family fell sometime after the Industrial Revolution at a time of rising incomes. But mortality rates among children were much higher in the pre-industrial world, with most of the mortality occurring in the first years of life. Thus if we count only children who survived to reproductive age the average completed family size was close to 2 for all societies before 1800. Further since children who died in the pre-industrial world tended to do so fairly early, the numbers of children in any household at any time in the pre-industrial world would typically be 3 or less. For example, of 1,000 children born in England in 1700–1724, nearly 200 would be dead within 6 months (Wrigley et al. 1997). Preindustrial families would look not unlike the families of America in the 1950s and 1960s. Preindustrial families faced remarkably similar tradeoffs between the number and quality of children as do modern families. The Industrial Revolution era in England itself saw an increase in completed family sizes, followed in the late nineteenth century by a decline back towards the Malthusian norm by the 1960s. Further we shall see that there is evidence for pre-industrial England that surviving children per family increased with income.

What would spark a switch of families towards fewer but better educated children? From the point of view of the individual family there must be some signal in the form of higher relative earnings for educated children. But why would such a change appear in the Malthusian economy? Since in this model, and that of Lucas below, there is only one type of agent we would not observe any wage premium associated with human capital. All agents have the same human capital. However, since the model is supposed to represent the essence of a world where families vary in the amount of human capital with which they endow their children, it is interesting to consider the wage differential between skilled and unskilled labor. Here, however, we find absolutely no evidence of any market signal to parents as we approach 1800 that they need to invest more in the education or training of their children. The skill premium is actually at its highest in the interval 1200–2000 in the earliest years, before the onset of the Black Death in 1348, when a craftsman earned nearly double the wage of a laborer. If there was ever an incentive to accumulate skills it was in the early economy. Thereafter it declines to a lower but relatively stable level from about 1370 until 1900, a period of over 500 years, before declining further in the twentieth century. Thus the time of the greatest market reward for skills and training was long before the Industrial Revolution.

Returning to the problem of what individual price signal encourages parents to increase the human capital of their children, we see the same issue with human capital explanations of the differences in economic performance between rich and poor countries in the modern world. Private returns to education seem to be as high in poor countries as in rich, and as high in poor countries now as they were at the time of the Industrial Revolution in England. Lucas (1988), which proposes human capital as the source of the differences in the modern world between income per capita in rich and poor economies, solves this problem by positing a human capital externality. But this does not explain why human capital would increase in pre-industrial England with a constant wage premium for skills. Even the Lucas (1988) solution of large external benefits is implausible on its face. Indian textile mills in the early twentieth century, for example, employed mainly illiterate workers, and there was little or no wage premium offered for literacy. But employers could easily determine literacy. Had there been any significant positive externality at the level of the workplace then they would have been induced to offer premiums to recruit literate workers. So the Lucas human capital externality has to operate mainly at the level of neighborhoods or cities. But then the process becomes quite mysterious.

We thus see a very poor match between the elements that would seem to go into a human capital story of the Industrial Revolution—the Industrial Revolution itself, the average size of families, and the premium paid in the labor market for skills. If human capital is the key to the Industrial Revolution, the trigger for its expansion in pre-industrial England remains mysterious if we assume a universal set of preferences for all societies.

Endogenous Growth Theories

None of the above theories explain why the Industrial Revolution had to happen, or why it happened in 1760 as opposed to 500 BC in Ancient Greece. Endogenous growth theories attempt to explain not just how the Industrial Revolution took place, but also why it occurred when it did. The problem in any such model is the creation of the "driver" that will change the state of the world in such a way that the Industrial Revolution comes about. Something has to be different about the world in 1770 than at any earlier date, despite the fact that in the static Malthusian economy on average every important economic variable should remain the same: wages, returns on capital, work hours, and capital per person.

The earliest example of such a potential endogenous growth theory is the elegant one of Michael Kremer (Kremer 1993). Kremer assumes that the social institutions that provide the incentives to individuals to create knowledge are the same in all societies. Each person has a given probability of producing a new idea. In this case the growth rate of knowledge will be a function of the size of the human community. The more people you are in contact with the more you get to benefit from the ideas of others. There was substantial but slow productivity growth in the world economy in the years before 1800, and that all got translated into a huge expansion of the world population. That larger population produces more ideas and more rapid growth. Sheer scale is what produces modern economic growth.

Kremer supports the argument with two sorts of evidence.

(1) The first is population growth rates for the world as a whole in the pre-industrial era. World population growth rates are faster the greater the size of populations. That implies, since Diamond (1997) contains many of the same ideas, merged also with consideration of the role of geography in creating the community that benefits from knowledge expansion, population growth rates and the rate of technological advance are proportionate, that productivity growth rates were speeding up over time as population grew.

(2) The second is population density, as an index of the level of technology in the pre-industrial world, for major isolated geographic areas—Eurasia, the Americas and Australia—as a function of the land area. The prediction is that the smaller the land area, and hence the potential population, the lower will be the rate of technological advance. In this case at any given time population density will depend on land area. This is found for the three cases examined.

Interesting though Kremer's ideas are, no matter how much population is a driver of the rate of technological advance, population alone cannot produce a discontinuity in the rate of technological advance circa 1800. The rate of technological advance seems to rise faster than population growth. At best productivity growth rates would be proportionate to population under the Kremer assumptions. This feature of the Kremer model, that it is hard to produce with an endogenous growth model a discontinuity of the required magnitude, is a general problem for endogenous growth models.

For Hanson and Prescott (2002) the driver is just the comparative productivity of a land using of producing a standard output versus a non-land using method. Output is produced using with a land using "Malthusian" sector where TFP growth rates are slow, and a "Solow" sector using only capital and labor where TFP growth rates are faster. This requires that the productivity of the land employing sector increases at only 3% per generation of 35 years, while the productivity of the Solow sector increases by 52% per generation. The authors show that with this specification the model can reproduce the gross features of the Industrial Revolution in terms of shares of labor devoted to each sector and output growth. Yet this calibration has some distinctly odd features. The implied annual interest rate is 4–4.5% in the modern Solovian era, but a mere 2% in the Malthusian era. A second empirical implication is that the productivity of land using technologies has increased more slowly since the Industrial Revolution than that of "Solow" technologies. And finally, oddly there is the implication that there is no discontinuity in productivity growth rates before and after the Industrial Revolution. Even in the Malthusian phase, before being used, the "industrial" sector is developing and becoming a viable competitor just as rapidly as later. It is all a matter of the shift in the relative size of each sector.

The Industrial Revolution in this model is inevitable. Once God sets the parameter of the initial state of the "Solow" technology it is just a matter of time. As in *Jaws,* we know from the setup that the "shark" is coming—the only uncertainty is when it will come.

The stark empirical difficulties faced by this model are the following.

(1) Productivity growth rates in the "industrial" sector *do* seem to have increased at the time of the Industrial Revolution. The Industrial Revolution is not the result of composition effects only.

(2) Productivity growth rates in "land-using" sectors such as agriculture have been as rapid as those in the rest of the economy since the Industrial Revolution, and also have increased markedly since the Industrial Revolution. Productivity growth rates increased sharply in the twentieth century. Indeed while TFP in agriculture in 1970 was about 4.2 times its level in 1800, TFP for the economy as a whole had increased only slightly faster, being 4.8 times the level in 1800. The reason this empirical problem does not cause problems for the Hansen and Prescott calibration is that by the time rapid productivity growth in agriculture begins in England, the country they model, the agricultural sector had shrunk to be a small share of the economy.

But there are other sources that point very clearly, despite this, to income having a strong effect on the numbers of surviving children in pre-industrial England. There is a clear association between household income and a child's chance of surviving the first year of life, with the richer parishes having less than half the infant mortality of the poorer ones. Indeed the crude measure of household income used here explains 62% of the variation in infant mortality rates.

Another source of data is the number of children listed in the wills of the rich and the poor. In seventeenth century England wills were made by people in a wide range of economic circumstances, and seemed to typically mention all surviving children. Wills were also generally made within days of death. Examining a sample of wills from Suffolk and London in the years 1620–1635 we find that in both town and countryside, as table 9 shows [see original text], literate testators left more surviving children than the illiterate. Given the huge range in numbers of surviving children per testator, from 0 to 13, the sample sizes are too small for London and for the towns to find statistically significant differences in numbers of survivors with literacy. But for the sample of testators whose residence was the countryside the difference is statistically significant. The literate were leaving more survivors (Clark and Hamilton 2003).

This raises the question of what features exactly of families were responsible for higher reproductive success? Is it occupation, literacy, or wealth? To investigate this further we considered a sample of wills where we can also calculate some approximation to the total value of the estate. What shows up very clearly is that other things being equal town residence correlates with fewer surviving children, but the other major correlate is the assets bequeathed by the testator. Testators with 500 pounds or more in assets would leave, other things equal, about 1.24 more surviving children than those with no assets.

The reproductive advantage of those bequeathing larger stocks of assets is not mainly because they are more likely to get married, or again because those with larger stocks of assets are just being observed later in the life cycle. The last three columns show the estimated coefficients when we regress reproductive success on the same measures, using only those who were, or had been, married by time of death. Even looking just at the married assets matter almost as much, and now literacy is a statistically significant predictor of reproductive success.

This strong association of assets and reproductive success is surprising since we have such a weak measure of the assets bequeathed. The implication would be that the real effects of wealth on reproductive success must be even stronger than the ones observed here.

Unfortunately we do not have information on the wills of the children to check to what extent parental characteristics were passed on to children. We do know that the greater the assets of parents at death, the greater the average bequest per child, despite there being more surviving children in these families. Thus at least at some point in their lives such children are well endowed with material assets relative to the average person.

Thus the conditions may well have existed in pre-industrial England for a selection towards certain cultural types in the population. Exactly what is being selected for is hard to tell since literacy and assets are highly correlated. Interestingly an examination of the numbers of surviving children in the frontier conditions of New France in the seventeenth century shows that if there was any survival advantage it was to the illiterate and low status individuals. And in the same community there was no gain in literacy rates between 1630 and 1730.

Material living conditions did not improve over the eons-long Malthusian era. Yet while the material conditions people were living in did not change, the suggestion of Galor and Moav that people themselves were changed by their long exposure to the Malthusian economy in settled agrarian societies finds support for pre-industrial England at least. There are indications that England was an extraordinarily stable society for 500 years before the Industrial Revolution, where the overwhelming source of deaths was from sicknesses that could be avoided through economic success. In this case institutional stability could have helped launch an Industrial Revolution, but through a very indirect effect on the prevailing cultural norms.

While this approach suggested by Galor and Moav seems promising, it like any endogenous growth theory is going to predict a relatively slow transition between pre-industrial stagnation and modern growth. However, this apparent failing may not be as damaging as it would appear.

The Timing and Pace of the Industrial Revolution

We have been following the traditional assumption, so far, that the Industrial Revolution was a relatively abrupt transition to modern productivity growth rates. Recent empirical work suggests that the Industrial Revolution may be a much less abrupt transition. Output per person was rising already in the years 1600–1689, before any institutional changes of the Glorious Revolution of 1688–1689. And indeed if we project forward this growth rate we would not be far off in estimating GDP per capita in the 1860s. Thus there are clear signs of growth beginning before the traditional date of the Industrial Revolution.

Thus the dating of the Industrial Revolution is not so clear as has traditionally been assumed. The true break from the Malthusian embrace will be difficult to date, and the changes may be much more gradual than traditionally assumed. This as noted bodes well for endogenous growth approaches, and badly for models based on a move between equilibria, or for models based on exogenous changes in property rights.

Conclusion

The Industrial Revolution remains one of history's great mysteries. We have seen in this survey that the attempts by economists to model this transition have been largely unsuccessful. The first approach emphasizing an exogenous switch in property rights stemming from political changes, despite its continuing popularity, fails in terms of the timing of political changes, and their observed effects on the incentives for innovation. The second approach, which looks for a shift between equilibria, again fails because there is little sign of any major changes in the underlying parameters of the economy which would lead to changed behavior by individuals.

The most promising class of models is those based on endogenous growth. The problem here is to find some kind of "driver" that is changing over time that will induce changes in productivity growth rates. Previously these models seemed to face insuperable difficulties in that they find it very hard to model the kind of one time upward shift in productivity growth rates that the Industrial Revolution seemed to involve. But as we gather more information on the empirics of the Industrial Revolution the transition between the old world of zero productivity growth rates and the new world of rapid productivity growth is much more gradual. This bodes well for endogenous growth models.

Notes

1. This article is not the place to prove this assertion, but Clark (2003a) shows that measured by calorie and protein consumption, work hours, heights, and life expectancy the average person in England in 1800, when England was probably the richest country in the world, was little better off than modern foragers and subsistence agriculture societies such as the Ache of Paraguay, the Hiwi of Venezuela, the !Kung of Botswana, or the Shipobo of Peru.

2. Again the reader will have to take this assertion on trust. Income per capita in England in 1450 was about one seventh of its level in the 1990s. That means that living standards in England in the fifteenth century (think Agincourt), based on the Penn world tables, exceeded those of countries such as India, Bolivia and most of Sub-Saharan Africa in 1992.

References

Abramovitz, Moses. 1956. "Resource and Output Trends in the United States since 1870," *American Economic Review,* 46 (May): 5–23.

Abramovitz, Moses. 1993. "The Search for the Sources of Growth: Areas of Ignorance, Old and New," *Journal of Economic History,* 53(2) (June): 217–243.

Acemoglu, Daron, James A. Robinson, and Simon Johnson. 2001. "The Colonial Origins of Comparative Economic Development: An Empirical Investigation," *American Economic Review*, 91: 1369–1401.

Acemoglu, Daron, James A. Robinson, and Simon Johnson. 2002. "Reversal of Fortune: Geography and Institutions in the Making of the Modern World," *Quarterly Journal of Economics*, 117: 1231–1294.

Becker, Gary, Kevin Murphy, and Robert Tamura. 1990. "Human Capital, Fertility and Economic Growth," *Journal of Political Economy*, 98: S12–37.

Clark, Gregory. 1996. "The Political Foundations of Modern Economic Growth: England, 1540–1800," *Journal of Interdisciplinary History*, 26: 563–588.

Clark, Gregory. 1998. "Land Hunger: Land as a Commodity and as a Status Good in England, 1500–1910," *Explorations in Economic History*, 35: 5982.

Clark, Gregory. 2002. "Farmland Rental Values and Agrarian History: England, 1500–1912," *European Review of Economic History,* 6: 281–309.

Clark, Gregory. 2005. "The Condition of the Working-Class in England, 1209–2004," *Journal of Political Economy,* 113: 1307–1340.

Clark, Gregory. 2007. A *Farewell to Alms: A Brief Economic History of the World.* Princeton: Princeton University Press.

Clark, Gregory, and Gillian Hamilton. 2006. "Survival of the Richest: The Malthusian Method in England, 1585–1638," *Journal of Economic History,* 66: 707–736.

Crafts, N. F. R. 1985. *British Economic Growth During the Industrial Revolution.* New York: Oxford University Press.

Crafts, N. F. R., and C. K. Harley. 1992. "Output Growth and the Industrial Revolution: A Restatement of the Crafts-Harley View," *Economic History Review,* 45:703–730.

Cressy, David. 1977. "Levels of Illiteracy in England, 1530-1730," *The Historical Journal,* 20: 1–23.

Deane, Phyllis, and W. A. Cole. 1967. *British Economic Growth, 1688–1959.* 2d ed. Cambridge: Cambridge University Press.

Delong, Brad, and Larry Summers. 1991. "Equipment Investment and Economic Growth," *Quarterly Journal of Economics,* 106: 445–502.

De Vries, Jan 1994. "The Industrial Revolution and the Industrious Revolution," *Journal of Economic History,* 54: 249–270.

Diamond, Jared M. 1997. *Guns, Germs, and Steel: The Fates of Human Societies.* New York: W. W. Norton.

Duncan-Jones, Richard. 1990. *Structure and Scale in the Roman Economy.* Cambridge: Cambridge University Press.

Evans, Nesta. 1987. *The Wills of the Archdeaconry of Sudbury, 1630–35.* Suffolk Records Society, Vol. 29. Woodbridge, Suffolk: The Boydell Press.

Fischer, Stanley, ed. 1987. *Macroeconomics Annual.* Cambridge, Mass.: MIT Press.

Galor, Oded, and Omer Moav. 2002. "Natural Selection and the Origin of Economic Growth," *Quarterly Journal of Economics,* 117: 1133–1191.

Galor, Oded, and David N. Weil. 2000. "Population, Technology and Growth: From Malthusian Stagnation to the Demographic Transition and Beyond," *American Economic Review,* 90: 806–828.

Griliches, Zvi. 1994. "Productivity, R&D, and the Data Constraint," *American Economic Review,* 84: 1–23.

Griliches, Zvi. 1996. "The Discovery of the Residual: A Historical Note," *Journal of Economic Literature,* 34: 1324–1330.

Hair, P. E. H. 1971. "Deaths from Violence in Britain: A Tentative Secular Survey," *Population Studies,* 25: 5–24.

Hamilton, Gillian, and Aloysius Siow. 1999. "Marriage and Fertility in a Catholic Society: Eighteenth Century Quebec." Working Paper, University of Toronto.

Hanawalt, Barbara A. 1976. "Violent Death in England in the Fourteenth and Early Fifteenth Centuries," *Comparative Studies in Society and History,* 18: 297–320.

Hanawalt, Barbara A. 1979. *Crime and Community in Medieval England, 1300–48.*

Hansen, G., and Edward C. Prescott. 2002. "Malthus to Solow," *American Economic Review,* 92: 1205–1217.

Harley, Knick. 1993. "Reassessing the Industrial Revolution: A Macro View," in Joel Mokyr (ed.), *The British Industrial Revolution: An Economic Assessment.* Boulder, Colo.: Westview Press, 1993, 227–266.

Harley, Knick. 1997. "Cotton Textile Prices and the Industrial Revolution." Working Paper, University of Western Ontario, February.

Hill, Kim, and A. M. Hurtado. 1996. *Ache Life History: The Ecology and Demography of a Foraging People.*

Hopkins, Keith. 1966. "On the Probable Age Structure of the Roman Population," *Population Studies*, 20: 245–264.

Houston, R. A. 1982. "The Development of Literacy: Northern England, 1640–1750," *Economic History Review*, New Series, 35: 199–216.

Jones, Charles I. 1995. "R&D-Based Models of Economic Growth," *Journal of Political Economy*, 103: 759–784.

Jones, Charles I. 2001. "Was the Industrial Revolution Inevitable? Economic Growth Over the Very Long Run." *Advances in Macroeconomics*, 1. http://www.bepress .com/bejm/advances/.

Jones, Charles I. 2002. *Introduction to Economic Growth*. 2d ed. New York: W. W. Norton.

Kremer, Michael. 1993. "Population Growth and Technological Change: One Million B.C. to 1990," *Quarterly Journal of Economics*, 107: 681–716.

Landers, John. 1993. *Death and the Metropolis: Studies in the Demographic History of London, 1670–1830*. Cambridge: Cambridge University Press.

Long, Pamela. 1991. "Invention, Authorship, 'Intellectual Property,' and the Origin of Patents: Notes Towards a Conceptual History," *Technology and Culture*, 32: 846–884.

Lucas, Robert. 1988. "On the Mechanics of Economic Development," *Journal of Monetary Economics*, 22: 3–42.

Lucas, Robert E. 2002. "The Industrial Revolution: Past and Future," in Robert E. Lucas, *Lectures on Economic Growth*. Cambridge: Harvard University Press.

McCloskey, Donald. 1981. "1780–1860: A Survey," in R. Floud and D. N. McCloskey, *The Economic History of Britain since 1700*, Vol. I, 103–127.

McCloskey, Donald. 1994. "1780–1860: A Survey," in R. Floud and D. N. McCloskey, *The Economic History of Britain since 1700*, 2d ed., Vol. I, 242–270.

Mokyr, Joel. 1999. "Introduction," in Joel Mokyr (ed.), *The Industrial Revolution: An Economic Analysis*. Boulder: Westview Press.

Mokyr, Joel. 2005. "Long-term Economic Growth and the History of Technology," in Philippe Aghion and Steven Durlauf, *Handbook of Economic Growth*. Elsevier, 1113–1180.

North, Douglass C. 1981. *Structure and Change in Economic History*. New York: Norton.

North, Douglass C. 1994. "Economic Performance Through Time." *American Economic Review*, 84: 359–368.

North, Douglass, and R. P. Thomas. 1973. *The Rise of the Western World*. Cambridge: Cambridge University Press.

North, Douglass, and Barry Weingast. 1989. "Constitutions and Commitment: Evolution of Institutions Governing Public Choice in Seventeenth Century England," *Journal of Economic History*, 49: 803–832.

Oulton, Nicholas. 2001. "Measuring Capital Services in the United Kingdom." Bank of England, *Quarterly Bulletin.*

Psacharopoulos, George. 1994. "Returns to Investment in Education: A Global Update," *World Development*, 22: 1325–1343.

Romer, Paul M. 1986. "Increasing Returns and Long-Run Growth," *Journal of Political Economy*, 94: 1002–1037.

Romer, Paul M. 1987. "Crazy Explanations for the Productivity Slowdown," in Stanley Fischer (ed.), *Macroeconomics Annual 1987*. Cambridge, Mass.: MIT Press.

Romer, Paul M. 1990. "Endogenous Technological Change," *Journal of Political Economy*, 98: S71–102.

Rostow, Walt W. 1960. *The Stages of Economic Growth*. Cambridge: Cambridge University Press.

Rubinstein, W. D. 1981. *Men of Property: The Very Wealthy in Britain Since the Industrial Revolution*. London: Croom Helm.

Schofield, Roger. 1973. "Dimensions of Illiteracy, 1750–1850," *Explorations in Economic History*, 10: 437–454.

Sharma, Ram Sharan. 1983. *Perspectives in Social and Economic History of Early India*. New Delhi: Munshiram Manoharlal.

Solow, Robert M. 1956. "A Contribution to the Theory of Economic Growth," *Quarterly Journal of Economics*, 70: 65–94.

Stokey, Nancy L. 2001. "A Quantitative Model of the British Industrial Revolution," Carnegie Rochester Conference Series on Public Policy, 55: 55–109.

Wrigley, E. A., R. S. Davies, J. E. Oeppen, and R. S. Schofield. 1997. *English Population History from Family Reconstruction: 1580–1837*. New York: Cambridge University Press.

PART 3

The Other Gap:
Domestic Income Inequality

11

Economic Growth and Income Inequality

SIMON KUZNETS

Most debate on the internal gap between rich and poor people in developing nations begins with this seminal presidential address delivered by Simon Kuznets to the American Economic Association in 1954. The address, portions of which are reprinted here, uses limited data from Germany, the United Kingdom, and the United States to show that since the 1920s, and perhaps even earlier, there has been a trend toward equalization in the distribution of income. Kuznets discusses in some detail the possible causes for this trend, examining those factors in the process of industrialization that tend to counteract the concentration of savings in the hands of the wealthy. That particular discussion is not included here, but the interested reader can consult the original piece. Our interest lies in Kuznets's conclusion that the central factor in equalizing income must have been the rising incomes of the poorer sectors outside of the traditional agricultural economy. Kuznets introduces the critically important notion of the "Inverted U-curve" (although he does not label it as such in the address), arguing that there seems to be increasing inequality in the early phases of industrialization, followed by declines in the later phases only. Finally, Kuznets opens the debate over the relevance of these findings for the developing nations by examining data from India, Ceylon (Sri Lanka), and Puerto Rico. The findings that income inequality in the developing countries is greater than that in the advanced countries and that such inequality may be growing form the basis of virtually all subsequent research and debate on this subject. ■

Reprinted with permission from the *American Economic Review,* vol. 45 (March 1955): 1, 3–6, 17–26.

THE CENTRAL THEME OF THIS CHAPTER IS THE CHARACTER AND CAUSES OF LONG-term changes in the personal distribution of income. Does inequality in the distribution of income increase or decrease in the course of a country's economic growth? What factors determine the secular level and trends of income inequalities?

These are broad questions in a field of study that has been plagued by looseness in definitions, unusual scarcity of data, and pressures of strongly held opinions. . . .

Trends in Income Inequality

Forewarned of the difficulties, we turn now to the available data. These data, even when relating to complete populations, invariably classify units by income for a given year. From our standpoint, this is their major limitation. Because the data often do not permit many size groupings, and because the difference between annual income incidence and longer-term income status has less effect if the number of classes is small and the limits of each class are wide, we use a few wide classes. This does not resolve the difficulty; and there are others due to the scantiness of data for long periods, inadequacy of the unit used—which is, at best, a family and very often a reporting unit—errors in the data, and so on through a long list. Consequently, the trends in the income structure can be discerned but dimly, and the results considered as preliminary informed guesses.

The data are for the United States, England, and Germany—a scant sample, but at least a starting point for some inferences concerning long-term changes in the presently developed countries. The general conclusion suggested is that the relative distribution of income, as measured by annual income incidence in rather broad classes, has been moving toward equality—with these trends particularly noticeable since the 1920s but beginning perhaps in the period before the first world war.

Let me cite some figures, all for income before direct taxes, in support of this impression. In the United States, in the distribution of income among families (excluding single individuals), the shares of the two lowest quintiles rise from 13.5 percent in 1929 to 18 percent in the years after the second world war (average of 1944, 1946, 1947, and 1950); whereas the share of the top quintile declines from 55 to 44 percent, and that of the top 5 percent from 31 to 20 percent. In the United Kingdom, the share of the top 5 percent of units declines from 46 percent in 1880 to 43 percent in 1910 or 1913, to 33 percent in 1929, to 31 percent in 1938, and to 24 percent in 1947; the share of the lower 85 percent remains fairly constant between 1880 and 1913, between 41 and 43 percent, but then rises to 46 percent in 1929 and 55 percent in 1947. In Prussia, income inequality increases slightly between 1875 and 1913—the shares of the top quintile rising from 48 to 50 percent, of the top 5 percent from 26 to 30 percent; the share of the lower 60 percent, however, remains about the same. In Saxony, the change between 1880 and 1913 is minor: the share of the two lowest quintiles declines from 15 to 14.5 percent; that of the third quintile rises from 12 to 13 percent, of the fourth quintile from 16.5 to about 18 percent; that of the top quintile declines from 56.5 to 54.5 percent, and of the top 5 percent from 34 to 33 percent. In Germany as a whole, relative income inequality drops fairly sharply from 1913 to the 1920s, apparently due to decimation of large fortunes and property incomes during the war and inflation, but then begins to return to prewar levels during the depression of the 1930s.[1]

Even for what they are assumed to represent, let alone as approximations to shares in distribution by secular income levels, the data are such that differences of two or three percentage points cannot be assigned significance. One must judge by the general weight and consensus of the evidence—which unfortunately is limited to a few countries. It justifies a tentative impression of constancy in the relative distribution of income before taxes, followed by some narrowing of relative income inequality after the first world war—or earlier.

Three aspects of this finding should be stressed. First, the data are for income before direct taxes and exclude contributions by government (e.g., relief and free assistance). It is fair to argue that both the proportion and progressivity of direct taxes and the proportion of total income of individuals accounted for by government assistance to the less privileged economic groups have grown during recent decades. This is certainly true of the United States and the United Kingdom, but in the case of Germany is subject to further examination. It follows that the distribution of income after direct taxes and including free contributions by government would show an even greater narrowing of inequality in developed countries with size distributions of pretax, ex-government-benefits income similar to those for the United States and the United Kingdom.

Second, such stability or reduction in the inequality of the percentage shares was accompanied by significant rises in real income per capita. The countries now classified as developed have enjoyed rising per capita incomes except during catastrophic periods such as years of active world conflict. Hence, if the shares of groups classified by their annual income position can be viewed as approximations to shares of groups classified by their secular income levels, a constant percentage share of a given group means that its per capita real income is rising at the same rate as the average for all units in the country; and a reduction in inequality of the shares means that the per capita income of the lower-income groups is rising at a more rapid rate than the per capita income of the upper-income groups.

The third point can be put in the form of a question. Do the distributions by annual incomes properly reflect trends in distribution by secular incomes? As technology and economic performance rise to higher levels, incomes are less subject to transient disturbances, not necessarily of the cyclical order that can be recognized and allowed for by reference to business cycle chronology, but of a more irregular type. If in the earlier years the economic fortunes of units were subject to greater vicissitudes—poor crops for some farmers, natural calamity losses for some nonfarm business units—if the over-all proportion of individual entrepreneurs whose incomes were subject to such calamities, more yesterday but some even today, was larger in earlier decades, these earlier distributions of income would be more affected by transient disturbances. In these earlier distributions the temporarily unfortunate might crowd the lower quintiles and depress their shares unduly, and the temporarily fortunate might dominate the top quintile and raise its share unduly—proportionately more than in the distributions for later years. If so, distributions by longer-term average incomes might show less reduction in inequality than do the distributions by annual incomes; they might even show an opposite trend.

One may doubt whether this qualification would upset a narrowing of inequality as marked as that for the United States, and in as short a period as twenty-five years. Nor is it likely to affect the persistent downward drift in the spread of the distributions in the United Kingdom. But I must admit a strong element of judgment in deciding how far this qualification modifies the finding of long-term stability followed by reduction in income inequality in the few developed countries for which it is observed or is likely to be revealed by existing data. The important point is that the qualification is relevant; it suggests need for further study if we are to learn much from the available data concerning the secular income structure; and such study is likely to yield results of interest in themselves in their bearing upon the problem of trends in temporal instability of income flows to individual units or to economically significant groups of units in different sectors of the national economy. . . .

Hence we may conclude that the major offset to the widening of income inequality associated with the shift from agriculture and the countryside to industry and the city must have been a rise in the income share of the lower groups within the nonagricultural sector of the population. This provides a lead for exploration in what seems to me a most promising direction: consideration of the pace and character of the economic growth of the urban population, with particular reference to the relative position of lower-income groups. Much is to be said for the notion that once the early turbulent phases of industrialization and urbanization had passed, a variety of forces converged to bolster the economic position of the lower-income groups within the urban population. The very fact that, after a while, an increasing proportion of the urban population was "native," i.e., born in cities rather than in the rural areas, and hence more able to take advantage of the possibilities of city life in preparation for the economic struggle, meant a better chance for organization and adaptation, a better basis for securing greater income shares than was possible for the newly "immigrant" population coming from the countryside or from abroad. The increasing efficiency of the older, established urban population should also be taken into account. Furthermore, in democratic societies the growing political power of the urban lower-income groups led to a variety of protective and supporting legislation, much of it aimed to counteract the worst effects of rapid industrialization and urbanization and to support the claims of the broad masses for more adequate shares of the growing income of the country. Space does not permit the discussion of demographic, political, and social considerations that could be brought to bear to explain the offsets to any declines in the shares of the lower groups, declines otherwise deducible from the trends suggested in the numerical illustration.

Other Trends Related
to Those in Income Inequality

One aspect of the conjectural conclusion just reached deserves emphasis because of its possible interrelation with other important elements in the process and theory of economic growth. The scanty empirical evidence suggests that the narrowing of income inequality in the developed countries is relatively recent and probably did not characterize the earlier stages of their growth. Likewise, the various factors that have been suggested above would explain stability and narrowing in income inequality in the later rather than in the earlier phases of industrialization and urbanization. Indeed, they would suggest widening inequality in these early phases of economic growth, especially in the older countries where the emergence of the new industrial system had shattering effects on long-established pre-industrial economic and social institutions. This timing characteristic is particularly applicable to factors bearing upon the lower-income groups: the dislocating effects of the agricultural and industrial revolutions, combined with the "swarming" of population incident upon a rapid decline in death rates and the maintenance or even rise of birth rates, would be unfavorable to the relative economic position of lower-income groups. Furthermore, there may also have been a preponderance in the earlier periods of factors favoring maintenance or increase in the shares of top-income groups: in so far as their position was bolstered by gains arising out of new industries, by an unusually rapid rate of creation of new fortunes, we would expect these forces to be relatively stronger in the early phases of industrialization than in the later when the pace of industrial growth slackens.

One might thus assume a long swing in the inequality characterizing the secular income structure: widening in the early phases of economic growth when the transition from the pre-industrial to the industrial civilization was most rapid; becoming stabilized for a while; and then narrowing in the later phases. This long secular swing would be most pronounced for older countries where the dislocation effects of the earlier phases of modern economic growth were most conspicuous; but it might be found also in the "younger" countries like the United States if the period preceding marked industrialization could be compared with the early phases of industrialization, and if the latter could be compared with the subsequent phases of greater maturity.

If there is some evidence for assuming this long swing in relative inequality in the distribution of income before direct taxes and excluding free benefits from government, there is surely a stronger case for assuming a long swing in inequality of income net of direct taxes and including government benefits. Progressivity of income taxes and, indeed, their very importance characterize only the more recent phases of development of the presently developed countries; in narrowing income inequality they must have accentuated the downward phase of the long swing, contributing to the reversal of trend in the secular widening and narrowing of income inequality.

No adequate empirical evidence is available for checking this conjecture of a long secular swing in income inequality;[2] nor can the phases be dated precisely. However, to make it more specific, I would place the early phase in which income inequality might have been widening from about 1780 to 1850 in England; from about 1840 to 1890, and particularly from 1870 on in the United States; and from the 1840s to the 1890s in Germany. I would put the phase of narrowing income inequality somewhat later in the United States and Germany than in England—perhaps beginning with the first world war in the former and the last quarter of the nineteenth century in the latter.

Is there a possible relation between this secular swing in income inequality and the long swing in other important components of the growth process? For the older countries a long swing is observed in the rate of growth of population—the upward phase represented by acceleration in the rate of growth reflecting the early reduction in the death rate which was not offset by a decline in the birth rate (and in some cases was accompanied by a rise in the birth rate); and the downward phase represented by a shrinking in the rate of growth reflecting the more pronounced downward trend in the birth rate. Again, in the older countries, and also perhaps in the younger, there may have been a secular swing in the rate of urbanization, in the sense that the proportional additions to urban population and the measures of internal migration that produced this shift of population probably increased for a while—from the earlier much lower levels; but then tended to diminish as urban population came to dominate the country and as the rural reservoirs of migration became proportionally much smaller. For old, and perhaps for young countries also, there must have been a secular swing in the proportions of savings or capital formation to total economic product. Per capita product in pre-industrial times was not large enough to permit as high a nationwide rate of saving or capital formation as was attained in the course of industrial development: this is suggested by present comparisons between net capital formation rates of 3 to 5 percent of national product in underdeveloped countries and rates of 10 to 15 percent in developed countries. If then, at least in the older countries, and perhaps even in the younger ones—prior to initiation of the process of modern development—we begin with low secular levels in the savings proportions, there would be a rise in the early phases to appreciably higher levels. We also know that during recent periods the net capital formation proportion, and even the gross, failed to rise and perhaps even declined.

Other trends might be suggested that would possibly trace long swings similar to those for inequality in income structure, rate of growth of population, rate of urbanization and internal migration, and the proportion of savings or capital formation to national product. For example, such swings might be found in the ratio of foreign trade to domestic activities; in the aspects, if we could only measure them properly, of government activity that bear upon market forces (there must have been a phase of increasing freedom of market forces, giving way to greater intervention by government). But the suggestions already made suffice to indicate that the long swing in income inequality must be viewed as part of a wider process of economic growth, and interrelated with similar movements in other elements. The long alternation in the rate of growth of population can be seen partly as a cause, partly as an effect of the long swing in income inequality which was associated with a secular rise in real per capital income levels. The long swing in income inequality is also probably closely associated with the swing in capital formation proportions— in so far as wider inequality makes for higher, and narrower inequality for lower, countrywide savings proportions.

Comparison of Developed and Underdeveloped Countries

What is the bearing of the experience of the developed countries upon the economic growth of underdeveloped countries? Let us examine briefly the data on income distribution in the latter, and speculate upon some of the implications.

As might have been expected, such data for underdeveloped countries are scanty. For the present purpose, distributions of family income for India in 1949–50, for Ceylon in 1950, and for Puerto Rico in 1948 were used. While the coverage is narrow and the margin of error wide, the data show that income distribution in these underdeveloped countries is somewhat *more* unequal than in the developed countries during the period after the second world war. Thus the shares of the lower 3 quintiles are 28 percent in India, 30 percent in Ceylon, and 24 percent in Puerto Rico—compared with 34 percent in the United States and 36 percent in the United Kingdom. The shares of the top quintile are 55 percent in India, 50 percent in Ceylon, and 56 percent in Puerto Rico, compared with 44 percent in the United States and 45 percent in the United Kingdom.[3]

This comparison is for income before direct taxes and excluding free benefits from governments. Since the burden and progressivity of direct taxes are much greater in developed countries, and since it is in the latter that substantial volumes of free economic assistance are extended to the lower-income groups, a comparison in terms of income net of direct taxes and including government benefits would only accentuate the wider inequality of income distributions in the underdeveloped countries. Is this difference a reliable reflection of wider inequality also in the distribution of *secular* income levels in underdeveloped countries? Even disregarding the margins of error in the data, the possibility raised earlier in this chapter that transient disturbances in income levels may be more conspicuous under conditions of primitive material and economic technology would affect the comparison just made. Since the distributions cited reflect the annual income levels, a greater allowance should perhaps be made for transient disturbances in the distributions for the underdeveloped than in those for the developed countries. Whether such a correction would obliterate the difference is a matter on which I have no relevant evidence.

Another consideration might tend to support this qualification. Underdeveloped countries are characterized by low average levels of income per capita, low enough to raise the question of how the populations manage to survive. Let us assume that these countries represent fairly unified population groups, and exclude, for the moment, areas that combine large native populations with small enclaves of nonnative, privileged minorities, e.g., Kenya and Rhodesia, where income inequality, because of the excessively high income shares of the privileged minority, is appreciably wider than even in the underdeveloped countries cited above.[4] On this assumption, one may infer that in countries with low average income, the secular level of income in the lower brackets could not be below a fairly sizable proportion of average income—otherwise, the groups could not survive. This means, to use a purely hypothetical figure, that the secular level of the share of the lowest decile could not fall far short of 6 or 7 percent, i.e., the lowest decile could not have a per capita income less than six- or seven-tenths of the countrywide average. In more advanced countries, with higher average per capita incomes, even the *secular* share of the lowest bracket could easily be a smaller fraction of the countrywide average, say as small as 2 or 3 percent for the lowest decile, i.e., from a fifth to a third of the countrywide average—without implying a materially impossible economic position for that group. To be sure, there is in all countries continuous pressure to raise the relative position of the bottom-income groups; but the fact remains that the lower limit of the proportional share in the secular income structure is higher when the real countrywide per capita income is low than when it is high.

If the long-term share of the lower-income groups is larger in the underdeveloped than in the average countries, income inequality in the former should be narrower, not wider as we have found. However, if the lower brackets receive larger shares, and at the same time the very top brackets also receive larger shares—which would mean that the intermediate income classes would not show as great a progression from the bottom—the net effect may well be wider inequality. To illustrate, let us compare the distributions for India and the United States. The first quintile in India receives 8 percent of total income, more than the 6 percent share of the first quintile in the United States. But the second quintile in India receives only 9 percent, the third 11, and the fourth 16; whereas in the United States, the shares of these quintiles are 12, 16, and 22 respectively. This is a rough statistical reflection of a fairly common observation relating to income distributions in underdeveloped compared with developed countries. The former have no "middle" classes: there is a sharp contrast between the preponderant proportion of population whose average income is well below the generally low countrywide average, and a small top group with a very large relative income excess. The developed countries, on the other hand, are characterized by a much more gradual rise from low to high shares, with substantial groups receiving more than the high countrywide income average, and the top groups securing smaller shares than the comparable ordinal groups in underdeveloped countries.

It is, therefore, possible that even the distributions of secular income levels would be more unequal in underdeveloped than in developed countries— not in the sense that the shares of the lower brackets would be lower in the former than in the latter, but in the sense that the shares of the very top groups would be higher and that those of the groups below the top would all be significantly lower than a low countrywide income average. This is even more likely to be true of the distribution of income net of direct taxes and inclusive of free government benefits. But whether a high probability weight can be attached to this conjecture is a matter for further study.

In the absence of evidence to the contrary, I assume that it is true: that the secular income structure is somewhat more unequal in underdeveloped countries than in the more advanced—particularly in those of Western and Northern Europe and their economically developed descendants in the New World (the United States, Canada, Australia, and New Zealand). This conclusion has a variety of important implications and leads to some pregnant questions, of which only a few can be stated here.

In the first place, the wider inequality in the secular income structure of underdeveloped countries is associated with a much lower level of average income per capita. Two corollaries follow—and they would follow even if the income inequalities were of the same relative range in the two groups of countries. First, the impact is far sharper in the underdeveloped countries, where the failure to reach an already low countrywide average spells much greater material and psychological misery than similar proportional deviations from the average in the richer, more advanced countries. Second, positive savings are obviously possible only at much higher relative income levels in the underdeveloped countries: if in the more advanced countries some savings are possible in the fourth quintile, in the underdeveloped countries savings could be realized only at the very peak of the income pyramid, say by the top 5 or 3 percent. If so, the concentration of savings and of assets is even more pronounced than in the developed countries; and the effects of such concentration in the past may serve to explain the peculiar characteristics of the secular income structure in underdeveloped countries today.

The second implication is that this unequal income structure presumably coexisted with a low rate of growth of income per capita. The underdeveloped countries today have not always lagged behind the presently developed areas in level of economic performance; indeed, some of the former may have been the economic leaders of the world in the centuries preceding the last two. The countries of Latin America, Africa, and particularly those of Asia, are underdeveloped today because in the last two centuries, and even in recent decades, their rate of economic growth has been far lower than that in the Western world—and low indeed, if any growth there was, on a per capita basis. The underlying shifts in industrial structure, the opportunities for internal mobility and for economic improvement, were far more limited than in the more rapidly growing countries now in the developed category. There was no hope, within the lifetime of a generation, of a significantly perceptible rise in the level of real income, or even that the next generation might fare much better. It was this hope that served as an important and realistic compensation for the wide inequality in income distribution that characterized the presently developed countries during the earlier phases of their growth.

The third implication follows from the preceding two. It is quite possible that income inequality has not narrowed in the underdeveloped countries within recent decades. There is no empirical evidence to check this conjectural implication, but it is suggested by the absence, in these areas, of the dynamic forces associated with rapid growth that in the developed countries checked the upward trend of the upper-income shares that was due to the cumulative effect of continuous concentration of past savings; and it is also indicated by the failure of the political and social systems of underdeveloped countries to initiate the governmental or political practices that effectively bolster the weak positions of the lower-income classes. Indeed, there is a possibility that inequality in the secular income structure of underdeveloped countries may have widened in recent decades—the only qualification being that where there has been a recent shift from colonial to independent status, a privileged, *nonnative* minority may have been eliminated. But the implication, in terms of the income distribution among the *native* population proper, still remains plausible.

The somber picture just presented may be an oversimplified one. But I believe that it is sufficiently realistic to lend weight to the questions it poses— questions as to the bearing of the recent levels and trends in income inequality, and the factors that determine them, upon the future prospect of underdeveloped countries within the orbit of the free world.

The questions are difficult, but they must be faced unless we are willing completely to disregard past experience or to extrapolate mechanically oversimplified impressions of past development. The first question is: Is the pattern of the older developed countries likely to be repeated in the sense that in the early phases of industrialization in the underdeveloped countries income inequalities will tend to widen before the leveling forces become strong enough first to stabilize and then reduce income inequalities? While the future cannot be an exact repetition of the past, there are already certain elements in the present conditions of underdeveloped societies, e.g., "swarming" of population due to sharp cuts in death rates unaccompanied by declines in birth rates, that threaten to widen inequality by depressing the relative position of lower-income groups even further. Furthermore, if and when industrialization begins, the dislocating effects on these societies, in which there is often an old hardened crust of economic and social institutions, are likely to be quite sharp—so sharp as to destroy the positions of some of the lower groups more rapidly than opportunities elsewhere in the economy may be created for them.

The next question follows from an affirmative answer to the first. Can the political framework of the underdeveloped societies withstand the strain which further widening of income inequality is likely to generate? This query is pertinent if it is realized that the real per capita income level of many underdeveloped societies today is lower than the per capita income level of the presently developed societies before *their* initial phases of industrialization. And yet the stresses of the dislocations incident to early phases of industrialization in the developed countries were sufficiently acute to strain the political and social fabric of society, force major political reforms, and sometimes result in civil war.

The answer to the second question may be negative, even granted that industrialization may be accompanied by a rise in real per capita product. If, for many groups in society, the rise is even partly offset by a decline in their proportional share in total product; if, consequently, it is accompanied by widening of income inequality, the resulting pressures and conflicts may necessitate drastic changes in social and political organization. This gives rise to the next and crucial question: How can either the institutional and political framework of the underdeveloped societies or the processes of economic growth and industrialization be modified to favor a sustained rise to higher levels of economic performance and yet avoid the fatally simple remedy of an authoritarian regime that would use the population as cannon-fodder in the fight for economic achievement? How to minimize the cost of transition and avoid paying the heavy price—in internal tensions, in long-run inefficiency in providing means for satisfying wants of human beings as individuals—which the inflation of political power represented by authoritarian regimes requires?

Facing these acute problems, one is cognizant of the dangers of taking an extreme position. One extreme—particularly tempting to us—is to favor repetition of past patterns of the now developed countries, patterns that, under the markedly different conditions of the presently underdeveloped countries, are almost bound to put a strain on the existing social and economic institutions and eventuate in revolutionary explosions and authoritarian regimes. There is danger in simple analogies; in arguing that because an unequal income distribution in Western Europe in the past led to accumulation of savings and financing of basic capital formation, the preservation or accentuation of present income inequalities in the underdeveloped countries is necessary to secure the same result. Even disregarding the implications for the lower-income groups, we may find that in at least some of these countries today the consumption propensities of upper-income groups are far higher and savings propensities far lower than were those of the more puritanical upper-income groups of the presently developed countries. Because they may have proved favorable in the past, it is dangerous to argue that completely free markets, lack of penalties implicit in progressive taxation, and the like are indispensable for the economic growth of the now underdeveloped countries. Under present conditions the results may be quite the opposite—withdrawal of accumulated assets to relatively "safe" channels, either by flight abroad or into real estate; and the inability of governments to serve as basic agents in the kind of capital formation that is indispensable to economic growth. It is dangerous to argue that, because in the past foreign investment provided capital resources to spark satisfactory economic growth in some of the smaller European countries or in Europe's descendants across the seas, similar effects can be expected today if only the underdeveloped countries can be convinced of the need of a "favorable climate." Yet, it is equally dangerous to take the opposite position and claim that the present problems are entirely new and that we must devise solutions that are the product of imagination unrestrained by knowledge of the past, and therefore full of romantic violence. What we need, and I am afraid it is but a truism, is a clear perception of past trends and of conditions under which they occurred, as well as knowledge of the conditions that characterize the underdeveloped countries today. With this as a beginning, we can then attempt to translate the elements of a properly understood past into the conditions of an adequately understood present.

Notes

1. The following sources were used in calculating the figures cited: *United States.* For recent years we used *Income Distribution by Size, 1944–1950* (Washington, 1953) and Selma Goldsmith and others, "Size Distribution of Income Since the Mid-Thirties," *Rev. Econ. Stat.,* Feb. 1954, XXXVI, 1–32; for 1929, the Brookings Institution

data as adjusted in Simon Kuznets, *Shares of Upper Groups in Income and Savings* (New York, 1953), p. 220.

United Kingdom. For 1938 and 1947, Dudley Seers, *The Levelling of Income Since 1938* (Oxford, 1951), p. 39; for 1929, Colin Clark, *National Income and Outlay* (London, 1937) Table 47, p. 109; for 1880, 1910, and 1913, A. Bowley, *The Change in the Distribution of the National Income, 1880–1913* (Oxford, 1920).

Germany. For the constituent areas (Prussia, Saxony and others) for years before the first world war, based on S. Prokopovich, *National Income of Western European Countries* (published in Moscow in the 1920s). Some summary results are given in Prokopovich, "The Distribution of National Income," *Econ. Jour.,* March 1926, XXXVI, 69–82. See also, "Das Deutsche Volkseinkommen vor und nach dem Kriege," *Einzelschrift zur Stat. des Deutschen Reichs,* no. 24 (Berlin, 1932), and W. S. and E. S. Woytinsky, *World Population and Production* (New York, 1953) Table 192, p. 709.

2. Prokopovich's data on Prussia, from the source cited in footnote 1, indicate a substantial widening in income inequality in the early period. The share of the lower 90 percent of the population declines from 73 percent in 1854 to 65 percent in 1875; the share of the top 5 percent rises from 21 to 25 percent. But I do not know enough about the data for the early years to evaluate the reliability of the finding.

3. For sources of these data see "Regional Economic Trends and Levels of Living," submitted at the Norman Waite Harris Foundation Institute of the University of Chicago in November 1954 (in press in the volume of proceedings). This paper, and an earlier one, "Underdeveloped Countries and the Pre-industrial Phases in the Advanced Countries: An Attempt at Comparison," prepared for the World Population Meetings in Rome held in September 1954 (in press) discuss issues raised in this section.

4. In one year since the second world war, the non-African group in Southern Rhodesia, which accounted for only 5 percent of total population, received 57 percent of total income; in Kenya, the minority of only 2.9 percent of total population, received 51 percent of total income; in Northern Rhodesia, the minority of only 1.4 percent of total population, received 45 percent of total income. See United Nations, *National Income and Its Distribution in Underdeveloped Countries,* Statistical Paper, Ser. E, no. 3, 1951, Table 12, p. 19.

12

Should Equity Be a Goal of Economic Policy?

IMF FISCAL AFFAIRS DEPARTMENT

In Chapter 3, Robert Hunter Wade discusses the expanding external gap and warns against policymakers ignoring it. In this chapter, International Monetary Fund staff working in the IMF Fiscal Affairs Department pose the question, should governments be concerned with issues of equity? After concluding that widespread economic expansion has not been met with declining inequalities, the authors attempt to determine the impact of globalization on the distribution of income. They conclude by suggesting that one of the more promising strategies for economic growth with equity involves investing in human capital. The reader should also consult Chapter 29 for an argument based on human capital. ■

OVER THE PAST DECADE, GLOBAL OUTPUT HAS GROWN BY MORE THAN 3 PERCENT a year and inflation has slowed in most regions. The fruits of this growth have not been shared equally, however, and income disparities have grown in many countries, developed as well as developing. One of the most pressing issues facing policymakers today is how to respond to these trends. To what extent are growth and equity complementary, and to what extent is there a trade-off between the two?

Why Is Equity Important?

The answers to these questions depend on how equity is defined. Different societies have different perceptions of what is equitable, and these social and cultural norms shape the policies they will adopt to promote equity. Although there is a consensus that extreme inequality of income, wealth, or opportunity is unfair and that efforts should be made to raise the incomes of the poorest members of society, there is little agreement on the desirability of greater income equality for its own sake or on what constitutes a fair distribution of income. Equity issues are especially knotty because they are inextricably intertwined with social values. Nonetheless, economic policymakers are devoting greater attention to them for a number of reasons:

• Some societies view equity as a worthy goal in and of itself because of its moral implications and its intimate link with fairness and social justice.

• Policies that promote equity can help, directly and indirectly, to reduce poverty. When incomes are more evenly distributed, fewer individuals fall below the poverty line. Equity-enhancing policies, particularly such investment in human capital as education, can, in the long run, boost economic growth, which, in turn, has been shown to alleviate poverty.

• Heightened awareness of the discrimination suffered by certain groups because of their gender, race, or ethnic origin has focused attention on the need to ensure that these groups have adequate access to government services and receive fair treatment in the labor market.

• Many of today's policies will affect the welfare of future generations, which raises the issue of intergenerational equity. For instance, the provision of very generous pension benefits to today's retirees could be at the expense of tomorrow's retirees—an important issue in many transition and industrial countries.

• Policies that promote equity can boost social cohesion and reduce political conflict. To be effective, most policies require broad political support, which is more likely to be forthcoming when the distribution of income is seen as fair. However, macroeconomic adjustment that entails growth-enhancing structural reforms such as privatization may increase unemployment and worsen inequality in the short run. In such circumstances, well-targeted social safety nets to shelter the consumption levels of the poor are critically important.

Growing Inequality

Income inequality varies greatly from region to region. It is greatest in Latin America and sub-Saharan Africa, and lowest in Eastern Europe; other regions fall between these two extremes. In Latin America, the average "Gini coefficient"—the most commonly used measure of inequality, with 0 representing perfect equality and 1 representing total inequality—is nearly 0.5. The average Gini coefficient in sub-Saharan Africa is slightly lower, but there is considerable variation among countries. Income inequality has a regional dimension in both Africa and Latin America—average incomes are significantly higher in urban areas than in rural areas.

In recent years, income inequality has been increasing in a large number of countries. This increase has been most striking in the economies in transition to market-oriented systems, where the average Gini coefficient had been about 0.25 until the late 1980s; by the mid-1990s, it had risen to more than 0.30. Although this may not appear to be a large increase, it is quite significant for such a short period of time, since Gini coefficients tend to be relatively stable in countries over long periods. In the past decade, income inequality has also increased in several Group of Seven countries (for example, Germany, Japan, the United Kingdom, and the United States) and is beginning to rise in some East Asian countries (China and Thailand).

Much of the debate about income distribution has centered on wage earnings. But wages tell only part of the story. The distribution of wealth (and, by implication, capital income) is more concentrated than labor income. In Africa and Latin America, unequal ownership of land has been identified as an important factor in the overall distribution of income. Furthermore, in recent years, there has been a shift from labor to capital income (including from self-employment) in many countries. In transition economies, this shift has been due primarily to the privatization of state-owned assets. The analysis of trends in nonlabor income in countries with well-developed capital markets and pension funds is more complicated. Pension funds and other financial institutions receive a sizable portion of capital income, and the share of capital income in total household income typically changes over the life cycle of the individuals in the household.

Is Globalization to Blame?

Globalization has linked the labor, product, and capital markets of economies around the world. Increased trade, capital and labor movements, and technological progress have led to greater specialization in production and the dispersion of specialized production processes to geographically distant locations. Developing countries, with their abundant supply of unskilled labor, have a comparative advantage relative to developed countries in the production of unskilled-labor-intensive goods and services. As a result, production of these goods in developed countries has come under increased competitive pressure. Economic theory tells us this should apply downward pressure on the relative compensation of unskilled workers in developed countries and upward pressure on the compensation of their counterparts in developing countries.

On the basis of this theory, some have claimed that globalization is to blame for growing income inequality in developed countries. Others argue that the widening gap between the wages of skilled workers and unskilled workers in the industrial countries is due to the development and dispersion of skill-intensive technologies rather than to increased trade. Several empirical studies have tried to gauge the relative importance of trade versus technological progress for the decline in wages of unskilled workers in developed countries. Estimates of the contribution of increased trade to the total increase of the wage differential between unskilled and skilled workers range from negligible to 50 percent. This large variation reflects the structure of production in developed countries and the share of the labor market that is in direct competition with low-skilled workers in developing countries.

The debate regarding the effect of globalization on income distribution in developing countries mirrors the debate on developed countries. Although, all other things being equal, increased openness would be expected to boost the relative wage of unskilled workers in developing countries, experience has been mixed. Evidence suggests that the relative wages of unskilled workers rose in East Asian countries in the 1960s and 1970s but fell in Latin America in the 1980s and early 1990s. There are two possible explanations for why wages fell in Latin America: first, the opening up of developing Asian countries—Bangladesh, India, China, Indonesia, and Pakistan—where unskilled labor is even more abundant; second, the availability of new production technologies that are biased toward skilled labor.

Globalization's effect on income distribution appears to be determined to some extent by a country's level of development and the technologies available to it. Similarly, exposure to international competition may change institutions (for example, trade unions), and thereby affect income distribution. Some observers contend that, because of the mobility of capital, globalization limits the ability of union workers to achieve a "union wage premium," decreasing the bargaining power of workers vis-à-vis capital. In addition, globalization may lead to sharp short-run changes in the distribution of income, as barriers to trade are reduced and the distribution of production is reallocated among sectors.

Many argue that globalization makes it more difficult for governments to carry out equitable policies. Increasingly mobile capital and labor have limited the ability of governments to levy taxes and transfer them to those affected by globalization. To the extent that capital is more mobile than labor, the incidence of taxes to finance safety nets for those affected by globalization is shifted to labor. . . .

Summary

Despite widespread economic expansion, income gaps have widened during the past decade in many parts of the world, including in the industrial countries. This trend has heightened concerns about the treatment of equity in the formulation of economic policy. Equity and growth can be complementary: some policies that promote equity—particularly investment in human capital—can boost growth in the long run and thus alleviate extreme poverty, increase social cohesion, and reduce the scope for political conflict. Policy choices are not always so easy, however: when growth and equity do not go hand in hand, when and how should governments intervene?

The strategies that countries have adopted vary widely. The most effective tool for redistributing income is fiscal policy. And of the two sides of the budget—taxation and spending—the expenditure side, especially spending on health and education, has offered the better opportunities for reducing income inequality over the long term. But governments have also pursued income redistribution through labor market measures, monetary policy, and the overall stance of macroeconomic policy.

An important question is whether governments should focus on outcomes (such as decreasing broad measures of income inequality) or on ensuring that all members of society have equal opportunities (for example, through policies that facilitate mobility among income classes and by setting up a well-functioning judicial system and reducing the scope for corruption). In all these efforts, governments face difficult obstacles: lack of financial resources, difficult-to-reach target groups, weak administrative capacity, and legal and political constraints. A consensus is forming nevertheless that governments should sometimes intervene to ensure not only that the size of the pie increases, but that everybody gets a fair share.

13

Inequality and Insurgency

EDWARD N. MULLER AND MITCHELL A. SELIGSON

What are the consequences of the widespread domestic income inequality that has been noted in Part 3 of this volume? In this chapter Edward Muller and Mitchell Seligson conduct a cross-national test using a large database. They find that when income inequality is high, the probability of domestic political violence increases substantially. This finding suggests that income inequality can lead to uprisings, guerrilla movements, and civil wars, as have occurred in Vietnam, Central America, and elsewhere. Since the violence invariably causes considerable destruction of property, not to speak of the lives lost, economic growth is adversely affected. Thus, in addition to creating normative problems, income inequality seems to be responsible for violence and, in turn, slowed economic growth. The inescapable conclusion is that income inequality matters a great deal, for when it is high, a vicious circle of violence and slowed growth is the result. ■

MANY STUDENTS OF DOMESTIC POLITICAL CONFLICT CONSIDER INEQUALITY IN THE distribution of land and/or lack of land ownership (landlessness) to be among the more fundamental economic preconditions of insurgency and revolution (e.g., Huntington 1968; Midlarsky 1981, 1982; Midlarsky and Roberts 1985; Paige 1975; Prosterman 1976; Prosterman and Riedinger 1982; Russett 1964; Tanter and Midlarsky 1967). Huntington (1968, 375), whose writing on the subject has been particularly influential, advanced a strong version of the land

---

Reprinted with permission of the American Political Science Association from *American Political Science Review,* vol. 81, no. 2 (1987): 425–450.

maldistribution hypothesis as follows: "Where the conditions of land-owner-ship are equitable and provide a viable living for the peasant, revolution is un-likely. Where they are inequitable and where the peasant lives in poverty and suffering, revolution is likely, if not inevitable, unless the government takes prompt measures to remedy these conditions." However, because mass revolu-tions are rare events, it is more plausible to relax the postulate that revolution is an inevitable consequence of land maldistribution and to restate the hypoth-esis: the greater the maldistribution of land, the greater the probability of mass-based political insurgency and, consequently, the greater the *vulnerability* of a country to revolution from below. This weaker, necessary-but-not-sufficient version of the land-maldistribution-leads-to-revolution hypothesis directs atten-tion to the relationship between land distribution and mass political violence.

The land maldistribution hypothesis is based on the assumption that dis-content resulting from a highly concentrated distribution of land and/or lack of land ownership (landlessness) in agrarian societies is an important direct cause of mass political violence. Advocates of what has come to be called the "re-source mobilization" approach to the explanation of collective protest and vi-olence (e.g., Gamson 1975; Oberschall 1973; Tilly 1978) reject such discon-tent hypotheses for the reason that inequality and discontent are more or less always present in virtually all societies and that consequently the most direct and influential explanatory factor must not be discontent per se but rather the *organization* of discontent. Thus Skocpol (1979, 112–57), who is skeptical of discontent theories of revolution, argues that the peasant revolts that were a crucial insurrectionary ingredient in the French, Russian, and Chinese revolu-tions occurred not because of the maldistribution of landholdings but rather because communities of French, Russian, and Chinese peasants had sufficient autonomy from local landlords to enable them to mobilize collectively. By contrast, Midlarsky (1982, 15–20), a proponent of discontent theory, explains the peasant revolts in each of these cases by the fact that rapid population growth severely exacerbated land inequality until a level of deprivation was reached that no longer could be tolerated.

Two contemporary cases cited by Midlarsky and Roberts (1985) in support of the land maldistribution hypothesis are El Salvador and Nicaragua.[1] Com-pared with other middle-income developing countries, population growth in El Salvador and Nicaragua was above average during the 1960s and 1970s (see World Bank 1981, tbl. 17). Maldistribution of land also was a serious problem, as the Gini coefficient of land concentration was .80 for Nicaragua and .81 for El Salvador (values well above the global mean of .60) and agricultural house-holds without land (i.e., tenants, sharecroppers, and agricultural laborers) amounted to 40% of the total labor force in El Salvador circa 1970, which was the highest level of landlessness in the world at that time (data are not available for Nicaragua).[2] Each country subsequently experienced a relatively high rate of mass political violence, which in the Nicaraguan case culminated in revolution.

But the seemingly obvious conclusion that land maldistribution must have been a primary cause of political violence in El Salvador and Nicaragua ignores the fact that, during the same period of time, two other Central American states, Costa Rica and Panama, remained quite peaceful despite the presence of exactly the same preconditions supposed to have caused the insurgency in El Salvador and Nicaragua. Costa Rica and Panama experienced above-average population growth (in fact, Costa Rica's 3.4% annual population-growth rate during 1960–70 not only exceeded the 2.9% rate registered by El Salvador and Nicaragua but was also among the highest in the entire world); land was concentrated in the hands of the few to about the same degree in Costa Rica (the Gini coefficient was .82) and Panama (Gini coefficient of .78) as in El Salvador and Nicaragua; and the amount of landlessness in Costa Rica (24%) and in Panama (36.2%) ranked ninth and third highest in the world, respectively. Nevertheless, during 1970–77 Panama registered only a single death from political violence, and there were no instances of deadly political violence in Costa Rica (see Taylor and Jodice 1983, vol. 2, tbl. 2.7).

Comparison of Costa Rica and Panama with El Salvador and Nicaragua thus raises the issue of the general validity of the land maldistribution hypothesis: Are Costa Rica and Panama merely exceptions to the rule, or is maldistribution of land in reality a minor or even irrelevant factor in the process that generates insurgency and revolution? That question is significant not only because inequality is frequently assumed in academic writing to be an important determinant of political instability; it also has profound policy implications because land reform has traditionally been a cornerstone of U.S. efforts to promote political stability in developing countries.

Inequality, Resource Mobilization, and the Structure of the State

We argue that theories emphasizing land maldistribution as a fundamental precondition of insurgency and revolution are misspecified. They attribute direct causal significance to an inequality variable that plays only a relatively small, indirect part in the generation of mass political violence. We hypothesize that the more important direct cause of variation in rates of political violence cross-nationally is inequality in the distribution of income rather than maldistribution of land. This hypothesis is predicated on the following assumptions:

1. Inequality in the contemporary world generates discontent;
2. Although inequality is present to some degree in all societies, some societies are significantly more inegalitarian than others;
3. Inequality in the distribution of land and inequality in the distribution of income are not necessarily tightly connected; in particular, they are

sufficiently independent of each other that an effect of one on a response variable such as the rate of political violence does not necessarily imply that the other will have a similar effect;

4. Given the existence of inequality-based discontent, it is more difficult
   to mobilize peasant communities than urban populations for political
   protest; peasants normally become the foot soldiers of insurgent
   movements only if they are effectively organized by a "vanguard" of
   urban professional revolutionaries.

From these assumptions we derive the following postulates:

1. A high level of income inequality nationwide significantly raises the
   probability that at least some dissident groups will be able to organize
   for aggressive collective action. This is because, first, the pool of discontented persons from which members can be drawn will include the
   more easily mobilized urban areas; and, second, it may be possible for
   urban revolutionaries to establish cross-cutting alliances with groups
   in the countryside.
2. A high level of agrarian inequality does not necessarily raise the probability that dissident groups will be able to organize for aggressive collective action; this is because the pool of discontented persons from
   which members can be drawn may be restricted to the countryside,
   which is difficult to mobilize; consequently, we predict that if income
   inequality is relatively low, the rate of political violence will tend to
   be relatively low, even if agrarian inequality is relatively high;
   whereas if income inequality is relatively high, the rate of political
   violence will tend to be relatively high, even if agrarian inequality is
   relatively low.

Our inequality hypothesis, which is based on an integration of discontent
(or relative deprivation) arguments (e.g., Gurr 1970) with the resource mobilization approach, can be illustrated by the cases of Costa Rica and Venezuela,
where egalitarian redistribution of income occurred despite persisting high
agrarian inequality; and the case of Iran, where income inequality worsened,
especially in urban areas, despite an egalitarian land reform.

Costa Rica circa 1960 had a relatively inegalitarian distribution of land
(the 1963 Gini coefficient was .78) and an extremely inegalitarian distribution
of income (the richest 20% of families received 61% of total personal income
in 1961). During the decade of the 1960s the distribution of land in Costa Rica
became slightly more concentrated (the 1973 Gini coefficient was .82). The
distribution of income, however, was substantially altered in an egalitarian direction by democratically elected reformist administrations who pursued wel-
fare-state policies similar to those of European social democratic govern-

ments. By 1970 the share of national income accruing to the richest quintile of Costa Rican households had been reduced to 50%.[3] As mentioned above, violent conflict was absent from Costa Rican politics during the 1970s.

Venezuela was a similarly inegalitarian society circa 1960, when a democratic regime was inaugurated. The 1956 Gini index of land concentration was .91—the second highest in the world next to Peru—and the richest quintile of Venezuelan households received 59% of total personal income in 1962. During the 1960s the distribution of land in Venezuela remained highly concentrated (the 1971 Gini coefficient was .91), but the distribution of income became more egalitarian—although not as dramatically so as in Costa Rica—due to a combination of reformist administrations and an expanding petroleum-based economic pie (by 1970 the income share of the richest quintile of households had been reduced to 54%). Deaths from political violence in Venezuela registered a sharp decline over this period (according to Taylor and Jodice 1983, vol. 2, tbl. 2.7, they amounted to 1,392 during the years 1958–62; 155 during 1963–67; 53 during 1968–72; and 9 during 1973–77). . . .

Of course, income inequality is not the only cause of mass political violence. In Panama, for example, income was distributed very unequally circa 1970, as the richest 20% of households earned 62% of total national income. But by the early 1970s, General Omar Torrijos Herrera, who had led a successful coup d'etat by officers of the national guard in 1968, had crushed all opposition, established firm censorship of the media, and taken control of the judiciary. Ratings of political rights and civil liberties in Panama during the mid-1970s on a scale of one to seven (most free to least free) averaged 6.5.[4] During this period (1973–77) the Torrijos regime in Panama was the most repressive in the Western Hemisphere next to Cuba, where the rating of political rights and civil liberties averaged 6.9. Inequality-induced discontent presumably existed in Panama, and it probably was relatively widespread, but there was little or no opportunity to organize it.

By contrast, Panama's next-door neighbor to the northwest, Costa Rica, enjoyed the distinction in the mid-1970s of being the oldest democracy in Latin America. Since 1949 Costa Rica had held regularly scheduled free and fair elections, the media were uncensored, unions were free to organize, the judiciary was independent of the executive and legislative branches of government, and citizens were not subject to arbitrary arrest. Costa Rica's political and civil rights ratings averaged a maximum score of 1.0 during 1973–77.

The "open" and "closed" political systems of Costa Rica and Panama exemplify polar extremes of regime repressiveness. Differences in regime structure are relevant to the explanation of cross-national variation in mass political violence because they can be assumed to affect three important variables emphasized in some versions of resource mobilization theory (e.g., McAdam 1982): (1) the extent to which dissident groups are able to develop strong organizations, (2) their belief in the likelihood of success of collective action, and (3) the range of political opportunities available to them for achieving their goals.

In the context of an extremely repressive regime, dissident groups are severely restricted in their ability to organize; their belief in the likelihood of success of collective action will probably be low; and opportunities to engage in collective action of any kind will be quite limited. Consequently, under the condition of a high level of regime repressiveness, rational actors most likely will attach a relatively low utility to violent collective action, and the rate of mass political violence therefore should be relatively low.

In the context of a nonrepressive or "democratic" regime, dissident groups will not face significant restrictions on their ability to organize for collective action, and their belief in the likelihood of achieving at least some success from collective action will probably be relatively high. Moreover, a democratic regime structure will afford a variety of opportunities for dissident groups to participate legally and peacefully in the political process. Because the costs of peaceful collective action will be lower than those of violent collective action and because the likelihood of success of peaceful collective action will be reasonably high, rational actors under the condition of a nonrepressive regime structure presumably will usually attach a much higher utility to peaceful as opposed to violent collective action, and, therefore, the rate of mass political violence here too should be relatively low.

In the context of a semirepressive regime, it is possible for dissident groups to develop relatively strong organizations. However, opportunities to engage in nonviolent forms of collective action that effectively exert influence on the political process are limited. Semirepressive regimes allow only for, in Green's (1984, 154) apt terminology, "pseudoparticipation . . . an elaborate charade of the participatory process." Polities with pseudoparticipation typically have elections that are not free and fair, legislatures that are little more than debating societies, and a judiciary that is not independent of the will of the executive; the media are subject to censorship at the whim of the executive; and citizens are subject to arbitrary arrest and detention by security forces, which are under the exclusive control of the executive. In short, semirepressive regimes erect a facade of participatory institutions but do not permit popular input to significantly influence governmental output. Because opportunities for genuine participation are restricted, many politically activated citizens may come to perceive civil disobedience and violence as being more efficacious than legal means of pseudoparticipation; and since the expected costs of insurgency may not be perceived to be prohibitive, rational actors may well attach a relatively high utility to aggressive political behavior. Therefore, it is plausible to expect that the rate of mass political violence cross-nationally will be highest under semirepressive authoritarian regimes.

The analysis of the causes of the Iranian revolution by Green (1982, 1984) documents in detail how the Shah vacillated between fully restricting mass participation and allowing pseudoparticipation and concludes that "the effects of such tactics served to increase popular hostility among those socially mobilized Iranians eager to have a measure of influence over the manner in which their society was ruled" (Green, 1984, 155). Green's case study description is corroborated by global comparative measures of regime repressiveness, which show that Iran in the late 1950s was classified as having a "semi-competitive" regime (Coleman 1960); was scored for 1960 and 1965 as intermediate (34.9 and 45.0, respectively) on a 0–100 scale of extent of political democracy (Bollen 1980); was ranked circa 1969 at an intermediate level on a scale of opportunity for political opposition (Dahl 1971); received a mean rating of 5.7 on political and civil rights for 1973–77; and had shifted in 1978 to a mean rating of 5.0 on political and civil rights. Thus, while pursuing a strategy of economic development that had the short-term consequence of increasing inequality in the distribution of income, the Pahlavi government would appear to have added fuel to the fire by following a semirepressive political development strategy that allowed opposition groups to organize but did not enable them to participate effectively.

If one takes income inequality and the repressiveness of the regime into account simultaneously, it might be argued that each variable could have an independent causal impact on the likelihood of mass political violence. An equally plausible specification of the joint relationship is that discontent resulting from income inequality will affect political violence only (or most strongly) in countries with semirepressive regime structures; whereas in countries with nonrepressive regime structures, inequality-induced discontent will tend to be channeled into peaceful participation; and in countries with repressive regime structures, it will be borne apathetically or else perhaps lead to various kinds of nonpolitical deviant behavior. . . .

A Cross-National Test of the Causal Model

There have been no studies reported to date that compare the causal importance of land maldistribution versus income inequality as determinants of mass political violence cross-nationally.[5] Until the 1970s, reasonably reliable information on the distribution of land and income was available for only a limited number of countries. Thus in Hibbs's (1973) comprehensive cross-national study of determinants of mass political violence during the 1948–67 period, inequality variables had to be excluded because of insufficient data. We now have been able to compile a relatively comprehensive data set on inequality circa 1970 [appendix in original—Eds.]. Information on land inequality is available for approximately three-quarters of the population of independent political units in 1970, while information on landlessness and income inequality is available for approximately one-half of the population. Regionally, these data are quite comprehensive for Europe and the Americas. In regard to land-lessness and, especially, income distri-bution, coverage is poor for states in the Middle East and North Africa, and it is somewhat limited for the states of sub-Saharan Africa. Since it is unlikely that much new data on inequality circa 1970 will emerge in the future, results using the current data set can probably be regarded as being about as definitive as possible for this time period.

Measurement of the Dependent Variable

Political violence is measured by the natural logarithm of the death rate from domestic conflict per one million population.[6] Annual death counts are from Table 2.7 of Taylor and Jodice (1983, vol. 2). Current political violence is the logged sum of annual deaths from domestic political conflict during 1973–77 divided by midinterval population; lagged political violence is the logged sum of annual deaths from domestic political conflict during 1968–72 divided by midinterval population. Countries where domestic political conflict overlaps with major interstate wars are excluded: Kampuchea, Laos, and South Viet-nam for the 1968–77 period; and Pakistan for the 1968–72 period (where an extremely high death rate reflects the conflict between India and Pakistan in 1971 over the secession of Bangladesh). Ireland also is excluded for the 1973–77 period because the relatively high death rate there reflects a spillover from the Northern Ireland conflict.

In the vast majority of countries, the death rate from political violence per one million population is less than 50. A few countries register very extreme scores, however; for example, Zimbabwe's 1973–77 death rate from political violence was 544 per million and Argentina's death rate was 177 per million. Even after logging, countries with political violence death rates of 50 or more almost always show up as outliers in regression equations (i.e., they usually have extremely high standardized residuals). Consequently, in order to reduce the problem of extreme scores on the dependent variable, it is desirable to set a ceiling on the death rate. The upper limit that we have selected is 50 deaths per million. The adjusted death rate variables thus range from a minimum value of 0 to a maximum value of 50 or more; and the range of the logged death rate variables is from 0 to 3.93.

Measurement of the Independent Variables

The data on land inequality circa 1970 encompass 85 states in which agricul-ture was not collectivized. Land inequality is measured by the Gini coefficient of land concentration. A weighted index of land inequality is the geometric mean of the Gini coefficient (expressed as a percentage) and the percentage of the labor force employed in agriculture in 1970 (see Taylor and Jodice 1983, vol. 1). Apart from measurement of the extent to which land is concentrated in the hands of the few, we also take into account a second aspect of land mal-distribution, landlessness, as measured by agricultural households without land as a proportion of the total labor force. These data are derived from estimates by Prosterman and Riedinger (1982) of the proportion in 64 countries of agricultural households without land.

Income inequality is measured by the size of the share of personal income accruing to the richest quintile of recipients, based on information about the nationwide distribution of income in 63 countries compiled principally from publications of the World Bank. Although some previous studies have used Gini coefficients of income concentration, this measure tends to be unduly sensitive to inequality in the middle of the distribution, whereas inequality in reference to the top of the distribution probably is more relevant to political violence. In any event, income shares also have a more direct meaning than Gini coefficients and are currently more frequently used in research on income inequality.

Regime repressiveness is measured by a country's 1973–77 average annual combined rating on 7-point rank-order scales of political rights and civil liberties that have been reported by Raymond D. Gastil since 1973 (the data are from Taylor and Jodice 1983). A semirepressive regime structure is defined operationally as a mean political rights and civil liberties rank in the range of 2.6–5.5. These cutpoints are identical to those used by Gastil for classifying political systems as "free" (1.0–2.5), "partly free" (2.6–5.5), and "not free" (5.6–7.0).

The indicator of governmental acts of coercion is the negative sanctions variable (imposition of sanctions) from Taylor and Jodice 1983 (vol. 2, tbl. 3.1). Current negative sanctions is the frequency of negative sanctions summed over the years 1973–77 and divided by midinterval total population in millions; lagged negative sanctions are the 1968–72 frequency per one million midinterval population. The negative sanctions variables are expressed as natural logarithms (after adding an increment of one).

The indicator of intensity of separatism is an ordinal scale developed by Ted and Erika Gurr. The data for circa 1975 are from Taylor and Jodice 1983, 55–57 and tbl. 2.5. We express intensity of separatism as a dummy variable, scored 1 (i.e., high intensity) if groups or regions actively advocating greater autonomy were forcibly incorporated into the state (codes 3 and 4) and 0 (i.e., low intensity) otherwise (codes 0, 1, and 2).[7]

Level of economic development is measured by energy consumption per capita in 1970 (from Taylor and Jodice 1983, vol. 1). Values of this variable are expressed as natural logarithms.

Land Maldistribution, Income Inequality, and Political Violence

According to what is generally considered to be the most appropriate specification of the land inequality hypothesis (e.g., Huntington 1968; Nagel 1976;

Prosterman 1976), the strongest effect on political violence should be observed when inequality in the distribution of land is weighted by the proportion of the labor force employed in the agricultural sector of the economy. This specification implies a multiplicative interaction between land inequality and the size of the agricultural labor force, which we call *agrarian inequality,* defined operationally as the geometric mean of Gini land concentration and the percentage of the labor force employed in agriculture (i.e., the square root of the product of these variables). . . .

Results

The results of testing the inequality hypotheses in the context of a multivariate model of determinants of political violence are summarized in Figure 13.1. All of the evidence that we have considered points to the presence of a robust, positive monotonic (positively accelerated) relationship between income inequality and political violence that is independent of the other variables in the model. The effect of income inequality on political violence may be enhanced by the presence of a semirepressive regime, but the evidence is not conclusive in that regard, so we represent the possibility of an interaction between income inequality and semirepressiveness by dashed arrows. The other solid arrows linking explanatory variables to political violence also denote relationships that hold for change as well as level of violence and seem to be robust. We have tested the regime-repressiveness hypothesis with a dummy variable in this study (in order to take into account the possibility of an interaction with income inequality). It should be noted, however, that the same kind of effect appears if regime repressiveness is expressed as a continuous quantitative variable—that is, if the semirepressive-regime dummy variable is replaced by

Figure 13.1   Observed Causal Paths in the Multivariate Causal Model

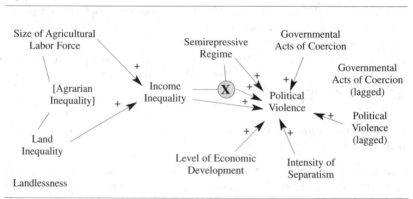

regime repressiveness and its square, a statistically significant nonmonotonic-inverted-U-curve relationship between regime repressiveness and political violence is consistently observed in multivariate equations that include income inequality and the other explanatory variables. We have not tested for the possibility of an instantaneous reciprocal relationship between political violence and governmental acts of coercion (see Hibbs 1973) because that is a complex topic requiring a separate paper. From preliminary work, however, we are confident that it is valid to infer the presence of a positive effect of current governmental acts of coercion on current political violence. . . .

The only completely irrelevant variable in the model is landlessness, a finding that runs counter to the strong claim of causal importance for this variable made by Prosterman (1976). Moreover, at least as a general determinant of mass political violence, the condition of high agrarian inequality also fails to warrant the strong causal claims made for it by many scholars. The components of agrarian inequality, land inequality and size of the agricultural labor force, affect income inequality and, therefore, are indirectly relevant to political violence, but neither the weighted index of agrarian inequality nor land inequality per se has any direct effect on political violence.

Discussion

The finding that agrarian inequality is relevant only to the extent that it is associated with inequality in the nationwide distribution of income has important policy implications. Land reform in third world countries all too often is considered to be a panacea for problems of inequality. However, as Huntington (1968, 385) points out, redistribution of land is the most difficult of reforms for modernizing governments because it almost always entails some degree of outright confiscation. And our study indicates that land redistribution is also not necessarily the most meaningful of reforms. If land redistribution is carried through to the point of actually effecting an egalitarian redistribution of income, as seems to have been the case in countries as diverse as Taiwan and Egypt, and/or if other economic development policies do not exacerbate income inequality, then land reform can make a contribution to the promotion of political stability. However, there are cases such as Bolivia and Mexico in which land reform has not been associated with egalitarian income redistribution. Land reform without income redistribution is probably at best merely a temporary palliative; and at worst, as the case of Iran demonstrates, it can be quite counterproductive by alienating powerful conservative groups such as the nobility and the clergy. Indeed, by simultaneously encouraging both land reform and a policy of rapid economic growth that ignored inegalitarian distributional consequences, U.S. advisors to the Shah would appear unwittingly to have exacerbated the economic preconditions of revolution in Iran.

If the effect of income inequality on change in political violence and its level, observed for 60 and 62 cases, is reliable and more or less generalizable across time in the contemporary world (at least for nontraditional societies where modern values like equality can be assumed to have become salient), it follows that redistribution of income must be ranked as one of the more meaningful reforms that a modernizing government can undertake in the interest of achieving political stability. Unfortunately, redistribution of income may conflict not only with the class interests of many third world governments but also with their predilection for rapid industrialization. The Shah's great dream of surpassing Sweden by the year 2000 was dashed in part by his single-minded concern with economic growth and the raising of per capita income. As Green (1982, 70–71) points out, "the premise of the Pahlavi development ethos rested on the assumption that economic development was more important than political rights or justice." Iran in the years immediately preceding the revolution indeed registered an extraordinary growth of per capita gross national product, which averaged an increase of 13.3% annually during 1970–78, the highest rate of growth of GNP per capita in the world (see Taylor and Jodice 1983, vol. 1, tbl. 3.6); but at the same time that per capita income was increasing phenomenally, the distribution of that income was apparently becoming more concentrated at the top, presumably heightening perceptions of economic injustice. It is important to emphasize, however, that there is no necessary trade-off between rapid economic growth and income inequality. Taiwan's average annual growth of GNP per capita during 1960–78 was 6.6% (see World Bank 1980, tbl. 1), a rate that, although surpassed by Iran (the world leader excluding Romania), was nevertheless almost twice as high as the average rate (3.7%) for all middle-income countries. At the same time (1964–78), the income share of the richest 20% of households in Taiwan declined from 41.1% to 37.2% (see Tsiang 1984, tbl. 9). Thus, by following a different set of economic policies than the Shah, the government of Taiwan achieved growth with equity. And the death rate from political violence in Taiwan during 1973–77 was .06, as compared with Iran's rate of .91. . . .

Notes

A version of this paper was presented at the 1985 Midwest Political Science Association meeting in Chicago, April 18–21. Support for this research was provided by National Science Foundation Grant SES83-2021.

1. Midlarsky and Roberts distinguish between these cases in regard to the dynamics of coalition formation leading to different kinds of revolutionary movements. Although both countries had inegalitarian distributions of land, creating a potential for insurgency in each case, the revolutionary movement in El Salvador was more narrowly class-based than in Nicaragua, due to differences in population density that produced greater land scarcity in El Salvador than in Nicaragua. This difference is thought to have enhanced the likelihood of a successful revolution in Nicaragua.

2. Unless otherwise noted, data on land and income distribution referred to in the text are either from Table A-1 [see original work] or, for years other than those in Table A-1, from the sources cited therein.

3. Based on a study reported by Céspedes (1979). Trejos (1983) reports the income share of the richest 20% of households in Costa Rica as 51.1% in 1971, 52.1% in 1974, and 53% in 1977.

4. These and all subsequent data on civil and political liberties referred to in the text are calculated from the data file of the *World Handbook of Political and Social Indicators*. For a description of the ratings, see Taylor and Jodice 1983 (1:58–65).

5. The only previous research on this topic is reported in Midlarsky 1981, where income distribution is measured by an index of intersectoral inequality. As Sigelman and Simpson (1977, 111) have pointed out, however, this index "is at best a second-rate measurement proxy for personal income, lacking theoretical interest of its own."

6. Deaths from political violence are an attribute of political-protest events like riots, armed attacks, and assassinations. Deaths are thus a summary measure of the intensity of political-protest events. Deaths are used in preference to a composite index for the following reasons: (1) a single-variable indicator is more easily interpretable than a composite measure; (2) deaths will necessarily correlate very strongly with a composite measure such as that constructed by Hibbs (1973), which includes deaths, armed attacks, and assassinations; and (3) there is probably less reporting bias for deaths than for indicators such as armed attacks (see Weede 1981). Death *rate* is preferred over raw counts because the former is an indicator of the extent to which the regime is threatened by insurgency, which depends not on the absolute frequency of political violence but rather on its frequency relative to size of population (for further discussion of this issue see Linehan 1976; Muller 1985; and Weede 1981). The logarithmic transformation is theoretically appropriate because death rate from political violence is expected to vary as a positively accelerated function of inequality; it is also necessary because of the presence of extreme values—although the problem of extreme values still exists after logging. An increment of one is added to each death score before logging because the log of zero is undefined.

7. In testing the multivariate model across 62 cases, the following countries are missing data on intensity of separatism: Barbados, Gabon, Honduras, Ivory Coast, Malawi, Nepal, Sierra Leone, and Trinidad and Tobago. Based on country descriptions from Banks 1976, these countries were scored zero on intensity of separatism.

References

Ahluwalia, Montak S. 1976. Inequality, Poverty, and Development. *Journal of Development Economics* 3:307–42.

Bandura, Albert. 1973. *Aggression: A Social Learning Analysis*. Englewood Cliffs, NJ: Prentice-Hall.

Banks, Arthur S., ed. 1976. *Political Handbook of the World: 1976*. New York: McGraw-Hill.

Bharier, Julian. 1971. *Economic Development in Iran 1900–1970*. New York: Oxford University Press.

Bollen, Kenneth A. 1980. Issues in the Comparative Measurement of Political Democracy. *American Sociological Review* 45:370–90.

Bornschier Volker, and Peter Heintz, eds. 1979. *Compendium of Data for World System Analysis*. Zurich: Soziologisches Institut der Universität.

Buss, Arnold H. 1961. *A Psychology of Aggression*. New York: Wiley.

Céspedes, Victor H. 1979. *Evolución de la distribución del ingreso en Costa Rica.* Serie divulgación económica, No. 18. Costa Rica: Ciudad Universitaria Rodrigo Facio.

Coleman, James S. 1960. Conclusion: The Political Systems of the Developing Areas. In *The Politics of the Developing Areas,* ed. Gabriel A. Almond and James S. Coleman. Princeton: Princeton University Press.

Dahl, Robert A. 1971. *Polyarchy.* New Haven: Yale University Press.

Fei, John C. H., Gustav Ranis, and Shirley W. Y. Kuo. 1979. *Growth with Equity: The Taiwan Case.* New York: Oxford University Press.

Food and Agriculture Organization of the United States. 1981. *Nineteen Seventy World Census of Agriculture: Analysis and International Comparison of the Results.* Rome: author.

Gamson, William A. 1975. *The Strategy of Social Protest.* Homewood, IL: Dorsey.

Green, Jerrold D. 1982. *Revolution in Iran.* New York: Praeger.

Green, Jerrold D. 1984. Countermobilization as a Revolutionary Form. *Comparative Politics* 16:153–69.

Gurr, Ted Robert. 1970. *Why Men Rebel.* Princeton: Princeton University Press.

Hardy, Melissa A. 1979. Economic Growth, Distributional Inequality, and Political Conflict in Industrial Societies. *Journal of Political and Military Sociology* 5:209–27.

Hibbs, Douglas A. 1973. *Mass Political Violence.* New York: Wiley.

Huntington, Samuel P. 1968. *Political Order in Changing Societies.* New Haven: Yale University Press.

Jabbari, Ahmad. 1981. Economic Factors in Iran's Revolution: Poverty, Inequality, and Inflation. In *Iran: Essays on a Revolution in the Making,* ed. Ahmad Jabbari and Robert Olson. Lexington, KY: Mazda.

Jain, Shail. 1975. *Size Distribution of Income.* Washington, DC: World Bank.

Keddie, Nikki R. 1968. The Iranian Village before and after Land Reform. *Journal of Contemporary History* 3:69–91.

Leal, Maria Angela. 1983. Heritage of Hunger: Population, Land, and Survival. In *Revolution in Central America,* ed. Stanford Central America Action Network. Boulder, CO: Westview.

Linehan, William J. 1976. Models for the Measurement of Political Instability. *Political Methodology* 3:441–86.

McAdam, Doug. 1982. *Political Process and the Development of Black Insurgency.* Chicago: University of Chicago Press.

Midlarsky, Manus I. 1981. The Revolutionary Transformation of Foreign Policy: Agrarianism and Its International Impact. In *The Political Economy of Foreign Policy Behavior,* ed. Charles W. Kegley and Patrick J. McGowan. Beverly Hills, CA: Sage.

Midlarsky, Manus I. 1982. Scarcity and Inequality. *Journal of Conflict Resolution* 26:3–38.

Midlarsky, Manus I., and Kenneth Roberts. 1985. Class, State, and Revolution in Central America: Nicaragua and El Salvador Compared. *Journal of Conflict Resolution* 29:163–93.

Muller, Edward N. 1985. Income Inequality, Regime Repressiveness, and Political Violence. *American Sociological Review* 50:47–61.

Muller, Edward N. 1986. Income Inequality and Political Violence: The Effect of Influential Cases. *American Sociological Review* 51:441–45.

Nagel, Jack. 1976. Erratum. *World Politics* 28:315.

Norusis, Marija J. 1986. *SPSS/PC+.* Chicago: SPSS.

Oberschall, Anthony. 1973. *Social Conflict and Social Movements.* Englewood Cliffs, NJ: Prentice-Hall.

Paige, Jeffery M. 1975. *Agrarian Revolution.* New York: Free Press.

Paukert, Felix. 1973. Income Distribution at Different Levels of Development: A Survey of Evidence. *International Labour Review* 108:97–125.

Prosterman, Roy L. 1976. IRI: A Simplified Predictive Index of Rural Instability. *Comparative Politics* 8:339–54.

Prosterman, Roy L., and Jeffrey M. Riedinger. 1982. Toward an Index of Democratic Development. In *Freedom in the World: Political Rights and Civil Liberties 1982,* ed. Raymond D. Gastil. Westport, CT: Greenwood Press.

Roberti, Paolo. 1974. Income Distribution: A Time-Series and a Cross-Section Survey. *Economic Journal* 84:629–38.

Russett, Bruce M. 1964. Inequality and Instability: The Relation of Land Tenure to Politics. *World Politics* 16:442–54.

Sawyer, Malcolm. 1976. Income Distribution in OECD Countries. *OECD Economic Outlook,* Occasional Studies, July, 3–36.

Seligson, Mitchell A., Richard Hough, John Kelley, Stephen Miller, Russell Derossier, and Fred L. Mann. 1983. *Land and Labor in Guatemala: An Assessment.* Washington, DC: Agency for International Development and Development Associates.

Sigelman, Lee, and Miles Simpson. 1977. A Cross-National Test of the Linkage between Economic Inequality and Political Violence. *Journal of Conflict Resolution* 21:105–28.

Skocpol, Theda. 1979. *States and Social Revolutions.* New York: Cambridge University Press.

Tanter, Raymond, and Manus I. Midlarsky. 1967. A Theory of Revolution. *Journal of Conflict Resolution* 11:264–80.

Taylor, Charles L., and Michael C. Hudson. 1972. *World Handbook of Political and Social Indicators.* 2d ed. New Haven: Yale University Press.

Taylor, Charles L., and David A. Jodice. 1983. *World Handbook of Political and Social Indicators.* 3d ed. Vols. 1 and 2. New Haven: Yale University Press.

Tilly, Charles. 1969. Collective Violence in European Perspective. In *Violence in America: Historical and Comparative Perspectives,* ed. Hugh Davis Graham and Ted Robert Gurr. New York: Signet Books.

Tilly, Charles. 1978. *From Mobilization to Revolution.* Reading, MA: Addison-Wesley.

Trejos, Juan Diego. 1983. *La distribución del ingreso de las familias Costarricenses: Algunas caracteristicas en 1977.* San Jose: Instituto investigaciones en ciencias económicas, Universidad de Costa Rica, No. 50.

Tsiang, S. C. 1984. Taiwan's Economic Miracle: Lessons in Economic Development. In *World Economic Growth,* ed. Arnold C. Harberger. San Francisco: Institute for Contemporary Studies.

United States Agency for International Development. 1983. *Country Development Strategy Statement: Jamaica, FY 1985.* Washington, DC: Government Printing Office.

Webb, Richard C. 1976. The Distribution of Income in Peru. In *Income Distribution in Latin America,* ed. Alejandro Foxley. New York: Cambridge University Press.

Weede, Erich. 1981. Income Inequality, Average Income, and Domestic Violence. *Journal of Conflict Resolution* 25:639–53.

Weede, Erich. 1986. Income Inequality and Political Violence Reconsidered. *American Sociological Review* 51:438–41.

World Bank. 1979, 1980, 1981, 1982, 1983, 1984, 1985. *World Development Report.* New York: Oxford University Press.

PART 4

The Classic Thesis:
Convergence or Divergence?

14

The Five Stages of Growth

W. W. ROSTOW

Early research on economic underdevelopment suggested that the problem was only short-term and that in the end all countries would become rich. In this excerpt from W. W. Rostow's classic work, The Stages of Economic Growth, *Rostow outlines this optimistic scenario by positing five stages of economic development all societies eventually experience as they mature into industrialized developed countries: tradition, the preconditions for takeoff, the takeoff, the drive to maturity, and the age of high mass consumption. Although this tremendously influential publication did not focus specifically on the causes of the gaps, the author suggests the reason they arise and their potential resolution. As a country moves out of the traditional stage and prepares for economic takeoff, its economy begins to grow much faster than the economies of countries that remain in the first stage. The gap between rich and poor would then be explained by the fact that not all countries enter the development process at the same time. Thus the gap between rich and poor countries would be expected to disappear as the countries progress into the later stages of growth. As a country progresses through the stages of development, those who adopt the new economic rules and succeed accumulate the profits of their success, and internal inequality arises. As more people join the monied economy and play by the new rules, the extent of the inequality should diminish.* ■

Reprinted with permission of Cambridge University Press from *The Stages of Economic Growth* by W. W. Rostow, pp. 4–12. New York: Cambridge University Press, 1990.

IT IS POSSIBLE TO IDENTIFY ALL SOCIETIES, IN THEIR ECONOMIC DIMENSIONS, AS lying within one of five categories: the traditional society, the preconditions for take-off, the take-off, the drive to maturity, and the age of high mass-consumption.

The Traditional Society

First, the traditional society. A traditional society is one whose structure is developed within limited production functions, based on pre-Newtonian science and technology, and on pre-Newtonian attitudes towards the physical world. Newton is here used as a symbol for that watershed in history when men came widely to believe that the external world was subject to a few knowable laws, and was systematically capable of productive manipulation.

The conception of the traditional society is, however, in no sense static; and it would not exclude increases in output. Acreage could be expanded; some *ad hoc* technical innovations, often highly productive innovations, could be introduced in trade, industry and agriculture; productivity could rise with, for example, the improvement of irrigation works or the discovery and diffusion of a new crop. But the central fact about the traditional society was that a ceiling existed on the level of attainable output per head. This ceiling resulted from the fact that the potentialities which flow from modern science and technology were either not available or not regularly and systematically applied.

Both in the longer past and in recent times the story of traditional societies was thus a story of endless change. The area and volume of trade within them and between them fluctuated, for example, with the degree of political and social turbulence, the efficiency of central rule, the upkeep of the roads. Population— and, within limits, the level of life—rose and fell not only with the sequence of the harvests, but with the incidence of war and of plague. Varying degrees of manufacture developed; but, as in agriculture, the level of productivity was limited by the inaccessibility of modern science, its applications, and its frame of mind.

Generally speaking, these societies, because of the limitation on productivity, had to devote a very high proportion of their resources to agriculture; and flowing from the agricultural system there was an hierarchical social structure, with relatively narrow scope—but some scope—for vertical mobility. Family and clan connexions played a large role in social organization. The value system of these societies was generally geared to what might be called a long-run fatalism; that is, the assumption that the range of possibilities open to one's grandchildren would be just about what it had been for one's grandparents. But this long-run fatalism by no means excluded the short-run option that, within a considerable range, it was possible and legitimate for the individual to strive to improve his lot, within his lifetime. In Chinese villages, for example, there was an endless struggle to acquire or to avoid losing land, yielding a situation where land rarely remained within the same family for a century.

Although central political rule—in one form or another—often existed in traditional societies, transcending the relatively self-sufficient regions, the centre of gravity of political power generally lay in the regions, in the hands of those who owned or controlled the land. The landowner maintained fluctuating but usually profound influence over such central political power as existed, backed by its entourage of civil servants and soldiers, imbued with attitudes and controlled by interests transcending the regions.

In terms of history then, with the phrase "traditional society" we are grouping the whole pre-Newtonian world: the dynasties in China; the civilization of the Middle East and the Mediterranean; the world of medieval Europe. And to them we add the post-Newtonian societies which, for a time, remained untouched or unmoved by man's new capability for regularly manipulating his environment to his economic advantage.

To place these infinitely various, changing societies in a single category, on the ground that they all shared a ceiling on the productivity of their economic techniques, is to say very little indeed. But we are, after all, merely clearing the way in order to get at the subject of this book; that is, the post-traditional societies, in which each of the major characteristics of the traditional society was altered in such ways as to permit regular growth: its politics, social structure, and (to a degree) its values, as well as its economy.

The Preconditions for Take-off

The second stage of growth embraces societies in the process of transition; that is, the period when the preconditions for take-off are developed; for it takes time to transform a traditional society in the ways necessary for it to exploit the fruits of modern science, to fend off diminishing returns, and thus to enjoy the blessings and choices opened up by the march of compound interest.

The preconditions for take-off were initially developed, in a clearly marked way, in Western Europe of the late seventeenth and early eighteenth centuries as the insights of modern science began to be translated into new production functions in both agriculture and industry, in a setting given dynamism by the lateral expansion of world markets and the international competition for them. But all that lies behind the break-up of the Middle Ages is relevant to the creation of the preconditions for take-off in Western Europe. Among the Western European states, Britain, favoured by geography, natural resources, trading possibilities, social and political structure, was the first to develop fully the preconditions for take-off.

The more general case in modern history, however, saw the stage of preconditions arise not endogenously but from some external intrusion by more advanced societies. These invasions—literal or figurative—shocked the traditional society and began or hastened its undoing; but they also set in motion ideas and sentiments which initiated the process by which a modern alternative to the traditional society was constructed out of the old culture.

The idea spreads not merely that economic progress is possible, but that economic progress is a necessary condition for some other purpose, judged to be good: be it national dignity, private profit, the general welfare, or a better life for the children. Education, for some at least, broadens and changes to suit the needs of modern economic activity. New types of enterprising men come forward—in the private economy, in government, or both—willing to mobilize savings and to take risks in pursuit of profit or modernization. Banks and other institutions for mobilizing capital appear. Investment increases, notably in transport, communications, and in raw materials in which other nations may have an economic interest. The scope of commerce, internal and external, widens. And, here and there, modern manufacturing enterprise appears, using the new methods. But all this activity proceeds at a limited pace within an economy and a society still mainly characterized by traditional low-productivity methods, by the old social structure and values, and by the regionally based political institutions that developed in conjunction with them.

In many recent cases, for example, the traditional society persisted side by side with modern economic activities, conducted for limited economic purposes by a colonial or quasi-colonial power.

Although the period of transition—between the traditional society and the take-off—saw major changes in both the economy itself and in the balance of social values, a decisive feature was often political. Politically, the building of an effective centralized national state—on the basis of coalitions touched with a new nationalism, in opposition to the traditional landed regional interests, the colonial power, or both, was a decisive aspect of the preconditions period; and it was, almost universally, a necessary condition for take-off. . . .

The Take-off

We come now to the great watershed in the life of modern societies: the third stage in this sequence, the take-off. The take-off is the interval when the old blocks and resistances to steady growth are finally overcome. The forces making for economic progress, which yielded limited bursts and enclaves of modern activity, expand and come to dominate the society. Growth becomes its normal condition. Compound interest becomes built, as it were, into its habits and institutional structure.

In Britain and the well-endowed parts of the world populated substantially from Britain (the United States, Canada, etc.) the proximate stimulus for take-off was mainly (but not wholly) technological. In the more general case, the take-off awaited not only the build-up of social overhead capital and a surge of technological development in industry and agriculture, but also the emergence to political power of a group prepared to regard the modernization of the economy as serious, high-order political business.

During the take-off, the rate of effective investment and savings may rise from say, 5 percent of the national income to 10 percent or more; although where heavy social overhead capital investment was required to create the technical preconditions for take-off the investment rate in the preconditions period could be higher than 5 percent, as, for example, in Canada before the 1890s and Argentina before 1914. In such cases capital imports usually formed a high proportion of total investment in the preconditions period and sometimes even during the take-off itself, as in Russia and Canada during their pre-1914 railway booms.

During the take-off new industries expand rapidly, yielding profits a large proportion of which are reinvested in new plants; and these new industries, in turn, stimulate, through their rapidly expanding requirement for factory workers, the services to support them, and for other manufactured goods, a further expansion in urban areas and in other modern industrial plants. The whole process of expansion in the modern sector yields an increase of income in the hands of those who not only save at high rates but place their savings at the disposal of those engaged in modern sector activities. The new class of entrepreneurs expands; and it directs the enlarging flows of investment in the private sector. The economy exploits hitherto unused natural resources and methods of production.

New techniques spread in agriculture as well as industry, as agriculture is commercialized, and increasing numbers of farmers are prepared to accept the new methods and the deep changes they bring to ways of life. The revolutionary changes in agricultural productivity are an essential condition for successful take-off; for modernization of a society increases radically its bill for agricultural products. In a decade or two both the basic structure of the economy and the social and political structure of the society are transformed in such a way that a steady rate of growth can be, thereafter, regularly sustained.

. . . One can approximately allocate the take-off of Britain to the two decades after 1783; France and the United States to the several decades preceding 1860; Germany, the third quarter of the nineteenth century; Japan, the fourth quarter of the nineteenth century; Russia and China the quarter-century or so preceding 1914; while during the 1950s India and China have, in quite different ways, launched their respective take-offs.

The Drive to Maturity

After take-off there follows a long interval of sustained if fluctuating progress, as the now regularly growing economy drives to extend modern technology over the whole front of its economic activity. Some 10–20 percent of the national income is steadily invested, permitting output regularly to outstrip the increase in population. The make-up of the economy changes unceasingly as technique improves, new industries accelerate, older industries level off. The economy finds its place in the international economy: goods formerly imported are produced at home; new import requirements develop, and new export commodities to match them. The society makes such terms as it will with the requirements of modern efficient production, balancing off the new against the older values and institutions, or revising the latter in such ways as to support rather than to retard the growth process.

Some sixty years after take-off begins (say, forty years after the end of take-off) what may be called maturity is generally attained. The economy, focused during the take-off around a relatively narrow complex of industry and technology, has extended its range into more refined and technologically often more complex processes; for example, there may be a shift in focus from the coal, iron, and heavy engineering industries of the railway phase to machine-tools, chemicals, and electrical equipment. This, for example, was the transition through which Germany, Britain, France, and the United States had passed by the end of the nineteenth century or shortly thereafter. But there are other sectoral patterns which have been followed in the sequence from take-off to maturity. . . .

Formally, we can define maturity as the stage in which an economy demonstrates the capacity to move beyond the original industries which powered its take-off and to absorb and to apply efficiently over a very wide range of its resources—if not the whole range—the most advanced fruits of (then) modern technology. This is the stage in which an economy demonstrates that it has the technological and entrepreneurial skills to produce not everything, but anything that it chooses to produce. It may lack (like contemporary Sweden and Switzerland, for example) the raw materials or other supply conditions required to produce a given type of output economically; but its dependence is a matter of economic choice or political priority rather than a technological or institutional necessity.

Historically, it would appear that something like sixty years was required to move a society from the beginning of take-off to maturity. Analytically the explanation for some such interval may lie in the powerful arithmetic of compound interest applied to the capital stock, combined with the broader consequences for a society's ability to absorb modern technology of three successive generations living under a regime where growth is the normal condition. But, clearly, no dogmatism is justified about the exact length of the interval from take-off to maturity.

The Age of High Mass-Consumption

We come now to the age of high mass-consumption, where, in time, the leading sectors shift towards durable consumers' goods and services: a phase from which Americans are beginning to emerge; whose not unequivocal joys Western Europe and Japan are beginning energetically to probe; and with which Soviet society is engaged in an uneasy flirtation.

As societies achieved maturity in the twentieth century two things happened: real income per head rose to a point where a large number of persons gained a command over consumption which transcended basic food, shelter, and clothing; and the structure of the working force changed in ways which increased not only the proportion of urban to total population, but also the proportion of the population working in offices or in skilled factory jobs—aware of and anxious to acquire the consumption fruits of a mature economy.

In addition to these economic changes, the society ceased to accept the further extension of modern technology as an overriding objective. It is in this post-maturity stage, for example, that, through the political process, Western societies have chosen to allocate increased resources to social welfare and security. The emergence of the welfare state is one manifestation of a society's moving beyond technical maturity; but it is also at this stage that resources tend increasingly to be directed to the production of consumers' durables and to the diffusion of services on a mass basis, if consumers' sovereignty reigns. The sewing-machine, the bicycle, and then the various electric-powered household gadgets were gradually diffused. Historically, however, the decisive element has been the cheap mass automobile with its quite revolutionary effects—social as well as economic—on the life and expectations of society.

For the United States, the turning point was, perhaps, Henry Ford's moving assembly line of 1913–14; but it was in the 1920s, and again in the post-war decade, 1946–56, that this stage of growth was pressed to, virtually, its logical conclusion. In the 1950s Western Europe and Japan appeared to have fully entered this phase, accounting substantially for a momentum in their economies quite unexpected in the immediate post-war years. The Soviet Union is technically ready for this stage, and, by every sign, its citizens hunger for it; but Communist leaders face difficult political and social problems of adjustment if this stage is launched.

Beyond Consumption

Beyond, it is impossible to predict, except perhaps to observe that Americans, at least, have behaved in the past decade as if diminishing relative marginal utility sets in, after a point, for durable consumers' goods; and they have chosen, at the margin, larger families—behavior in the pattern of Buddenbrooks dynamics.[1] Americans have behaved as if, having been born into a system that provided economic security and high mass-consumption, they placed a lower valuation on acquiring additional increments of real income in the conventional form as opposed to the advantages and values of an enlarged family. But even in this adventure in generalization it is a shade too soon to create—on the basis of one case—a new stage-of-growth, based on babies, in succession to the age of consumers' durables: as economists might say, the income-elasticity of demand for babies may well vary from society to society. But it is true that the implications of the baby boom along with the not wholly unrelated deficit in social overhead capital are likely to dominate the American economy over the next decade rather than the further diffusion of consumers' durables.

Here then, in an impressionistic rather than an analytic way, are the stages-of-growth which can be distinguished once a traditional society begins its modernization: the transitional period when the preconditions for take-off are created generally in response to the forces making for modernization; the take-off itself; the sweep into maturity generally taking up the life of about two further generations; and then, finally, if the rise of income has matched the spread of technological virtuosity (which, as we shall see, it need not immediately do) the diversion of the fully mature economy to the provision of durable consumers' goods and services (as well as the welfare state) for its increasingly urban—and then suburban—populations. Beyond lies the question of whether or not secular spiritual stagnation will arise, and, if it does, how man might fend it off. . . .

Notes

1. In Thomas Mann's novel of three generations, the first sought money; the second, born to money, sought social and civic position; the third, born to comfort and family prestige, looked to the life of music. The phrase is designed to suggest, then, the changing aspirations of generations, as they place a low value on what they take for granted and seek new forms of satisfaction.

15

Productivity Growth, Convergence, and Welfare: What the Long-Run Data Show

WILLIAM J. BAUMOL

In this chapter William Baumol provides empirical analysis of convergence theory and finds that for a sample of sixteen countries between 1870 and 1979, labor productivity and its growth are inversely related. Convergence theorists have long argued that not all countries will experience convergence because they lack the social capacity to utilize technology to achieve rapid growth. Baumol turns to the post–World War II era (1950–1980) to see if this relationship can be found for all countries. Using real GDP/pc and growth rates as proxies for labor productivity, Baumol finds that the poorest countries have the slowest rGDP/pc growth, thus failing to converge with the rich. The rest of the countries belong to what Baumol calls a "convergence club." Hence, if Baumol is correct, convergence will take place, but will exclude the poorest countries from the process, meaning that the gap will widen between them and the rest of the world. ■

> No matter how refined and how elaborate the analysis, if it rests solely on the short view it will still be . . . a structure built on shifting sands.
> —Jacob Viner (1958, pp. 112–131)

RECENT YEARS HAVE WITNESSED A REEMERGENCE OF INTEREST ON THE PART OF economists and the general public in issues relating to long-run economic growth. There has been a recurrence of doubts and fears for the future—

Reprinted with permission from the *American Economic Review*, vol. 76 (December 1986): 1072–1084.

aroused in this case by the protracted slowdown in productivity growth since the late 1960s, the seeming erosion of the competitiveness of U.S. industries in world markets, and the spectre of "deindustrialization" and massive structural unemployment. These anxieties have succeeded in redirecting attention to long-run supply-side phenomena that formerly were a central preoccupation of economists in the industrializing West, before being pushed aside in the crisis of the Great Depression and the ensuing triumph of Keynesian ideas.

Anxiety may compel attention, but it is not necessarily an aid to clear thinking. For all the interest now expressed in the subject of long-run economic growth and policies ostensibly directed to its stimulation, it does not seem to be widely recognized that adequate economic analysis of such issues calls for the careful study of economic history—if only because it is there that the pertinent evidence is to be found. Economic historians have provided the necessary materials, in the form of brilliant insights, powerful analysis as well as a surprising profusion of long-period data. Yet none of these has received the full measure of attention they deserve from members of the economics profession at large.

To dramatize the sort of reorientation long-term information can suggest, imagine a convincing prediction that over the next century, U.S. productivity growth will permit a trebling of per capita GNP while cutting nearly by half the number of hours in the average work year, and that this will be accompanied by a sevenfold increase in exports. One might well consider this a very rosy forecast. But none of these figures is fictitious. For these developments in fact lay before the United Kingdom in 1870, just as its economic leadership began to erode.

This chapter outlines some implications of the available long-period data on productivity and related variables—some tentative, some previously noted by economic historians, and some throwing a somewhat surprising light on developments among industrialized nations since World War II. Among the main observations that will emerge here is the remarkable convergence of output per labor hour among industrialized nations. Almost all of the leading free enterprise economies have moved closer to the leader, and there is a strong inverse correlation between a country's productivity standing in 1870 and its average rate of productivity growth since then. Postwar data suggest that the convergence phenomenon also extends to both "intermediate" and centrally planned economies. Only the poorer less developed countries show no such trend.

It will also emerge that over the century, the U.S. productivity growth rate has been surprisingly steady, and despite frequently expressed fears, there is no sign recently of any *long-term* slowdown in growth of either total factor productivity or labor productivity in the United States. And while, except in wartime, *for the better part of a century,* U.S. productivity growth rates have been low relative to those of Germany, Japan, and a number of other countries, this may be no more than a manifestation of the convergence phenomenon which requires countries that were previously behind to grow more rapidly. Thus, the chapter will seek to dispel these and a number of other misapprehensions apparently widespread among those who have not studied economic history.

Nonspecialists may well be surprised at the remarkably long periods spanned in time-series contributed by Beveridge, Deane, Kuznets, Gallman, Kendrick, Abramovitz, David, and others. The Phelps Brown-Hopkins indices of prices and real wages extend over seven centuries. Maddison, Feinstein (and his colleagues), and Kendrick cover productivity, investment, and a number of other crucial variables for more than 100 years. Obviously, the magnitudes of the earlier figures are more than a little questionable, as their compilers never cease to warn us. Yet the general qualitative character of the time paths is persuasive, given the broad consistency of the statistics, their apparent internal logic and the care exercised in collecting them. In this chapter, the period used will vary with topic and data availability. In most cases, something near a century will be examined, using primarily data provided by Angus Maddison (1982) and R.C.O. Matthews, C. H. Feinstein, and J. C. Odling-Smee (1982—henceforth, M-F-O).

Magnitude of the Accomplishment

The magnitude of the productivity achievement of the past 150 years resists intuitive grasp, and contrasts sharply with the preceding centuries. As the *Communist Manifesto* put the matter in 1848, with remarkable foresight, "The bourgeoisie, during its rule of scarce one hundred years, has created more massive and more colossal productive forces than have all preceding generations together." There obviously are no reliable measures of productivity in antiquity, but available descriptions of living standards in Ancient Rome suggest that they were in many respects higher than in eighteenth-century England (see Colin Clark, 1957, p. 677). This is probably true even for the lower classes—certainly for the free urban proletariat, and perhaps even with the inclusion of slaves. An upper-class household was served by sophisticated devices for heating and bathing not found in eighteenth-century homes of the rich. A wealthy Roman magically transported into an eighteenth-century English home would probably have been puzzled by the technology of only a few products—clocks, window panes, printed books and newspapers, and the musket over the fireplace.

It is true that even during the Middle Ages (see, for example, Carlo Cipolla, 1976), there was substantial technological change in the workplace and elsewhere. Ship design improved greatly. Lenses and, with them, the telescope and microscope appeared in the sixteenth century, and the eighteenth century brought the ship's chronometer which revolutionized water transport by permitting calculation of longitude. Yet, none of this led to rates of productivity growth anywhere near those of the nineteenth and twentieth centuries.

Nonhistorians do not usually recognize that initially the Industrial Revolution was a fairly minor affair for the economy as a whole. At first, much of the new equipment was confined to textile production (though some progress in fields such as iron making had also occurred). And, as David Landes (1969) indicates, an entrepreneur could undertake the new types of textile operations with little capital, perhaps only a few hundred pounds, which (using the Phelps Brown-Hopkins data) translates into some 100,000 1980 dollars. Jeffrey Williamson (1983) tells us that in England during the first half-century of the Industrial Revolution, real per capita income grew only about 0.3 percent per annum,[1] in contrast with the nearly 3 percent achieved in the Third World in the 1970s (despite the decade's economic crises).

Table 15.1 shows the remarkable contrast of developments since 1870 for Maddison's 16 countries. We see (col. 1) that growth in output per work-hour ranged for the next 110 years from approximately 400 percent for Australia all the way to 2500 percent (in the case of Japan). The 1100 percent increase of labor productivity in the United States placed it somewhat below the middle of the group, and even the United Kingdom managed a 600 percent rise. Thus, after not manifesting any substantial long-period increase for at least 15 centuries, in the course of 11 decades the median increase in productivity among the 16 industrialized leaders in Maddison's sample was about 1150 percent. The rise in productivity was sufficient to permit output per capita (col. 2) to increase more than 300 percent in the United Kingdom, 800 percent in West

Table 15.1   Total Growth from 1870 to 1979:[a] Productivity, GDP per Capita, and Exports, Sixteen Industrialized Countries[b]

	Real GDP per Work-Hour	Real GDP per Capita	Volume of Exports
Australia	398	221	—
United Kingdom	585	310	930
Switzerland	830	471	4,400
Belgium	887	439	6,250
Netherlands	910	429	8,040
Canada	1,050	766	9,860
United States	1,080	693	9,240
Denmark	1,098	684	6,750
Italy	1,225	503	6,210
Austria	1,270	643	4,740
Germany	1,510	824	3,730
Norway	1,560	873	7,740
France	1,590	694	4,140
Finland	1,710	1,016	6,240
Sweden	2,060	1,083	5,070
Japan	2,480	1,661	293,060

Source: Angus Maddison (1982, pp. 8, 212, 248–53).
Notes: a. In 1970 U.S. dollars.
b. Shown in percent.

Germany, 1700 percent in Japan, and nearly 700 percent in France and the United States. Using Robert Summers and Alan Heston's sophisticated international comparison data (1984), this implies that in 1870, U.S. output per capita was comparable to 1980 output per capita in Honduras and the Philippines, and slightly below that of China, Bolivia, and Egypt!

The growth rates of other pertinent variables were also remarkable. One more example will suffice to show this. Table 15.1, which also shows the rise in volume of exports from 1870 to 1979 (col. 3), indicates that the median increase was over 6,000 percent.

The Convergence of National Productivity Levels

There is a long and reasonably illustrious tradition among economic historians centered on the phenomenon of convergence. While the literature devoted to the subject is complex and multifaceted, as revealed by the recent reconsideration of these ideas by Moses Abramovitz (1985), one central theme is that forces accelerating the growth of nations who were latecomers to industrialization and economic development give rise to a long-run tendency towards convergence of levels of per capita product or, alternatively, of per worker product. Such ideas found expression in the works of Alexander Gerschenkron (see, for example, 1952), who saw his own views on the advantages of "relative backwardness" as having been anticipated in important respects by Thorstein Veblen's writings on the penalties of being the industrial leader (1915). Although such propositions also have been challenged and qualified (for example, Edward Ames and Nathan Rosenberg, 1963), it is difficult to dismiss the idea of convergence on the basis of the historical experience of the industrialized world. (For more recent discussions, see also the paper by Robin Marris, with comments by Feinstein and Matthews in Matthews, 1982, pp. 12–13, 128–147, as well as Dennis Mueller, 1983.)

Using 1870–1973 data on gross domestic product (GDP) per work-year for 7 industrialized countries, M-F-O have shown graphically that those nations' productivity levels have tended to approach ever closer to one another. . . .[2]

The convergence toward the vanguard (led in the first decades by Australia—see Richard Caves and Laurence Krause, 1984—and the United Kingdom and, approximately since World War I, by the United States) is sharper than it may appear to the naked eye. In 1870, the ratio of output per work-hour in Australia, then the leader in Maddison's sample, was about eight times as great as Japan's (the laggard). By 1979, that ratio for the leader (the United States) to the laggard (still Japan) had fallen to about 2. The ratio of the standard deviation from the mean of GDP per work-hour for the 16 countries has also fallen quite steadily, except for a brief but sharp rise during World War II.

The convergence phenomenon and its pervasiveness are confirmed by Figure 15.1, on which my discussion will focus. The horizontal axis indicates each Maddison country's absolute level of GDP per work-hour in 1870. The vertical axis represents the growth rate of GDP per work-hour in the 110 years since 1870. The high inverse correlation between the two is evident. Indeed, we obtain an equation (subject to all sorts of statistical reservations)[3]

$$\textit{Growth Rate } (1870\text{--}1979) = 5.25 - 0.75ln \, (\textit{GDP} \text{ per } \textit{WorkHr, } 1870),$$
$$R^2 = 0.88.$$

That is, with a very high correlation coefficient, the higher a country's productivity level in 1870 the more slowly that level grew in the following century.

Implications of the Inverse Correlation: Public Goods Property of Productivity Policy

The strong inverse correlation between the 1870 productivity levels of the 16 nations and their subsequent productivity growth record seems to have a startling implication. Of course, hindsight always permits "forecasts" of great accuracy—that itself is not surprising. Rather, what is striking is the apparent implication that *only one variable,* a country's 1870 GDP per work-hour, or its relation to that of the productivity leader matters to any substantial degree, and that other variables have only a peripheral influence. It seems not to have mattered much whether or not a particular country had free markets, a high propensity to invest, or used policy to stimulate growth. Whatever its behavior, that nation was apparently fated to land close to its predestined position in Figure 15.1.

However, a plausible alternative interpretation is that while national policies and behavior patterns do substantially affect productivity growth, the spillovers from leader economies to followers are large—at least among the group of industrial nations. If country A's extraordinary investment level and superior record of innovation enhance its own productivity, they will almost automatically do the same in the long run for industrialized country B, though perhaps to a somewhat more limited extent. In other words, for such nations a successful productivity-enhancing measure has the nature of a public good. And because the fruits of each industrialized country's productivity-enhancement efforts are ultimately shared by others, each country remains in what appears to be its predestined *relative* place along the growth curve of Figure 15.1. I will note later some considerations which might lead one to doubt that the less developed countries will benefit comparably from this sharing process.

Figure 15.1   Productivity Growth Rate, 1870–1979 vs. 1870 Level (in percent)

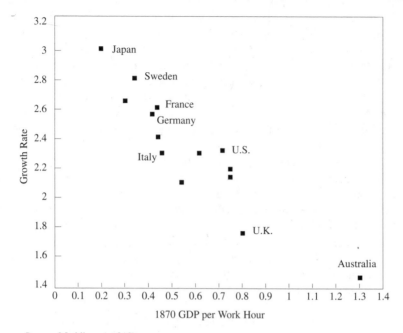

Source: Maddison (p. 212).

This sharing of productivity growth benefits by industrialized countries involves both innovation and investment. The innovation-sharing process is straightforward. If industry in country A benefits from a significant innovation, those industries in other countries which produce competing products will find themselves under pressure to obtain access to the innovation, or to an imitation or to some other substitute. Industrialized countries, whose product lines overlap substantially and which sell a good deal in markets where foreign producers of similar items are also present, will find themselves constantly running in this Schumpeterian race, while those less developed countries which supply few products competing with those of the industrialized economies will not participate to the same degree.

There is reason to suspect that the pressures for rapidity in imitation of innovation in industrial countries have been growing. The explosion in exports reported in Table 15.1 has given them a considerably larger share of gross national product than they had in 1870. This suggests that more of each nation's output faces the direct competition of foreign rivals. Thus, the penalties for failure to keep abreast of innovations *in other countries* and to imitate them where appropriate have grown.

Second, the means required for successful imitations have improved and expanded enormously. World communications are now practically instantaneous, but required weeks and even months at the birth of the Industrial Revolution. While today meetings of scientists and technicians are widely encouraged, earlier mercantilist practices entailed measures by each country to prevent other nations from learning its industrial techniques, and the emigration of specialized workers was often forbidden. Though figures in this arena are difficult to interpret, much less substantiate, one estimate claims that employment in "information activities" in the United States has grown from less than 1 percent of the labor force in 1830 to some 45 percent today (James Beniger, forthcoming, p. 364, leaning heavily on Marc Porat, 1977). Presumably, growth of the information sector in other industrialized nations has been similar. This must surely facilitate and speed the innovative, counterinnovative, and imitative tasks of the entrepreneur. The combination of direct U.S. manufacturing investment in Europe, and the technology transfer activities of multinational corporations in the postwar era were also of great significance (see, for example, David Teece, 1976). All of this, incidentally, suggests that as the forces making for convergence were stronger in the postwar era than previously, the rate of convergence should have been higher. The evidence assembled by Abramovitz (1985) on the basis of Maddison's data indicates that this is in fact what has happened.

The process that has just been described, then, provides mutual benefits, but it inherently helps productivity laggards more than leaders. For the laggards have more to learn from the leaders, and that is why the process makes for convergence.

Like innovation, investment, generally considered the second main source of growth in labor productivity, may also exhibit international public good properties. Suppose two industrialized countries, A and B, each produce two traded products: say automobiles and shoes, with the former more capital intensive. If A's investment rate is greater than B's then, with time, A's output mix will shift toward the cars while B's will move toward shoes. The increased demand for auto workers in A will raise their real wages, while A's increased demand for imports of B's shoes will raise real wages in B, and will raise the *value* of gross domestic product per labor hour in that country. Thus, even investment in country A automatically tends to have a spillover effect on value productivity and real wages *in those other countries that produce and trade in a similar array of goods.*

While, strictly speaking, the factor-price equalization theorem is not applicable to my discussion because it assumes, among other things, that technology is identical in all the countries involved, it does suggest why (for the reasons just discussed) a high investment rate may fail to bring a relative wage advantage to the investing country. In practice, the conditions of the theorem are not satisfied precisely, so countries in which investment rates are relatively high do seem to obtain increased relative real wages. Yet the analysis suggests that the absolute benefits are contagious—that one country's successful investment policy will also raise productivity and living standards in other industrialized countries.[4]

Thus, effective growth policy does contribute to a nation's living standards, but it may also help other industrialized countries and to almost the same degree; meaning that relative deviations from the patterns indicated in Figure 15.1 will be fairly small, just as the diagram shows. (However, see Abramovitz, 1985, for a discussion of the counterhypothesis, that growth of a leader creates "backwash" effects inhibiting growth of the followers.)

All this raises an obvious policy issue. If productivity growth does indeed have such public good properties, what will induce each country to invest the socially optimal effort and other resources in productivity growth, when it can instead hope to be a free rider? In part, the answer is that in Western capitalistic economies, investment is decentralized and individual firms can gain little by free riding on the actions of investors in other economies, so that the problem does not appear to be a serious one at the national policy level.

Is Convergence Ubiquitous?

Does convergence of productivity levels extend beyond the free-market industrialized countries? Or is the convergence "club" a very exclusive organization? While century-long data are not available for any large number of countries, Summers and Heston provide pertinent figures for the 30-year period 1950–80 (data for more countries are available for briefer periods).[5] Instead of labor productivity figures, they give output per capita, whose trends can with considerable reservations be used as a rough proxy for those in productivity, as Maddison's figures confirm.

Figure 15.2 tells the story. Constructed just like Figure 15.1, it plots the 1950–80 real growth rate of GDP per capita for all 72 Summers-Heston countries against the initial (1950) level of this variable. The points form no tight relationship, and unlike those for the industrial countries, the dots show no negatively sloping pattern. Indeed, a regression yields a slightly positive slope. Thus, rather than sharing in convergence, some of the poorest countries have also been growing most slowly.

Figure 15.2 brings out the patterns more clearly by surrounding the set of points representing Maddison's 16 countries with a thin boundary and the centrally planned economy points[6] with a heavier boundary. We see that the Maddison country points lie near a sort of upper-right-hand boundary, meaning that most of them had the high incomes in 1950 (as was to be expected) and, for any given per capita income, the highest growth rates between 1950 and 1980. This region is very long, narrow, and negatively sloped, with the absolute

Figure 15.2   Growth Rate, 1950–80, GDP/pc vs. 1950 Level, 72 Countries

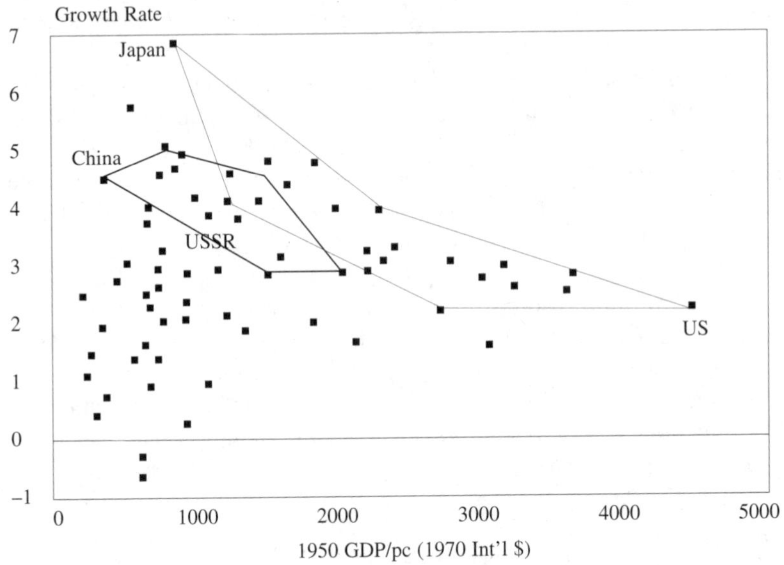

Source: Summers and Heston, 1984.

slope declining toward the right. As in the Figure 15.1, productivity data for a 110-year period, this is exactly the shape one expects with convergence. Second, we see that the centrally planned economies are members of a convergence club of their own, forming a negatively sloping region lying below and to the left of the Maddison countries. The relationship is less tight, so convergence within the group is less pronounced, but it is clearly there.

Finally, there is the region of remaining points (aside from the rightmost non-Maddison points in the graph) which lies close to the origin of the graph and occupies something like a distorted circle without any apparent slope. The points closest to the origin are less developed countries which were poor in 1950, and have grown relatively slowly since. They show no convergence among themselves, much less with other groups.

A few numbers suggest the difference in performance of various subgroups of the 72 countries. Using a four-set classification Summers, I. B. Kravis and Heston (1984, p. 254) provide Gini coefficients by decade from 1950 to 1980. For their set of industrialized countries, this coefficient falls precipitously from 0.302 in 1950 to 0.129 in 1980–a sharp drop in inequality. For the centrally planned economies the drop is much smaller—from 0.381 to 0.301. The middle-income group exhibits an even smaller decline, from 0.269 to 0.258. But the low-income countries underwent a small *rise* over the period, from 0.103 to 0.112, and the world as a whole experienced a tiny rise from 0.493 to 0.498.

There has also been little convergence among the groups. For the entire period, Summers et al. report (p. 245) an average annual growth rate in per capita real GDP of 3.1 percent for industrialized countries, 3.6 percent for centrally planned economies, 3.0 percent for middle-income market economies, and only 1.5 percent for the low-income group, with a world average group rate of 2.7 percent.

This suggests that there is more than one convergence club. Rather, there are perhaps three, with the centrally planned and the intermediate groups somewhat inferior in performance to that of the free-market industrialized countries. It is also clear that the poorer less developed countries are still largely barred from the homogenization processes. Since any search for "the causes" of a complex economic phenomenon of reality is likely to prove fruitless, no attempt will be made here to explain systematically why poorer less developed countries have benefited to a relatively small degree from the public good properties of the innovations and investments of other nations. But part of the explanation may well be related to product mix and education. A less developed country that produces no cars cannot benefit from the invention and adoption of a better car-producing robot in Japan (though it does benefit to a lesser degree from new textile and rice-growing technology), nor can it benefit from the factor-price equalization effect of the accompanying Japanese investments, since it cannot shift labor force out of its (nonexistent) auto industry as the theorem's logic requires. Lack of education and the associated skills prevent both the presence of high-tech industries and the effective imitation (adoption) of the Japanese innovation. Obviously, there is much more to any reasonably fuller explanation of the exclusion of many less developed countries from the convergence process, but that is not my purpose here. . . .

Notes

1. This observation does not quite seem to square with Charles Feinstein's estimates (1972, pp. 82–94) which indicate that while output per worker in the United Kingdom increased 0.2 percent per year between 1761 and 1800, between 1801 and 1830 the growth rate leaped up to 1.4 percent per annum. He estimates that total factor productivity behaved similarly. However, between 1801 and 1810, total annual investment fell to 10 percent of gross domestic product, in comparison with its 14 percent rate in the immediately preceding and succeeding periods.

2. Space prevents extensive consideration of Paul Romer's (1985) objection to the evidence offered for the convergence hypothesis provided here and elsewhere, i.e., that the sample of countries studied is an *ex post* selection of successful economies. Successes, by definition, are those which have done best relative to the leader. However, the Summers-Heston 1950–80 data for 72 countries represented in Figure 15.2 do permit an ex ante selection. Tests ranking countries both by 1950 and by 1960 GDP levels confirm that

even an *ex ante* sample of the wealthiest countries yields a pattern of convergence which, while less pronounced than that calculated from an *ex post* group, is still unambiguous.

3. The high correlation should not be taken too seriously. Aside from the reasons why its explanation may be misunderstood that are presently discussed in the text, the tight fit of the data points is undoubtedly ascribable in good part to several biasing features of the underlying calculation. First, the 1870 figures were calculated by Maddison using backward extrapolation of growth rates, and hence their correlation is hardly surprising. Second, since growth rate, r, is calculated by solving $y_t = e^{rt}y^0$ for r, to obtain $r = (\ln y_t - \ln y_0)/t$, where $y_t = GDP$ per capita in period t, a regression equation $r = f(y_0)$ contains the same variable, y_0 on both sides of the equation, thus tending to produce a spurious appearance of close relationship. Indeed, if the convergence process were perfect, so that we would have $y_t = k$ with k the same for every country in the sample, every dot in the diagram would necessarily perfectly fit the curve $r = lnk/t - lny_0/t$, and the r^2 would be unity, identically. The 72-country data depicted in Figure 12.2 hardly constitute a close fit (the R^2 is virtually zero), and do not even yield a negatively sloping regression line. Thus, a relationship such as that in Figure 12.1 is no tautology, nor even a foregone conclusion.

In addition, if the 1870 productivity levels are measured with considerable error, this must result in some significant downward bias in the regression coefficient on $ln(GDP$ per $WorkHr$, 1870). This is a point distinct from the one concerning the size of the correlation coefficient, although the latter is affected by the fact that relatively large measurement errors in the 1870 productivity levels enter as inversely correlated measurement errors in the 1870–1979 growth rate. The argument that this bias is not sufficient to induce a negative correlation in the 72-country sample may not be wholly germane, as the relative seriousness of the measurement errors in the initial and terminal observations may be much the same for observations confined to the period 1950–80.

4. It must be conceded that the longer-run data do not seem to offer impressive support for the hypothesis that the forces of factor-price equalization have, albeit imperfectly, extended the benefits of exceptional rates of investment from those economies that carried out the successful investment programs to other industrialized economies. Since we have estimates of relative real wages, capital stock, and other pertinent variables for the United Kingdom and Germany, these have been compared below:

	Period	Ratio: German Increase to U.K. Increase[b]
Real Wages	1860–1980	4.25
GDP per Labor Hour	1870–1979	2.35
Capital Stock[a]	1870–1979	6.26
Capital Stock per Worker	1870–1979	3.8
Capital Stock per Capita	1870–1979	5.4

Sources: Real wages, same as in Note 6 [of original text; not included here]; all other data from Maddison.

Notes: a. Net nonresidential fixed tangible capital stock.

b. (German 1979 figure/German 1870 figure)/(U.K. 1979 figure/U.K. 1987 figure) with appropriate modification of the dates for the wage figures.

If the public goods attribute hypothesis about the effects of investment in one country were valid and if factor-price equalization were an effective force, we would expect the relative rise in German real wages and in productivity to be small (on some criterion) in comparison with the relative increase in its capital stock. However, the figures do not seem to exhibit such a pattern.

5. There are at least two sources of such data: the World Bank and the University of Pennsylvania group. Here I report only data drawn from the latter, since their international comparisons have been carried out with unique sophistication and insight. Instead of translating the different currencies into one another using inadequate exchange rate comparisons, they use carefully constructed indices of relative purchasing power. I have also replicated my calculations using World Bank data and obtained exactly the same qualitative results.

6. The centrally planned economies are Bulgaria, China, Czechoslovakia, East Germany, Hungary, Poland, Romania, USSR, and Yugoslavia. The 5 countries with relatively high 1950 incomes included neither in Maddison's sample nor in the planned group are, in descending order of GDP per capita, Luxembourg, New Zealand, Iceland, Venezuela, and Argentina. The countries with negative growth rates are Uganda and Nigeria.

References

Abramovitz, Moses. 1979. "Rapid Growth Potential and Its Realization: The Experience of the Capitalist Economies in the Postwar Period," in Edmond Malinvaud, ed., *Economic Growth and Resources, Proceedings of the Fifth World Congress of the International Economic Association,* Vol. 1, London: Macmillan.

————. 1985. "Catching Up and Falling Behind," delivered at the Economic History Association, September 20, 1985.

Ames, Edward and Rosenberg, Nathan. 1963. "Changing Technological Leadership and Industrial Growth," *Economic Journal* 73 (March): 13–31.

Beniger, James R. Forthcoming. *The Control Revolution: Technological and Economic Origins of the Information Society.* Cambridge: Harvard University Press.

Caves, Richard E. and Krause, Lawrence B. 1984. *The Australian Economy: A View from the North.* Washington: The Brookings Institution.

Cipolla, Carlo M. 1976. *Before the Industrial Revolution: European Society and Economy, 1000–1700.* New York: W. W. Norton.

Clark, Colin. 1957. *The Conditions of Economic Progress,* 3rd ed. London: Macmillan.

Darby, Michael. 1984. "The U.S. Productivity Slowdown: A Case of Statistical Myopia," *American Economic Review,* 74 (June): 301–322.

David, Paul A. 1977. "Invention and Accumulation in America's Economic Growth: A Nineteenth-Century Parable," in K. Brunner and A. H. Meltzer, eds., *International Organization, National Policies and Economic Development,* pp. 179–228. Amsterdam: North-Holland.

Deane, Phyllis and Cole, W. A. 1962. *British Economic Growth 1688–1959.* Cambridge: Cambridge University Press.

Feinstein, Charles. 1972. *National Income, Expenditure and Output of the United Kingdom, 1855–1965.* Cambridge: Cambridge University Press.

Gerschenkron, Alexander. 1952. "Economic Backwardness in Historical Perspective," in Bert F. Hoselitz, ed., *The Progress of Underdeveloped Areas.* Chicago: University of Chicago Press.

Landes, David S. 1969. *The Unbound Prometheus.* Cambridge: Cambridge University Press.

Lawrence, Robert Z. 1984. *Can America Compete?* Washington: The Brookings Institution.

Maddison, Angus. 1982. *Phases of Capitalist Development.* New York: Oxford University Press.

Marx, Karl and Engels, Friedrich. 1946. *Manifesto of the Communist Party* (1848). London: Lawrence and Wishart.

Matthews, R.C.O. 1982. *Slower Growth in the Western World.* London: Heinemann.

———, Feinstein, C. H. and Odling-Smee, J. C. 1982. *British Economic Growth, 1856–1973.* Stanford: Stanford University Press.

McCloskey, D. N. 1981. *Enterprise and Trade in Victorian Britain.* London: Allen & Unwin.

Mueller, Dennis C. 1983. *The Political Economy of Growth.* New Haven: Yale University Press.

Phelps Brown, E. H. and Hopkins, S. V. 1955. "Seven Centuries of Building Wages," *Economica,* 22 (August): 195–206.

———. 1956. "Seven Centuries of the Prices of Consumables," *Economica,* 23 (November): 296–314.

Porat, Marc Uri. 1977. "The Information Economy, Definitions and Measurement," Office of Telecommunications, Special Publication, 77-12(1), U.S. Department of Commerce, Washington.

Romer, Paul M. 1985. "Increasing Returns and Long Run Growth," Working Paper No. 27. University of Rochester, October.

Summers, Robert and Heston, Alan. 1984. "Improved International Comparisons of Real Product and Its Composition, 1950–1980," *Review of Income and Wealth,* 30 (June): 207–262.

Summers, Robert, Kravis, I. B., and Heston, Alan. 1986. "Changes in World Income Distribution," *Journal of Policy Modeling,* 6 (May): 237–269.

Teece, David J. 1976. *The Multinational Corporation and the Resources Cost of International Technology Transfer.* Cambridge: Ballinger.

U.S. Bureau of Census. 1973. *Long Term Economic Growth 1860–1970.* Washington, D.C., June.

Veblen, Thorstein. 1915. *Imperial Germany and the Industrial Revolution.* New York: Macmillan.

Viner, Jacob. 1958. *The Long View and the Short.* Glencoe: Free Press.

Williamson, Jeffrey G. 1983. "Why Was British Growth So Slow During the Industrial Revolution?" Unpublished, Harvard Institute of Economic Research.

16

Productivity Growth, Convergence, and Welfare: Comment

J. Bradford De Long

In the previous chapter, William Baumol confirmed the expectations of convergence theory by finding that between 1870 and 1979, productivity rates of poorer countries grew more rapidly than those of richer countries. In this chapter, J. Bradford De Long argues that because only countries that converged by 1979 were included in the data set used by Baumol, convergence was ensured. When De Long corrects for this sample-selection bias, convergence disappears. De Long then analyzes other variables to determine if the pattern of growth that he found can be explained. He does not find an association between democracy in 1870 and subsequent growth. De Long did find a significant relationship between religion and growth: Protestant cultures grew faster. But the author notes that the correlations will not hold for long given the growth rates of countries such as Japan and Italy. The optimistic view that there is a process of economic homogenization, a closing of the gap between rich and poor, is not sustained by the data. As the author concludes, "It pushes us away from the belief that even the nations of the now industrial West will have roughly equal standards of living in 2090 or 2190." ∎

ECONOMISTS HAVE ALWAYS EXPECTED THE "CONVERGENCE" OF NATIONAL PRODUCtivity levels. The theoretical logic behind this belief is powerful. The per capita income edge of the West is based on its application of the storehouse of industrial and administrative technology of the Industrial Revolution. This storehouse

Reprinted with permission from the *American Economic Review,* vol. 78, no. 5 (1986): 1038–1048.

is open: modern technology is a public good. The benefits of tapping this store-house are great, and so nations will strain every nerve to assimilate modern technology and their incomes will converge to those of industrial nations.

William Baumol (1986) argues that convergence has shown itself strongly in the growth of industrial nations since 1870.[1] According to Baumol, those nations positioned to industrialize are much closer together in productivity now than a century ago. He bases this conclusion on a regression of growth since 1870 on 1870 productivity for sixteen countries covered by Angus Maddison (1982).[2]

Baumol's finding of convergence might—even though Baumol himself does not believe that it should—naturally be read to support two further conclusions. First, slow relative growth in the United States since World War II was inevitable: convergence implies that in the long run divergent national cultures, institutions, or policies cannot sustain significant productivity edges over the rest of the developed world. Second, one can be optimistic about future development. Maddison's sixteen all assimilated modern technology and converged; perhaps all developing nations will converge to Western living standards once they acquire a foundation of technological literacy.

But when properly interpreted Baumol's finding is less informative than one might think. For Baumol's regression uses an *ex post* sample of countries that are now rich and have successfully developed. By Maddison's choice, those nations that have not converged are excluded from his sample because of their resulting present relative poverty. Convergence is thus all but guaranteed in Baumol's regression, which tells us little about the strength of the forces making for convergence among nations that in 1870 belonged to what Baumol calls the "convergence club."

Only a regression run on an *ex ante* sample, a sample not of nations that have converged but of nations that seemed in 1870 likely to converge, can tell us whether growth since 1870 exhibits "convergence." The answer to this *ex ante* question—have those nations that a century ago appeared well placed to appropriate and utilize industrial technology converged?—is no. . . .

Maddison (1982) compiles long-run national income and aggregate productivity data for sixteen successful capitalist nations.[3] Because he focuses on nations which (a) have a rich data base for the construction of historical national accounts and (b) have successfully developed, the nations in Maddison's sixteen are among the richest nations in the world today. Baumol regresses the average rate of annual labor productivity growth over 1870–1979 on a constant and on the log of labor productivity in 1870 for this sample. He finds the inverse relationship of the first line of Table 16.1. The slope is large enough to erase by 1979 almost all initial income gaps, and the residual variance is small.

Regressing the log difference in per capita income between 1870 and 1979 on a constant and the log of per capita income in 1870 provides a slightly stronger case for convergence, as detailed in the second line of Table 16.1. The

Table 16.1   Regressions Using Maddison's Sixteen

Independent Variable	Dependent Variable	Constant	Slope Coefficient	Standard Error of Estimate	R^2
Natural Log of 1870 Productivity	Annual Percent Productivity Growth	5.251	−0.749 .075	.14	.87
Natural Log of 1870 Income	Log Difference of 1979 and 1870 Income	8.457	−0.995 .094	.15	.88

Source: Data from Maddison (1982).

logarithmic income specification offers two advantages. The slope has the intuitive interpretation that a value of minus one means that 1979 and 1870 relative incomes are uncorrelated, and extension of the sample to include additional nations becomes easier.

Baumol's regression line tells us little about the strength of forces making for convergence since 1870 among industrial nations. The sample suffers from selection bias, and the independent variable is unavoidably measured with error. Both of these create the appearance of convergence whether or not it exists in reality. Sample selection bias arises because any nations relatively rich in 1870 that have not converged fail to make it into Maddison's sixteen. Maddison's sixteen thus include Norway but not Spain, Canada but not Argentina, and Italy but not Ireland. . . .

The unbiased sample used here meets three criteria. First, it is made up of nations that had high potential for economic growth as of 1870, in which modern economic growth had begun to take hold by the middle of the nineteenth century. Second, inclusion in the sample is not conditional on subsequent rapid growth. Third, the sample matches Baumol's as closely as possible, both because the best data exist for Maddison's sixteen and because analyzing an unbiased sample close to Baumol's shows that different conclusions arise not from different estimates but from removing sample selection and errors in variables' biases.

Per capita income in 1870 is an obvious measure of whether a nation was sufficiently technologically literate and integrated into world trade in 1870 to be counted among the potential convergers. . . .

. . . The choice of cutoff level itself requires balancing three goals: including only nations which really did in 1870 possess the social capability for rapid industrialization; including as many nations in Baumol's sample as possible; and building as large a sample as possible. . . .

If the convergence club membership cutoff is set low enough to include all Maddison's sixteen, then nations with 1870 incomes above 300 1975 dollars are included. This sample covers half the world. All Europe including

Russia, all of South America, and perhaps others (Mexico and Cuba?) were richer than Japan in 1870. This sample does not provide a fair test of convergence. The Japanese miracle is a miracle largely because there was little sign in 1870 that Japan—or any nation as poor as Japan—was a candidate for rapid industrialization.

The second poorest of Maddison's sixteen in 1870 was Finland. Taking Finland's 1870 income as a cutoff leads to a sample in which Japan is removed, while Argentina, Chile, East Germany,[4] Ireland, New Zealand, Portugal, and Spain are added. . . .

All the additional nations have strong claims to belong to the 1870 convergence club. All were well integrated into the Europe-based international economy. All had bright development prospects as of 1870. . . . Argentina, Chile, and New Zealand were grouped in the nineteenth century with Australia and Canada as countries with temperate climates, richly endowed with natural resources, attracting large-scale immigration and investment, and exporting large quantities of raw and processed agricultural commodities. They were all seen as natural candidates for the next wave of industrialization.

Ireland's economy was closely integrated with the most industrialized economy in the world. Spain and Portugal had been the technological leaders of Europe during the initial centuries of overseas expansion—their per capita incomes were still above the European mean in the 1830s (Paul Bairoch, 1981)—and had retained close trading links with the heart of industrial Europe. Coke was used to smelt iron in Asturias in the 1850s, and by 1877 3,950 miles of railroad had been built in Spain. It is difficult to see how one could exclude Portugal and Spain from the convergence club without also excluding nations like Sweden and Finland.

Baumol's sample failed to include those nations that should have belonged to any hypothetical convergence club but that nevertheless did not converge. The enlarged sample might include nations not in the 1870 convergence club. Consider Kuwait today: Kuwait is rich, yet few would take its failure to maintain its relative standard of living over the next fifty years as evidence against convergence. For Kuwait's present wealth does not necessarily carry with it the institutional capability to turn oil wealth into next generation's industrial wealth. . . .

The volume of overseas investment poured into the additional nations by investors from London and Paris between 1870 and 1913 tells us that investors thought these nations' development prospects good. Herbert Feis' (1930) standard estimates of French and British overseas investment [the interested reader should refer to Table 2, p. 1,143 of the original article] show the six non-European nations among the top ten[5] recipients of investment per capita from France and Britain, and four of the five top recipients of investment belong to the once-rich twenty-two.[6] Every pound or franc invested is an explicit bet that the recipient country's rate of profit will remain high and an implicit bet that its rate of economic growth will be rapid. The coincidence of the nations added on a per capita income basis and the nations that would have been added on a foreign investment basis is powerful evidence that these nations do belong in the potential convergence club.

Errors in estimating 1870 income are unavoidable and produce equal and opposite errors in 1870–1979 growth. These errors therefore create the appearance of convergence where it does not exist in reality. . . .[7]

From one point of view, the relatively poor quality of much of the nineteenth century data is not a severe liability for this chapter. Only if there is less measurement error than allowed for will the results be biased against convergence. A more direct check on the importance of measurement error can be performed by examining convergence starting at some later date for which income estimates are based on a firmer foundation. A natural such date is 1913.[8] The relationship between initial income and subsequent growth is examined for the period 1913–1979 in Table 16.2.

The longer 1870–1979 sample of Table 16.3 . . . is slightly more hospitable to convergence than is the 1913–1979 sample, but for neither sample do the regression lines reveal a significant inverse relationship between initial income and subsequent growth. When it is assumed that there is no measurement error

Table 16.2   Maximum Likelihood Estimation for the Once-Rich Twenty-Two, 1913–1979

p	Slope Coefficient B	Standard Error of Slope	Standard Error of Regression	Standard Error in 1870 PCI
0.0	−.333	.116	.171	.000
0.5	−.140	.136	.151	.107
1.0	0.021	.158	.133	.133
2.0	0.206	.191	.106	.150
Infinity	0.444	.238	.000	.167

Source: Data from Maddison (1982).

Table 16.3   Maximum Likelihood Estimation for the Once-Rich Twenty-Two, 1870–1979

p	Slope Coefficient B	Standard Error of Slope	Standard Error of Regression	Standard Error in 1870 PCI
0.0	−.566	.144	.207	.000
0.5	−.292	.192	.192	.136
1.0	0.110	.283	.170	.170
2.0	0.669	.463	.134	.190
Infinity	1.381	.760	.000	.196

Source: Data from Maddison (1982).

in 1870 income, there is a large negative slope to the regression line. But even in this case the residual disturbance term is large. When measurement error variance is assumed equal to half disturbance variance, the slope is slightly but not significantly negative.

For the central case of equal variances growth since 1870 is unrelated to income in 1870. There is no convergence. Those countries with income edges have on average maintained them. If measurement error is assumed larger than the regression disturbance there is not convergence but divergence. Nations rich in 1870 or 1913 have subsequently widened relative income gaps. The evidence can be presented in other ways. The standard deviations of log income are given in Table 16.4. Maddison's sixteen do converge: the standard deviation of log income in 1979 is only 35 percent of its 1870 value. But the appearance of convergence is due to selection bias: the once-rich twenty-two have as wide a spread of relative incomes today as in 1870.

The failure of convergence to emerge for nations rich in 1870 is due to the nations—Chile, Argentina, Spain, and Portugal. In the early 1970s none of these was a democracy. Perhaps only industrial nations with democratic political systems converge. A dummy variable for democracy over 1950–80 is significant in the central ($p = 1$) case in the once-rich twenty-two regression in a at the 1 percent level, as detailed in Table 16.5.

But whether a nation is a democracy over 1950–80 is not exogenous but is partly determined by growth over the preceding century. As of 1870 it was

Table 16.4   Standard Deviations of Log Output for Maddison's Sixteen and the Once-Rich Twenty-Two

Sample	1870	1913	1979
Maddison's 16	.411	.355	.145
Once-Rich 22	.315	.324	.329

Source: Data from Maddison (1982).

Table 16.5   Democracy over 1950–1980 and Long-Run Growth for the Once-Rich Twenty-Two, 1870–1979

p	Slope Coefficient B	Standard Error of Slope	Coefficient on Democracy Variable	Standard Error	Standard Error in 1870 PCI	Standard Error of Regression
0.0	−.817	.277	.495	.085	.155	.000
0.5	−.744	.203	.476	.084	.154	.109
1.0	−.599	.208	.437	.090	.150	.150
2.0	0.104	.227	.248	.071	.131	.185
Infinity	1.137	.019	.044	.003	.000	.198

Source: Data from Maddison (1982).

not at all clear which nations would become stable democracies. Of the once-rich twenty-two, France, Austria (including Czechoslovakia), and Germany were empires; Britain had a restricted franchise; Spain and Portugal were semiconstitutional monarchies; the United States had just undergone a civil war; and Ireland was under foreign occupation. That all of these countries would be stable democracies by 1950 seems *ex ante* unlikely. Table 16.6 shows that shifting to an *ex ante* measure of democracy[9] removes the correlation. Whether a nation's politics are democratic in 1870 has little to do with growth since. The elective affinity of democracy and opulence is not one way with democracy as cause and opulence as effect.

There is one striking *ex ante* association between growth over 1870–1979 and a predetermined variable: a nation's dominant religious establishment. As Table 16.7 shows, a religious establishment variable that is one for Protestant, one-half for mixed, and zero for Catholic nations is significantly correlated with growth as long as measurement error variance is not too high.[10]

This regression is very difficult to interpret.[11] It does serve as an example of how culture may be associated with substantial divergence in growth

Table 16.6   Democracy in 1870 and Long-Run Growth for the Once-Rich Twenty-Two, 1870–1979

p	Slope Coefficient B	Standard Error of Slope	Coefficient on Democracy Variable	Standard Error	Standard Error in 1870 PCI	Standard Error of Regression
0.0	−.567	.342	.001	.091	.207	.000
0.5	−.272	.322	−.038	.094	.192	.136
1.0	0.164	.454	−.095	.115	.169	.169
2.0	0.742	.976	−.170	.180	.131	.155
Infinity	1.231	.167	−.195	.022	.000	.194

Source: Data from Maddison (1982).

Table 16.7   Dominant Religion in 1870 and Long-Run Growth for the Once-Rich Twenty-Two, 1870–1979

p	Slope Coefficient B	Standard Error of Slope	Coefficient on Democracy Variable	Standard Error	Standard Error in 1870 PCI	Standard Error of Regression
0.0	−.789	.252	.429	.088	.166	.000
0.5	−.688	.225	.403	.088	.164	.116
1.0	−.470	.248	.347	.098	.158	.158
2.0	0.375	.232	.132	.061	.132	.187
Infinity	1.199	.021	−.003	.004	.000	.197

Source: Data from Maddison (1982).

performance. But "Protestantism" is correlated with many things—early specialization in manufacturing (for a given level of income), a high investment ratio, and a northern latitude, to name three. Almost any view—except a belief in convergence—of what determines long-run growth is consistent with this correlation between growth and religious establishment. Moreover, this correlation will not last: neither fast grower Japan nor fast grower Italy owes anything to the Protestant ethic. The main message of Table 16.7 is that, for the once-rich twenty-two, a country's religious establishment has been a surprisingly good proxy for the social capability to assimilate modern technology.

The long-run data do not show convergence on any but the most optimistic reading. They do not support the claim that those nations that should have been able to rapidly assimilate industrial technology have all converged. Nations rich among the once-rich twenty-two in 1870 have not grown more slowly than the average of the sample. And of the nations outside this sample, only Japan has joined the industrial leaders.

This is not to say that there are no forces pushing for convergence. Convergence does sometimes happen. Technology is a public good. Western Europe (except Iberia) and the British settlement colonies of Australia, Canada, and the United States are now all developed. Even Italy, which seemed outside the sphere of advanced capitalism two generations ago, is near the present income frontier reached by the richest nations. The convergence of Japan and Western Europe toward U.S. standards of productivity in the years after World War II is an amazing achievement, and this does suggest that those present at the creation of the post–World War II international order did a very good job. But others—Spain, Portugal, Ireland, Argentina, and Chile—that one would in 1870 have thought capable of equally sharing this prosperity have not done so.[12] The capability to assimilate industrial technology appears to be surprisingly hard to acquire, and it may be distressingly easy to lose.

The forces making for "convergence" even among industrial nations appear little stronger than the forces making for "divergence." The absence of convergence pushes us away from a belief that in the long run technology transfer both is inevitable and is the key factor in economic growth. It pushes us away from the belief that even the nations of the now industrial West will have roughly equal standards of living in 2090 or 2190. And the absence of convergence even among nations relatively rich in 1870 forces us to take seriously arguments like Romer's (1986) that the relative income gap between rich and poor may tend to widen.

Notes

1. Consider Baumol (1986): "Among the main observations . . . is the remarkable convergence. . . . [T]here is a strong inverse correlation between a country's productiv-

ity . . . in 1870 and its . . . productivity growth since then," and Baumol (1987): "Even more remarkable . . . is the convergence in . . . living standards of the leading industrial countries. . . . In 1870 . . . productivity in Australia, the leader, was 8 times . . . Japan's (the laggard). By 1979, the ratio . . . had fallen to about two."

2. Moses Abramovitz (1986) follows the behavior of these sixteen over time and notes that even among these nations "convergence" is almost entirely a post–World War II phenomenon. Abramovitz' remarks on how the absence of the "social capability" to grasp the benefits of the Industrial Revolution may prevent even nations that could benefit greatly from industrializing are well worth reading. Also very good on the possible determinants of the social capability to assimilate technology are Irma Adelman and Cynthia Taft Morris (1980), Gregory Clark (1987), and Richard Easterlin (1981).

3. Maddison's focus on nations that have been economically successful is deliberate; his aim in (1964), (1982), and (1987) is to investigate the features of successful capitalist development. In works like Maddison (1970, 1983) he has analyzed the long-run growth and development of less successful nations.

4. Perhaps only nations that have remained capitalist should be included in the sample, for occupation by the Red Army and subsequent relative economic stagnation have no bearing on whether the forces making for convergence among industrial capitalist economies are strong. There is only one centrally planned economy in the unbiased sample, and its removal has negligible quantitative effects on the estimated degree of convergence.

5. The foreign investment figures do provide a powerful argument for adding other Latin American nations—Mexico, Brazil, and Cuba—to the sample of those that ought to have been in the convergence club. Inclusion of these nations would weigh heavily against convergence.

6. Japan would not merit inclusion in the 1870 convergence club on the basis of foreign investment before World War I, for Japanese industrialization was not financed by British capital. Foreign investors' taste for Japan was much less, investment being equal to about one pound sterling per head and far below investment in such nations as Venezuela, Russia, Turkey, and Egypt. Admittedly, Japan was far away and not well known, but who would have predicted that Japan would have five times the measured per capita GNP of Argentina by 1979?

7. By contrast, errors in measuring 1979 per capita income induce no systematic bias in the relationship between standard of living in 1870 and growth since, although they do diminish the precision of coefficient estimates.

8. The data for 1913 are much more plentiful and solid than for other years in the early years of the twentieth century because of the concentration of historians' efforts on obtaining a pre–World War I benchmark. Beginning the sample at 1913 does mean that changes in country's "social capability" for development as a result of World War I appear in the error term in the regression. If those nations that suffered most badly in World War I were nations relatively poor in World War I, there would be cause for alarm that the choice of 1913 had biased the sample against finding convergence when it was really present. But the major battlefields of World War I lay in and the largest proportional casualties were suffered by relatively rich nations at the core of industrial Europe.

9. Defined as inclusion of the electorate of more than half the adult male population.

10. The once-rich twenty-two are split into nations that had Protestant religious establishments in 1870 (Australia, Denmark, Finland, E. Germany, Netherlands, New Zealand, Norway, Sweden, U.K., and United States), intermediate nations—nations

that either were split in established religion in 1870 or that had undergone violent and prolonged religious wars between Protestant and Catholics in the centuries after the Protestant Reformation—(Belgium, Canada, France, West Germany, and Switzerland), and nations that had solid Catholic religious establishments in 1870 (Argentina, Austria, Chile, Ireland, Italy, Portugal, and Spain). This classification is judgmental and a matter of taste: are the Netherlands one of the heartlands of the Protestant Ethic or are they one of the few nations tolerant and pluralistic on matters of religion in the seventeenth century?

11. The easy explanation would begin with the medieval maxim *homo mercato vix aut numquam placere potest Deo:* the merchant's business can never please God. Medieval religious discipline was hostile to market capitalism, the Protestant Reformation broke this discipline down in some places, and capitalism flourished most and modern democratic growth took hold strongest where this breakdown of medieval discipline had been most complete.

But this easy explanation is at best incomplete. Initially the Reformation did not see a relaxation of religious control. Strong Protestantism—Calvin's Geneva or Cromwell's Republic of the Saints—saw theology and economy closely linked in a manner not unlike the Ayatollah's Iran. And religious fanaticism is not often thought of as a source of economic growth.

Nevertheless the disapproval of self-interested profit seeking by radical Protestantism went hand-in-hand with seventeenth century economic development. And by 1800 profit seeking and accumulation for accumulation's sake had become morally praiseworthy activities in many nations with Protestant religious establishments. How was the original Protestant disapproval for the market transformed? Accounting for the evolution of the economic ethic of the Protestant West from Jean Calvin to Cotton Mather to Benjamin Franklin to Andrew Carnegie is a deep puzzle in economic history. The best analysis may still be the psychological account given by Max Weber (1958). Originally published in 1905.

12. One can find good reasons—ranging from the Red Army to landlord political dominance to the legacy of imperialism—for the failure of each of the additional nations to have reached the world's achieved per capita income frontier in 1979. But the fact that there are good reasons for the relative economic failure of each of these seven nations casts substantial doubt on the claim that the future will see convergence, for "good reasons" for economic failure will always be widespread. It is a safe bet that in 2090 one will be able ex post to identify similar "good reasons" lying behind the relative economic decline of those nations that will have fallen out of the industrial core.

References

Abramovitz, M. 1986. "Catching Up, Forging Ahead, and Falling Behind," *Journal of Economic History,* June, 46: 385–406.

Adelman, I. and C. T. Morris. 1980. "Patterns of Industrialization in the Nineteenth and Early Twentieth Centuries," in Paul Uselding, ed., *Research in Economic History,* Vol. 5, Greenwich: JAI Press, 217–46.

Bairoch, P. 1981. "The Main Trends in National Economic Disparities Since the Industrial Revolution," in P. Bairoch and M. Lévy-Leboyer, eds., *Disparities in Economic Development Since the Industrial Revolution,* New York: St. Martin's Press.

Baumol, W. 1987. "America's Productivity 'Crisis'," *The New York Times,* February 15, 3:2.

———. 1986. "Productivity Growth, Convergence, and Welfare," *American Economic Review,* December, 76: 1072–85.

Clark, G. 1987. "Why Isn't the Whole World Developed? Lessons from the Cotton Mills," *Journal of Economic History,* March, 47: 141–74.

Easterlin, R. 1981. "Why Isn't the Whole World Developed?," *Journal of Economic History,* March, 41: 1–19.

Feis, H. 1930. *Europe, The World's Banker,* New Haven: Yale.

Maddison, A. 1987. "Growth and Slowdown in Advanced Capitalist Economies," *Journal of Economic Literature,* June, 25: 649–98.

———. 1983. "A Comparison of Levels of GDP per Capita in Developed and Developing Countries, 1700–1980," *Journal of Economic History,* March, 43: 27–41.

———. 1982. *Phases of Capitalist Development,* Oxford: Oxford University Press.

———. 1970. *Economic Progress and Policy in Developing Countries,* London: Allen & Unwin.

———. 1964. *Economic Growth in the West,* New York: The Twentieth Century Fund.

Romer, P. 1986. "Increasing Returns and Long Run Growth," *Journal of Political Economy,* October, 94: 1002–37.

Weber, M. 1958. *The Protestant Ethic and the Spirit of Capitalism,* New York: Scribner's. Originally published in 1905.

PART 5

Culture and Development

17

The Achievement Motive in Economic Growth

DAVID C. MCCLELLAND

In this chapter, David C. McClelland, a psychologist, expands upon ideas developed by Max Weber, who examined the relationship between the Protestant ethic and the rise of capitalism. McClelland posits a more generalized psychological attribute he calls the "need for Achievement," or n Achievement. In this discussion, which is a summary of a book on the subject, McClelland presents some very interesting historical data he believes help explain the rise and decline of Athenian civilization. Turning to the present century, he produces data that show a close association between national levels of n Achievement and rates of economic growth. In seeking to determine what produces this psychological characteristic, McClelland finds that it is not hereditary but rather is instilled in people. It is therefore possible, he claims, to teach people how to increase their need to achieve and by so doing stimulate economic growth in developing countries. McClelland has been responsible for establishing training and management programs in developing countries in hopes that a change in the psychological orientation of public officials will help speed economic growth. ▪

FROM THE BEGINNING OF RECORDED HISTORY, MEN HAVE BEEN FASCINATED BY THE fact that civilizations rise and fall. Culture growth, as A. L. Kroeber has demonstrated, is episodic, and sometimes occurs in quite different fields.[1] For example, the people living in the Italian peninsula at the time of ancient Rome produced a great civilization of law, politics, and military conquest; and at another time, during the Renaissance, the inhabitants of Italy produced a great civilization of art, music, letters, and science. What can account for such cultural flowerings? In our time we have theorists like Ellsworth Huntington, who stresses the importance of climate, or Arnold J. Toynbee, who also feels the right amount of challenge from the environment is crucial though he conceives of the environment as including its psychic effects. Others, like Kroeber, have difficulty imagining any general explanation; they perforce must accept the notion that a particular culture happens to hit on a particularly happy mode of self-expression, which it then pursues until it becomes overspecialized and sterile.

My concern is not with all culture growth, but with economic growth. Some wealth or leisure may be essential to development in other fields—the arts, politics, science, or war—but we need not insist on it. However, the question of why some countries develop rapidly in the economic sphere at certain times and not at others is in itself of great interest, whatever its relation to other types of culture growth. Usually, rapid economic growth has been explained in terms of "external" factors—favorable opportunities for trade, unusual natural resources, or conquests that have opened up new markets or produced internal political stability. But I am interested in the *internal* factors—in the values and motives men have that lead them to exploit opportunities, to take advantage of favorable trade conditions; in short, to shape their own destiny. . . .

Whatever else one thinks of Freud and the other psychoanalysts, they performed one extremely important service for psychology: once and for all, they persuaded us, rightly or wrongly, that what people said about their motives was not a reliable basis for determining what those motives really were. In his analyses of the psychopathology of everyday life and of dreams and neurotic symptoms, Freud demonstrated repeatedly that the "obvious" motives—the motives that the people themselves thought they had or that a reasonable observer would attribute to them—were not, in fact, the real motives for their often strange behavior. By the same token, Freud also showed the way to a better method of learning what people's motives were. He analyzed dreams and free associations: in short, fantasy or imaginative behavior. Stripped of its air of mystery and the occult, psychoanalysis has taught us that one can learn a great deal about people's motives through observing the things about which they are spontaneously concerned in their dreams and waking fantasies. About ten or twelve years ago, the research group in America with which I was connected decided to take this insight quite seriously and to see what we could learn about human motivation by coding objectively what people spontaneously thought about in their waking fantasies.[2] Our method was to collect such free fantasy, in the form of brief stories written about pictures, and to count the frequency with which certain themes appeared—rather as a medical technician counts the frequency with which red or white corpuscles appear in a blood sample. We were able to demonstrate that the frequency with which certain "inner concerns" appeared in these fantasies varied systematically as a function of specific experimental conditions by which we aroused or induced motivational states in the subjects. Eventually we were able to isolate several of these inner concerns, or motives, which, if present in great frequency in the fantasies of a particular person, enabled us to know something about how he would behave in many other areas of life.

Chief among these motives was what we termed "the need for Achievement" (n Achievement)—a desire to do well, not so much for the sake of social recognition or prestige, but to attain an inner feeling of personal accomplishment. This motive is my particular concern in this chapter. Our early laboratory studies showed that people "high" in n Achievement tend to work harder at certain tasks; to learn faster; to do their best work when it counts for the record, and not when special incentives, like money prizes, are introduced; to choose experts over friends as working partners; etc. Obviously, we cannot here review the many, many studies in this area. About five years ago, we became especially interested in the problem of what would happen in a society if a large number of people with a high need for achievement should happen to be present in it at a particular time. In other words, we became interested in a social-psychological question: What effect would a concentration of people with high n Achievement have on a society?

It might be relevant to describe how we began wondering about this. I had always been greatly impressed by the very perceptive analysis of the connection between Protestantism and the spirit of capitalism made by the great German sociologist, Max Weber.[3] He argues that the distinguishing characteristic of Protestant business entrepreneurs and of workers, particularly from the pietistic sects, was not that they had in any sense invented the institutions of capitalism or good craftsmanship, but that they went about their jobs with a new perfectionist spirit. The Calvinistic doctrine of predestination had forced them to rationalize every aspect of their lives and to strive hard for perfection in the positions in this world to which they had been assigned by God. As I read Weber's description of the behavior of these people, I concluded that they must certainly have had a high level of n Achievement. Perhaps the new spirit of capitalism Weber describes was none other than a high need for achievement—if so, then n Achievement has been responsible, in part, for the extraordinary economic development of the West. Another factor served to confirm this hypothesis. A careful study by M. R. Winterbottom had shown that boys with high n Achievement usually came from families in which the mothers stressed early self-reliance and mastery.[4] The boys whose mothers did not encourage their early self-reliance, or did not set such high standards of excellence, tended to develop lower need for achievement. Obviously, one of the key characteristics of the Protestant Reformation was its emphasis on self-reliance. Luther stressed the "priesthood of all believers" and translated the Bible so that every man could have direct access to God and religious thought. Calvin accentuated a rationalized perfection in this life for everyone. Certainly, the character of the Reformation seems to have set the stage, historically, for parents to encourage their children to attain earlier self-reliance and achievement. If the parents did in fact do so, they very possibly unintentionally produced the higher level of *n* Achievement in their children that was, in turn, responsible for the new spirit of capitalism.

This was the hypothesis that initiated our research. It was, of course, only a promising idea; much work was necessary to determine its validity. Very early in our studies, we decided that the events Weber discusses were probably only a special case of a much more general phenomenon—that it was *n* Achievement as such that was connected with economic development, and that the Protestant Reformation was connected only indirectly in the extent to which it had influenced the average *n* Achievement level of its adherents. If this assumption is correct, then a high average level of *n* Achievement should be equally associated with economic development in ancient Greece, in modern Japan, or in a preliterate tribe being studied by anthropologists in the South Pacific. In other words, in its most general form, the hypothesis attempts to isolate one of the key factors in the economic development, at least, of all civilizations. What evidence do we have that this extremely broad generalization will obtain? By now, a great deal has been collected—far more than I can summarize here; but I shall try to give a few key examples of the different types of evidence.

First, we have made historical studies. To do so, we had to find a way to obtain a measure of *n* Achievement level during time periods other than our own, whose individuals can no longer be tested. We have done this—instead of coding the brief stories written by an individual for a test, we code imaginative literary documents: poetry, drama, funeral orations, letters written by sea captains, epics, etc. Ancient Greece, which we studied first, supplies a good illustration. We are able to find literary documents written during three different historical periods and dealing with similar themes: the period of economic growth, 900 B.C.–475 B.C. (largely Homer and Hesiod); the period of climax, 475 B.C.–362 B.C.; and the period of decline, 362 B.C.–100 B.C. Thus, Hesiod wrote on farm and estate management in the early period; Xenophon, in the middle period; and Aristotle, in the late period. We have defined the period of "climax" in economic, rather than in cultural, terms, because it would be presumptuous to claim, for example, that Aristotle in any sense represented a "decline" from Plato or Thales. The measure of economic growth was computed from information supplied by F. Heichelheim in his *Wirtschaftsgeschichte des Altertums.*[5] Heichelheim records in detail the locations throughout Europe where the remains of Greek vases from different centuries have been found. Of course, these vases were the principal instrument of Greek foreign trade, since they were the containers for olive oil and wine, which were the most important Greek exports. Knowing where the vase fragments have been found, we could compute the trade area of Athenian Greece for different time periods. We purposely omitted any consideration of the later expansion of Hellenistic Greece, because this represents another civilization; our concern was Athenian Greece.

When all the documents had been coded, they demonstrated—as predicted—that the level of *n* Achievement was highest during the period of growth prior to the climax of economic development in Athenian Greece. (See Figure 17.1.) In other words, the maximum *n* Achievement level preceded the maximum economic level by at least a century. Furthermore, that high level

Figure 17.1   Average *n* Achievement Level (plotted at midpoints of periods of growth, climax, and decline of Athenian civilization as reflected in the extent of her trade area)

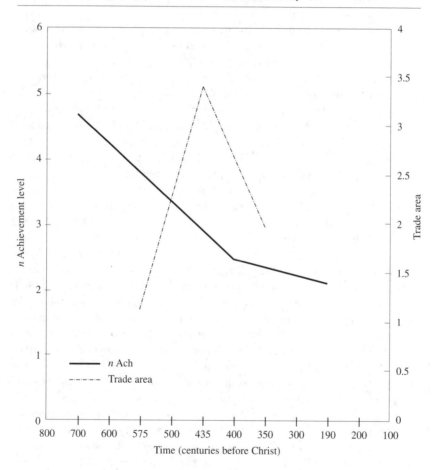

Note: Trade area measured for the sixth, fifth, and fourth centuries B.C. only.

had fallen off by the time of maximum prosperity, thus foreshadowing subsequent economic decline. A similar methodology was applied, with the same results, to the economic development of Spain in the sixteenth century[6] and to two waves of economic development in the history of England (one in the late sixteenth century and the other at the beginning of the industrial revolution, around 1800).[7] The n Achievement level in English history (as determined on the basis of dramas, sea captains' letters, and street ballads) rose, between 1400–1800, *twice,* a generation or two before waves of accelerated economic growth (incidentally, at times of Protestant revival). This point is significant because it shows that there is no "necessary" steady decline in a civilization's entrepreneurial energy from its earlier to its later periods. In the Spanish and English cases, as in the Greek, high levels of n Achievement preceded economic decline. Unfortunately, space limitations preclude more detailed discussion of these studies here.

We also tested the hypothesis by applying it to preliterate cultures of the sort that anthropologists investigate. At Yale University, an organized effort has been made to collect everything that is known about all the primitive tribes that have been studied and to classify the information systematically for comparative purposes. We utilized this cross-cultural file to obtain the two measures that we needed to test our general hypothesis. For over fifty of these cultures, collections of folk tales existed that I. L. Child and others had coded,[8] just as we coded literary documents and individual imaginative stories, for n Achievement and other motives. These folk tales have the character of fantasy that we believe to be so essential for getting at "inner concerns." In the meantime, we were searching for a method of classifying the economic development of these cultures, so that we could determine whether those evincing high n Achievement in their folk tales had developed further than those showing lower n Achievement. The respective modes of gaining a livelihood were naturally very different in these cultures, since they came from every continent in the world and every type of physical habitat; yet we had to find a measure for comparing them. We finally thought of trying to estimate the number of full-time "business entrepreneurs" there were among the adults in each culture. We defined "entrepreneur" as "anyone who exercises control over the means of production and produces more than he can consume in order to sell it for individual or household income." Thus an entrepreneur was anyone who derived at least 75 percent of his income from such exchange or market practices. The entrepreneurs were mostly traders, independent artisans, or operators of small firms like stores, inns, etc. Nineteen cultures were classified as high in n Achievement on the basis of their folk tales; 74 percent of them contained some entrepreneurs. On the other hand, only 35 percent of the twenty cultures that were classified as low in n Achievement contained any entrepreneurs (as we defined it) at all. The difference is highly significant statistically (Chi square = 5.97, $p < .02$). Hence data about primitive tribes seem to confirm the hypothesis that high n Achievement leads to a more advanced type of economic activity.

But what about modern nations? Can we estimate their level of n Achievement and relate it to their economic development? The question is obviously one of the greatest importance, but the technical problems of getting measures of our two variables proved to be really formidable. What type of literary document could we use that would be equally representative of the motivational levels of people in India, Japan, Portugal, Germany, the United States, and Italy? We had discovered in our historical studies that certain types of literature usually contain much more achievement imagery than others. This is not too serious as long as we are dealing with time changes within a given culture; but it is very serious if we want to compare two cultures, each of which may express its achievement motivation in a different literary form. At last, we decided to use children's stories, for several reasons. They exist in standard form in every modern nation, since all modern nations are involved in teaching their children to read and use brief stories for this purpose. Furthermore, the stories are imaginative; and, if selected from those used in the earliest grades, they are not often influenced by temporary political events. (We were most impressed by this when reading the stories that every Russian child reads. In general, they cannot be distinguished, in style and content, from the stories read in all the countries of the West.)

We collected children's readers for the second, third, and fourth grades from every country where they could be found for two time periods, which were roughly centered around 1925 and around 1950. We got some thirteen hundred stories, which were all translated into English. In all, we had twenty-one stories from each of twenty-three countries about 1925, and the same number from each of thirty-nine countries about 1950. Code was used on proper names, so that our scorers would not know the national origins of the stories. The tales were then mixed together, and coded for n Achievement (and certain other motives and values that I shall mention only briefly).

The next task was to find a measure of economic development. Again, the problem was to ensure comparability. Some countries have much greater natural resources; some have developed industrially sooner than others; some concentrate in one area of production and some in another. Economists consider national income figures in per capita terms to be the best measure available; but they are difficult to obtain for all countries, and it is hard to translate them into equal purchasing power. Ultimately, we came to rely chiefly on the measure of electricity produced: the units of measurement are the same all over the world; the figures are available from the 1920s on; and electricity is the *form* of energy (regardless of how it is produced) that is essential to modern economic development. In fact, electricity produced per capita correlates with estimates of income per capita in the 1950s around .90 anyway. To equate for differences in natural re-sources, such as the amount of water power available, etc., we studied *gains* in kilowatt hours produced per capita between 1925 and 1950. The level of electrical production in 1925 is, as one would expect, highly correlated with the size of the gain between then and 1950. So it was necessary to resort to a regression analysis; that is, to calculate, from the average regression of gain on level for all countries, how much gain a particular country should have shown between 1925 and 1950. The actual gain could then be compared with the expected gain, and the country could be classified as gaining more or less rapidly than would have been expected on the basis of its 1925 performance. The procedure is directly comparable to what we do when we predict, on the basis of some measure of I.Q., what grades a child can be expected to get in school, and then classify him as an "under-" or "over-achiever."

The correlation between the n Achievement level in the children's readers in 1925 and the growth in electrical output between 1925 and 1950, as compared with expectation, is a quite substantial .53, which is highly significant statistically. It could hardly have arisen by chance. Furthermore, the correlation is also substantial with a measure of gain over the expected in per capita income, equated for purchasing power by Colin Clark. To check this result more definitively with the sample of forty countries for which we had reader estimates of n Achievement levels in 1950, we computed the equation for gains in electrical output in 1952–58 as a function of level in 1952. It turned out to be remarkably linear when translated into logarithmic units, as is so often the case with simple growth functions. Table 17.1 presents the performance of each of the countries, as compared with predictions from initial level in 1952, in standard score units and classified by high and low n Achievement in 1950. Once again we found that n Achievement levels predicted significantly ($r = .43$) the countries which would perform more or less rapidly than expected in terms of the average for all countries. The finding is more striking than the earlier one, because many Communist and underdeveloped countries are included in the sample. Apparently, n Achievement is a precursor of economic growth—and not only in the Western style of capitalism based on the small entrepreneur, but also in economies controlled and fostered largely by the state.

For those who believe in economic determinism, it is especially interesting that n Achievement level in 1950 is *not* correlated either with *previous* economic growth between 1925 and 1950, or with the level of prosperity in 1950. This strongly suggests that n Achievement is a *causative* factor—a change in the minds of men which produces economic growth rather than being produced by it. In a century dominated by economic determinism, in both Communist and Western thought, it is startling to find concrete evidence for psychological determinism, for psychological developments as preceding and presumably causing economic changes.

The many interesting results which our study of children's stories yielded have succeeded in convincing me that we chose the right material to analyze. Apparently, adults unconsciously flavor their stories for young children with

Table 17.1 **Rate of Growth in Electrical Output (1952–1958) and National**
_n_ Achievement Levels in 1950

National _n_ Achievement levels (1950)[a]	Country	Deviation from Expected Growth Rate[b]	National _n_ Achievement Levels (1950)[a]	Country	Deviations from Expected Growth Rate[b]
Above Expectation Growth Rate			Below Expectation Growth Rate		
High _n_ Achievement Countries					
3.62	Turkey	+1.38			
2.71	India[c]	+1.12			
2.38	Australia	+0.42			
2.32	Israel	+1.18			
2.33	Spain	+0.01			
2.29	Pakistan[d]	+2.75			
2.29	Greece	+1.18	3.38	Argentina	−0.56
2.29	Canada	+0.08	2.71	Lebanon	−0.67
2.24	Bulgaria	+1.37	2.38	France	−0.24
2.24	U.S.A.	+0.47	2.33	South Africa	−0.06
2.14	West Germany	+0.53	2.29	Ireland	−0.41
2.10	U.S.S.R.	+1.61	2.14	Tunisia	−1.87
2.10	Portugal	+0.76	2.10	Syria	−0.25
Low _n_ Achievement Countries					
1.95	Iraq	+0.29	2.05	New Zealand	−0.29
1.86	Austria	+0.38	1.86	Uruguay	−0.75
1.67	U.K.	+0.17	1.81	Hungary	−0.62
1.57	Mexico	+0.12	1.71	Norway	−0.77
0.86	Poland	+1.26	1.62	Sweden	−0.64
			1.52	Finland	−0.08
			1.48	Netherlands	−0.15
			1.33	Italy	−0.57
			1.29	Japan	−0.04
			1.20	Switzerland[e]	−1.92
			1.19	Chile	−1.81
			1.05	Denmark	−0.89
			0.57	Algeria	−0.83
			0.43	Belgium	−1.65

Notes: Correlation of _n_ Achievement level (1950) x deviations from expected growth rate = .43, $p < .01$.

a. Deviations in standard score units. The estimates are computed from the monthly average electrical production figures, in millions Kwh, for 1952 and 1958, from United Nations, _Monthly Bulletin of Statistics_ (January, 1960), and _World Energy Supplies,_ 1951–1954 and 1955–1958 (Statistical Papers, Series 3). The correlation between log level 1952 and log gain 1952–1958 is .976. The regression equation based on these thirty-nine countries, plus four others from the same climatic zone on which data are available (China-Taiwan, Czechoslovakia, Rumania, Yugoslavia), is: log gain (1952–1958) = .9229 log level (1952) + .0480. Standard scores deviations from mean gain predicted by the regression formula (M = −.01831) divided by the standard deviation of the deviations from the mean predicted gain (SD = .159).

b. Based on twenty-one children's stories from second-, third-, and fourth-grade readers in each country.

c. Based on six Hindi, seven Telegu, and eight Tamil stories.

d. Based on twelve Urdu and eleven Bengali stories.

e. Based on twenty-one German Swiss stories, mean = .91; twenty-one French Swiss stories, mean = 1.71; overall mean obtained by weighting German mean double to give approximately proportionate representation of the two main ethnic populations.

the attitudes, the aspirations, the values, and the motives that they hold to be most important.

I want to mention briefly two other findings, one concerned with economic development, the other with totalitarianism. When the more and less rapidly developing economies are compared on all the other variables for which we scored the children's stories, one fact stands out. In stories from those countries which had developed more rapidly in both the earlier and later periods, there was a discernible tendency to emphasize, in 1925 and in 1950, what David Riesman has called "other-directedness"—namely, reliance on the opinion of particular others, rather than on tradition, for guidance in social behavior.[9] *Public opinion* had, in these countries, become a major source of guidance for the individual. Those countries which had developed the mass media further and faster—the press, the radio, the public-address system—were also the ones who were developing more rapidly economically. I think that "other-directedness" helped these countries to develop more rapidly because public opinion is basically more flexible than institutionalized moral or social traditions. Authorities can utilize it to inform people widely about the need for new ways of doing things. However, traditional institutionalized values may insist that people go on behaving in ways that are no longer adaptive to a changed social and economic order.

The other finding is not directly relevant to economic development, but it perhaps involves the means of achieving it. Quite unexpectedly, we discovered that every major dictatorial regime which came to power between the 1920s and 1950s (with the possible exception of Portugal's) was foreshadowed by a particular motive pattern in its stories for children: namely, a low need for affiliation (little interest in friendly relationships with people) and a high need for power (a great concern over controlling and influencing other people).

The German readers showed this pattern before Hitler; the Japanese readers, before Tojo; the Argentine readers, before Perón; the Spanish readers, before Franco; the South African readers, before the present authoritarian government in South Africa; etc. On the other hand, very few countries which did not have dictatorships manifested this particular motive combination. The difference was highly significant statistically, since there was only one exception in the first instance and very few in the second. Apparently, we stumbled on a psychological index of ruthlessness—i.e., the need to influence other people (n Power), unchecked by sufficient concern for their welfare (n Affiliation). It is interesting, and a little disturbing, to discover that the German readers of today still evince this particular combination of motives, just as they did in 1925. Let us hope that this is one case where a social science generalization will not be confirmed by the appearance of a totalitarian regime in Germany in the next ten years.

To return to our main theme—let us discuss the precise ways that higher n Achievement leads to more rapid economic development, and why it should lead to economic development rather than, for example, to military or artistic development. We must consider in more detail the mechanism by which the concentration of a particular type of human motive in a population leads to a complex social phenomenon like economic growth. The link between the two social phenomena is, obviously, the business entrepreneur. I am not using the term "entrepreneur" in the sense of "capitalist": in fact, I should like to divorce "entrepreneur" entirely from any connotations of ownership. An entrepreneur is someone who exercises control over production that is not just for his personal consumption. According to my definition, for example, an executive in a steel production unit in Russia is an entrepreneur.

It was Joseph Schumpeter who drew the attention of economists to the importance that the activity of these entrepreneurs had in creating industrialization in the West. Their vigorous endeavors put together firms and created productive units where there had been none before. In the beginning, at least, the entrepreneurs often collected material resources, organized a production unit to combine the resources into a new product, and sold the product, Until recently, nearly all economists—including not only Marx, but also Western classical economists—assumed that these men were moved primarily by the "profit motive." We are all familiar with the Marxian argument that they were so driven by their desire for profits that they exploited the workingman and ultimately forced him to revolt. Recently, economic historians have been studying the actual lives of such entrepreneurs and finding—certainly to the surprise of some of the investigators—that many of them seemingly were not interested in making money as such. In psychological terms, at least, Marx's picture is slightly out of focus. Had these entrepreneurs been above all interested in money, many more of them would have quit working as soon as they had made all the money that they could possibly use. They would not have continued to risk their money in further entrepreneurial ventures. Many of them, in fact, came from pietistic sects, like the Quakers in England, that prohibited the enjoyment of wealth in any of the ways cultivated so successfully by some members of the European nobility. However, the entrepreneurs often seemed consciously to be greatly concerned with expanding their businesses, with getting a greater share of the market, with "conquering brute nature," or even with altruistic schemes for bettering the lot of mankind or bringing about the kingdom of God on earth more rapidly. Such desires have frequently enough been labeled as hypocritical. However, if we assume that these men were really motivated by a desire for achievement rather than by a desire for money as such, the label no longer fits. This assumption also simplifies further matters considerably. It provides an explanation for the fact that these entrepreneurs were interested in money without wanting it for its own sake, namely, that money served as a ready quantitative index of how well they were doing—e.g., of how much they had achieved by their efforts over the past year. The need to achieve can never be satisfied by money; but estimates of profitability in money terms can supply direct knowledge of how well one is doing one's job.

The brief consideration of the lives of business entrepreneurs of the past suggested that their chief motive may well have been a high *n* Achievement. What evidence have we found in support of this? We made two approaches to the problem. First, we attempted to determine whether individuals with high *n* Achievement behave like entrepreneurs; and second, we investigated to learn whether actual entrepreneurs, particularly the more successful ones, in a number of countries, have higher *n* Achievement than do other people of roughly the same status. Of course, we had to establish what we meant by "behave like entrepreneurs"—what precisely distinguishes the way an entrepreneur behaves from the way other people behave?

The adequate answers to these questions would entail a long discussion of the sociology of occupations, involving the distinction originally made by Max Weber between capitalists and bureaucrats. Since this cannot be done here, a very brief report on our extensive investigations in this area will have to suffice. First, one of the defining characteristics of an entrepreneur is *taking risks* and/or innovating. A person who adds up a column of figures is not an entrepreneur—however carefully, efficiently, or correctly he adds them. He is simply following established rules. However, a man who decides to add a new line to his business is an entrepreneur, in that he cannot know in advance whether this decision will be correct. Nevertheless, he does not feel that he is in the position of a gambler who places some money on the turn of a card. Knowledge, judgment, and skill enter into his decision making; and, if his choice is justified by future developments, he can certainly feel a sense of personal achievement from having made a successful move.

Therefore, if people with high *n* Achievement are to behave in an entrepreneurial way, they must seek out and perform in situations in which there is some moderate risk of failure—a risk which can, presumably, be reduced by increased effort or skill. They should not work harder than other people at routine tasks, or perform functions which they are certain to do well simply by doing what everyone accepts as the correct traditional thing to do. On the other hand, they should avoid gambling situations, because, even if they win, they can receive no sense of personal achievement, since it was not skill but luck that produced the results. (And, of course, most of the time they would lose, which would be highly unpleasant to them.) The data on this point are very clear-cut. We have repeatedly found, for example, that boys with high *n* Achievement choose to play games of skill that incorporate a moderate risk of failure. . . .

Another quality that the entrepreneur seeks in his work is that his job be a kind that ordinarily provides him with accurate knowledge of the results of his decisions. As a rule, growth in sales, in output, or in profit margins tells him very precisely whether he has made the correct choice under uncertainty or not. Thus, the concern for profit enters in—profit is a measure of success. We have repeatedly found that boys with a high *n* Achievement work more efficiently when they know how well they are doing. Also, they will not work harder for money rewards; but if they are asked, they state that greater money rewards should be awarded for accomplishing more difficult things in games of skill. In the ring-toss game, subjects were asked how much money they thought should be awarded for successful throws from different distances. Subjects with high n Achievement and those with low n Achievement agreed substantially about the amounts for throws made close to the peg. However, as the distance from the peg increased, the amounts awarded for successful throws by the subjects with high n Achievement rose more rapidly than did the rewards by those with low n Achievement. Here, as elsewhere, individuals with high n Achievement behaved as they must if they are to be the success-ful entrepreneurs of society. They believed that greater achievement should be recognized by quantitatively larger reward.

What produces high n Achievement? Why do some societies produce a large number of people with this motive, while other societies produce so many fewer? We conducted long series of researches into this question. I can present only a few here.

One very important finding is essentially a negative one: n Achievement cannot be hereditary. Popular psychology has long maintained that some races are more energetic than others. Our data clearly contradict this in connection with n Achievement. The changes in n Achievement level within a given pop-ulation are too rapid to be attributed to heredity. For example, the correlation between respective n Achievement levels in the 1925 and 1950 samples of readers is substantially zero. Many of the countries that were high in n Achievement at one or both times may be low or moderate in n Achievement now, and vice versa. Germany was low in 1925 and is high now; and certainly the hereditary makeup of the German nation has not changed in a generation.

However, there is substantiating evidence that n Achievement is a motive which a child can acquire quite early in life, say, by the age of eight or ten, as a result of the way his parents have brought him up. . . . The principal results . . . indicate the differences between the parents of the "high n Achievement boys" and the parents of boys with low n Achievement. In general, the moth-ers and the fathers of the first group set higher levels of aspiration in a num-ber of tasks for their sons. They were also much warmer, showing positive emotion in reacting to their sons' performances. In the area of authority or dominance, the data are quite interesting. The mothers of the "highs" were more domineering than the mothers of the "lows," but the *fathers* of the "highs" were significantly *less* domineering than the fathers of the "lows." In other words, the fathers of the "highs" set high standards and are warmly in-terested in their sons' performances, but they do not directly interfere. This gives the boys the chance to develop initiative and self-reliance.

What factors cause parents to behave in this way? Their behavior cer-tainly is involved with their values and, possibly, ultimately with their religion or their general world view. At present, we cannot be sure that Protestant parents are more likely to behave this way than Catholic parents—there are too many subgroup variations within each religious portion of the community: the Lutheran father is probably as likely to be authoritarian as the Catholic father. However, there does seem to be one crucial variable discernible: the extent to which the religion of the family emphasizes individual, as contrasted with ritual, contact with God. The preliterate tribes that we studied in which the religion was the kind that stressed the individual contact had higher n Achievement; and in general, mystical sects in which this kind of religious self-reliance dominates have had higher n Achievement.

The extent to which the authoritarian father is away from the home while the boy is growing up may prove to be another crucial variable. If so, then one incidental consequence of prolonged wars may be an increase in n Achievement, because the fathers are away too much to interfere with their sons' development of it. And in Turkey, N. M. Bradburn found that those boys tended to have higher n Achievement who had left home early or whose fathers had died before they were eighteen.[10] Slavery was another factor which played an important role in the past. It probably lowered n Achievement—in the slaves, for whom obedience and responsibility, but not achievement, were obvious virtues; and in the slave-owners, because household slaves were often disposed to spoil the owner's children as a means for improving their own positions. This is both a plausible and a probable reason for the drop in n Achievement level in ancient Greece that occurred at about the time the middle-class entrepreneur was first able to afford, and obtain by conquest, as many as two slaves for each child. The idea also clarifies the slow economic development of the South in the United States by attributing its dilatoriness to a lack of n Achievement in its elite; and it also indicates why lower-class American Negroes, who are closest to the slave tradition, possess very low n Achievement.[11]

I have outlined our research findings. Do they indicate ways of accelerating economic development? Increasing the level of n Achievement in a country suggests itself as an obvious first possibility. If n Achievement is so important, so specifically adapted to the business role, then it certainly should be raised in level, so that more young men have an "entrepreneurial drive." The difficulty in this excellent plan is that our studies of how n Achievement originates indicate that the family is the key formative influence; and it is very hard to change on a really large scale. To be sure, major historical events like wars have taken authoritarian fathers out of the home; and religious reform movements have sometimes converted the parents to a new achievement-oriented ideology. However, such matters are not ordinarily within the policymaking province of the agencies charged with speeding economic development.

Such agencies can, perhaps, effect the general acceptance of an achievement-oriented ideology as an absolute *sine qua non* of economic development. Furthermore, this ideology should be diffused not only in business and governmental circles, but throughout the nation, and in ways that will influence the thinking of all parents as they bring up their children. As B. C. Rosen and R. G. D'Andrade found, parents must, above all, set high standards for their children. The campaign to spread achievement-oriented ideology, if possible, could also incorporate an attack on the extreme authoritarianism in fathers that impedes or prevents the development of self-reliance in their sons. This is, however, a more delicate point, and attacking this, in many countries, would be to threaten values at the very center of social life. I believe that a more indirect approach would be more successful. One approach would be to take the boys out of the home and to camps. A more significant method would be to promote the rights of women, both legally and socially—one of the ways to undermine the absolute dominance of the male is to strengthen the rights of the female! Another reason for concentrating particularly on women is that they play the leading role in rearing the next generation. Yet, while men in underdeveloped countries come in contact with new achievement-oriented values and standards through their work, women may be left almost untouched by such influences. But if the sons are to have high n Achievement, the mothers must first be reached.

It may seem strange that a chapter on economic development should discuss the importance of feminism and the way children are reared; but this is precisely where a psychological analysis leads. If the motives of men are the agents that influence the speed with which the economic machine operates, then the speed can be increased only through affecting the factors that create the motives. Furthermore—to state this point less theoretically—I cannot think of evinced substantial, rapid long-term economic development where women have not been somewhat freed from their traditional setting of "Kinder, Küche und Kirche" and allowed to play a more powerful role in society, specifically as part of the working force. This generalization applies not only to the Western democracies like the United States, Sweden, or England, but also to the USSR, Japan, and now China.

In the present state of our knowledge, we can conceive of trying to raise n Achievement levels only in the next generation—although new research findings may soon indicate n Achievement in adults can be increased. Most economic planners, while accepting the long-range desirability of raising n Achievement in future generations, want to know what can be done during the next five to ten years. This immediacy inevitably focuses attention on the process or processes by which executives or entrepreneurs are selected. Foreigners with proved entrepreneurial drive can be hired, but at best this is a temporary and unsatisfactory solution. In most underdeveloped countries where government is playing a leading role in promoting economic development, it is clearly necessary for the government to adopt rigid achievement-oriented standards of performance like those in the USSR.[12] A government manager or, for that matter, a private entrepreneur, should have to produce "or else." Production targets must be set, as they are in most economic plans; and individuals must be held responsible for achieving them, even at the plant level. The philosophy should be one of "no excuses accepted." It is common for government officials or economic theorists in underdeveloped countries to be weighed down by all the difficulties which face the economy and render its rapid development difficult or impossible. They note that there is too rapid population growth, too little capital, too few technically competent people, etc. Such obstacles to growth are prevalent, and in many cases they are immensely hard to overcome; but talking about them can provide merely a comfortable rationalization for mediocre performance. It is difficult to fire an administrator, no matter how poor his performance, if so many objective reasons exist for his doing badly. Even worse, such rationalization permits, in the private sector, the continued employment of incompetent family members as executives. If these private firms were afraid of being penalized for poor performance, they might be impelled to find more able professional managers a little more quickly. I am not an expert in the field, and the mechanisms I am suggesting may be far from appropriate. Still, they may serve to illustrate my main point: if a country short in entrepreneurial talent wants to advance rapidly, it must find ways and means of ensuring that only the most competent retain positions of responsibility. One of the obvious methods of doing so is to judge people in terms of their *performance*—and not according to their family or political connections, their skill in explaining why their unit failed to produce as expected, or their conscientiousness in following the rules. I would suggest the use of psychological tests as a means of selecting people with high *n* Achievement; but, to be perfectly frank, I think this approach is at present somewhat impractical on a large enough scale in most underdeveloped countries.

Finally, there is another approach which I think is promising for recruiting and developing more competent business leadership. It is the one called, in some circles, the "professionalization of management." Frederick Harbison and Charles A. Myers have recently completed a worldwide survey of the efforts made to develop professional schools of high-level management. They have concluded that, in most countries, progress in this direction is slow.[13] Professional management is important for three reasons: (1) It may endow a business career with higher prestige (as a kind of profession), so that business will attract more of the young men with high *n* Achievement from the elite groups in backward countries; (2) It stresses *performance* criteria of excellence in the management area—i.e., what a man can do and not what he is; (3) Advanced management schools can themselves be so achievement-oriented in their instruction that they are able to raise the *n* Achievement of those who attend them.

Applied toward explaining historical events, the results of our researches clearly shift attention away from external factors and to man—in particular, to his motives and values. That about which he thinks and dreams determines what will happen. The emphasis is quite different from the Darwinian or Marxist view of man as a creature who *adapts* to his environment. It is even different from the Freudian view of civilization as the sublimation of man's primitive urges. Civilization, at least in its economic aspects, is neither adaptation nor sublimation; it is a positive creation by a people made dynamic by a high level of *n* Achievement. Nor can we agree with Toynbee, who recognizes the importance of psychological factors as "the very forces which actually decide the issue when an encounter takes place," when he states that these factors "inherently are impossible to weigh and measure, and therefore to estimate scientifically in advance."[14] It is a measure of the pace at which the behavioral sciences are developing that even within Toynbee's lifetime we can demonstrate that he was mistaken. The psychological factor responsible for a civilization's rising to a challenge is so far from being "inherently impossible to weigh and measure" that it has been weighed and measured and scientifically estimated in advance; and, so far as we can now tell, this factor is the achievement motive.

Notes

1. A. L. Kroeber, *Configurations of Culture Growth* (Berkeley, Calif., 1944).

2. J. W. Atkinson (Ed.), *Motives in Fantasy, Action, and Society* (Princeton, N.J., 1958).

3. Max Weber, *The Protestant Ethic and the Spirit of Capitalism,* trans. Talcott Parsons (New York, 1930).

4. M. R. Winterbottom, "The Relation of Need for Achievement to Learning and Experiences in Independence and Mastery," in Atkinson, *op. cit.,* pp. 453–478.

5. F. Heichelheim, *Wirtschaftsgeschichte des Altertums* (Leiden, 1938).

6. J. B. Cortés, "The Achievement Motive in the Spanish Economy Between the Thirteenth and the Eighteenth Centuries," *Economic Development and Cultural Change,* IX (1960), 144–163.

7. N. M. Bradburn and D. E. Berlew, "Need for Achievement and English Economic Growth," *Economic Development and Cultural Change,* 1961.

8. I. L. Child, T. Storm, and J. Veroff, "Achievement Themes in Folk Tales Related to Socialization Practices," in Atkinson, *op. cit.,* pp. 479–492.

9. David Riesman, with the assistance of Nathan Glazer and Reuel Denney, *The Lonely Crowd* (New Haven, Conn., 1950).

10. N. M. Bradburn, "The Managerial Role in Turkey" (unpublished Ph.D. dissertation, Harvard University, 1960).

11. B. C. Rosen, "Race, Ethnicity, and Achievement Syndrome," *American Sociological Review,* XXIV (1959), 47–60.

12. David Granick, *The Red Executive* (New York, 1960).

13. Frederick Harbison and Charles A. Myers, *Management in the Industrial World* (New York, 1959).

14. Arnold J. Toynbee, *A Study of History* (abridgment by D. C. Somervell; Vol. I; New York, 1947).

18

Underdevelopment Is a State of Mind

LAWRENCE E. HARRISON

After twenty years of working for the United States Agency for International Development (USAID), Lawrence Harrison has concluded that Latin America's culture explains its lack of development. As should be clear by now, the cultural approach blames the poor for their poverty. According to Harrison, Latin Americans have become so preoccupied with a belief in the self-defeating "myths" of dependency and imperialism that they are paralyzed to the point that they do not use the resources they have to develop. At its heart, the process of development is one of human creative capacity, the ability to imagine, conceptualize, and so on. If a country is to tap the creative energy of its people, the government must establish an environment that encourages and uses all of its people's abilities. ■

What Makes Development Happen?

Development, most simply, is improvement in human well-being.[1] Most people today aspire to higher standards of living, longer lives, and fewer health problems; education for themselves and their children that will increase their earning capacity and leave them more in control of their lives; a measure of stability and tranquility; and the opportunity to do the things that give them pleasure and satisfaction. A small minority will take exception to one or more

Reprinted with permission from *Underdevelopment Is a State of Mind: The Latin American Case,* by Lawrence E. Harrison (Cambridge, MA: The Center for International Affairs, Harvard University), pp. 1–9. © 1985 by the President and Fellows of Harvard College.

of these aspirations. Some others may wish to add one or more. For the purposes of this chapter, however, I think the list is adequate.

The enormous gap in well-being between the low-income and the industrialized countries is apparent from . . . table [18.1], the source of which is the World Bank's *World Development Report* 1982. . . .

What explains the gap? What have the industrialized countries done that the low-income countries have not? Why was the Marshall Plan a monumental success, the Alliance for Progress much less successful? What makes development happen or not happen?

There are those who will say that what the industrialized countries have done that the low-income countries have not is to exploit the low-income countries; that development is a zero-sum game; that the rich countries are rich because the poor countries are poor. This is doctrine for Marxist-Leninists and it has wide currency throughout the Third World. To be sure, colonial powers often did derive great economic advantage from their colonies, and U.S. companies have made a lot of money in Latin America and elsewhere in the Third World, particularly during the first half of this century. But the almost exclusive focus on "imperialism" and "dependency" to explain underdevelopment has encouraged the evolution of a paralyzing and self-defeating mythology. The thesis of this chapter is in diametrical contrast. It looks inward rather than outward to explain a society's condition.

I believe that the creative capacity of human beings is at the heart of the development process. What makes development happen is our ability to imagine, theorize, conceptualize, experiment, invent, articulate, organize, manage, solve problems, and do a hundred other things with our minds and hands that contribute to the progress of the individual and of human-kind. Natural resources, climate, geography, history, market size, governmental policies, and many other factors influence the direction and pace of progress. But the engine is human creative capacity.

The economist Joseph Schumpeter (1883–1950) singled out the entrepreneurial geniuses—the Henry Fords of the world—as the real creators of wealth and progress, as indeed they must have appeared in the early years of Schumpeter's life. Economist and political scientist Everett Hagen was less elitist:

Table 18.1   Gap in Well-Being: Low-Income and Industrialized Countries

	Low-Income Countries	Industrialized Countries
Total population (mid-1980)	2.2 billion	671 million
Annual average population growth rate (1970–80)	2.1 percent	.8 percent
Average per capita gross national product (1980)	$260	$10,320
Average life expectancy at birth (1980)	57 years	74 years
Average adult literacy (1977)	50 percent	99 percent

"The discussion of creativity refers . . . not merely to the limiting case of genius but to the quality of creativity in general, in whatever degree it may be found in a given individual."[2]

My *own* belief is that the society that is most successful at helping its people—*all* its people—realize their creative potential is the society that will progress the fastest.

It is not just the entrepreneur who creates progress, even if we are talking narrowly about material-economic progress. The inventor of the machine employed by the entrepreneur; the scientist who conceived the theory that the inventor turned to practical use; the engineer who designed the system to mass-produce the machine; the farmer who uses special care in producing a uniform raw material to be processed by the machine; the machine operator who suggests some helpful modifications to the machine on the basis of long experience in operating it—all are contributing to growth. So is the salesman who expands demand for the product by conceiving a new use for it. So, too, are the teachers who got the scientist, the inventor, and the engineer interested in their professions and who taught the farmer agronomy.[3]

Production takes place within a broader society, and the way that society functions affects the productive process. Good government can assure stability and continuity, without which investment and production will falter. Good government can provide a variety of services that facilitate production. And the policies government pursues, e.g., with respect to taxation, interest rates, support prices for agricultural products, will importantly affect producer decisions. Thus, the creativity and skill of government officials play a key role in economic development. It can be argued, in fact, that an effective government policymaker— e.g., a Treasury Secretary—is worth many Henry Fords.[4] W. Arthur Lewis observes, "The behaviour of government plays as important a role in stimulating or discouraging economic activity as does the behaviour of entrepreneurs, or parents, or scientists, or priests."[5]

But our definition of development is far broader than just the productive dimension of human existence. It also embraces the social dimension, particularly health, education, and welfare. It is government that bears the principal responsibility for progress in these sectors, and, as with economic progress, innovation and creativity are at the root of social progress. The people who conceive the policies that expand and improve social services are thus comparable in their developmental impact to industrial entrepreneurs, as are public-sector planners, administrators, technicians, and blue-collar workers to their private-sector counterparts.

It is not difficult to see how this view of what makes development happen can be extended to virtually all forms of work, intellectual and physical, performed within a society. While it is obvious that the contribution of some will be greater than that of others, and while the role of gifted people can be enormously important, all can contribute. It is thus probably more accurate, at least in the contemporary world, to think of development as a process of millions of small breakthroughs than as a few monumental innovations, the work of geniuses. A society that smoothes the way for these breakthroughs is a society that will progress.

How does a society encourage the expression of human creative capacity? Basically, in seven ways:

1. Through creation of an environment in which people expect and receive fair treatment.
2. Through an effective and accessible education system: one that provides basic intellectual and vocational tools; nurtures inquisitiveness, critical faculties, dissent, and creativity; and equips people to solve problems.
3. Through a health system that protects people from diseases that debilitate and kill.
4. Through creation of an environment that encourages experimentation and criticism (which is often at the root of experimentation).
5. Through creation of an environment that helps people both discover their talents and interests and mesh them with the right jobs.
6. Through a system of incentives that rewards merit and achievement (and, conversely, discourages nepotism and "pull").
7. Through creation of the stability and continuity that make it possible to plan ahead with confidence. Progress is made enormously more difficult by instability and discontinuity.

Two Examples in Nicaragua

My recent experience in Nicaragua provides two examples that symbolize what societies can do to nurture or frustrate human creative capacity.

The United States ambassador to Nicaragua during my two years there was Lawrence A. Pezzullo. Larry Pezzullo grew up in the Bronx, the son of an immigrant Italian butcher. His mother, also an immigrant, was illiterate. He attended public schools in New York City, served in the U.S. Army in Europe during World War II, and returned to New York to attend Columbia University under the GI bill. Following graduation, he taught in a public high school on Long Island for six years, then joined the Foreign Service. He rose steadily through the ranks, served as deputy assistant secretary of state for congressional affairs from 1975 to 1977, and was named ambassador to Uruguay in 1977. He became ambassador to Nicaragua in July 1979, simultaneous with the installation of the revolutionary Government of National Reconstruction.

Larry Pezzullo is a person of extraordinary talent. He has great capacity for understanding complicated political processes. But he also has a flair for conceiving and orchestrating responses to the circumstances he faces, and an unerring sense of timing. He is a diplomatic entrepreneur who, in Nicaragua, was the right man in the right place at the right time. (He has since become executive director of Catholic Relief Services.)

Rosa Carballo was born into similar humble circumstances, but in Nicaragua. She is a woman in her sixties, highly intelligent, dignified, and self-disciplined. She has a profound understanding of human nature and sees well below the surface of the political process in her country. With those qualities, she might well have been a successful professional in another society. In Nicaragua she is a domestic servant. She is effectively illiterate.

I want to note in passing that, today, there are few countries that could not virtually eradicate illiteracy within a generation if the will to do so existed.

Values and Attitudes That Foster Progress

We now have to ask what values and attitudes foster the conditions that facilitate the expression of human creative capacity—and development. . . .

The society's world view is the source of its value and attitude systems. The world view is formed by a complex of influences, including geography, economic organization, and the vagaries of history. The world view and its related value and attitude systems are constantly changing, but usually at a very slow pace, measurable in decades or generations. The world view is expressed at least in part through religion.

Of crucial importance for development are: (1) the world view's time focus—past, present, or future; (2) the extent to which the world view encourages rationality; and (3) the concepts of equality and authority it propagates.

If a society's major focus is on the past—on the glory of earlier times or in reverence of ancestors—or if it is absorbed with today's problems of survival, the planning, organizing, saving, and investment that are the warp and woof of development are not likely to be encouraged. Orientation toward the future implies the possibility of change and progress. And that possibility, as Max Weber stressed in his landmark work *The Protestant Ethic and the Spirit of Capitalism,* must be realizable in this life. The Calvinist concepts of "calling" and "election" force the eyes of the faithful toward the future. So do the basic tenets of Judaism: "Judaism clings to the idea of Progress. The Golden Age of Humanity is not in the past, but in the future."[6]

If the society's world view encourages the belief that humans have the capacity to know and understand the world around them, that the universe operates according to a largely decipherable pattern of laws, and that the scientific method can unlock many secrets of the unknown, it is clearly imparting a set of attitudes tightly linked to the ideas of progress and change. If the world view explains worldly phenomena by supernatural forces, often in the form of numerous capricious gods and goddesses who demand obeisance from humans, there is little room for reason, education, planning, or progress.

Many world views propagate the idea of human equality, particularly in the theme of the Golden Rule and its variations. The idea is stressed more in some ethical systems than in others. It is obviously present in both the Protestant and Catholic ethical systems. But Weber argues that the traditional Catholic focus on the afterlife, in contrast to the Protestant (and Jewish) focus on life in this world, vitiates the force of the ethical system, particularly when that focus is accompanied by the cycle of transgression/confession/absolution.[7] One possible consequence may be a relatively stronger Protestant orientation toward equality and the community, and a relatively stronger Catholic orientation toward hierarchy and the individual.

Directly related to the idea of equality is the concept of authority. Subsequent chapters [in the original book—*Eds.*] observe repeatedly the negative consequences of authoritarianism for growth of individuals and societies. There may well be truth in the belief of Weber and others that traditional Catholicism, with its focus on the afterlife and the crucial role of the church hierarchy and the priest, encouraged a dependency mindset among its adherents that was an obstacle to entrepreneurial activity. Martin Luther, by contrast, preached "the priesthood of all believers";[8] "every Christian had to be a monk all his life."[9]

But there are also some religions—including, to be sure, some Protestant denominations—whose basic tenets embrace the idea of inequality. Traditional Hinduism comes immediately to mind, as do Gunnar Myrdal's comments on South Asia:

> . . . Social and economic stratification is accorded the sanction of religion.
> . . . The inherited stratification implies low social and spatial mobility, little free competition in its wider sense, and great inequalities.[10]

It should be an hypothesis for further study that people in this region are not inherently different from people elsewhere, but that they live and have lived for a long time under conditions very different from those in the Western world, and that this has left its mark upon their bodies and minds. Religion has, then, become the emotional container of this whole way of life and work and by its sanction has rendered it rigid and resistant to change.[11]

The fundamental questions of future versus past orientation, encouragement or discouragement of rationality, and emphasis on equality versus emphasis on authority strongly influence three other cultural factors that play an important role in the way a society develops: (1) the extent of identification with others, (2) the rigor of the ethical system, and (3) attitudes about work.

Several of the people whose works are discussed . . . (e.g., Weber, Myrdal, David McClelland) have emphasized the importance for progress of a radius of identification and trust that embraces an entire society. There is evidence that the extended family is an effective institution for survival but an obstacle to development.[12] Weber observes, "The great achievement of ethical religions, above all of the ethical and ascetistic sects of Protestantism, was to shatter the fetters of the sib [i.e., the extended family]."[13]

The social consequences of widespread mistrust can be grave. Samuel Huntington makes the point:

> . . . the absence of trust in the culture of the society provides formidable obstacles to the creation of public institutions. Those societies deficient in stable and effective government are also deficient in mutual trust among their citizens, in national and public loyalties, and in organization skills and capacity. Their political cultures are often said to be marked by suspicion, jealousy, and latent or actual hostility toward everyone who is not a member of the family, the village, or, perhaps, the tribe. These characteristics are found in many cultures, their most extensive manifestation perhaps being in the Arab world and in Latin America. . . . In Latin America . . . traditions of self-centered individualism and of distrust and hatred for other groups in society have prevailed.[14]

A whole set of possibilities opens up when trust is extended beyond the family, possibilities that are likely to be reflected in both economic and social development. Myrdal observes, ". . . a more inclusive nationalism then becomes a force for progress . . . a vehicle for rationalism and for the ideals of planning, equality, social welfare, and perhaps democracy."[15] In such an environment, the idea of cooperation will be strengthened, with all that implies for modern production techniques, community problem-solving, and political stability. The idea of compromise, which is central to the working of a pluralistic system, is also reinforced.[16] When the idea of compromise—i.e., that a relationship is important enough to warrant seeking to avoid confrontation, even if some concession is necessary—is weak, the likelihood of confrontation is increased. Constant confrontation undermines stability and continuity, which, as noted earlier, are crucial to development.

There is a gap in all societies between the stated ethical system and the extent to which that system is honored in practice. Religions' treatment of ethical issues obviously has something to do with the size of the gap. Broad identification among the members of a society will strengthen the impact of the ethical system. Where the radius of identification and trust is small, there may effectively be no operative ethical system.

The rigor of the effective ethical system will shape attitudes about justice, which are central to several major development issues. If the members of a society expect injustice, the ideas of cooperation, compromise, stability, and continuity will be undermined. Corruption and nepotism will be encouraged. And the self-discipline necessary to keep a society working well (e.g., payment of taxes, resistance to the temptation to steal) will be weakened. The system of criminal and civil jurisprudence will be politicized and corrupted and will not be taken seriously by the citizenry. The idea of justice is also central to crucial social issues: the fairness of income distribution, availability of educational opportunities and health services, and promotion by merit.

Another link to these questions of radius of identification, rigor of the effective ethical system, and justice is the idea of dissent.[17] Its acceptance is fundamental to a functioning pluralistic political system, and it is clearly related to the idea of compromise. But it is also an important idea for creativity: what the inventor and the entrepreneur do is a kind of creative dissent.

Attitudes about work link back to several of these ideas, but particularly to future orientation. If the idea of progress is well established in the culture, there is a presumption that planning and hard work will be rewarded by increased income and improved living conditions. When the focus is on the present, on day-to-day survival, the ceiling on work may be the amount necessary to survive.

This brings us back to the seven conditions that encourage the expression of human creative capacity:

1. The expectation of fair play
2. Availability of educational opportunities
3. Availability of health services
4. Encouragement of experimentation and criticism
5. Matching of skills and jobs
6. Rewards for merit and achievement
7. Stability and continuity

Taken together, the seven conditions describe a functional modern democratic capitalist society. The extent to which countries realize their potential is determined, I believe, by the extent to which these conditions exist . . . [T]he seven conditions substantially exist in the fifteen countries whose per-capita gross national product (GNP) is the highest in the world (excluding four oil-rich Arab countries). These same fifteen countries accounted for 83 percent of the Nobel Prize winners from 1945 to 1981. . . .

Notes

1. "Development" and "progress" are used synonymously in this chapter.

2. Everett E. Hagen, *On the Theory of Social Change. How Economic Growth Begins,* p. 88.

3. Hagen makes similar points on p. 11 of *On the Theory of Social Change.*

4. This point is elaborated in Lawrence E. Harrison, "Some Hidden Costs of the Public Investment Fixation," pp. 20–23.

5. W. Arthur Lewis, *The Theory of Economic Growth,* p. 376.

6. The words of a former Chief Rabbi of Great Britain in J. H. Hertz (ed.), *The Pentateuch and Haftorahs,* p. 196.

7. Clearly, contemporary Catholicism is moving toward the Protestant and Jewish focus on this life, particularly since Pope John XXIII.

8. Quoted in David C. McClelland, *The Achieving Society,* p. 48.

9. Max Weber, *The Protestant Ethic and the Spirit of Capitalism,* p. 121.

10. Gunnar Myrdal, *Asian Drama: An Inquiry into the Poverty of Nations,* p. 104.

11. Ibid., p. 112.

12. The conditions for human progress and happiness are still worse where trust extends no further than the nuclear family, as in Banfield's "Montegrano." In that case, both development and survival are threatened.

13. Max Weber, *The Religion of China,* p. 237.

14. Samuel P. Huntington, *Political Order in Changing Societies,* p. 28.

15. Myrdal, *Asian Drama,* p. 122.

16. It is, I believe, significant that there is no truly apt Spanish word for "compromise."

17. It also seems significant that there is no truly apt Spanish word for "dissent."

References

Hagen, E. E. 1962. *On the Theory of Social Change. How Economic Growth Begins.* Homewood, IL: Dorsey Press.

Harrison, L. E. 1970. "Some Hidden Costs of the Public Investment Fixation." *International Development Review* 12.

Hertz, J. H. (ed.). 1961. *The Pentateuch and Haftorahs.* London: Soncino Press.

Huntington, S. P. 1968. *Political Order in Changing Societies.* New York and London: Yale University Press.

Lewis, W. A. 1955. *The Theory of Economic Growth.* Homewood, IL: Richard D. Irwin, Inc.

McClelland, D. C. 1961. *The Achieving Society.* Princeton: D. Van Nostrand Co., Inc.

Myrdal, G. 1968. *Asian Drama. An Inquiry into the Poverty of Nations.* New York: Pantheon.

Weber, M. 1950. *The Protestant Ethic and the Spirit of Capitalism.* New York: Charles Scribner's Sons.

Weber, M. 1951. *The Religion of China.* New York: Macmillan.

World Bank. 1982. *World Development Report, 1982.*

19

The Confucian Ethic
and Economic Growth

HERMAN KAHN

*The most recent theory on the cultural origins of economic growth
derives from the observation that a group of countries that have
made spectacular strides since World War II (e.g., Japan, South Korea,
Taiwan) are Confucian societies. Until his death, Herman Kahn was director of the Hudson Institute think tank and was well-known as a
futurist. In this contribution, Kahn says that much of the success of
these nations can be attributed directly to their cultures. It is interesting to compare the attributes of Confucianism that Kahn suggests are
important for development with the attributes of n Achievement discussed in Chapter 17. It is also worth considering the implication of
Kahn's argument for those nations in Latin America, Africa, and elsewhere that have dramatically different traditions. Has the absence of
a "Confucian ethic" held back the development of these nations? If
so, is it likely to make closing the gap between them and the developed nations an impossible dream?* ■

MOST READERS OF THIS BOOK ARE FAMILIAR WITH THE ARGUMENT OF MAX WEBER
that the Protestant ethic was extremely useful in promoting the rise and spread
of modernization.[1] Most readers, however, will be much less familiar with the
notion that has gradually emerged in the last two decades that societies based
upon the Confucian ethic may in many ways be superior to the West in the pursuit of industrialization, affluence, and modernization. Let us see what some
of the strengths of the Confucian ethic are in the modern world.

Reprinted with permission from *World Economic Development: 1979 and Beyond*,
by Herman Kahn (Indianapolis: Hudson Institute, 1979), pp. 121–122, 124–125.

The Confucian Ethic

The Confucian ethic includes two quite different but connected sets of issues. First and perhaps foremost, Confucian societies uniformly promote in the individual and the family sobriety, a high value on education, a desire for accomplishment in various skills (particularly academic and cultural), and seriousness about tasks, job, family, and obligations. A properly trained member of a Confucian culture will be hard working, responsible, skillful, and (within the assigned or understood limits) ambitious and creative in helping the group (extended family, community, or company). There is much less emphasis on advancing individual (selfish) interests.

In some ways, the capacity for purposive and efficient communal and organizational activities and efforts is even more important in the modern world than the personal qualities, although both are important. Smoothly fitting, harmonious human relations in an organization are greatly encouraged in most neo-Confucian societies. This is partly because of a sense of hierarchy but even more because of a sense of complementarity of relations that is much stronger in Confucian than in Western societies.

The anthropologist Chie Nakane has pointed out that in Western societies there is a great tendency for "like to join like" in unions, student federations, women's groups, men's clubs, youth movements, economic classes, and so on.[2] This tends to set one group in society against another: students against teachers, employees against employers, youths against parents, and so on. In the Confucian hierarchic society, the emphasis is on cooperation among complementary elements, much as in the family (which is in fact the usual paradigm or model in a Confucian culture). The husband and wife work together and cooperate in raising the children; each has different assigned duties and responsibilities, as do the older and younger siblings and the grandparents. There is emphasis on fairness and equity, but it is fairness and equity in the institutional context, not for the individual as an individual. Synergism—complementarity and cooperation among parts of a whole—are emphasized, not equality and interchangeability. The major identification is with one's role in the organization or other institutional structure, whether it be the family, the business firm, or a bureau in the government.

Since the crucial issues in a modern society increasingly revolve around these equity issues and on making organizations work well, the neo-Confucian cultures have great advantages. As opposed to the earlier Protestant ethic, the modern Confucian ethic is superbly designed to create and foster loyalty, dedication, responsibility, and commitment and to intensify identification with the organization and one's role in the organization. All this makes the economy and society operate much more smoothly than one whose principles of identification and association tend to lead to egalitarianism, to disunity, to confrontation, and to excessive compensation or repression.

A society that emphasizes a like-to-like type of identification works out reasonably well as long as there is enough hierarchy, discipline, control, or motivation within the society to restrain excessive tendencies to egalitarianism, anarchy, self-indulgence, and so on. But as the society becomes more affluent and secular, there is less motivation, reduced commitment, more privatization, and increasingly impersonal and automatic welfare. Interest in group politics, group and individual selfishness, egoism, intergroup antagonisms, and perhaps even intergroup warfare all tend to increase. It becomes the old versus the young, insiders versus outsiders, men versus women, students versus teachers, and—most important of all—employees against employers. The tendencies toward anarchy, rivalry, and payoffs to the politically powerful or the organized militants become excessive and out of control.

For all these reasons we believe that both aspects of the Confucian ethic— the creation of dedicated, motivated, responsible, and educated individuals and the enhanced sense of commitment, organizational identity, and loyalty to various institutions—will result in all the neo-Confucian societies having at least potentially higher growth rates than other cultures. . . .

Whether or not one accepts our analysis of *why* neo-Confucian cultures are so competent in industrialization, the impressive data that support the final thesis are overwhelming. The performance of the People's Republic of China; of both North and South Korea; of Japan, Taiwan, Hong Kong, and Singapore; and of the various Chinese ethnic groups in Malaysia, Thailand, Indonesia, and the Philippines, discloses extraordinary talent (at least in the last twenty-five years) for economic development and for learning about and using modern technology. For example, the North Vietnamese operated one of the most complicated air defense networks in history more or less by themselves (once instructed by the Soviets), and the American army found that the South Vietnamese, if properly motivated, often went through training school in about half the time required by Americans. We do not gloss over the enormous differences among these neo-Confucian cultures. They vary almost as much as do European cultures. But all of them seem amenable to modernization under current conditions.

Notes

1. Max Weber, *The Protestant Ethic and the Spirit of Capitalism,* translated by Talcott Parsons (New York: Charles Scribner's Sons, 1930).

2. Chie Nakane, *Japanese Society* (Berkeley, Calif.: University of California Press, 1970).

20

The Effect of Cultural Values on Economic Development: Theory, Hypotheses, and Some Empirical Tests

JIM GRANATO, RONALD INGLEHART, AND DAVID LEBLANG

In this chapter, Jim Granato, Ronald Inglehart, and David Leblang examine the ties between cultural values and economic development. They utilize the "achievement motive" thesis developed by McClelland as a specific empirical point of reference. The authors test the theory using the World Values Survey, a database of interviews collected in many countries around the world. In this study, data are used for twenty-five countries, and strong evidence indicates that certain cultural values help to spur economic growth. In the same journal from which this chapter was drawn, however, the findings are disputed by other authors. The jury still seems to be out on this fascinating debate. ∎

DO CULTURAL FACTORS INFLUENCE ECONOMIC DEVELOPMENT? IF SO, CAN THEY BE measured and their effect compared with that of standard economic factors such as savings and investment? This article examines the explanatory power of the standard endogenous growth model and compares it with that of two types of cultural variables capturing motivational factors—achievement motivation and postmaterialist values. We believe that it is not an either/or proposition: cultural and economic factors play complementary roles. This belief is borne out empirically; we use recently developed econometric techniques to assess the relative merits of these alternative explanations.

Cultural factors alone do not explain all of the cross-national variation in economic growth rates. Every economy experiences significant fluctuations in

Reprinted with permission of Blackwell Publishing from *American Journal of Political Science*, vol. 40, no. 3 (August 1996): 607–631.

growth rates from year to year as a result of short-term factors such as techno-logical shocks or unforeseen circumstances that affect output. These could not be attributed to cultural factors, which change gradually. A society's economic and political institutions also make a difference. For example, prior to 1945, North Korea and South Korea had a common culture, but South Korea's eco-nomic performance has been far superior.

On the other hand, the evidence suggests that cultural differences are an im-portant part of the story. Over the past five decades, the Confucian-influenced economies of East Asia outperformed the rest of the world by a wide margin. This holds true despite the fact that they are shaped by a wide variety of eco-nomic and political institutions. Conversely, during the same period most African economies experienced low growth rates. Both societal-level and indi-vidual-level evidence suggests that a society's economic and political institu-tions are not the only factors determining economic development; cultural fac-tors are also important.

Traditionally, the literature presents culture and economic determinants of growth as distinct. Political economists and political sociologists view their re-spective approaches as mutually exclusive. One reason lies in the level of analysis employed and with this the underlying assumptions about human be-havior. Another reason is that we have had inadequate measures of cultural factors. Previous attempts to establish the role of culture either infer culture from economic performance or estimate cultural factors from impressionistic historical evidence. Both factors could be important, but until cultural factors are entered into a quantitative analysis, this possibility could not be tested.

By *culture,* we refer to a system of basic common values that help shape the behavior of the people in a given society. In most preindustrial societies, this value system takes the form of a religion and changes very slowly; but with industrialization and accompanying processes of modernization, these worldviews tend to become more secular, rational, and open to change.

For reasons discussed below, the cultures of virtually all preindustrial so-cieties are hostile to social mobility and individual economic accumulation. Thus, both medieval Christianity and traditional Confucian culture stigma-tized profit-making and entrepreneurship. But (as Weber argues), a Protestant version of Christianity played a key role in the rise of capitalism—and much later—a modernized version of Confucian society encourages economic growth, through its support of education and achievement.

The theory and evidence presented in this paper are organized as follows: section one discusses theories that deal with the effect of culture on economic development. This literature emphasizes the importance of motivational factors in the growth process. Section two introduces the data. This data, based on rep-resentative national surveys of basic values, enables us to construct two mea-sures of cultures—achievement motivation and postmaterialist values. Section three discusses the baseline endogenous growth model. We draw upon a recent paper by Levine and Renelt (1992) to specify this model, and we augment it with cultural variables. Section four is the multivariate analysis. Economic and cultural variables each explain unique aspects of the cross-national variation in economic growth. Using the *encompassing* principles we find that an improved and parsimonious explanation for economic growth comes from a model that includes both economic and cultural variables. Section four also examines the robustness of this economic-cultural model and finds that the specification is robust to alterations in the conditioning set of information, the elimination of influential cases, and variations in estimation procedure. Section five concludes.

Culture, Motivational Factors, and Economic Growth

We first discuss the literature that views achievement motivation as an essential component in the process of economic development, and then we explore how cultural measures from the World Values Survey can be used to examine the effect of motivation on growth.

The motivational literature stresses the role of cultural emphasis on economic achievement. It grows out of Weber's (1904–1905) Protestant Ethic thesis. This school of thought gave rise to the historical research of Tawney (1926, 1955), case studies by Harrison (1992), and empirical work by McClelland et al. (1953) and McClelland (1961) on achievement motivation. Inglehart (1971, 1977, 1990) extends this work by examining the shift from materialist to post-materialist value priorities. Although previous work mainly focuses on the political consequences of these values, their emergence represents a shift away from emphasis on economic accumulation and growth. These "new" values could be viewed as the erosion of Protestant Ethic among populations that experience high levels of economic security.

We suggest that Weber is correct in arguing that the rise of Protestantism is a crucial event in modernizing Europe. He emphasizes that the Calvinist version of Protestantism encourages norms favorable to economic achievement. But we view the rise of Protestantism as one case of a more general phenomenon. It is important, not only because of the specific content of early Protestant beliefs, but because this belief system undermines a set of religious norms that inhibit economic achievement and are common to most preindustrial societies.

Preindustrial economies are zero-sum systems: they are characterized by little or no economic growth which implies that upward social mobility only comes at the expense of someone else. A society's cultural system generally reflects this fact. Social status is hereditary rather than achieved, and social norms encourage one to accept one's social position in this life. Aspirations toward social mobility are sternly repressed. Such value systems help to maintain social solidarity but discourage economic accumulation.

Weber's emphasis on the role of Protestantism seems to capture an important part of reality. The Protestant Reformation combined with the emergence of scientific logic broke the grip of the medieval Christian Worldview on a significant part of Europe. Prior to the Reformation, Southern Europe was economically more advanced than Northern Europe. During the three centuries after the Reformation, capitalism emerged, mainly among the Protestant regions of Europe and the Protestant minorities in Catholic countries. Within this cultural context, individual economic accumulation was no longer rejected.

Protestant Europe manifested a subsequent economic dynamism that moved it far ahead of Catholic Europe. Shifting trade patterns, declining food production in Southern Europe and other factors also contributed to this shift, but the evidence suggests that cultural factors played a major role. Throughout the first 150 years of the Industrial Revolution, industrial development took place almost entirely within Protestant regions of Europe, and the Protestant portions of the New World. It was only during the second half of the twentieth century that an entrepreneurial outlook emerged in Catholic Europe and in the Far East. Both now show higher rates of economic growth than Protestant Europe. In short, the concept of the Protestant Ethic would be outdated if we take it to mean something that exists in historically Protestant countries. But Weber's more general concept, that certain cultural factors influence economic growth, is an important and valid insight.

McClelland et al. (1953) and McClelland's (1961) work on achievement motivation builds on the Weberian thesis but focuses on the values that were encouraged in children by their parents, schools, and other agencies of socialization. He hypothesizes that some societies emphasize economic achievement as a positive goal while others give it little emphasis. Since it was not feasible for him to measure directly the values emphasized in given societies through representative national surveys, McClelland attempts to measure them indirectly, through content analysis of the stories and school books used to educate children. He finds that some cultures emphasize achievement in their school books more heavily than others—and that the former showed considerably higher rates of economic growth than did the latter.

McClelland's work is criticized on various grounds. It is questioned whether his approach really measures the values taught to children, or simply those of textbook writers. Subsequently, writers of the dependency school argue that any attempt to trace differences in economic growth rates to factors within a given culture, rather than to global capitalist exploitation, is simply a means of justifying exploitation of the peripheral economies. Such criticism tends to discredit this type of research but is hardly an empirical refutation.

Survey research by Lenski (1963) and Alwin (1986) finds that Catholics and Protestants in the United States show significant differences in the values they emphasize as the most important things to teach children. These differences are more or less along the lines of the Protestant Ethic thesis. Alwin also demonstrates that these differences erode over time, with Protestants and Catholics gradually converging toward a common belief system.

The Data

The World Values Survey asks representative national samples of the publics in a number of societies, "Here is a list of qualities which children can be encouraged to learn at home. Which, if any, do you consider to be especially important?" This list includes qualities that reflect emphasis on autonomy and economic achievement, such as "thrift," "saving money and things," and "determination." Other items on the list reflect emphasis on conformity to traditional social norms, such as "obedience" and "religious faith."

We construct an index of achievement motivation that sums up the percentage in each country emphasizing the first two goals minus the percentage emphasizing the latter two goals. This method of index construction controls for the tendency of respondents in some societies to place relatively heavy emphasis on all of these goals, while respondents in other countries mention relatively few of them.

Figure 20.1 shows the simple bivariate relationship between this index and rates of per capita economic growth between 1960 and 1989. The zero-point on the achievement motivation index reflects the point where exactly as many people emphasize obedience and religion, as emphasize thrift and determination. As we move to the right, the latter values are given increasing emphasis. A given society's emphasis on thrift and determination *over* obedience and religious faith has a strong bivariate linkage with its rate of economic growth over the past three decades ($r = .66$; $p = .001$).

Though often stereotyped as having authoritarian cultures, Japan, China, and South Korea emerge near the pole that emphasizes thrift more heavily than obedience. The three East Asian societies rank highest on that dimension, while the two African societies included in this survey rank near the opposite end of the continuum, emphasizing obedience and religious faith.

The publics of India and the United States also fall toward the latter end of the scale. This is *not* an authoritarianism dimension. It reflects the balance between emphasis on two types of values. One set of values—thrift and determination—support economic achievement; while the other—obedience and religious faith—tend to discourage it, emphasizing conformity to traditional authority and group norms. These two types of values are not necessarily incompatible: some societies rank relatively high on both, while others rank relatively low on both. But, the relative *priority* given to them is strongly related to its growth rate.

Do cultural factors lead to economic growth, or does economic growth lead to cultural change? We believe that the causal flow can work in both

Figure 20.1 Economic Growth Rate by Achievement Motivation Scores of Public

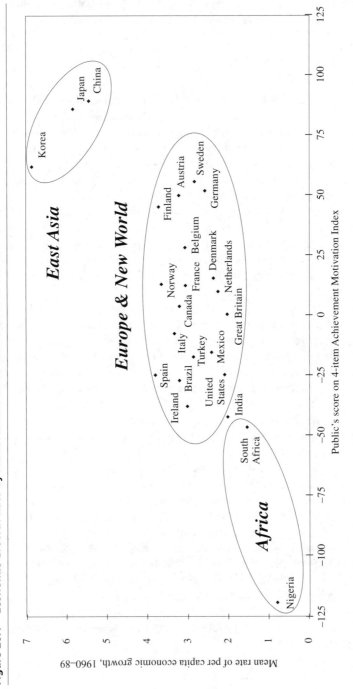

Note: Achievement Motivation Index is based on the percentage in each society who emphasized "Thrift" and "Determination" as important things for a child to learn *minus* the percentage emphasizing "Obedience" and "Religious Faith."

directions. For example, there is strong evidence that postmaterialist values emerge when a society attains relatively high levels of economic security. In this case, economic change reshapes culture. On the other hand, once these values become widespread, they are linked with relatively low subsequent rates of economic growth. Here, culture seems to be shaping economics—a parallel to the Weberian thesis, except that what is happening here is, in a sense, the rise of the Protestant Ethic in reverse.

Demonstrating causal connections is always difficult. In connection with our achievement motivation index, the obvious interpretation would be that emphasis on thrift and hard work, rather than on obedience and respect, is conducive to economic growth. The two most sensitive indicators of this dimension are thrift, on the one hand, and obedience on the other. For some time, economists have been aware that a nation's rate of gross domestic investment is a major influence on its long term growth rate. Investment, in turn, depends on savings. Thus, a society that emphasizes thrift produces savings, which leads to investment, and later to economic growth. We provide evidence below that this is probably the case. This does not rule out the possibility that economic growth might be conducive to thrift but this linkage is less obvious.

Emphasis on obedience is negatively linked with economic growth, for a converse reason. In preindustrial societies, obedience means conformity to traditional norms, which de-emphasize and even stigmatize economic accumulation. Obedience, respect for others, and religious faith all emphasize obligations to share with and support one's relatives, friends and neighbors. Such communal obligations are strongly felt in preindustrial societies. But from the perspective of a bureaucratized rational-legal society, these norms are antithetical to capital accumulation and conducive to nepotism. Furthermore, conformity to authority inhibits innovation and entrepreneurship.

The motivational component is also tapped by materialist/postmaterialist values, with postmaterialism having a negative relationship with economic growth. The achievement motivation variable is only modestly correlated with the materialist/postmaterialist dimension ($r = -.39$; $p = .0581$). Though both dimensions have significant linkages with economic growth, they affect it in different ways. The achievement motivation dimension seems to tap the transition from preindustrial to industrial values systems, linked with the modernization process.

The materialist/postmaterialist dimension reflects the transition to post-industrial society, linked with a shift away from emphasis on economic growth, toward increasing emphasis on protection of the environment and on the quality of life more generally. Previous research demonstrates that: (1) a gradual shift from materialist toward postmaterialist goals has been taking place throughout advanced industrial society; (2) that this shift is strongly related to the emergence of democracy ($r = .71$); but (3) that it has a tendency to be negatively linked with economic growth (Abramson and Inglehart 1995).

Multivariate Analysis

Our empirical approach is straightforward: we begin by estimating (via OLS) a baseline endogenous growth model that includes variables identified by Levine and Renelt (1992) as having robust partial correlations with economic growth. Using data for 25 countries[1] we first test the endogenous growth specification (Model 1 in Table 20.1). Following Equation [1], a nation's rate of per capita economic growth is regressed on its initial level of per capita income and human capital investment (education spending) as well as on its rate of physical capital accumulation. As expected, the results are quite compatible with the expectations of endogenous growth theory. The results of Model 1 are summarized as follows: (1) the significant negative coefficient on the initial level of per capita income indicates that there is evidence of "conditional convergence." That is, controlling for human and physical capital investment, poorer nations grow faster than richer nations; (2) investment in human capital (education spending) has a positive and statistically significant effect on subsequent economic growth; and (3) increasing the rate of physical capital accumulation increases a nation's rate of economic growth.

Table 20.1   OLS Estimation of Economic Growth Models Dependent
Variable: Mean Rate of per Capita Economic Growth (1960–1989)

Model Variable	Model 1	Model 2	Model 3	Model 4
Constant	−0.70	7.29*	3.16	2.40*
	(1.08)	(1.49)	(1.94)	(0.77)
Per Capita GDP in 1960	−0.63*		−0.42*	−0.43*
	(0.14)		(0.14)	(0.10)
Primary Education in 1960	2.69*		2.19*	2.09*
	(1.22)		(1.06)	(0.96)
Secondary Education	3.27*		1.21	
	(1.01)		(1.08)	
Investment	8.69*		3.09	
	(4.90)		(4.40)	
Achievement Motivation		2.07*	1.44*	1.88*
		(0.37)	(0.48)	(0.35)
Postmaterialism		−2.24*	−1.07	
		(0.77)	(1.03)	
R^2 Adjusted	.55	.59	.69	.70
SEE	.86	.83	.72	.71
LM ($x^2[1]$)	.42	.65	.68	.87
Jarque-Bera ($x^2[2]$)	.05	.30	.18	.57
White ($x^2[1]$)	.28	.24	.37	.18
SC	.119	−.117	−.095	−.352

Notes: Mean of dependent variable: 3.04; N is 25 for all models; standard errors in parentheses.
*t test: p < .05

Overall this baseline economic model performs well: it accounts for 55% of the variation in cross-national growth rates and is consistent with prior cross-national tests of the conditional convergence hypothesis (e.g., Barro 1991; Mankiw, Romer, and Weil 1992). Model 1 also passes all diagnostic tests, indicating that the residuals are not serially correlated[2] (LM test), are normally distributed (Jarque-Bera test), and homoskedastic (White test).

Model 2 in Table 20.1 regresses the rate of per capita economic growth on a constant and the two cultural variables. As expected, both achievement motivation and postmaterialism are significant predictors of economic growth and have the expected sign. Thus, the arguments of both Protestant Ethic and postmaterialist type theories cannot be rejected by this evidence. In addition, these variables, taken by themselves, do fairly well, accounting for 59% of the variance in growth rates. A glance at the diagnostics also indicates that the residuals are well behaved.

Comparing Competing Empirical Models: Encompassing Results

Both the economic and cultural models give similar goodness-of-fit performance. Each model's regressors are statistically significant. Yet, which model is superior? Or do both models possess explanatory factors that are missing in the other? . . .

In short, both models explain aspects of growth that the rival cannot. The implication is straightforward: growth rates are best understood as a consequence of both economic and cultural factors.

What happens when we combine the economic model with the cultural model? The results of this experiment are contained in Model 3. Beginning with the endogenous growth variables, adding the variables from Model 2 significantly alters the parameter estimates and standard errors on secondary education spending and physical capital investment. In fact, the coefficient on the physical capital investment variable changes dramatically. It decreases from 8.69 in Model 1 to 3.09 in Model 3. While this coefficient still has the expected sign, it is now far from significant.

Why is physical capital investment, a variable "robustly" correlated with economic growth in a number of other studies, now insignificant? Achievement motivation quite possibly is conducive to economic growth at least partly because it encourages relatively high rates of investment. Achievement motivation also has an important direct effect on economic growth rates, quite apart from its tendency to increase investment. Presumably the direct path from culture to economic growth reflects the effect of motivational factors on entrepreneurship and effort.

Returning to the analysis of Model 3 in Table 20.1, we now examine the direct effect of cultural values, particularly achievement motivation, on economic growth. As in Model 2, achievement motivation is positively and significantly related to economic growth. Combining Model 2 and Model 3 results in postmaterialism now being insignificant, however. This is probably due to the fact that countries with postmaterialist values are already fairly rich; the bivariate correlation between the initial level of wealth and postmaterialism is .75 and is significant at the .0000 level. Combining the regressors of these models (Model 3) we again have a model that does not violate any diagnostic test. In addition, the fit is more accurate (SEE).

Sensitivity Analysis

Table 20.1 contains an additional specification. In Model 4 we eliminate the three insignificant variables from Model 3—those for postmaterialism, investment, and secondary school enrollment—to check the stability of the remaining parameters. Model 4 is the most parsimonious and efficient model, explaining 70 percent of the variance in per capita growth rates with only three variables. . . .

Conclusion

The idea that economic growth is partly shaped by cultural factors has encountered considerable resistance. One reason for this resistance is because cultural values have been widely perceived as diffuse and permanent features of given societies: if cultural values determine economic growth, then the outlook for economic development seems hopeless, because culture cannot be changed. Another reason for opposition is that standard economic arguments supposedly suffice for international differences in savings and growth rates. For example, the standard life cycle model and not cultural arguments explains the difference in savings rates and growth rates between, say, Germany, Japan, and the United States.[3]

When we approach culture as something to be measured on a quantitative empirical basis, the illusion of diffuseness and permanence disappears. We no longer deal with gross stereotypes, such as the idea that "Germans have always been militaristic," or "Hispanic culture is unfavorable to development." We can move to the analysis of specific components of a given culture at a given time and place. Thus, we find that, from 1945 to 1975, West German political culture underwent a striking transformation from being relatively authoritarian to becoming increasingly democratic and participant (Baker, Dalton, and Hildebrandt 1981). And we find that, from 1970 to 1993, the United States and a number of West European societies experienced a gradual intergenerational shift from having predominantly materialist toward increasingly postmaterialist value priorities (Abramson and Inglehart 1995). Though these changes have been gradual, they demonstrate that central elements of culture can and do change.

Furthermore, empirical research can help identify specific components of culture that are relevant to economic development. One need not seek to change a society's entire way of life. The present findings suggest that one specific dimension—achievement motivation—is highly relevant to economic growth rates. In the short run, to change even a relatively narrow and well-defined cultural component such as this is not easy, but it should be far easier than attempting to change an entire culture. Furthermore, empirical research demonstrates that culture can and does change. Simply making parents, schools and other organizations aware of the potentially relevant factors may be a step in the right direction.

We find that economic theory already is augmented with "social norms" and "cultural" factors (Cole, Malaith, and Postlewaite 1992; Elster 1989; Fershtman and Weiss 1993). Where would cultural values fit theoretically in growth models? The economics literature is replete with models of savings behavior that focus on the "life cycle" and, more specifically, the bequest motive. Cultural variables matter here. Since savings and investment behavior holds an important place in growth models, a determination of how cultural and motivational factors can be used to augment these existing economic models, it seems to us, is the next step to uncovering a better understanding of economic growth.[4]

In the end, however, these arguments can only be resolved on the empirical battlefield. We use ordinary least squares regression to test economic and cultural models of growth on a cross section of 25 countries. We find that economic and cultural factors affect growth. . . .

The results in this article demonstrate that *both* cultural and economic arguments matter. Neither supplants the other. Future theoretical and empirical work is better served by treating these "separate" explanations as complementary.

Notes

1. The nations included in the multivariate analysis are: Austria, Belgium, Brazil, Canada, China, Denmark, Finland, France, Germany, Great Britain, India, Ireland, Italy, Japan, Korea, Mexico, Netherlands, Nigeria, Norway, South Africa, Spain, Sweden, Switzerland, Turkey, United States.

2. This is a check for spatial correlation between the errors of the cases.

3. In the post–World War II period, the life cycle model argues that since Japan and Germany had a substantial portion of their capital stock destroyed, the "permanent income" of the population was going to be less than was expected at the onset of the war. The lower capital-labor ratio contributes to lower real wages and higher interest rates. In response the public raised its savings rate to "smooth" its postretirement income. The United States, on the other hand, saw a significant increase in its capital

stock as a result of the war. This had the opposite effect since the higher capital-labor ratio depresses interest rates and raises real wages. The public's savings rate falls in this case since "permanent income" increases, while current consumption rises.

4. Institutional factors such as regime type and property rights have also been suggested as important determinants of economic growth (Helliwell 1994; Leblang 1996).

References

Abramson, Paul, and Ronald Inglehart. 1995. *Value Change in Global Perspective.* Ann Arbor: University of Michigan Press.

Achen, Christopher. 1982. *Interpreting and Using Regression.* Beverly Hills: Sage.

Alwin, Duane F. 1986. "Religion and Parental Child-Rearing Orientations: Evidence of a Catholic-Protestant Convergence." *American Journal of Sociology* 92:412–40.

Baker, Kendall L., Russell Dalton, and Kai Hildebrandt. 1981. *Germany Transformed* Cambridge: Harvard University Press.

Barro, Robert. 1991. "Economic Growth in a Cross Section of Countries." *Quarterly Journal of Economics* 106:407–44.

Bollen, Kenneth, and Robert Jackman. 1985. "Regression Diagnostics. An Expository Treatment of Outliers and Influential Cases." *Sociological Methods and Research* 13:510–42.

Chatterjee, S., and A. S. Hadi. 1988. *Sensitivity Analysis in Linear Regression.* New York: John Wiley.

Cole, Harold, George Malaith, and Andrew Postlewaite. 1992. "Social Norms, Savings Behavior, and Growth." *Journal of Political Economy* 100:1092–125.

Cook, R. D., and S. Weisberg. 1982. *Residuals* and *Influence in Regression.* London: Chapman and Hall.

Davidson, Ronald, and James MacKinnon. 1991. "Several Tests for Model Specification in the Presence of Alternative Hypotheses." *Econometrica* 49:781–93.

Elster, Jon. 1989. "Social Norms and Economic Theory." *Journal of Economic Perspectives* 3:99–117.

Fershtman, Chaim, and Yoram Weiss. 1993. "Social Status, Culture, and Economic Performance." *The Economic Journal* 103:946–59.

Fox, John. 1991. *Regression Diagnostics: An Introduction.* Sage University Paper on Quantitative Applications in the Social Sciences, 07-079. Newbury Park, CA: Sage.

Godfrey, Leslie. 1984. "On the Uses of Misspecification Checks and Tests of Nonnested Hypotheses in Empirical Econometrics." *Economic Journal* Supplement 96:69–81.

Granato, Jim, and Motoshi Suzuki. N.d. "The Use of the Encompassing Principle to Resolve Empirical Controversies in Voting Behavior: An Application to Voter Rationality in Congressional Elections." *Electoral Studies.* Forthcoming.

Hamilton, Lawrence. 1992. *Regression with Graphics: A Second Course in Applied Statistics.* Pacific Grove, CA: Brooks/Cole Publishing.

Harrison, Lawrence E. 1992. *Who Prospers? How Cultural Values Shape Economic and Political Success.* New York: Basic Books.

Helliwell, J. F. 1994. "Empirical Linkages Between Democracy and Growth." *British Journal of Political Science* 24:225–48.

Hendry, David, and Jean-Francois Richard. 1989. "Recent Developments in the Theory of Encompassing." In *Contributions to Operations Research and Econometrics:*

The XXth Anniversary of CORE, ed. B. Comet and H. Tulkens. Boston: MIT Press.

Inglehart, Ronald. 1971. "The Silent Revolution in Europe." *American Political Science Review* 4:991–1017.

Inglehart, Ronald. 1977. *The Silent Revolution: Changing Values and Political Styles.* Princeton: Princeton University Press.

Inglehart, Ronald. 1990. *Culture Shift in Advanced Industrial Society.* Princeton: Princeton University Press.

Jackman, Robert. 1987. "The Politics of Economic Growth in Industrialized Democracies, 1974–1980." *Journal of Politics* 49:242–56.

Leamer, Edward. 1983. "Let's Take the 'Con' Out of Econometrics." *American Economic Review* 73:31–43.

Leblang, David. 1996. "Property Rights, Democracy, and Economic Growth." *Political Research Quarterly* 49:5–26.

Lenski, Gerhard. 1963. *The Religious Factor.* New York: Anchor-Doubleday.

Levine, Ross, and David Renelt. 1992. "A Sensitivity Analysis of Cross-Country Growth Regressions." *American Economic Review* 82:942–63.

Lucas, Robert. 1988. "On the Mechanics of Economic Development." *Journal of Monetary Economics* 1:3–32.

Mankiw, N. Gregory, David Romer, and David Weil. 1992. "A Contribution to the Empirics of Economic Growth." *Quarterly Journal of Economics* 152:407–37.

McClelland, David. 1961. *The Achieving Society.* Princeton: Van Nostrand.

McClelland, David, et al. 1953. *The Achievement Motive.* New York: Appleton-Century-Crofts.

Mizon, Grayham, and Jean-Francois Richard. 1986. "The Encompassing Principle and Its Application to Non-nested Hypothesis Tests." *Econometrica* 54:657–78.

Mooney, Christopher, and Robert Duval. 1993. *Bootstrapping: A Nonparametric Approach to Statistical Inference.* Sage University Paper Series on Quantitative Applications in the Social Sciences, 07-095. Newbury Park, CA: Sage.

Romer, Paul. 1990. "Endogenous Technological Change." *Journal of Political Economy* 98:71–102.

Solow, Robert. 1956. "A Contribution to the Theory of Economic Growth." *Quarterly Journal of Economics* 70:65–94.

Stine, Robert. 1990. "An Introduction to Bootstrap Methods." *Sociological Methods and Research* 18:243–91.

Swan, Trevor. 1956. "Economic Growth and Capital Accumulation." *Economic Record* 22:334–61.

Tawney, Richard. 1926. *Religion and the Rise of Capitalism: A History.* Gloucester, MA: P. Smith.

Tawney, Richard. [1922] 1955. *The Acquisitive Society.* Reprint. New York: Harcourt Brace.

Welsch, Roy. 1980. "Regression Sensitivity Analysis and Bounded-Influence Estimation." In *Evaluation of Econometric Models,* ed. Jan Kmenta and James Ramsey. New York: Academic Press.

PART 6

Dependency and World Systems Theory: Still Relevant?

21

The Development of Underdevelopment

ANDRE GUNDER FRANK

This chapter is the classic work that initiated what would eventually grow into a tidal wave of "dependency theory" research. In it, the author argues against the classical theory of economics, as articulated in works such as W. W. Rostow's "Stages of Economic Growth" (see this volume, Chapter 14), in which all countries will eventually become developed. Gunder Frank takes a very long-term view, as do Diamond (Chapter 7) and Acemoglu et al. (Chapter 9), but from his perspective the cause of underdevelopment is that great colonial powers became wealthy at the expense of the colonies that they exploited and continue to exploit even after the formal colonial period ended. ■

WE CANNOT HOPE TO FORMULATE ADEQUATE DEVELOPMENT THEORY AND POLICY for the majority of the world's population who suffer from underdevelopment without first learning how their past economic and social history gave rise to their present underdevelopment. Yet most historians study only the developed metropolitan countries and pay scant attention to the colonial and underdeveloped lands. For this reason most of our theoretical categories and guides to development policy have been distilled exclusively from the historical experience of the European and North American advanced capitalist nations.

Since the historical experience of the colonial and underdeveloped countries has demonstrably been quite different, available theory therefore fails to reflect the past of the underdeveloped part of the world entirely, and reflects

Excerpted from Andre Gunder Frank, *Latin America: Underdevelopment or Revolution?* (New York: Monthly Review Press, 1969). Reprinted with permission from the Monthly Review Foundation.

the past of the world as a whole only in part. More important, our ignorance of the underdeveloped countries' history leads us to assume that their past and indeed their present resembles earlier stages of the history of the now developed countries. This ignorance and this assumption lead us into serious misconceptions about contemporary underdevelopment and development. Further, most studies of development and underdevelopment fail to take account of the economic and other relations between the metropolis and its economic colonies throughout the history of the world-wide expansion and development of the mercantilist and capitalist system. Consequently, most of our theory fails to explain the structure and development of the capitalist system as a whole and to account for its simultaneous generation of underdevelopment in some of its parts and economic development in others.

It is generally held that economic development occurs in a succession of capitalist stages and that today's underdeveloped countries are still in a stage, sometimes depicted as an original stage of history, through which the now developed countries passed long ago. Yet even a modest acquaintance with history shows that underdevelopment is not original or traditional and that neither the past nor the present of the underdeveloped countries resembles in any important respect the past of the now developed countries. The now developed countries were never underdeveloped, though they may have been undeveloped. It is also widely believed that the contemporary underdevelopment of a country can be understood as the product or reflection solely of its own economic, political, social, and cultural characteristics or structure. Yet historical research demonstrates that contemporary underdevelopment is in large part the historical product of past and continuing economic and other relations between the satellite underdeveloped and the now developed metropolitan countries. Furthermore, these relations are an essential part of the structure and development of the capitalist system on a world scale as a whole. A related and also largely erroneous view is that the development of these underdeveloped countries and, within them of their most underdeveloped domestic areas, must and will be generated or stimulated by diffusing capital, institutions, values, etc., to them from the international and national capitalist metropoles. Historical perspective based on the underdeveloped countries' past experience suggests that, on the contrary, in the underdeveloped countries economic development can now occur only independently of most of these relations of diffusion.

Evident inequalities of income and differences in culture have led many observers to see "dual" societies and economies in the underdeveloped countries. Each of the two parts is supposed to have a history of its own, a structure, and a contemporary dynamic largely independent of the other. Supposedly, only one part of the economy and society has been importantly affected by intimate economic relations with the "outside" capitalist world; and that part, it is held, became modern, capitalist, and relatively developed precisely because of this contact. The other part is widely regarded as variouly isolated, subsistence-based, feudal, or precapitalist, and therefore more underdeveloped.

I believe on the contrary that the entire "dual society" thesis is false and that the policy recommendations to which it leads will, if acted upon, serve only to intensify and perpetuate the very conditions of underdevelopment they are supposedly designed to remedy.

A mounting body of evidence suggests, and I am confident that future historical research will confirm, that the expansion of the capitalist system over the past centuries effectively and entirely penetrated even the apparently most isolated sectors of the underdeveloped world. Therefore, the economic, political, social, and cultural institutions and relations we now observe there are the products of the historical development of the capitalist system no less than are the seemingly more modern or capitalist features of the national metropoles of these underdeveloped countries. Analogously to the relations between development and underdevelopment on the international level, the contemporary underdeveloped institutions of the so-called backward or feudal domestic areas of an underdeveloped country are no less the product of the single historical process of capitalist development than are the so-called capitalist institutions of the supposedly more progressive areas. In this paper I should like to sketch the kinds of evidence which support this thesis and at the same time indicate lines along which further study and research could fruitfully proceed.

The Secretary General of the Latin American Center for Research in the Social Sciences writes in that Center's journal: "The privileged position of the city has its origin in the colonial period. It was founded by the Conqueror to serve the same ends that it still serves today; to incorporate the indigenous population into the economy brought and developed by that Conqueror and his descendants. The regional city was an instrument of conquest and is still today an instrument of domination."[1] The Instituto Nacional Indigenista (National Indian Institute) of Mexico confirms this observation when it notes that "the mestizo population, in fact, always lives in a city, a center of an intercultural region, which acts as the metropolis of a zone of indigenous population and which maintains with the underdeveloped communities an intimate relation which links the center with the satellite communities."[2] The Institute goes on to point out that "between the mestizos who live in the nuclear city of the region and the Indians who live in the peasant hinterland there is in reality a closer economic and social interdependence than might at first glance appear" and that the provincial metropoles "by being centers of intercourse are also centers of exploitation."[3]

Thus these metropolis-satellite relations are not limited to the imperial or international level but penetrate and structure the very economic, political, and social life of the Latin American colonies and countries. Just as the colonial and national capital and its export sector become the satellite of the Iberian (and later of other) metropoles of the world economic system, this satellite immediately becomes a colonial and then a national metropolis with respect to the productive sectors and population of the interior. Furthermore, the provincial capitals, which thus are themselves satellites of the national metropolis—and through the latter of the world metropolis—are in turn provincial centers around which their own local satellites orbit. Thus, a whole chain of constellations of metropoles and satellites relates all parts of the whole system from its metropolitan center in Europe or the United States to the farthest outpost in the Latin American countryside.

When we examine this metropolis-satellite structure, we find that each of the satellites, including now underdeveloped Spain and Portugal, serves as an instrument to suck capital or economic surplus out of its own satellites and to channel part of this surplus to the world metropolis of which all are satellites. Moreover, each national and local metropolis serves to impose and maintain the monopolistc structure and exploitative relationship of this system (as the Instituto Nacional Indigenista of Mexico calls it) as long as it serves the interests of the metropoles which take advantage of this global, national, and local structure to promote their own development and the enrichment of their ruling classes.

These are the principal and still surviving structural characteristics which were implanted in Latin America by the Conquest. Beyond examining the establishment of this colonial structure in its historical context, the proposed approach calls for study of the development—and underdevelopment—of these metropoles and satellites of Latin America throughout the following and still continuing historical process. In this way we can understand why there were and still are tendencies in the Latin American and world capitalist structure which seem to lead to the development of the metropolis and the underdevelopment of the satellite and why, particularly, the satellized national, regional, and local metropoles in Latin America find that their economic development is at best a limited or underdeveloped development.

That present underdevelopment of Latin America is the result of its centuries-long participation in the process of world capitalist development, I believe I have shown in my case studies of the economic and social histories of Chile and Brazil.[4] My study of Chilean history suggests that the Conquest not only incorporated this country fully into the expansion and development of the world mercantile and later industrial capitalist system but that it also introduced the monopolistic metropolis-satellite structure and development of capitalism into the Chilean domestic economy and society itself. This structure then penetrated and permeated all of Chile very quickly. Since that time and in the course of world and Chilean history during the epochs of colonialism, free trade, imperialism, and the present, Chile has become increasingly marked by the economic, social, and political structure of satellite underdevelopment. This development of underdevelopment continues today, both in Chile's still increasing satellization by the world metropolis and through the ever more acute polarization of Chile's domestic economy.

The history of Brazil is perhaps the clearest case of both national and regional development of underdevelopment. The expansion of the world economy since the beginning of the sixteenth century successively converted the Northeast, the Minas Gerais interior, the North, and the Center-South (Rio de Janeiro, São Paulo, and Paraná) into export economies and incorporated them into the structure and development of the world capitalist system. Each of these regions experienced what may have appeared as economic development during the period of its respective golden age. But it was a satellite development which was neither self-generating nor self-perpetuating. As the market or the productivity of the first three regions declined, foreign and domestic economic interest in them waned; and they were left to develop the underdevelopment they live today. In the fourth region, the coffee economy experienced a similar though not yet quite as serious fate (though the development of a synthetic coffee substitute promises to deal it a mortal blow in the not too distant future). All of this historical evidence contradicts the generally accepted theses that Latin America suffers from a dual society or from the survival of feudal institutions and that these are important obstacles to its economic development.

During the First World War, however, and even more during the Great Depression and the Second World War, São Paulo began to build up an industrial establishment which is the largest in Latin America today. The question arises whether this industrial development did or can break Brazil out of the cycle of satellite development and underdevelopment which has characterized its other regions and national history within the capitalist system so far. I believe that the answer is no. Domestically the evidence so far is fairly clear. The development of industry in São Paulo has not brought greater riches to the other regions of Brazil. Instead, it converted them into internal colonial satellites, de-capitalized them further, and consolidated or even deepened their underdevelopment. There is little evidence to suggest that this process is likely to be reversed in the foreseeable future except insofar as the provincial poor migrate and become the poor of the metropolitan cities. Externally, the evidence is that although the initial development of São Paulo's industry was relatively autonomous it is being increasingly satellized by the world capitalist metropolis and its future development possibilities are increasingly restricted.[5] This development, my studies lead me to believe, also appears destined to limited or underdeveloped development as long as it takes place in the present economic, political, and social framework.

We must conclude, in short, that underdevelopment is not due to the survival of archaic institutions and the existence of capital shortage in regions that have remained isolated from the stream of world history. On the contrary, underdevelopment was and still is generated by the very same historical process which also generated economic development: the development of capitalism itself. This view, I am glad to say, is gaining adherents among students of Latin America and is proving its worth in shedding new light on the problems of the area and in affording a better perspective for the formulation of theory and policy.[6]

The same historical and structural approach can also lead to better development theory and policy by generating a series of hypotheses about development and underdevelopment such as those I am testing in my current research. The hypotheses are derived from the empirical observation and theoretical assumption that within this world-embracing metropolis-satellite structure the metropoles tend to develop and the satellites to underdevelop. The first hypothesis has already been mentioned above: that in contrast to the development of the world metropolis which is no one's satellite, the development of the national and other subordinate metropoles is limited by their satellite status. It is perhaps more difficult to test this hypothesis than the following ones because part of its confirmation depends on the test of the other hypotheses. Nonetheless, this hypothesis appears to be generally confirmed by the non-autonomous and unsatisfactory economic and especially industrial development of Latin America's national metropoles, as documented in the studies already cited. The most important and at the same time most confirmatory examples are the metropolitan regions of Buenos Aires and São Paulo whose growth only began in the nineteenth century, was therefore largely untrammeled by any colonial heritage, but was and remains a satellite development largely dependent on the outside metropolis, first of Britain and then of the United States.

A second hypothesis is that the satellites experience their greatest economic development and especially their most classically capitalist industrial development if and when their ties to their metropolis are weakest. This hypothesis is almost diametrically opposed to the generally accepted thesis that development in the underdeveloped countries follows from the greatest degree of contact with and diffusion from the metropolitan developed countries. This hypothesis seems to be confirmed by two kinds of relative isolation that Latin America has experienced in the course of its history. One is the temporary isolation caused by the crises of war or depression in the world metropolis. Apart from minor ones, five periods of such major crises stand out and seem to confirm the hypothesis. These are: the European (and especially Spanish) depression of the seventeenth century, the Napoleonic Wars, the First World War, the depression of the 1930s, and the Second World War. It is clearly established and generally recognized that the most important recent industrial development—especially of Argentina, Brazil, and Mexico, but also of other countries such as Chile—has taken place precisely during the periods of the two World Wars and the intervening depression. Thanks to the consequent loosening of trade and investment ties during these periods, the satellites initiated marked autonomous industrialization and growth. Historical research demonstrates that the same thing happened in Latin America during Europe's seventeenth-century depression. Manufacturing grew in the Latin American countries, and several of them such as Chile became exporters of manufactured goods. The Napoleonic Wars gave rise to independence movements in Latin America, and these should perhaps also be interpreted as in part confirming the development hypothesis.

The other kind of isolation which tends to confirm the second hypothesis is the geographic and economic isolation of regions which at one time were relatively weakly tied to and poorly integrated into the mercantilist and capitalist system. My preliminary research suggests that in Latin America it was these regions which initiated and experienced the most promising self-generating economic development of the classical industrial capitalist type. The most important regional cases probably are Tucumán and Asunción, as well as other cities such as Mendoza and Rosario, in the interior of Argentina and Paraguay during the end of the eighteenth and the beginning of the nineteenth centuries. Seventeenth- and eighteenth-century São Paulo, long before coffee was grown there, is another example. Perhaps Antioquia in Colombia and Puebla and Querétaro in Mexico are other examples. In its own way, Chile was also an example since, before the sea route around the Horn was opened, this country was relatively isolated at the end of the long voyage from Europe via Panama. All of these regions became manufacturing centers and even exporters, usually of textiles, during the periods preceding their effective incorporation as satellites into the colonial, national, and world capitalist system.

Internationally, of course, the classic case of industrialization through non-participation as a satellite in the capitalist world system is obviously that of Japan after the Meiji Restoration. Why, one may ask, was resource-poor but unsatellized Japan able to industrialize so quickly at the end of the century while resource-rich Latin American countries and Russia were not able to do so and the latter was easily beaten by Japan in the War of 1904 after the same forty years of development efforts? The second hypothesis suggests that the fundamental reason is that Japan was not satellized either during the Tokugawa or the Meiji period and therefore did not have its development structurally limited as did the countries which were so satellized.

A corollary of the second hypothesis is that when the metropolis recovers from its crisis and reestablishes the trade and investment ties which fully reincorporate the satellites into the system, or when the metropolis expands to incorporate previously isolated regions into the world-wide system, the previous development and industrialization of these regions is choked off or channelled into directions which are not self-perpetuating and promising. This happened after each of the five crises cited above. The renewed expansion of trade and the spread of economic liberalism in the eighteenth and nineteenth centuries choked off and reversed the manufacturing development which Latin America had experienced during the seventeenth century, and in some places at the beginning of the nineteenth. After the First World War, the new national industry of Brazil suffered serious consequences from American economic invasion.

The increase in the growth rate of Gross National Product and particularly of industrialization throughout Latin America was again reversed and industry became increasingly satellized after the Second World War and especially after the post–Korean War recovery and expansion of the metropolis. Far from having become more developed since then, industrial sectors of Brazil and most conspicuously of Argentina have become structurally more and more underdeveloped and less and less able to generate continued industrialization and/or sustain development of the economy. This process, from which India also suffers, is reflected in a whole gamut of balance of payments, inflationary, and other economic and political difficulties, and promises to yield to no solution short of far-reaching structural change.

Our hypothesis suggests that fundamentally the same process occurred even more dramatically with the incorporation into the system of previously unsatellized regions. The expansion of Buenos Aires as a satellite of Great Britain and the introduction of free trade in the interest of the ruling groups of both metropoles destroyed the manufacturing and much of the remainder of the economic base of the previously relatively prosperous interior almost entirely. Manufacturing was destroyed by foreign competition, lands were taken and concentrated into latifundia by the rapaciously growing export economy, intraregional distribution of income became much more unequal, and the previously developing regions became simple satellites of Buenos Aires and through it of London. The provincial centers did not yield to satellization without a struggle. This metropolis-satellite conflict was much of the cause of the long political and armed struggle between the Unitarists in Buenos Aires and the Federalists in the provinces, and it may be said to have been the sole important cause of the War of the Triple Alliance in which Buenos Aires, Montevideo, and Rio de Janeiro, encouraged and helped by London, destroyed not only the autonomously developing economy of Paraguay but killed off nearly all of its population which was unwilling to give in. Though this is no doubt the most spectacular example which tends to confirm the hypothesis, I believe that historical research on the satellization of previously relatively independent yeoman-farming and incipient manufacturing regions such as the Caribbean islands will confirm it further.[7] These regions did not have a chance against the forces of expanding and developing capitalism, and their own development had to be sacrificed to that of others. The economy and industry of Argentina, Brazil, and other countries which have experienced the effects of metropolitan recovery since the Second World War are today suffering much the same fate, if fortunately still in lesser degree.

A third major hypothesis derived from the metropolis-satellite structure is that the regions which are the most underdeveloped and feudal-seeming today are the ones which had the closest ties to the metropolis in the past. They are the regions which were the greatest exporters of primary products to and biggest sources of capital for the world metropolis and which were abandoned by the metropolis when for one reason or another business fell off. This hypothesis also contradicts the generally held thesis that the source of a region's underdevelopment is its isolation and its pre-capitalist institutions.

This hypothesis seems to be amply confirmed by the former super-satellite development and present ultra-underdevelopment of the once sugar-exporting West Indies, Northeastern Brazil, the ex-mining districts of Minas Gerais in Brazil, highland Peru, and Bolivia, and the central Mexican states of Guanajuato, Zacatecas, and others whose names were made world famous centuries ago by their silver. There surely are no major regions in Latin America which are today more cursed by underdevelopment and poverty; yet all of these regions, like Bengal in India, once provided the life blood of mercantile and industrial capitalist development—in the metropolis. These regions' participation in the development of the world capitalist system gave them, already in their golden age, the typical structure of underdevelopment of a capitalist export economy. When the market for their sugar or the wealth of their mines disappeared and the metropolis abandoned them to their own devices, the already existing economic, political, and social structure of these regions prohibited autonomous generation of economic development and left them no alternative but to turn in upon themselves and to degenerate into the ultra-underdevelopment we find there today.

These considerations suggest two further and related hypotheses. One is that the latifundium, irrespective of whether it appears as a plantation or a hacienda today, was typically born as a commercial enterprise which created for itself the institutions which permitted it to respond to increased demand in the world or national market by expanding the amount of its land, capital, and labor and to increase the supply of its products. The fifth hypothesis is that the latifundia which appear isolated, subsistence-based, and semi-feudal today saw the demand for their products or their productive capacity decline and that they are to be found principally in the above-named former agricultural and mining export regions whose economic activity declined in general. These two hypotheses run counter to the notions of most people, and even to the opinions of some historians and other students of the subject, according to whom the historical roots and socioeconomic causes of Latin American latifundia and agrarian institutions are to be found in the transfer of feudal institutions from Europe and/or in economic depression.

The evidence to test these hypotheses is not open to easy general inspection and requires detailed analyses of many cases. Nonetheless, some important confirmatory evidence is available. The growth of the latifundium in nineteenth-century Argentina and Cuba is a clear case in support of the fourth hypothesis and can in no way be attributed to the transfer of feudal institutions during colonial times. The same is evidently the case of the postrevolutionary and contemporary resurgence of latifundia particularly in the north of Mexico, which produce for the American market, and of similar ones on the coast of Peru and the new coffee regions of Brazil. The conversion of previously yeoman-farming Caribbean islands, such as Barbados, into sugar-exporting economies at various times between the seventeenth and twentieth centuries and the resulting rise of the latifundia in these islands would seem to confirm the fourth hypothesis as well. In Chile, the rise of the latifundium and the creation of the institutions of servitude which later came to be called feudal occurred in the eighteenth century and have been conclusively shown to be the result of and response to the opening of a market for Chilean wheat in Lima.[8] Even the growth and consolidation of the latifundium in seventeenth-century Mexico—which most expert students have attributed to a depression of the economy caused by the decline of mining and a shortage of Indian labor and to a consequent turning in upon itself and ruralization of the economy—occurred at a time when urban population and demand were growing, food shortages became acute, food prices skyrocketed, and the profitability of other economic activities such as mining and foreign trade declined.[9] All of these and other factors rendered hacienda agriculture more profitable. Thus, even this case would seem to confirm the hypothesis that the growth of the latifundium and its feudal-seeming conditions of servitude in Latin America has always been and still is the commercial response to increased demand and that it does not represent the transfer or survival of alien institutions that have remained beyond the reach of capitalist development. The emergence of latifundia, which today really are more or less (though not entirely) isolated, might then be attributed to the causes advanced in the fifth hypothesis—i.e., the decline of previously profitable agricultural enterprises whose capital was, and whose currently produced economic surplus still is, transferred elsewhere by owners and merchants who frequently are the same persons or families. Testing this hypothesis requires still more detailed analysis, some of which I have undertaken in a study on Brazilian agriculture.[10]

All of these hypotheses and studies suggest that the global extension and unity of the capitalist system, its monopoly structure and uneven development throughout its history, and the resulting persistence of commercial rather than industrial capitalism in the underdeveloped world (including its most industrially advanced countries) deserve much more attention in the study of economic development and cultural change than they have hitherto received. Though science and truth know no national boundaries, it is probably new generations of scientists from the underdeveloped countries themselves who most need to, and best can, devote the necessary attention to these problems and clarify the process of underdevelopment and development. It is their people who in the last analysis face the task of changing this no longer acceptable process and eliminating this miserable reality.

They will not be able to accomplish these goals by importing sterile stereotypes from the metropolis which do not correspond to their satellite economic reality and do not respond to their liberating political needs. To change their reality they must understand it. For this reason, I hope that better confirmation of these hypotheses and further pursuit of the proposed historical, holistic, and structural approach may help the peoples of the underdeveloped countries to understand the causes and eliminate the reality of their development of underdevelopment and their underdevelopment of development.

Notes

1. *America Latina*, Año 6, No. 4, October–December 1963, p. 8.
2. Instituto Nacional Indigenista, *Los centros coordinadores indigenistas*, Mexico, 1962, p. 34.
3. Ibid., pp. 33–34, 88.
4. "Capitalist Development and Underdevelopment in Chile" and "Capitalist Development and Underdevelopment in Brazil" in *Capitalism and Underdevelopment in Latin America*, New York, Monthly Review Press, 1967.
5. Also see, "The Growth and Decline of Import Substitution," Economic Bulletin for Latin America, New York, IX, No. 1, March 1964 and Celso Furtado, *Dialectica do Desenvolvimiento*, Rio de Janeiro, Fundo de Cultura, 1964.
6. Others who use a similar approach, though their ideologies do not permit them to derive the logically following conclusions, are Anibal Pintos S.C., *Chile: Un caso de desarrollo frustado*, Santiago, Editorial Universitaria, 1957; Celso Furtado, *A formacao economica do Brasil*, Rio de Janeiro, Fundo de Cultura, 1959 (translated into English and published under the title *The Economic Growth of Brazil* by the University of California Press); and Caio Prado Junior, *Historia economica do Brasil*, São Paulo, Editora Brasiliense, 7th ed., 1962.
7. See for instance Ramon Guerra y Sanchez, *Azucar y poblacion en las Antillas*, Havana 1942, 2nd ed., also published as *Sugar and Society in the Caribbean*, New Haven, Yale University Press, 1964.
8. Mario Gongora, *Origen de los "inquilinos" de Chile central*, Santiago, Editorial Universitaria, 1960; Jean Borde and Mario Gongora, *Evolucion de la propiedad rural en el Valle del Puango*, Santiago, Instituto de Sociologia de la Universidad de Chile; Sergio Sepulveda, *El trigo chileno en el mercado mundial*, Santiago, Editorial Universitario, 1959.
9. Woodrow Borah makes depression the centerpiece of his explanation in "New Spain's Century of Depression," *Ibero-Americana*, Berkeley, No. 35, 1951. François Chevalier speaks of turning upon itself in the most authoritative study of the subject, "La formacion de los grandes latifundios en Mexico," Mexico, *Problemas Agricolas e Industriales de Mexico*, VIII, No. 1, 1956 (translated from the French and recently published by the University of California Press). The data which provide the basis for my contrary interpretation are supplied by these authors themselves. This problem is discussed in my "Con que modo de produccion conviene la gallina maiz en huevos de oro?" *El Gallo Illustrado, Suplemento de El Dia*, Mexico, Nos. 175 and 179, October 31 and November 28, 1965; and it is further analyzed in a study of Mexican agriculture under preparation by the author.
10. "Capitalism and the Myth of Feudalism in Brazilian Agriculture," in *Capitalism and Underdevelopment in Latin America*, cited footnote 4 above.

22

American Penetration and Canadian Development: A Case Study of Mature Dependency

HEATHER-JO HAMMER AND JOHN W. GARTRELL

Dependency theorists have found that extensive foreign capital pene-
tration dampens long-term economic growth, but, in a previous edi-
tion of this volume, Edward Muller asserted that up to that point, de-
pendency theory had been unable to explain how Canada—a country
highly penetrated by foreign investment—could be wealthy, fast
growing, and experiencing relatively low levels of income inequality.
In this chapter, Heather-Jo Hammer and John Gartrell argue that de-
pendency theorists had failed to acknowledge that a country could
be both a member of the core and a dependent country. After noting
some similarities between mature dependency and Peter Evans's de-
pendent development, the authors provide a model for Canada's ma-
ture dependence and offer evidence of a negative long-term effect
of change in American direct investment on change in Canadian eco-
nomic growth. ∎

THE DEPENDENCY PERSPECTIVE ON THE SOCIOLOGY OF DEVELOPMENT HAS HAD
difficulties in coming to terms with the Canadian situation. Canada seems to
fall between types of social formations, displaying the social relations of advanced capitalism and the economic structure of dependency (Drache 1983,
36). Indeed, the Innisian tradition of Canadian political economy[1] stems from
a perceived need for both original theory and distinctive methodology in the
explanation of Canadian development (Drache 1983, 38). There is little doubt
within the dependency perspective that Canada is "profoundly dependent" in

---

Reprinted with permission of the American Sociological Association and the authors from *American Sociological Review,* vol. 51, no. 2 (April 1986): 201–213.

the critical sense that it is extensively penetrated by American direct investment. Nevertheless, Canadian dependency is of a "different genre" than classic peripheral dependency (Portes 1976, 78). . . .

As a theory of development, dependency cannot adequately explain why core economies are not susceptible to the negative consequences of penetration as long as dependency is defined as a structural distortion that is evident exclusively in peripheral modes of development. We think that a demonstration of the negative structural effect of dependency is possible in the case of extensively penetrated core countries. The situation of "relative" core underdevelopment is described with the concept "mature dependency" (Hammer 1982, 1984a, 1984b). The differentiation of mature dependency from other forms of economic power dependency requires that the theory be liberated from its focus on the periphery and the semi-periphery, and the empirical studies be liberated from cross-national analysis. Our endeavour to specify a model of the structural effect of mature dependency on economic growth in Canada reflects Duvall's suggestion to merge dialectical analysis with time series methodology (Duvall 1978).

Mature Dependency and Canadian Development: Reformulating Dependency Theory

Dialectical analysis requires that each new situation of dependency be specified in a "search for differences and diversity" (Cardoso and Faletto 1979, xiii). Contrary to Caporaso and Zare (1981, 47) who state that "The questions of identification and measurement must be answered before theoretical ones can be raised," the dialectical method suggests that ". . . before measuring, previous elaboration of adequate theories and categories is required to give sense to the data" (Cardoso and Faletto 1979, xiii). In brief, Cardoso and Faletto's strategy is to establish the evidence on theoretical grounds and to interpret the data historically. Shifting to the language of empirical models, historical arguments must be interpreted in terms of the important context-defining variables that specify the form of dependency (Duvall 1978, 74).

The existing form of dependency that is most relevant to the Canadian case is Evans's (1979) statement of dependent development. There are some striking similarities between the Canadian and Brazilian developmental histories, particularly in relation to changes in the concentration of foreign capital. In both countries there is an historical shift from British portfolio to American direct investment, and from concentration in resources to concentration in industry. The key difference rests with the timing of the changes and the initial mode of incorporation into the world economy. During the period of Canada's initial industrialization at the end of the nineteenth century, American direct investment in Canadian manufacturing accounted for about 34 percent of total manufacturing investment, compared to less than 4 percent in Brazil. The proportion of American to total direct investment in Canadian manufacturing was 55.6 percent by 1924 (Lewis 1938); in Brazil, by 1929, American direct investment accounted for only 24 percent of total manufacturing investment (Evans 1979, 78). It was not until the 1950s that American direct investment in Brazilian manufacturing attained the concentration levels evident in Canada before the 1920s.

Most of the American [multinational enterprises] MNEs that are currently dominant in Canada had already been established by the end of 1920 (Gonick 1970, 62). By 1897, Canada accounted for about 25 percent of total American direct investment abroad. By 1913, there were 450 American branch plants in Canada, including such giants as Singer, Bell, and Houston Electric (now General Electric) (Field 1914). When the American MNEs asserted their interests in Canadian manufacturing, Canada was the eighth largest manufacturing country in the world, not a peripheral country in transition (Maizels 1963). In 1870, manufacturing accounted for 19 percent of Canada's gross national product, with the production of iron and steel leading the composition.

"Production moves to the periphery only after the technology has become routinized" (Evans 1979, 28). Therefore, the comparative advantage of the periphery in the international market becomes the low cost of its labor (Evans 1979, 28). In addition to the economic disarticulation that results from the lack of integration between subsidiary firms,[2] there exists a disarticulation between technology and social structure. The problem is evident in the failure of imported technology to absorb the huge reserves of underemployed agricultural labor that have been excluded from urban industrialization (Evans 1979, 29). For the elite, disarticulation is an obstacle to self-sustained, autocentric accumulation (Evans 1979, 29). For the masses, economic exclusion is followed by political repression in order to prevent a rise in wages that would mean a loss in comparative advantage (Evans 1979, 48). Evans (1979, 29) describes both exclusion and disarticulation as the constant features of dependency, in the case of dependent development.[3]

Certainly, there is evidence of internal economic disarticulation in Canada. The establishment and protection of foreign technology and the control of the market by oligopolistic MNEs has resulted in a miniature replica effect. The Canadian goods market is fragmented due to an excess of buyers and sellers relative to size, and the concentration of MNEs in central Canada has resulted in regional disparity (Britton and Gilmour 1978, 93–96). However, the only way one can argue for the exclusion of the Canadian masses is in a relative sense, and only in comparison to the U.S. Historically, the wage levels of Canadian workers have been considerably higher than the wage levels of European workers. In fact, when American direct investment moved into Canadian industry at the end of the 1800s, Canada was at a comparative "disadvantage" because of its high wage levels. Where the wage differential does show up is in comparison to American industrial wages which were 60 percent higher than those in Canada during the period (Logan 1937, 90). Firestone's (1958) research suggests that real productivity in Canada outstripped real wages, but this relationship was reversed in the 1930s.

Canada had a reserve army of unskilled labor working in resources, construction and agriculture, whose wage rates were tied to the boom-bust cycle of export-led growth rather than to the import of technology (Drache 1983). This relation is accounted for by Canada's unique situation of being extensively penetrated by MNE investment simultaneously in resource extraction and manufacturing (Gherson 1980). In this sense the Canadian economy remains classically dependent, in that its export composition is predominated by primary resources.[4] In 1913, Canada was exporting an average of 31 percent less finished manufactures than the largest seven manufacturing countries (Maizels 1963). It was not the case that Canada lacked domestic savings for investment in the technology needed to further develop the manufacturing sector. Instead, Canadian funds were being directed into an elaborate banking and financial system to support the domestic transportation and utilities infrastructure needed for the export of wheat (Laxer 1984).

Technology was being imported at a much faster rate than manufactured goods were being exported. Consequently, foreign capital inflows were solicited to maintain the overall rate of economic growth (Ingram 1957). Gonick (1970, 70) argues that the import-substitution mentality implicit in the Canadian National Policy of 1897 was motivated by the commercial capitalists' concern with protecting their trade monopoly in staple exports. The policy of establishing a tariff barrier around Canadian manufacturing was intended to force the American MNEs to finance the Canadian industrial sector in order to penetrate the Canadian market. Apart from sidestepping the Canadian tariff, the opportunity to compete under the terms of British preference in export trade was a further attraction to American direct investment. In addition, the MNEs were able to take advantage of tax benefits and offers of free land that were a result of the regional competition within Canada to attract investment (Scheinberg 1973, 85).

The Canadian railway and financial capitalists were the same central Canadian capitalists who stood to gain from the protection of Canadian manufacturing and from government assistance to the Canadian Pacific Railway. Levitt (1970, 50–51) explains that Canadian private capital flowed freely from railway enterprises into the financial sector and manufacturing industries. In dependent development, the industrial bourgeoisie has no choice but to ally with the state and foreign capital (Evans 1979), whereas in mature dependency, the position and privileges of the commercial industrialists are not contingent upon the tripartite alliance. The alliance is formed by invitation, not necessity.

Innis (1956) argues that even though Canada had liberal democratic institutions, it lacked "strong" popular and democratic traditions. He suggests that this anomaly is linked to Canada's historical dependence and the way Canada was settled. The white settlers who colonized Canada were either fleeing revolution or were exiled when their revolution failed. "It was the presence of a deeply entrenched counter-revolutionary tradition which fundamentally altered not only the liberal democratic character and institutions of Canada but class relations as well" (Drache 1983, 44). Nevertheless, the history of democratic government in Canada can hardly be described as repressive, particularly in comparison to the history of Brazilian government. Thus, the two constant features of dependent development, exclusion of the masses and disarticulation, are evident in Canada, but to a relatively small degree. We suggest that the historical evidence does not support the argument that Canada has experienced dependent development. Rather, Canadian dependency is mature.

Mature dependency diverges from dependent development in the following respects:

1. The mature dependent's economy is functionally complete at the time when the tripartite alliance is formed. External capital inputs are invited, not essential.
2. The economic disarticulation associated with MNE investment is superimposed upon an intact economy that has demonstrated the capacity for self-sustained, autocentric accumulation. Mature dependency is a concrete historical alternative to classic autocentric development rather than an advanced phase of dependent development.
3. Mature dependency does not require economic exclusion of the masses, nor does it result in the associated conditions of political repression.
4. Mature dependency is the condition that causes rich, industrialized core countries to exhibit relative underdevelopment vis-à-vis some of the other core countries on some criteria. The variability in relative status is determined, to a large extent, by the effectiveness of a state's development policy.

In contrast to its non-core counterparts, the mature dependent has abundant social, economic, and political resources that can be mobilized to regulate the negative effects of dependency (Duvall 1978, 69; Bornschier 1980, 166–67). The contemporary features of mature dependency reflect a slow, historical process that has extended over a period of at least 120 years. Similar to dependent development, mature dependency emerged during the period of classic colonial dependence on staple-export growth. The continuity between Canada's early reliance on staple exports and contemporary mature dependency is a result of the continued interest of the Canadian state and the dominant capital interests in the encouragement of American MNE investment.

The difficulty in modeling mature dependency empirically is that we do not expect that the negative structural effects associated with MNE penetration will be evident in a rich, industrialized host until after the division of labor within the multinationals has come to dominate economic structure and growth. The actual effect, according to the decapitalization thesis, will appear only when inflows of fresh foreign capital slow down, or as we will demonstrate for the Canadian case, in combination with actual disinvestment. Although 80 percent of total direct investment in Canada has been American (Government of Canada 1981, 10), British portfolio investment was the primary source of foreign long-term investment capital until 1926.

Circa 1926, American portfolio investment split the market with the U.K., and by 1933, total American long-term investment came to exceed total British investment. Yet, at the onset of World War I, American direct investment accounted for only 13.5 percent of total foreign long-term investment in Canada. Fully 73.2 percent of all foreign long-term investment capital in Canada was in the form of British portfolio investment, imported by the sale of government-guaranteed railway bonds in order to subsidize Canadian investments.

American economic domination was not perceived as a threat to the Canadian state (Marshall et al. 1976, 15), because of its relatively small proportion and because it was complementary to British and Canadian investment (Behrman 1970). Moreover, for the period 1930–1946, portfolio investment (American and British) accounted for twice as much foreign long-term investment as did American direct investment. Flows of portfolio capital generally contribute to economic growth whereas the structural effects of foreign direct investment reduce growth (Behrman 1970, 19). Direct investments are those in which control lies with the foreign investor (Aitken 1961, 24). The organizational form of foreign direct investment is the multinational (Evans 1979, 38). In contrast, portfolio investments involve the acquisition of foreign securities by individuals or institutions with limited control over the companies concerned. In fact, there is considerable agreement that portfolio investment does not involve foreign control at all (Aitken 1961, 24; Hood and Young 1979, 9; Levitt 1970, 58; Gonick 1970, 50). As an economy expands, the foreign sector recedes (Gonick 1970, 50), whereas foreign direct investment may well expand faster than the general economy due to its concentration in the most dynamic and profitable sectors.

World War II changed the balance of foreign capital investments in Canada. Prior to the war, foreign portfolio investment accounted for an average of 71 percent of total foreign capital investment. After World War II, the average dropped to 34.8 percent. American direct investment, which had accounted for only 19.3 percent of the pre-war average, increased to 42.9 percent of foreign long-term investment for the period after 1946. Although American direct exceeded British portfolio investment as a proportion of total foreign long-term investment for the first time in 1946, it took about six more years for American direct investment to emerge as the primary source of foreign capital investment in Canada. While World War II facilitated an important increase in Canadian-owned manufacturing, it also brought closer economic ties with the U.S. Prior to 1950, American direct investment was linked closely to changes in the Canadian economy, accelerating during periods of high tariffs and decelerating during periods of recession (Marshall et al. 1976, 21). Pope (1971, 24) and Aitken (1961, 104) suggest that by 1950, American direct investment had become so large that it not only exploited opportunities, it created them by molding the Canadian economic structure.

The acceleration of American direct investment in Canada during the post-war boom period (1946–1960) is related to both the loss of Canadian access to British portfolio investment and markets and the ascent of the American economy to world economic hegemony. However, the crucial years, according to Grant (1970, 8), were the early 1940s when it was decided that Canada would become a branch plant economy. Both the organization of the war and the postwar construction were carried out under the assumption that government supported business interests in all national economic decisions. World War II brought the Ogdensburg agreements of 1940 to establish a joint defense board, the Hyde Park Declaration on the specialization of munitions production in 1941, a Joint War Production Committee, and Article VII of the Lend-Lease Law, which provided for a reduction in trade barriers. At this point, states Scheinberg (1973), Canadian leaders did perceive a threat to sovereignty, but were not prepared to change course in a period of accelerated wartime production.

Levitt (1970) describes how American direct investment continued to flow into the Canadian economy after the recession of 1957–1958, despite rising rates of unemployment and a slowing of Canadian output. The most important feature of the post-recession expansion was that only a very small proportion of foreign investment actually involved the importation of foreign savings (Gonick 1970, 64). American direct investment was financed largely from corporate capital raised in Canada through the sale of Canadian resources extracted and processed by Canadian labor, or from the sale of branch plant manufactures back to Canadian consumers at tariff-protected prices (Levitt 1970, 63).

Levitt (1970, 63–64) estimates that between 1957 and 1964, American direct investment in manufacturing, petroleum and natural gas, and mining and smelting secured 73 percent of investment funds from retained earnings and depreciation reserves. The strongest cross-national evidence (Bornschier 1980a, 161) of the negative impact of MNE penetration on specific economic sectors is evident in two of the three areas of American concentration in Canada, manufacturing and mining and smelting.

Although the proportion of American direct investment declined in the late 1970s, Canada's liabilities to the U.S. continued to rise through the reinvestment of retained earnings. Since 1975, almost 90 percent of the net increase in the book value of the stock of foreign direct investment in Canada has been accounted for by this process (Government of Canada 1981, 10).

Within the post-war period, both Grant and Levitt select 1960 as an important turning point in Canadian economic history. Grant (1970, 8) argues that since 1960, Canada has developed as a "northern extension" of the continental economy. Levitt (1970, 65) divides the post-war period into a boom period followed by a period of stabilization and disinvestment that she dates precisely to 1960. Levitt describes the latter phase of Canadian economic history as the period of "American Corporate Imperialism." In our analysis, the specification of this structural break is critical in the demonstration of the long-term negative effect of American direct investment on Canadian economic growth. Bergesen (1982) emphasizes the importance of considering structural breaks in world economic development as parameters that delineate the time frame of analysis. World wars are structural breaks, and in the context of dependency analysis World War II takes on particular significance as the demarcation of the emergence of the MNEs as the basic organizational units of world production (Bergesen 1982, 33; Bornschier and Ballmer-Cao 1979, 488; Blake and Walters 1983, 87; Hood and Young 1979, 18), and the establishment of American direct investment as the dominant form of foreign investment capital in Canada. Our restriction of the time series analysis to the post–World War II period is consistent with the literature. . . .

Results

The results of the time series regression analysis support our hypothesis. Change in American direct investment for the post-war period has a negative effect on change in Canadian GNP after a lag of nine years. This effect is evident after 1960. The equation is reported in Table 22.1.

According to the full equation with all the variables included, IL9USDI has a negative effect on GNP of –1.88. As indicated by the value of the Durbin-Watson statistic (2.14), the model is free of autocorrelation. The coefficient for the long-term negative effect, specified as an interaction, is significant at the .025 level. The main effect of the lagged change in American direct investment (L9USDI) is small, negative and not significant for the entire post-war period. There is no evidence of a negative effect for the boom period (this run is not reported). The difference between the pre- and post-1960 series is significant at the .005 level. This difference . . . is equal to $4,709 million. Also significant at this level are the coefficients for the short-term (synchronous) effect of GFCF and USDI. As predicted by dependency theory, these effects are positive, and the immediate effect of change in American direct investment on change in Canadian economic growth is .42 larger than the GFCF coefficient. The main effect of the interaction term (IUSDI) is negative and not significant.

Although the Durbin-Watson statistic does not call for reestimation of the full equation, the variables are taken as first differences; therefore, the time-se-

Table 22.1   Change in American Direct Investment and Change in Canadian
Gross National Product: Ordinary Least Squares Time Series
Estimates for the Period 1947–1978

Variable	Estimated Coefficient	Standard Error	T
DIFF	4709.16	882.282	5.33748
GFCF	.992951	.253596	3.91549
USDI	1.31187	.441842	2.96909
L9USDI	−.118747	.207940	−.571065
IUSDI	−.560369	.615555	−.910347
IL9USDI	−1.87526	.899004	−2.08593

Sum of the squared residuals = .321235E+08.
Standard error of the regression = −1111.54.
Mean of the dependent variable = −3066.78.
Standard deviation = 1893.11.
Log of the likelihood function = −266.516.
Number of observations = 32.
Sum of the residuals = 3486.96.
Durbin-Watson statistic = 2.1452.

ries procedure does not calculate in R^2. For this reason, the Cochrane-Orcutt iterative procedure (see Pindyck and Rubinfeld 1981, 157) has been performed on the equation as a check on the amount of variance explained. The R^2 and the R^2 adjusted both exceed .90. Various specifications of this full model have been estimated, eliminating the nonsignificant variables. What is most remarkable about the restricted equations is the stability of the coefficients and reported statistics across the different models. In the equation that includes only the difference between the periods, GFCF, USDI and IL9USDI, the estimated long-term negative effect for the post-1960 period is −1.92, compared to −1.88 in the full model. The other statistics are comparably close (results are not reported).

The argument could be made that the negative effect of change in USDI is simply a reflection of an underlying business cycle of the Juglar type (7–10 years). If this were the case, it is likely that a similarly lagged GFCF would show a negative effect on change in GNP. In the equation which estimates both main and interaction effects, the Durbin-Watson statistic indicates a problem of autocorrelation (D.W. = 1.54). The Cochrane-Orcutt estimation indicates that the period difference and the short-term effect of change in GFCF are both significant at the .005 level. The coefficient for GFCF is 1.77. These are the only significant effects in the equation. The other coefficients are estimated with enormous standard errors. The R^2 and adjusted R^2 are reduced to .83 and .81 respectively.

American direct investment in Canada is part of the composite measure of total American long-term investment. If the structural effect of mature dependency is related to the organization of the multinationals, we would expect to see a similar structure in total American long-term investment, to the extent that direct investment is proportionally dominant. The other two components of total long-term investment, portfolio and miscellaneous investments, should not exhibit the dependency effect on growth when they are disaggregated from the composite. Because American miscellaneous investment in Canada has accounted for only about 2.7 percent of total American long-term investment since 1926 (Government of Canada 1978), we will elaborate on the total of investment and on portfolio investment disaggregated.

Again, the analyses support our hypotheses about the nature of mature dependency. Comparing the lagged effects of American long-term and American direct investment, there is a similarity in the magnitudes and relative size of the coefficients, although the lagged effect is not significant. The portfolio estimates exhibit very little similarity to the direct investment estimates, and the short-term effect of portfolio investment is not significant. In fact, there is no significant effect for any of the portfolio variables when the American direct investment model is used to structure the equation. The evidence suggests that foreign direct investment is the only component of foreign long-term capital investments that has a long-term negative effect on the growth of the host economy. Granted, the empirical demonstration of a structural economic effect of dependency is a narrow delineation of the complexity of the alliance of social forces whose coincidence of interests causes the internalization of MNE investment. In fact, Portes (1976, 77) describes the internal impact of the multinationals as a remolding of the domestic social structure. Although our demonstration is limited to the transformation of the domestic economic structure, the specificities of our model are clearly defined by the contextual specificity of the larger social structure.

The importance of the findings is enhanced by their application to Canada, a dependent and yet non-peripheral economy. In this sense the findings and the historical evidence upon which they are based, suggest that dependency theory requires some modification. According to economic theories of the internal markets of MNEs, it is possible for core countries to experience MNE-based dependency. The implications for the social structure of the dependent mature economy are not as devastating as they are in the periphery and the semi-periphery, but the structural effect on long-term economic growth is precisely the same.

Discussion and Conclusions

For the researcher interested in the demonstration of dependency effects in non-peripheral countries, model specification is the key directive in research design. Duvall (1978, 74) argues that the design of dependency research must incorporate the notion that context affects causal relations. "To effectuate this requirement, it is necessary to interpret verbal historicist arguments in terms of the important context-defining variables that are implied in the contextu- ally-specific analysis" (Duvall 1978, 74). The context of mature dependency is provided by both history and theory. The historical legacy of the process of incorporation into the world economy has resulted in a hierarchical division of labor that requires both the measurement of variation between different struc- tural positions and the measurement of variations within positions.

The restriction of current empirical studies of dependency to comparative non–time series designs has meant that events which are major sources of vari- ation in independent variables have been largely ignored (Esteb 1977, 13). In the case of Canada's mature dependency, a time series design is required to capture the structural break that occurs in 1960. Moreover, the cross-national analysis of core countries as a block has obscured the structural distinctions that differentiate Canada from other developed countries.

Dependency theory suggests that extensive foreign capital penetration will have a long-term negative effect on the host's economic growth. The crit- ical importance of theory in the design of dependency research is evident in variable selection, specification of the functional form of the relationship be- tween variables, and the identification of the structure of lagged effects. De- pendency theory has integrated organizational economics to explain how the dominance of multinational enterprises has changed the structure of the post- war world economy (see Evans 1979; dos Santos 1970; Cardoso and Faletto 1979). However, dependency theory has not seriously considered the implica- tions of cross-penetration within the core for the structure of developed economies.

New theories addressing the organizational economics of multinational enterprises suggest that the structural effect associated with dependency need not be confined to the peripheral economies of the world system. The couch- ing of dependency arguments in terms of peripheral modes of development does not accommodate "deviant" case analyses without some modification to the theory. Although Wallerstein himself waivers between essays, he classifies Canada, Australia and New Zealand as members of the semi-periphery in order to deal with the "doubtful" economic structures of these countries (see Wallerstein 1974; 1976). Evans (1979, 293) does the same. On this point, we must disagree with both theorists.

The theoretical definition of what constitutes the semi-periphery is admit- tedly imprecise; however, the term is used as a catch-all category for those coun- tries which cannot simply be considered "peripheral" and yet are structurally distinguishable from center countries (Evans 1979, 291; Wallerstein 1976). Wallerstein (1974) suggests that the coherence of the category is derived from the fact that the semi-periphery is formed by the more advanced exemplars of dependent development. According to Evans's (1979) theory or dependent development, Canada does not fit the category.

The resolution of the issue of Canada's status requires both theoretical and methodological innovation. We suggest that a country can be both a member of the core and dependent. The situation has been described by the concept "mature dependency." The demonstration of a negative long-term effect of change in American direct investment on change in Canadian economic growth provides strong evidence for the existence of mature dependency as a variation in core development. We suggest that future empirical research be directed into case-by-case analyses of core country dependency. Portes (1976) suggests that Australia may be a good candidate for analysis. The Canadian case was a good place to start, particularly because of the significance of retained earnings in Canada, a characteristic which sets Canada apart from other American dependencies (see Hood and Young 1979, 39). In conclusion, we may have inadvertently bridged the rift between the dialectical method of analysis and empirical dependency research. As we have demonstrated in this paper, theoretically and historically informed time series analysis is the appropriate design for modeling the contextual specificity of variations in dependency.

Notes

1. The Innisian tradition began with the work of Harold Innis in the 1930s. He explained Canadian development in terms of its domination by staple-export-led growth. The tradition is a reformulation or Marxism tailored to Canada's mode of capitalist accumulation. It negates the liberal argument Canada's development has been principally autonomous, introverted and autocentric (Drache 1983, 27).

2. "Firms in dependent countries buy their equipment and other capital goods from outside. so that the 'multiplier effect' of new investments is transferred back to the center" (Evans 1979, 28).

3. Because the masses are effectively barred from economic participation, "to allow them political participation would be disruptive. Social and cultural exclusion follow from political and economic exclusion" (Evans 1979, 29).

4. See Richards and Pratt (1979) on "advanced resource capitalism."

References

Aitken, Hugh G.J. 1961. *American Capital and Canadian Resources*. Cambridge, MA: Harvard University Press.

Behrman, Jack N. 1970. *National Interests and the Multinational Enterprise: Tensions Among the North Atlantic Countries*. Englewood Cliffs, NJ: Prentice-Hall.

Bergesen, Albert. 1982. "The Emerging Science of the World-System." *International Social Science Journal* 34:23–25.

Blake, David H. and Robert S. Walters. 1983. *The Politics of Global Economic Relations*. Englewood Cliffs, NJ: Prentice-Hall.

Bornschier, Volker. 1980. "Multinational Corporations, Economic Policy and National Development in the World System." *International Social Sciences Journal* 32:158–72.

Bornschier, Volker and Thanh-Huyen Ballmer-Cao. 1979. "Income Inequality: A Cross-national Study of the Relationship Between MNC-Penetration, Dimensions of the Power Structure and Income Distribution." *American Sociological Review* 44:487–506.

Britton, John H. and James A. Gilmour. 1978. *The Weakest Link—A Technological Perspective on Canadian Industrial Underdevelopment*. Ottawa: Science Council of Canada.

Caporaso, James A. and Behrouz Zare. 1981. "An Interpretation and Evaluation of Dependency Theory." 43–56 in *From Dependency to Development: Strategies to Overcome Underdevelopment and Inequality,* edited by Herald Manoz. Boulder, CO: Westview Press.

Cardoso, Fernando Henrique and Enzo Faletto. 1979. *Dependency and Development in Latin America.* Berkeley, CA: University of California Press.

dos Santos, Theotonio. 1970. "The Structure of Dependence." *American Economic Review* 60:231–36.

Drache, Daniel. 1983. "The Crisis of Canadian Political Economy Dependency Theory Versus the New Orthodoxy." *Canadian Journal of Political and Social Theory* 7:25–49.

Duvall, Raymond. 1978. "Dependency and Dependencia Theory: Notes Towards Precision of Concept and Argument." *International Organization* 32:51–78.

Duvall, Raymond and John Freeman. 1981. "The State and Dependent Capitalism." *International Studies Quarterly* 25:99–118.

Esteb, Nancy. 1977. "Methods for World System Analysis: A Critical Appraisal." Paper presented at the 72nd annual meetings of the American Sociological Association in Chicago, September 5–9.

Evans, Peter. 1979. *Dependent Development: The Alliance of Multinational, State, and Local Capital in Brazil.* Princeton, NJ: Princeton University Press.

Field, F. W. 1914. *Capital Investments in Canada.* Montreal: The Monetary Times of Canada.

Firestone, O. John. 1958. *Canada's Economic Development, 1867–1953.* London: Bowes and Bowes.

Gherson, Joan. 1980. "U.S. Investment in Canada." *Foreign Investment Review* 3:11–14.

Gonick, Cyril Wolfe. 1970. "Foreign Ownership and Political Decay." 44–73 in *Close the 49th Parallel etc.: The Americanization of Canada,* edited by Ian Lumsden. Toronto: University of Toronto Press.

Government of Canada. 1978. Canada's International Investment Position 1978. Ottawa: Minister of Supply and Services (catalogue no. 67-202).

————. 1981. Canada's International Investment Position 1978. Ottawa: Minister of Supply and Services (catalogue no. 67-202).

————. Statistics Canada. 1983. *National Income and Expenditure Accounts 1965–1982.* Ottawa: Minister of Supply and Services (catalogue no. 13-201) GNP CANSIM MATRIX 000531. GNP CANSIM MATRIX 000528.

Grant, George. 1970. *Lament for a Nation.* Toronto: McClelland and Stewart.

Hammer, Heather-Jo. 1982. "Multinational Corporations and National Development: American Direct Investment in Canada." Paper presented at the 10th annual congress meetings of the International Sociological Association in Mexico City, August 16–21.

————. 1984a. Comment on "Dependency Theory and Taiwan: Analysis of a Deviant Case." *American Journal of Sociology* 89:932–36.

————. 1984b. "Mature Dependency: The Effects of American Direct Investment on Canadian Economic Growth." Unpublished Ph.D. dissertation. Department of Sociology, University of Alberta, Edmonton, Canada.

Hood, Neil and Stephen Young. 1979. *The Economics of Multinational Enterprise.* London: Longman Group Limited.

Ingram, James C. 1957. "Growth in Capacity in Canada's Balance of Payments." *American Economic Review* 47:93–104.

Innis, Harold. 1956. *Essays in Canadian Economic History.* Toronto: Toronto University Press.

Laxer, Gordon. 1984. "Foreign Ownership and Myths About Canadian Development." *Review of Canadian Sociology and Anthropology* 22:311–45.

Levitt, Kari. 1970. *Silent Surrender: The Multinational Corporation in Canada.* Toronto: Macmillan.

Lewis. Cleona. 1938. *America's Stake in International Investments.* Washington, DC: Brookings Institute.

Logan, Harold. 1937. "Labour Costs and Labour Standards." 63–97 in *Labour in Canadian-American Relations,* edited by H. Innis. Toronto: University of Toronto Press.

Maizels, Alfred. 1963. *Industrial Growth and World Trade.* London: Cambridge University Press.

Marshall, Herbert, Frank A. Southard Jr. and Kenneth W. Taylor. 1976. *Canadian-American Industry: A Study in International Investment.* New Haven: Yale University Press.

Pindyck, Robert S. and Daniel Rubinfeld. 1981. *Econometric Methods and Economic Forecasting.* New York: McGraw-Hill.

Pope, William H. 1971. *The Elephant and the Mouse.* Toronto: McClelland and Stewart.

Portes, Alejandro. 1976. "On the Sociology of National Development: Theories and Issues." *American Journal of Sociology* 82:55–85.

Richards, John and Larry Pratt. 1979. *Prairie Capitalism: Power and Influence in the New West.* Toronto: McClelland and Stewart.

Scheinberg, Stephen. 1973. "Invitation to Empire: Tariffs and American Economic Expansion in Canada." 80–100 in *Enterprise and National Development: Essays on Canadian Business and Economic History,* edited by Glenn Porter and Robert D. Cuff. Toronto: Hakkert.

Stoneman, Colin. 1975. "Foreign Capital and Economic Growth." *World Development* 3:11–26.

Wallerstein, Immanuel. 1974. "Dependence in an Interdependent World: The Limited Possibilities of Transformation Within the Capitalist World Economy." *African Studies Review* 17:1–26.

————. 1976. "Semi-Peripheral Countries and the Contemporary World Crisis." *Theory and Society* 3:461–83.

23

The Irish Case of Dependency: An Exception to the Exception?

Denis O'Hearn

*According to dependency/world systems theory, transnational corpora-
tion (TNC) penetration depresses growth and worsens income inequality. In the previous chapter, Heather-Jo Hammer and John Gartrell
point to the relatively high degree of TNC penetration and income
equality in Canada, questioning why TNC investment in developing
countries has one outcome but in penetrated developed countries another. In this chapter, Denis O'Hearn addresses Irish dependency and
its record of economic growth and income inequality, arguing that
some countries have regimes that make them vulnerable to dependency relations while others do not. He reports that Ireland's growth
was undermined by decapitalization. He also notes that radical free
trade policies in Ireland are also related to rising income inequality.* ■

FOR THE PAST 20 YEARS, THE APPROACH LOOSELY TERMED AS *DEPENDENCY* ENJOYED
popularity in development studies, particularly among radical scholars. Many
studies concentrated on the connections between foreign penetration, economic
growth, and income distribution. Baran (1957) and others emphasized the *tendencies* of foreign penetration to limit economic growth in the LDCs. Later
works (Frank 1969) implied "laws" of development, relating proximity to the
"metropole" with underdevelopment in the periphery. A series of analysts then
attempted to "test" the hypotheses that foreign penetration caused (1) low growth
rates and (2) inequality in LDCs (Chase-Dunn 1975; Bornschier 1980; Biersteker 1978; Bornschier and Ballmer-Cao 1979; Evans and Timberlake 1980).

Reprinted with permission of the American Sociological Association and the authors from *American Sociological Review* (1989): 578–594.

Within the past few years some scholars have strongly challenged the dependency approach. A number of empirical analyses concentrated on "exceptions" to dependency, particularly from East Asia (for a review, see Chakravarty 1987). In place of dependency, these analysts propose a return to orthodox principles of neoclassical development economics and modernization theory. . . .

In place of dependency, a series of trade theorists give the following reasons for the "gang of four's" [Taiwan, South Korea, Singapore, and Hong Kong—eds.] success:

a. maintenance of an outward-looking orientation throughout the rapid growth phase of these countries;
b. maintenance of a very hospitable climate for foreign investment;
c. and finally, "keeping the prices right," by which they imply a relatively low real price of labour, a relatively high real rate of interest and "realistic" exchange rates (Chakravarty 1987).

Sociological and political accounts of the success in East Asia concentrate less on openness to foreign penetration than on political and class variables—the nature of the colonial and post-colonial relationship with Japan, the emphasis on labor-intensive enterprises, and the absence of an entrenched bourgeoisie. In fairness, many of these "non-economic" analyses have taken great pains to point out that South Korea and Taiwan are special or deviant cases and, therefore, do not in themselves constitute a threat to the dependency approach. Barrett and Whyte, for example, argue that Taiwan is a "deviant case" of dependency theory because foreign penetration was linked neither to stagnation nor inequality (Barrett and Whyte 1982; see also Cummings 1984).

In the present chapter, I will challenge the new modernizationism in development studies by presenting the case study of Ireland (i.e., the 26 southern counties). Ireland represents not only an "exception" to the "exceptions" in the so-called gang of four. It is in many ways a truer representation of the open, foreign-dominated, free-enterprise regime that the new modernizationists prescribe. In development terms, it is also an abject failure. This is especially significant because Ireland has for 30 years been in the heart of European economic integration. For 15 years, Ireland has "enjoyed" full membership in the European Economic Community, one of the dominant economic powers of the "modern industrial West." Indeed, this close relationship to the core, in classical "dependency" terms, directly contributed to Ireland's development problems.

Specificity of Irish Dependency

Ireland is an island about the size of the state of Maine, lying 30–60 miles from the British mainland. Its population is about four and a half million, well below its mid-19th century population of eight million. Its modern history is dominated by British occupation, four major waves of emigration, and several famines, including the famous mid-19th century "potato famine." In the 19th century, Irish peasants won limited ownership of farms and limited rights against British landlords. Ireland's traditional industrial area, around Belfast, was based on shipbuilding and linen-making for the British empire. Industry in the rest of the island was impeded by British laws, which removed Irish tariffs on industrial goods and outlawed certain lines of industry and exports.

Ireland was partitioned in 1921, at the end of a war of independence. Britain retained six of the nine counties of the province of Ulster, which included industrial Belfast and the largest adjoining area with a built-in settler majority. The southern state of today, therefore, comprises an area of about four-fifths of the island, with a population of about 3 million.

The new postcolonial state in 1932 embarked on an attempt to build native industry through a classical program of import-substituting industrialization (ISI), with high levels of tariff protection. Despite an economic war waged by Britain against Ireland, this program was quite successful: between 1931 and 1947 the number of manufacturing establishments employing more than 10 grew by 63 percent, and those employing over a hundred more than doubled. In the same period, industrial employment grew by about 80 percent, from 110,588 to 197,605 (O'Hearn 1988, pp. 82, 89). But in the mid-1950s, because of rising dollar trade deficits, external political pressures tied to Marshall Aid and European integration, and economic recession, the Irish regime changed the industrialization program from ISI to export-led industrialization (ELI). The new ELI regime had three distinguishing characteristics: (1) radical free trade, (2) radical free enterprises, and (3) foreign industrial domination.

Radical Free Trade

Unlike many developing countries, which followed a "stop-and-go" pattern of deprotection and reprotection, Ireland was forced to free its trade rapidly and totally. The removal of protection began after Ireland joined the Organisation for European Economic Cooperation (OEEC) in the 1950s—a prerequisite for receiving Marshall Aid—and ended when Ireland joined the EEC in 1972. Table 23.1 clearly shows the fall of tariff receipts during ELI, beginning in 1959 when OEEC free trade pressures became severe. In 1972, tariff revenues as a percentage of total Irish government revenues fell by almost 6 percent. Four years later, as a result of Ireland's terms of accession to the EEC, tariff revenues fell to practically nil.[1]

As a result, the Irish market was penetrated by competing imports. Between 1960 and 1980, imports took over the Irish market in nearly every category of manufactured goods. In footwear and clothing, imports rose from 8 percent of domestic consumption in 1960, to 70–80 percent in 1980. In

Table 23.1   Revenues from Customs Tariffs, and as Percentage of Total Net Government Receipts (million Irish punts[a])

Year	(1) Tariff Revenue	(2) Total Revenue	(1) As Percentage of (2)	Year	(1) Tariff Revenue	(2) Total Revenue	(1) As Percentage of (2)
1954	37	83	44.6	1970	88	338	26.0
1955	37	85	43.5	1971	92	398	27.2
1956	39	89	43.8	1972	101	469	21.5
1957	45	94	47.9	1973	117	540	21.7
1958	47	97	48.5	1974	139	665	20.8
1959	48	98	49.0	1975	176	901	19.5
1960	45	103	43.7	1976	25	1222	2.0
1961	41	107	38.3	1977	29	1445	2.0
1962	45	119	37.8	1978	35	1709	2.0
1963	47	129	36.4	1979	39	1991	2.0
1964	50	145	34.5	1980	46	2584	1.8
1965	56	177	31.6	1981	58	3274	1.8
1966	58	194	29.9	1982	62	4014	1.5
1967	68	222	30.6	1983	77	4503	1.7
1968	70	248	28.2	1984	94	5115	1.8
1969	76	282	27.0				

Source: Irish Revenue Commissioners (various years).
Note: a. The punt is the Irish currency. Its value was tied to the British pound until Ireland joined the European Money System in 1979.

nonelectrical machinery, the share of imports during the same period rose from 55 to 98 percent.

The results for Irish-owned industry were disastrous (Table 23.2). Between 1973 and 1986, 85 to 90 percent of the jobs in pre-1955 clothing and textiles firms were lost. Three-fourths of the jobs in domestic miscellaneous manufacturing and over half of the jobs in domestic chemicals and metals were lost. In the pre-ELI Irish manufacturing sector as a whole, half of the jobs held in 1973 were lost by 1986 (60 percent in the nonfood sector). Of course, this demolition of protected nationalist industry *could* be viewed as "restructuring"—that is, clearing out inefficient and unprofitable sectors to make way for more profitable "modern" sectors. To validate the dependency approach, therefore, we must show that the new industry which replaced domestic manufacturing was not conducive to economic growth.

Radical Free Enterprise

From its inception, the ISI regime was based strictly on principles of "private enterprise." Interventions by the state into the "business of business" were few, and state industry was limited (in 1945 there were three infrastructural and two industrial state companies). These principles were intensified under ELI. The state's role was to market Ireland as a profitable location for business—to pro-

Table 23.2   Changes of Employment and Number of Firms in Domestic "Old" and "Adapted" Industry from 1973 to 1986, Ireland

	Employment			Number of Firms		
Sector	1973	1986	Percent Change	1973	1986	Percent Change
Food	27,601	17,330	−37.2	598	448	−25.1
Drink	3,804	3,197	−16.0	77	56	−27.3
Textiles	8,561	894	−89.6	120	43	−64.2
Clothing	8,084	1,231	−84.8	213	78	−63.4
Wood	5,186	2,769	−46.6	361	284	−21.3
Paper	8,446	4,453	−47.3	218	176	−19.3
Clay	9,861	7,519	−23.8	211	161	−23.7
Chemical	2,245	1,047	−53.4	64	28	−56.3
Metals	12,148	5,172	−57.4	354	239	−32.5
Other mfg.	3,267	766	−76.6	132	71	−46.2
Nonfood	58,825	23,851	−59.5	1,673	1,080	−35.4
Total	90,230	44,378	−50.8	2,348	1,584	−32.5

Source: Author's calculations from IDA Employment Surveys.

vide incentives for industry to locate in Ireland and to find firms that would respond to the incentives. After that, new foreign firms could avoid any kind of scrutiny. The disposition of profits is left entirely in the hands of the firm. No profits taxes are paid on most manufactured exports, and profits may be freely repatriated. Means of production are freely imported, and output is freely exported. The regime does not pressure TNCs to use Irish inputs or to create other linkages. In the words of an Irish Minister for Industry and Commerce at the beginning of ELI, "we aim to convince [U.S. industrialists] that Ireland is the best possible location because of its attitude to private enterprise. . . . the more profits they make the better we will like it" (Dail Eireann 1958).

Foreign Domination

The Irish regime perceives foreign industry as a substitute for—not a complement to—domestic industry. An early and influential proponent of ELI captured the Irish attitude, saying, "By far the most hopeful means of getting good management, technical knowledge, and capital all at once is from subsidiaries of large foreign companies. . . . a plant which is paid for by foreign capital is a great deal better than one which has to be paid for from the scanty saving of the Republic" (Carter 1957). Since the inception of ELI, the regime relies *first and foremost* on the attraction of new foreign capital for industrial expansion. . . .

During the first half of the 1960s, TNCs created more than half of the new manufacturing jobs. After 1965, at least 70 to 80 percent of the new manufacturing jobs were in TNCs (O'Hearn 1987).

Ireland's adherence to free trade, free enterprise, and foreign industrial domination sets it apart from "exceptional" cases, such as South Korea and Taiwan. Regimes in these countries are characterized by strong state intervention in business, widespread use of selective protection and import-substitution, and a definite preference for domestic industry. The "free market" in Singapore, another high-growth East Asian economy, has been described as a "myth" (Lim 1983; see also Rodan 1985; Islam and Kirkpatrick 1986).[2] . . .

Results I: Slow Economic Growth

How do the specificities of the Irish case affect the relation of foreign penetration to economic growth and inequality? Are the relations of "dependency" at work in Ireland? . . .

Linkages

Even if the resources for investment and expansion are available, productive outlets for investment must be found. For many years, orthodox development theorists stressed the desirability of balanced growth among economic sectors, to avoid bottlenecks and realization problems (see Nurkse 1953; Lewis 1955). Albert Hirschman (1958) challenged this orthodoxy in his seminal work *The Strategy of Economic Development*. According to Hirschman, investment opportunities are created by the imbalanced development of the economy. Bottlenecks and gaps induce productive investment to correct or fill them.

Hirschman lists three kinds of linkages, or investment inducements. (1) If a firm buys inputs locally, it induces someone to produce them (*backward linkages*). (2) If a firm makes a product which may be processed further, it may induce a local firm to make a new product (*forward linkages*). (3) If a firm's activities contribute to the state's economic resources (through taxes and import duties), it creates *fiscal linkages*. Hirschman's analysis of linkages is behind more recent concepts such as *disarticulation* between "modern" and "traditional" economic sectors (Amin 1974) and *economic dualism* (Myint 1970; Singer 1970).

Fiscal linkages are probably negative in Ireland because (1) the typical TNC pays no taxes due to "free enterprise" tax provisions and pays no import duties due to free trade, and (2) large incentives and infrastructural costs are incurred by the state to attract foreign investment. Since TNCs in Ireland export nearly all of their product, forward linkages are few. The only possible significant linkages from TNC operations in Ireland are *backward* linkages.

Irish data on backward linkages are sparse. There were surveys of industrial firms in 1966, 1971, 1974, and 1983 (Survey Team 1967; O hUiginn 1972; McAleese 1977). Unfortunately, the coverage and classification of firms differ among the surveys, so longitudinal comparisons are awkward. But it is still possible to construct a fairly good picture of TNCs' backward linkages. Buckley (1974) found that TNCs in 1971 purchased only 31.5 percent of their material inputs from Irish sources, while Irish firms purchased 68.3 percent locally. McAleese and McDonald (1978) found that new (post–1955) nonfood TNCs purchased 11.2 percent of their inputs in Ireland, while new domestic firms purchased 22.2 percent locally. Thus, we can conclude that (a) the rate of TNC-related linkages is very low, (b) domestic firms have twice as many linkages as TNCs, and (c) the rate of linkages created by new domestic industry is also low. It is important to note that linkages were reduced in Ireland not only by the predominance of TNCs in new industry, but also because free trade encouraged (or forced) *domestic* firms to turn to foreign sources of supply. . . .

TNCs' backward linkages in Ireland are also extremely low relative to other dependent countries. Table 23.3 compares the proportions of material inputs that are locally purchased by manufacturing subsidiaries of U.S. TNCs in Ireland, Brazil, and Mexico. TNCs' local purchases are uniformly lower in Ireland, particularly in the "modern" sectors. In manufacturing as a whole, U.S. affiliates purchased 76.4 percent of their material inputs locally in Brazil and 68.5 percent in Mexico, but less than 20 percent in Ireland. While this confirms the extremely low level of TNC-induced linkages in Ireland by comparison with other semiperipheral countries, it also indicates the importance of specificities of Irish development. In particular, the most important causes of low linkages in Ireland—unlike Mexico and Brazil—are (1) the predominance

Table 23.3   Locally Purchased Materials as Percentage of Total Material Inputs in U.S. Affiliates Operating in Brazil, Mexico, and Ireland

| | | | Ireland | |
| | | | U.S. | All |
Sector	Brazil	Mexico	TNCs	TNCs
Food	89.5	96.8	73.0	70.7
Textiles	*	94.1	13.8	18.1
Paper	91.4	93.5	33.3	55.3
Chemicals	44.7	54.8	19.3	18.2
Rubber	92.7	88.5	3.1	1.5
Clay/cement	81.7	66.7	15.3	49.6
Metals	83.8	90.8	7.0	15.4
Nonelectric machinery	63.6	45.7	12.6	15.4
Electric machinery	60.0	61.6	10.9	11.2
Transport	97.1	60.7	8.9	18.6
Instruments	11.2	44.7	21.9	18.9
Other	74.0	97.6	19.2	19.2
Total	76.4	68.5	19.7	27.7

Source: IDA Components of Sales Survey data, Connor (1977).
Note: Irish data are for 1983; Brazilian and Mexican data are for 1972.

of TNC production for export rather than for local markets, and (2) the degree of free enterprise (absence of local-content regulations).

In an economy such as Ireland's, where the regime emphasizes the attraction of new foreign capital, and where imports have swamped the domestic consumer market, *linkages* are an important source of investment opportunities. The scarcity of linkages between TNCs and the local Irish economy means that the contribution of new TNCs to growth is practically restricted to the activities of the TNCs themselves. Foreign investment creates few multipliers that lead to the growth of domestic investment.

Foreign Penetration and Growth

The logic of the Irish development regime is deceptively simple, as is the logic of modernizationist analysis in general: attract as much foreign investment as possible, the foreign investors will export a lot, exports will bring new resources into the country, and economic development will surely follow, along with jobs and prosperity.

Irish ELI was *spectacularly* successful at attracting foreign investment and increasing exports. Real foreign investment grew at an annual rate of 25 percent between 1955 and 1983. Real exports grew by 7.5 percent annually between 1955 and 1985 (8.3 percent after 1972), and manufactured exports by more than 10 percent (calculated from OECD 1987). If foreign investments and exports are the key to growth, the Irish economy should have expanded especially rapidly during the 1970s and 1980s.

The actual Irish growth experience was very different (Table 23.4). Throughout ELI, gross fixed capital formation (GFCF) grew annually by only 5 percent. Since 1972 (when Ireland joined the EEC) per capita GFCF grew by less than 2 percent. Annual rates of growth of per capita GNP were even slower. At its highest, per capita GNP grew at an annual rate of 3.4 percent (1965–1970). During ELI as a whole, the annual growth rate of per capita GNP was a mere 2.3 percent. Most significantly, the annual per capita economic growth rate fell to 0.4 percent during the post-EEC period, and was negative (–1.25 percent) in the 1980s.

These rates of growth are strikingly low compared to rates of growth in other countries. Ireland's annual rate of economic growth over the 30 years of ELI was the lowest in Europe, well below rates of growth in the European periphery (4–6 percent) and the average rates of growth for upper-income LDCs (about 5 percent), and far below the "exceptional" East Asian economies (6–8 percent). Even in its so-called "miracle years" of the 1960s, Ireland's annual growth rate of per capita GNP never reached 4 percent over any five-year period. Can this poor growth performance be associated with foreign penetration, free trade, and free enterprise?[3]

Growth of output and investment became slower as foreign penetration became higher, and growth rates became particularly low (and finally nega-

Table 23.4   Annual Percentage Rates of Growth of Gross Fixed Capital Formation (GFCF) and GNP during ELI, 1955–85 (constant 1958 Irish punts)

Years	GFCF	Per Capita GFCF	GFCF (mfg.)	GNP	Per Capita GNP	Net Output (mfg.)
1955–60	–3.91	–3.31	3.6	1.22	1.83	4.4
1960–65	11.88	11.59	14.64	3.41	3.14	7.75
1965–70	6.34	5.87	7.82	3.9	3.41	8.23
1970–75	3.48	1.98	6.51	3.33	1.81	5.61
1975–80	6.89	5.34	6.61	3.53	2.16	6.99
1980–85	–0.39	–1.02	–6.12	–0.45	–1.25	6.88
1955–72	6.73	6.53	11.3	3.4	3.19	7.44
1972–85	3.24	1.97	1.61	1.65	0.38	5.9
1955–85	5.83	5.02	7.74	3.15	2.34	6.92

Source: Central Statistics Office (various years); OECD (1987).

Note: Five-year rates of growth for each variable x are calculated according to the following formula: [log $x(t+5)$ – log $x(t)$] / 5. Rates of growth for longer periods are calculated by least-square regression of the log of the variable on time in years.

tive) after Ireland joined the EEC and was forced into full-fledged free trade. *Every industrial sector except chemicals and metals experienced significantly lower rates of growth of net output after Ireland's accession to the EEC than in the pre-EEC period of ELI* (O'Hearn 1988, chap. 14). Textiles and clothing experienced negative post-EEC growth rates. Food, drink, wood, paper, and clay were stagnant after 1972. Only metals, chemicals, and other manufacturing experienced annual growth rates of more than 5 percent after Ireland entered the EEC and embarked on full free trade. . . .

Results II: Income Distribution

The second major claim of dependency is that foreign penetration either increases inequality or prevents its decrease. Here again most of the existing evidence is from cross-sectional studies, which do not adequately explain how the effects of dependency may unfold over time (for a review of findings, see Bornschier 1980b). Dependency posits three major types of arguments about foreign penetration and inequality: (1) arguments about structural unemployment and poverty, (2) arguments about class inequality, and (3) arguments about wage inequality.

Structural Unemployment and Poverty

Foreign penetration may cause unemployment for several reasons, two of which are particularly relevant in the Irish case. (*a*) Radical free trade and discrimination in favor of foreign industry may cause widescale displacement of domestic industry. To this may be added the migration of farmers to the cities and towns, which may further swell the ranks of the unemployed. (*b*) If new foreign industry is more capital-intensive than domestic industry, or is concentrated in capital- (or materials-) intensive sectors, the employment created per unit of foreign investment may be too low to offset employment *losses* associated with foreign-penetration (Rubinson 1976; Bornschier and Ballmer-Cao 1979).

Although Irish income distribution data are scarce,[4] structural unemployment has certainly been a major cause of inequality since Ireland joined the EEC. In Table 23.5 I show the distribution of direct incomes in 1973 and 1980. Unemployment is the source of the major differences between the two distributions. In 1973, the lowest 10 percent of Irish households received less than 1 percent of direct incomes, while the next decile received 1.7 percent. By 1980, the lowest decile received no direct income, while the next decile received a mere 0.7 percent of total incomes. Today, with unemployment exceeding 20 percent, the lowest *two* deciles receive no direct income. To the extent the ELI regime caused unemployment in Ireland, it unquestionably *caused* higher inequality of direct incomes.

Apart from industrial closures, rising capital intensity is the major cause of unemployment. Assets per hour of labor expended in Irish industry grew during ELI (1955–82) at an annual rate of 5.3 percent (O'Hearn 1988). Not only did highly capital-intensive foreign operations penetrate Irish industry, but the regime's generous capital grants encouraged local firms to replace labor with machines. These factors added considerably to unemployment in the 1970s and 1980s.

An important difference between the Irish case and other situations of dependency, however, is the degree to which popular demands for social welfare

Table 23.5   Distribution of Incomes and Tax Payments, by Decile, 1973 and 1980

Decile	Direct Income 1973	Direct Income 1980	Gross Income 1973	Gross Income 1980	Indirect Tax, 1980
1	—	Nil	2.9	2.6	10.0
2	1.7	0.7	4.4	4.2	
3	4.4	3.5	5.3	5.1	6.7
4	6.1	5.7	6.5	6.2	7.2
5	7.6	7.5	7.5	7.4	8.3
6	9.0	9.3	8.8	8.8	9.6
7	11.0	11.2	10.3	10.4	11.1
8	13.5	13.9	12.4	12.7	12.5
9	17.0	18.0	15.5	16.1	14.6
10	29.6	30.1	26.3	26.5	20.1
	99.9	99.9	99.9	100.0	100.1

Source: Roche (1984); Revenue Commissioners (1985).

have been met. Ireland's proximity to England, its claim to full European membership and "modernity," and its national aspirations to regain its northern territory all contributed to pressures on the regime to keep its social welfare benefits roughly in line with Britain's. At the same time, Britain's claim over the North of Ireland necessitated the introduction of social welfare benefits there at the same level as existed in England. Thus, when postwar welfare reforms were introduced in Britain, Ireland followed with a similar, if slightly less "grandiose" scheme. As a result, the distribution of *gross* incomes in Ireland is more equitable than direct incomes (Table 23.5), although the share of the bottom 20 percent of families is still falling. Unfortunately, data more recent than 1980 are not available. Social welfare cutbacks have increased dramatically in the 1980s because of severe public and foreign debt crisis in Ireland. When the effects of these cutbacks on gross income distribution are accounted, it will surely be shown that inequality rose significantly.

Finally, the introduction of free trade in Ireland led to a massive loss of tariff revenues for the state. As a result, highly regressive value-added taxes were introduced in 1964, and the rates were rapidly increased during the 1970s and 1980s. Indirect (value-added and excise) taxes now account for more than half of government revenues. As shown in Table 23.5, the proportion of *indirect* taxes paid by low-income receivers is much greater than the proportion of income they receive. Since indirect taxes have risen considerably during ELI—they made up 19.8 percent of government revenues in 1955 and 50.5 percent of revenues in 1985—they have added considerably to inequality over time. Thus, free trade is responsible for yet another dimension of income inequality in terms of spending power.

Class Inequality

Explanations of inequality that concentrate on income differences among classes emphasize the aspects of foreign penetration that increase elite power and decrease working-class power. Some analysts concentrate on the tendency of local elites to use their alliances with foreign capital in order to resist popular demands for income redistribution (Rubinson 1976; Bornschier and Ballmer-Cao 1979). Others concentrate on the power of TNCs to resist labor demands and weaken labor organization. A structural argument emphasizes that the high proportion of unskilled workers in TNC subsidiaries increases the number of the lowest industrial wage earners, while the failure to locate skilled work in subsidiaries leaves a gap in the middle ranges of the income scale. At the same time, foreign penetration may encourage the expansion of low-paying service jobs (Evans and Timberlake 1980).

Certain specific characteristics of the Irish case tend to make some of these effects inoperable. The most obvious is the difference between the Irish political system—where overt authoritarianism is largely avoided—and regimes in other developing countries. A related difference is the degree to which the very rich elites in pre-independence Ireland were *absentee* elites, since England was so close. Very rich landlords and very rich capitalists in Ireland tended to remove their incomes to England, where they do not figure in Irish income distribution statistics. Therefore, 20th-century Ireland never developed the kind of measurable elite-mass inequality that is observed throughout the developing world.

These special Irish characteristics are reflected in the movement of upper income shares between 1973 and 1980 (Table 23.5). The increases of higher-income shares that are associated with falling low-income shares are spread throughout the top 50 percent of income earners. The share of the top 20 percent of income receivers grew only a little, from 46.6 percent to 48.1 percent of total incomes. No identifiable small elite in Ireland appeared to benefit greatly from the worsening position of the lowest-income receivers. This is because the lost income of the lowest 20 percent was due less to lower wages than to the complete loss of wages. Wage earners who remained employed may not be better off absolutely but still moved up to higher income deciles as the unemployed filled up lower deciles.

The lack of significant "bunching" of income shares in the higher deciles is also consistent with the structural argument that there are few new high-salaried professionals and managers in TNC subsidiaries. Evidence in support of this conclusion comes from studies of the skill structure of TNCs in Ireland. In the electronics industry, for example, Wickham (1986) finds a large concentration of employees in assembly operations, and a particular preponderance of women in these occupations.

The most significant change of class inequality to come out of dependent Irish industrialization is absent from Irish income distribution statistics. This change involves the large-scale movement of incomes from wages to profits, and within profits from domestic industry to the TNCs. The high levels of profit repatriations simply reflect the rapid rise of TNC profits, and the duality of profit rates between foreign and domestic industry. During TNC-penetration (1955–85), the surplus-share of incomes rose by 2 percent a year in manufacturing as a whole, and by 3.5 percent annually in electronics and 6.4 percent in pharmaceuticals (O'Hearn 1988, chap. 16).

The level of *international* inequality that is engendered by dependency is clearly shown in Table 23.6, where I report profit rates in 1981 by economic sector and nationality of ownership. The duality of profit rates is particularly large in the "modern" sectors—electronics, pharmaceuticals, and other manufacturing—and a few "traditional" sectors such as drink, wood, and clay. Profits in certain foreign sectors—soft drinks, pharmaceuticals, healthcare, computers, instrument engineering, and others—were well in excess of 25 percent of sales and in some cases as high as *60 percent.* Overall, non-British TNCs' profit rates in Ireland av-

Table 23.6   Profit Rates by Sector and Country of Ownership, Irish Manufacturing, 1983

Sector	(a) Irish	(b) British	(c) Other Foreign	c/a
Food	2.26	3.01	5.23	2.31
Drink	9.29	18.60	26.95	2.90
Textiles	0.90	7.23	2.09	2.32
Clothing	−1.88	6.71	1.33	—
Wood	0.98	1.55	27.68	28.24
Paper	0.95	1.63	8.12	8.55
Clay	4.13	−8.90	27.32	6.62
Chemicals	−12.04	3.04	5.34	—
Pharmaceutical	10.15	22.02	48.66	4.79
Metals	1.09	5.52	10.25	9.40
Electric	−1.47	−196.00	22.65	—
Other	3.74	5.62	25.09	6.70
Total	1.82	7.03	22.09	12.14

Source: Author's calculations from IDA Components of Sales Survey.
Note: Profit rate refers to pretax profits as a percentage of total sales.

eraged 22 percent, while domestic firms' profit rates averaged less than 2 percent. It is clearly possible, therefore, that the effects of dependency on inequality *among countries* are much greater than its effects on local inequality.

Finally, the relationship between elites, TNCs, and trade union power may differ significantly in Ireland from many other cases of dependency. The Irish working class developed in close proximity to the highly-unionized British working class. Trade unionists were involved in the struggle for national liberation, and their support for early nationalist governments was very important. By 1958, 92 percent of Irish industrial workers were unionized (Registrar of Friendly Societies 1959). At the same time, the uneasy alliance between governments and trade unions, which is an important factor that neutralizes working-class opposition to foreign penetration, led most unions to become nonmilitant. For many years, the IDA advised TNCs who located in Ireland to recognize trade unions. An incoming TNC commonly made a "sweetheart" agreement with an Irish trade union, giving it sole organizing rights in return for guarantees of labor peace. Recently, however, as the Irish regime became desperate for new TNC investments, they acceded to the wishes of the latest wave of entrants—the "yuppie" U.S. electronic firms—and dropped their pressure for unionization of TNC subsidiaries. The first major TNC to "go nonunion" was the computer firm Digital, which is now one of the largest employers in the country. The consequences on interclass income distribution of these successes of TNC power over Irish trade unions have yet to be worked out.

Wage Inequality

The effects of foreign penetration on wage differentials have probably been the most widely discussed aspect of dependency and inequality. Much has been written about *dualism,* where a thriving foreign-dominated "modern" sector exists alongside a stagnant "traditional" sector (Myint 1970; Singer 1970). According to this approach, wages in the "modern" sectors are expected to be higher than in the "traditional" sectors, and this encourages *wage* inequality.

On the other hand, the expectation that subsidiaries' employment structures are weighted toward unskilled jobs, with the more skilled and professional positions kept in the parent country, contradicts the *dualism* argument. If TNCs concentrate their employment in unskilled assembly trades, they *decrease* wage inequality, even if their unskilled workers are paid more than unskilled workers in domestic firms. Finally, in a labor-rich economy, with high unemployment—and particularly with a highly educated working class as in Ireland—there may be little reason to expect the TNCs to pay higher wages than local firms. This is particularly true where centralized wage-setting or wage-bargaining structures exist, as they do not only in Ireland, but also in some of the East Asian economies (e.g., Singapore).

There is little evidence that foreign penetration caused significant *wage* inequality in Ireland. Average wage rates within industrial sectors in 1983 were quite similar among Irish, British, and other foreign firms (Table 23.7). Neither are wage rates particularly high in the "modern" sectors. Wages in electronics, metals, and "other manufacturing" are at or below the average for industry.

Table 23.7   Wages by Sector and Country of Ownership, Irish
                    Manufacturing, 1983 (annual wage per capita in Irish punts)

Sector	Irish	British	Other Foreign
Food	9,445	10,822	9,600
Drink	12,694	15,840	12,652
Textiles	6,545	7,025	9,208
Clothing	5,619	5,567	4,838
Wood	7,114	10,383	4,039
Paper	12,787	9,276	9,781
Clay	12,424	13,821	15,561
Chemicals	15,455	10,191	12,925
Pharmaceutical	9,720	10,675	13,830
Metals	8,967	10,520	9,139
Electric	7,861	10,202	9,867
Other	7,664	9,251	8,837
Total	9,502	9,235	9,307

Source: Author's calculations from IDA Components of Sales Survey.

Among foreign sectors, only chemicals and pharmaceuticals have relatively high average wages. Clearly, the sectoral differentials in wage rates are tied to the structure of the labor force within those sectors. Electronics, healthcare products, textiles, and clothing have a high proportion of female assembly-type workers. The drink and chemicals industries are highly capital-intensive and have a higher proportion of technical and other skilled workers.

Specific local factors are more important than foreign penetration or "duality" in determining the Irish wage distribution. The Irish wage bargaining structure—where wages are negotiated in a series of centralized "wage rounds" with tripartite participation of capital, trade unions, and the state—is the most important determinant of wage distribution. It is in the area of wage determination that the specificities of dependent cases, rather than any general "laws" of dependency, are likely to be most important.

Still, there are important dependency-related trends—economic decline, capital intensity, and unemployment—which have a strong influence in favor of *income* (as opposed to wage) inequality. These "pure dependency" effects of foreign penetration on income distribution differ significantly from other developing regimes, where localized political factors—often connected with authoritarian regimes—play a more important role in determining inequality.

Conclusions

The "dependency" approach to development studies has come under fire in recent years because of the seemingly "deviant" cases of East Asia. Proponents of modernization cite Taiwan and South Korea as instances where foreign penetration was *not* accompanied by either slow growth or rising inequality. They imply that other developing countries may also achieve rapid growth *with* equality by following a radical regime of free trade, free enterprise, and openness to foreign enterprise.

Unfortunately for the new modernizationists, neither South Korea nor Taiwan is really characterized by these traits. Both regimes intervene strongly in business, use selective protection and import-substitution, and have a definite preference for domestic industry. If South Korea, Taiwan, and even Singapore are "getting the prices right," it is because of their regimes' extensive intervention, not their reliance on "the market."

Ireland, on the other hand, has closely followed the prescriptions of the modernizationists. Since the 1950s, it has been highly penetrated by foreign industry, in preference to domestic industry; it removed its protective barriers and allows free movement of goods and profits in and out of the country; it disdained any form of control of business, including the use of indirect economic instruments such as credit and foreign exchange manipulations.

Ireland has also grown at a snail's pace and, recently, experienced negative economic growth. While the level of inequality has been reduced by social welfare policies—a remnant of the country's proximity to Europe—there is an underlying trend toward rising inequality, resulting from slow growth and tax policies that are forced by free trade and free enterprise. Since Ireland is among the top five debtor countries in the world (foreign debt as a percentage of GNP), the regime has already begun social welfare cutbacks that will drive it toward greater inequality. It is a classic case of "dependent" relations: slow growth and inequality caused by foreign penetration.[5]

There are other countries that are like Ireland in many respects, although the *specific* nature of dependent relations always differs significantly from country to country. The present analysis of Ireland does not resolve the problems of using dependency as a general approach to the study of development. Rather, it demonstrates how dependency-type mechanisms may thrive in a liberal, open atmosphere. Liberalness and openness, however, do not predominate in the periphery today—deviations from liberal regimes reinforce the need to rigorously examine the specificity of dependent situations. Thus, the Peruvian case of export-led "bonanza development"—where the state tries to maximize its share of TNC profits—is quite different from Irish ELI, where the state tries to maximize TNC investment and depend on trickle-down. The Brazilian case, where the state attempts to maximize linkages of TNCs with local capital, differs from the Irish regime, where linkages are simply hoped for.

Still, there are strong pressures afoot for liberalization, as proposed by the new modernizationists. These pressures are seen less in East Asia, however, than in places like Mexico and in the conditional lending of the IMF. The experience of foreign penetration, limited growth, and inequality—despite the exceptional cases of East Asia—is still much more common among developing countries than so-called "success." Students of development may have a lot to learn from the "exceptions"—particularly about ways to bring about economic development while avoiding the extreme authoritarianism of the East Asian cases. They have still more to learn from careful comparative historical analyses of specific cases of dependent development. The route of free trade, free enterprise, foreign penetration, and the new modernizationism is not the way to go.

Notes

1. Care should be taken not to confuse tariff revenues with categories such as "taxes on international trade and transactions" (e.g., in *World Development Report*). For Ireland, the latter is primarily excise taxes on alcohol and tobacco, a consumption tax which has partly replaced tariffs as a source of government revenues. Excise taxes are not a form of protection because locally produced alcoholic drinks and tobacco products are taxed at the same rate as imports. In addition, because excise taxes are

placed on goods that are highly price inelastic, they have a limited effect on consumption of taxed items.

2. Apart from the level of state intervention in Singapore, its special characteristics as a city-state—like Hong Kong—reduce its usefulness as a "model of development" (Rodan 1985, pp. 9–10).

3. Critics of the present approach may suggest that Ireland's poor per capita growth performance is caused by its high rate of population growth. This is not the case. It is true that Ireland has the highest rate of natural increase in Western Europe, and that population grew more rapidly in the 1960s and 1970s than in previous periods (when it actually declined, because of emigration). Thus, population growth did exacerbate the slow growth of the 1970s. In the 1980s, however, Irish population is again declining—emigration is reaching its highest levels ever (see Irish Census of Population 1986). Most experts agree that emigration and population decline will continue at a rapid rate for some years to come, barring an unforeseen economic recovery. While there is some reciprocity Irish population growth rates (which change according to emigration rates) clearly respond to economic growth rates more than they "cause" them.

4. The Irish census contains no questions about income. There are a few tax-based surveys of income distribution, but these have gaps in coverage, because many people pay no income taxes. A few household budget surveys were conducted (in 1951/52, 1965/66, 1973, and 1981) and these seem to provide the best information on income distribution. For existing studies of Irish income distribution. see Stark (1977) and Roche (1984).

5. A similar analysis could be made regarding the North of Ireland. It has also experienced severe economic decline and inequality during the postwar period. The reasons for stagnation and inequality in the North, however, are quite different from the South. Stagnation is mainly a result of the decline in importance to England of shipbuilding and natural fibers. The North has been allowed to decline as part of a British regional policy which favors Southern England at the expense of the so-called "Celtic fringe" and the old industrial regions of Northern England. In other words, Britain has largely withdrawn economically from its Northern Irish colony, although it refuses to withdraw militarily and politically. Inequality in the North of Ireland, unlike the South, is affected not only by class relations and economic decline, but also by sectarianism. The unemployment rate among the settler ("Protestant") population, for example, remains below the British average, at the expense of the native ("Catholic") population, which suffers unemployment averaging over 35 percent (above 80 percent in some Catholic areas).

References

Amin, S. 1974. *Accumulation on a World Scale.* New York: Monthly Review.

Baran, P. 1957. *The Political Economy of Growth.* New York: Monthly Review.

Barrett, R. E., and M. K. Whyte. 1982. "Dependency Theory and Taiwan: Analysis of a Deviant Case." *American Journal of Sociology* 87: 1064–89.

Biersteker, T. 1978. *Distortion or Development? Contending Perspectives on the Multinational Corporation.* Cambridge, MA: M.I.T. Press.

Bornschier, V. 1980a. "Multinational Corporations and Economic Growth: A Cross-National Test of the Decapitalization Thesis." *Journal of Development Economics* 7: 191–210.

———. 1980b. "Multinational Corporations, Economic Policy and National Development in the World System." *International Social Sciences* 32: 158–71.

Bornschier, V., and T.-H. Ballmer-Cao. 1978. "Income Inequality: A Cross-National Study of the Relationships between MNC-Penetration, Dimensions of the Power Structure and Income Distribution." *American Sociological Review* 44: 487–506.

Buckley, P. J. 1974. "Some Aspects of Foreign Private Investment in the Manufacturing Sector of the Economy of the Irish Republic." *Economic and Social Review* 5: 301–21.

Carter, C. 1957. "The Irish Economy Viewed from Without." *Studies* 46: 137–43.

Central Statistics Office. Various years. *National Income Accountants.* Dublin: Stationery Office.

Chakravarty, S. 1987. "Marxist Economics and Contemporary Developing Economies." *Cambridge Journal of Economics* 11: 3–22.

Chase-Dunn, C. 1975. "The Effects of International Economic Dependence on Development and Inequality." *American Sociological Review* 40: 720–38.

Connor, J. M. 1977. *The Market Power of Multinationals: A Quantitative Analysis of U.S. Corporations in Brazil and Mexico.* New York: Praeger.

Cummings, B. 1983. "The Origins and Development of the Northeast Asian Political Economy: Industrial Sectors, Product Cycles, and Political Consequences." *International Organization* 38: 1–40.

Dail Eireann. 1958. Parliamentary Debates 165. Dublin: Stationery Office.

Evans, P., and M. Timberlake. 1980. "Dependence, Inequality, and Growth in Less Developed Countries." *American Sociological Review* 45: 531–52.

Frank, A. G. 1969. *Latin America: Underdevelopment or Revolution.* New York: Monthly Review.

Hirschman, A. O. 1958. *The Strategy of Economic Development.* New York: Norton.

Islam, I., and C. Kirkpatrick. 1986. "Export-Led Development, Labour-Market Conditions and the Distribution of Income: The Case of Singapore." *Cambridge Journal of Economics.* 10: 113–27.

Lewis, W. A. 1955. *Theory of Economic Growth.* Homewood, IL: Irwin.

Lim, L. 1983. "Singapore's Success: The Myth of the Free Market Economy." *Asian Survey* 23: 752–64.

McAleese, D. 1977. *A Profile of Grant-Aided Industry in Ireland.* Dublin: Institute of Public Administration.

McAleese, D., and D. McDonald. 1978. "Employment Growth and the Development of Linkages in Foreign-Owned and Domestic Manufacturing Enterprises." *Oxford Bulletin of Economics and Statistics* 40: 321–39.

Myint, H. 1970. "Dualism and the International Integration of the Underdeveloped Economies." *Banca Nazionale del Lavoro Quarterly Review* 93: 128–56.

Nurkse, R. 1953. *Problems of Capital Formation in Underdeveloped Countries.* Oxford: Oxford University Press.

O'Hearn, Denis. 1987. "Estimates of New Foreign Manufacturing Employment in Ireland (1956–1972)." *Economic and Social Review* 18: 173–88.

———. 1988. *Export-led Industrialization in Ireland: A Specific Case of Dependent Development.* Ph.D. diss., University of Michigan.

O hUiginn, P. 1972. *Regional Development and Industrial Location in Ireland. Volume 1, Locational Decisions and Experiences of New Industrial Establishments 1960–1970.* Dublin: An Foras Forbartha.

Organization for Economic Cooperation and Development. (OECD). 1987. *National Accounts: Main Aggregates 1960–1985.* Paris: OECD.

Registrar of Friendly Societies (Ireland). 1959. *Annual Report.* Dublin: Stationery Office.

Revenue Commissioners (Ireland). Various years. *Annual Report.* Dublin: Stationery Office.

Roche, J. D. 1984. *Poverty and Income Maintenance Policies in Ireland.* Dublin: Institute of Public Administration.

Rodan, G. 1985. *Singapore's "Second Industrial Revolution": State Intervention and Foreign Investment.* Kuala Lumpur: ASEAN-Australian Joint Research Project.

Rubinson, R. 1976. "The World Economy and the Distribution of Income within States: A Cross-National Study." *American Sociological Review* 41: 638–50.

Singer, H. 1970. "Dualism Revisited: A New Approach to the Problems of the Dual Society in Developing Countries." *Journal of Development Studies* 7: 60–75.

Stark, T. 1977. *The Distribution of Income in Eight Countries.* London: HMSO.

Survey Team. 1967. *Survey of Grant-Aided Industry, 1967.* Dublin: Stationery Office.

U.S. Department of Commerce. 1980. "U.S. Direct Investment Abroad." *Survey of Current Business* 60: 16–38.

Wickham, J. 1986. *Trends in Employment and Skill in the Irish Electronics Industry.* Report to National Board for Science and Technology, Dublin.

World Bank. 1981. *World Development Report 1981.* Washington, DC: World Bank.

24

Transnational Corporations in World Development: Still the Same Harmful Effects in an Increasingly Globalized World Economy?

MARK HERKENRATH AND VOLKER BORNSCHIER

For over three decades dependency and world systems theory scholars have produced evidence that when developing nations opened their doors to investments by transnational corporations, their long-run economic growth was dampened and income inequality worsened. In this study the authors examine the role of transnational corporations (TNCs) in the process of globalization and seek to determine if TNCs' potentially harmful impact on developing countries' levels of inequality and rates of economic growth has changed. ■

DURING THE LAST DECADES OF THE 20TH CENTURY THE WORLD HAS EXPERIENCED AN impressive increase in the amount and relative importance of border-crossing economic interlinkages. Transnational corporations (TNCs) whose organizational structures transcend polities and connect various national societies have been playing a leading role in this process. The TNC system has grown substantially and gained historically unprecedented power in the political world-economy (UNCTAD 2000: Overview). The old question of how transnational corporations affect economic and social development in their host countries thus arises with renewed relevance.

The findings of previous research result in a quite bleak picture. Although standard economic theory argues transnational firms to be important catalysts of development and worldwide convergence, numerous cross-national studies on data from the late 1960s and early 1970s support the opposite view of *dependencia* and world-system theorists. They all show that TNC affiliates rather

Excerpted from the *Journal of World Systems Research* 9, 1 (Winter 2003): 105–139, http://jwsr.ucr.edu/archive/vol9/number1/pdf/jwsr-v9n1-herkenborn.pdf. Reprinted with the permission of the authors.

303

add to inequality and underdevelopment than to socio-economic progress in their host countries (Bornschier and Chase-Dunn 1985; Dixon and Boswell 1996a, b). These results, however, do not necessarily hold for the contemporary era. As the impressive growth of the TNC system since the 1960s (and, with increased velocity, since the 1980s) has been accompanied by various qualitative transformations, the effects of TNC presence on national development might have changed as well (Hübner 1998). It is thus necessary to analyze more recent data and compare the results with previous findings. Up to now, surprisingly few studies have addressed this problem and assessed the actual applicability of previous results to this contemporary era of increased global economic integration. The present study aims at closing this gap. We review the most recent literature on the relation between TNC presence and income inequality, and we also explore the effect of TNC presence on economic growth by means of new cross-national analyses based on data from the 1980s and early 1990s.

Three Theoretical Positions

The question of how TNCs influence national development has generated a long-lasting and intense scholarly debate. Two "classical" positions can be distinguished in this debate: the conventional position derived from standard economic theory, and the pessimistic position proposed by dependencia theorists and most proponents of the world-system approach. In the next sections we briefly review the two approaches in order to derive from them the hypotheses that will guide our study. Moreover, we discuss a third approach, which is termed the "skeptical" position. In contending that TNC presence may have positive and negative effects, this promising new perspective not only combines elements of the two classical positions but also puts the state and issues of "dependency management" back on the agenda. It should be noted, however, that the skeptical approach has not (yet) produced testable hypotheses. We are thus unable to assess its validity by means of cross-national testing.

The Conventional Position

The core arguments of the conventional position are well known, since they reflect common sense in standard economics as well as modernization theory. Late development, conventionalists contend, is a function of capital inflows, the creative adaptation of imported technology and the diffusion of modern perspectives among the population. Since TNCs and their affiliates provide all of these badly needed resources—fresh capital, new ideas and technologies, and modern values—right on the spot, they may help their host countries to achieve faster development and catch-up in the world system. Hence, countries with a marked TNC presence should be better off than countries where foreign firms are absent or less actively involved.

Regarding the effects on income distribution, proponents of the conventional position are somewhat less optimistic and concede that TNC activities may well create further inequality. TNC presence is argued to foster the process of industrialization that, in turn, creates dualistic structures and inequality. However, given that the effect of TNC activities is transmitted by economic success and further development, it necessarily follows Kuznets' famous inverted U-curve. Once the turning point is reached, FDI-induced development should actually start lowering the level of inequality. Thus, the hypothesized effect is neither direct nor long lasting. Rather, inequality has to be seen as a necessary but temporary price to be paid for the economic success brought about by TNCs and their investment.

The hypotheses of this position then read as follows:

H1.1 A stronger TNC presence is associated with more income inequality. This, however, is caused by the contribution of TNCs to growing income.

H1.2 The presence of TNCs is an advantage since their inputs accelerate convergence.

Hypotheses relating to conditional relations/interactions:

H1.3 Since TNCs provide technology and modern outlooks, the income-generating productivity of domestic investment should be greater the larger the presence of TNCs in a host country.

H1.4 Since the resources provided by TNCs are particularly scarce at low levels of development, the positive effect of TNC presence is more significant in poorer countries than in others.

The Pessimistic Position

The pessimistic position is based on a more realistic view of the divergent interests of TNCs and national governments. According to the proponents of this view, TNCs enter foreign markets to do profitable business there without paying any attention to the needs of the majority of the host country's population. TNC affiliates do business according to, and within, the global logic of capital accumulation of their parent corporations. Yet, the pessimistic position contends, they are not only economic actors. At the same time they are involved as "national corporate citizens" in the political economy of the host country and, like any other interest group, try to influence the government to act in their favor. Although this behavior is normal politics it alters power constellations and preferences in the national political economy. Since TNC affiliates are normally among the largest corporations in the host countries, and since the huge resources of their parent corporations abroad back them, they have substantial influence on the agenda of the host government.

Whereas the optimal agenda for developing country governments aims at moving up in the worldwide division of labor (by improving the value added in ever more sophisticated branches of the economy), this is not a high priority item on the agenda of TNCs. Foreign firms, indeed, choose a given host country exactly because of the relative availability of resources and relative prices that the government would or should want to change in order to achieve upward mobility in the worldwide division of labor. Thus, countries that are highly "penetrated" by foreign firms will find it difficult to propose and successfully implement an agenda of economic upgrading against the opposition of foreign interests.

According to the pessimistic position, the hierarchical division of labor within transnational corporations—the most important functions are performed in core countries, while more specialized and less sophisticated value-added activities are transferred to the periphery—not only corresponds with the existing stratification of the world system but also perpetuates it. The TNC system thus stabilizes the division of the world into different sections with unequal access to sophisticated economic activities and differing opportunities to generate national income. A national political economy that enters late development with the supposed help of TNCs will find it difficult to actually improve its position in the worldwide division of labor, and the optimal or potential convergence is hampered.

With regard to inequality, the argument is similar to the one proposed by the conventional position (H1.1): TNC presence leads to higher inequality. But unlike conventionalists, who claim a transitory impact, pessimists contend that inequality generated by TNC activities becomes institutionalized and, thus, enduring. Bornschier and Ballmer-Cao (1979), for example, claim that TNC presence affects various aspects of the internal power distribution, which, in turn, are related to overall income inequality. TNC presence, they argue, alters traditional social relations, the power distribution among formal organizations, the bargaining position of labor, and the way in which resources provided by the state authorities affect life-chances.

The hypotheses of the pessimistic position thus read as follows:

H2.1 More pronounced TNC presence is related to higher income inequality. This is not a transitory but, rather, a permanent relationship, since TNC presence transforms power relations in the host country.

H2.2 Higher TNC presence does not add to growth and may even hinder convergence once fresh TNC investment slows down.

Hypotheses relating to interactions/conditional effects:

H2.3 As a consequence of the altered political economy, total (domestic) investment contributes relatively little to economic growth in countries with strong TNC presence as compared to more independent countries. This is because the powerful TNC affiliates claim inputs and infrastructure from the state that could otherwise be used to support the bulk of medium- and small-sized domestic companies.

H2.4 The lower the level of development, the more the bargaining process between host country governments and TNCs is likely to result in solutions that favor the latter. Since the resources needed to reach a fairer bargain are particularly scarce in the poorest countries, the supposed negative effect of TNC presence should be more pronounced there.

The Skeptical Position

In addition to the classical positions discussed so far, the most recent editions of UNCTAD's World Investment Reports (particularly UNCTAD 1999) and a few other publications (Blomström/Kokko 1996; Khor 2000; Kiely 1998) propose an innovative third perspective. We have decided to call this new approach "skeptical" because it accuses both the pessimistic as well as the conventional position of being over-simplistic and too one-sided. According to the proponents of the skeptical approach, TNC presence is neither unequivocally good nor unequivocally bad for host country development. Rather, the net effect of TNC presence is argued to vary in accordance with the quality of policy packages adopted by different countries.

More specifically, the adherents of the skeptical position acknowledge the potential problems related to TNC presence, and they make clear that "FDI promises more than it delivers" (Kumar, cit. in Khor 2000:39). At the same time it is claimed that "politics matter," and that a reasonable "dependency management" may make a difference. Kiely (1996:60), for example, contends that "[s]tates in the Third World are not simply passive victims of the activities of TNCs, and some have quite successfully regulated the activities of foreign capital for their own developmental ends." In other words, the effects of TNC presence on income inequality and economic growth are argued to be ambiguous. In some cases, the skeptical approach claims, TNC activities are associated with high inequality and low economic growth. In other cases, however, host country governments may prevent these negative effects from working by pursuing successful countervailing policies.

The main problem with this new approach is that it represents a research program rather than a well-elaborated theory. The principal questions are still unanswered (i.e., the skeptical position does not give any detailed indication of which policies could prevent the negative effects of TNC presence from working). Nor is it made clear under what conditions a country is able to adopt such measures. In the case of UNCTAD's World Investment Reports these questions are deliberately avoided. The authors contend that there is no generally applicable package of "intelligent" TNC policies, and that "[a]ny good strategy must be context specific, reflecting the level of economic development, the resource base, the specific technological context and the competitive setting" (UNCTAD 1999: 315). Other researchers simply state that questions related to host country policies vis-à-vis foreign TNCs require further research (Blomström/Kokko 1996: 33). Fact is that the skeptical approach has not yet produced any testable hypotheses.

New Findings and Their Interpretation

In our own analyses we try to replicate the previous studies on the 1980s and, at the same time, to overcome their weaknesses. Thus, we investigate a much larger sample than Herkenrath (1999)—namely 84 cases, including a subsample of 63 less developed countries—and also test for the conditional model that has been neglected by de Soysa and Oneal (1999). All analyses are carried out with data for 1980–90 as well as 1985–95 in order to enable direct comparisons with the two other studies that use contemporary data. . . .

The results reported in table 1 [see the original article for the table][1] refer to the direct effect of TNC presence on economic growth predicted in hypotheses H1.2 and H2.2. The first thing worth noting is the equations' great explanatory power. Adjusted R-squares range from 0.71 to 0.75, indicating that more than two-thirds of the observed variance in GDP per capita growth can be explained by the predictors we included. Except for the TNC-related variables FIR and DUMMY all predictors turn out to have significant, and sometimes substantial, effects on the dependent variable. The results clearly confirm the assumptions of standard economic theory. The regressions of growth on domestic investment as well as on trade openness both show the presumed positive slopes, while the significant positive coefficient for market size nicely illustrates the existence of growth-enhancing scale effects. We also find a significant positive effect for human capital.

In the period 1980–90 we observe a marked convergence effect, which indicates that less developed economies tend to grow substantially faster than others do (ceteris paribus). This result, however, is not robust. In the second period (1985–95), the negative regression of GDP per capita growth on the initial level of development is significantly different from zero only in the total

---

1. The tables and numerous explanatory endnotes have been removed for the sake of space. The interested reader is referred to the original article for the tables and supporting evidence. The article can be found at: http://jwsr.ucr.edu/archive/vol9/number1/pdf/jwsr-v9n1-herkenborn.pdf. —Eds.

sample of 84 countries. In the sub-sample of 63 less developed countries, from which the highly industrialized benchmark countries were removed, the effect "disappears." The world's poorest countries do not seem to benefit from a greater growth potential than countries on a medium level of development. It should be noted, though, that this finding does not come totally unexpected. Dixon and Boswell (1996a, 1996b) as well as Firebaugh (1992) discover no convergence effect within their samples either.

Concerning the variable "foreign investment rate" (FIR), our results require further explanation. At first glance, the insignificant coefficients for FIR seem to suggest that fresh TNC investment (as measured by FDI inward stock growth rates) has no effect on GDP per capita growth whatsoever. This impression, however, is misleading. It should be noted that our models also control for total domestic investment, and that this measure already includes investment by TNC affiliates. Due to this restrictive condition, our foreign investment rate represents the marginal contribution of TNC investment; i.e., FIR simply measures whether foreign-controlled investment contributes relatively more to economic growth than total investment does (Borensztein et al. 1995). Yet, as indicated by our results, there is no such effect. Unlike most other studies on the subject, but in accordance with the results of Herkenrath (1999), we can thus conclude that TNC investment does not outperform investment by local entrepreneurs when it comes to encouraging economic progress.

As regards the effect of TNC presence, the results . . . are straightforward. Introducing our dichotomous TNC dummy does not improve the explanatory power of the test models at all, and in neither period nor sample is it a significant predictor of economic growth. While contradicting all empirical results for the late 1960s, this result clearly confirms the findings of most contemporary studies. Using a dummy variable instead of measuring TNC presence on higher scale-level seems to make no difference. We are as unable to detect a systematic linear and unconditional effect from TNC presence on national development as de Soysa and Oneal (1999) or Herkenrath (1999) are. Our results thus confirm the conclusion that, for the 1980s and early 1990s, the hypothesis H1.2 of the conventional position as well as H2.2 of the pessimistic position need to be rejected. Yet, contrary to de Soysa and Oneal (1999), we do not conclude that contemporary TNCs are harmless and of no relevance for their host countries.

This interpretation would be premature, since there are alternative interpretations of equal, or even greater, plausibility. It should be noted, for instance, that the present findings are also in perfect accordance with the skeptical position's claim that dependence on TNC presence still tends to have unfavorable effects, except in those (few) countries where the activities of foreign firms are regulated by adequate policies.

We must concede, however, that our decision to use a dichotomous measure of TNC presence in the above analyses is not entirely unproblematic.

While the transformation of the actual FDI data into a dummy variable drastically reduces the effects of measurement error, it also minimizes all "sound" information the original measure may have contained. Thus, to put it in the words of an anonymous reviewer, "the cure may have killed the cat." To address this problem, we reestimate the models . . . with several alternative specifications of TNC presence. . . . [T]he results . . . reveal no surprise whatsoever. None of the various measures of TNC presence show a significant effect on GDP per capita growth, irrespective of what period and what sample of countries we analyze. . . .

[Next], we investigate the validity of the hypotheses H1.3 and H2.3, which claim that the presence of foreign TNCs shapes, in one way or another, the growth-spurring effect of domestic investment. The results mainly re-confirm the existence of the growth-adverse conditional effect discovered by Dixon and Boswell (1996b), since the corresponding slope dummy, the interaction term "TNC dummy * domestic investment rate," reveals a significant negative coefficient. Thus, the conventional assumption H.3 has to be rejected. Although TNC affiliates may bring modern and efficient Western technologies into their host countries, we find absolutely no evidence of total domestic investment being more productive in those contexts where TNCs hold a dominant position. The contrary is the case: in countries with a more pronounced presence of foreign firms, local investment appears to contribute relatively less to economic growth than elsewhere. This result stands for two phenomena: On the one hand, we can conclude that foreign firms tend to supplant local firms in the more profitable branches of the economy and push them into those sectors where private and social returns on investment are lower. On the other hand, our findings show that many developing countries tend to promote the presence of foreign firms by offering them attractive production sites with high-quality infrastructure while neglecting the domestic sector. In these cases, domestic firms often lack the basic conditions for a frictionless production and, thus, yield below average.

The explanatory power of this conditional relation is by no means negligible. As compared to the models for 1980–90 in table 1 [see original article], the adjusted R-squares increase by 4 percentage points for the total sample and 3 percentage points for the LDC-sample when the slope dummy is included. (Note that the latter increase in the explained variance corresponds very nicely with the results of Dixon and Boswell for the late 1960s and early 1970s; see Dixon and Boswell 1996a: table 1, and 1996b: table 1).

[Finally we] address hypotheses H1.4 and H2.4. We analyze whether TNC presence produces a particularly positive, or negative, effect in the poorest and most backward countries. It could be argued that the additive models do not reveal any significant TNC effects simply because these effects vary in accordance with the level of development. Yet, table 3 [see original article] shows that there are no such conditional relations at work. The corresponding slope dummy, the interaction term "TNC dummy * level of development," is never a significant predictor in our models. Thus, the conventional assumption of accelerated convergence—TNCs are supposed to produce particularly positive effects in the least developed countries—cannot be upheld. Yet the same is true for the pessimistic claim that TNCs tend to produce their worst consequences in the world's most backward economies.

Conclusions and Discussion

Regarding income inequality as the dependent variable, all empirical studies included in our survey "[see the literature review in the original article] indicate that there is a notable and statistically significant positive (i.e., "harmful") relationship with TNC presence. It can be shown that, ceteris paribus, countries with high levels of dependence on foreign transnationals suffer from comparatively high levels of income concentration. To some extent, this relation seems to be influenced by the fact that TNCs preferably invest in unequal countries with relatively abundant cheap labor and wealthy elites. Yet, several studies show that the positive regression slope is still valid when the effect of reverse causation is controlled for (Beer and Boswell 2002; Kentor 2001). We can therefore conclude that the activities of TNC affiliates indeed tend to augment income inequality and "may in fact benefit elite segments of the population over others" (Beer and Boswell 2002: 52). This finding supports the expectations of the pessimistic position proposed by many dependencia and world-system theorists. It is important to note, however, that the corresponding regression coefficients show relatively large standard errors. One could thus argue that the studies we surveyed rather support the skeptical approach towards TNCs than the pessimistic position. Possibly, the presence of foreign transnationals leads to an increase in income concentration only under a laissez faire regime, whereas in the (fewer) countries with apt and development-oriented bureaucracies this tendency is offset by adequate political measures.

Although many advocates of corporate globalization contend that high TNC-induced inequality may be the price for accelerated economic development, the present analyses of data on the 1980s and the 1990s reveal no statistically significant effect from TNC presence on GDP per capita growth. Contrary to the predictions of standard economic theory, TNC affiliates do not systematically spur economic progress within their host countries. Nor do the activities of TNCs contribute to faster convergence of national incomes on a global level. In other words, TNCs are by no means "automatic" and systematic catalysts of socio-economic development, and the corresponding premises and principles underlying the Washington Consensus turn out to be mistaken. Although praised again and again by the most powerful organizations in the contemporary world system, unconditional openness towards TNC investment is not an appropriate remedy for underdevelopment. Governments in the South and everywhere should refrain from trying to attract TNC investment à tout prix. As indicated by our additional tests with interactive equations, tax incentives for foreign investors and other TNC-friendly policies probably just diminish the important growth-generating capacity of the (neglected) local sector.

Then again, our findings not only contradict the optimistic view on TNCs proposed by standard economic theory. Concerning growth as the dependent variable, our results are at odds with the pessimistic position as well. We find no empirical support for the assumption that economic growth in developing countries is directly and systematically hampered by the presence of foreign-owned firms. In this respect, our contemporary results differ substantially from the findings for the late 1960s and the 1970s. The earlier results, which unequivocally supported a critical and pessimistic view on TNCs' activities, cannot be replicated. The negative effect of TNC presence on the growth-generating capacity of domestic investment discovered earlier by Dixon and Boswell (1996b) has remained, but the generally negative impact on growth and convergence seems to have weakened.

This withering away of a previously strong statistical effect leads us to a further question. How come a relation not significantly different from zero supplanted the negative growth effect of TNC presence found in the 1960s and 1970s? Following de Soysa and Oneal (1999), it could be argued that TNCs per se have become harmless for economic growth. This interpretation does not seem overly convincing, though. Neither the will of foreign transnationals to generate maximum economic profits, nor their ability to rationally pursue this aim, has been subject to fundamental changes. In our opinion, the recent results and the fact that they differ from older findings should be interpreted in the light of the skeptical position presented in section 2 [of the original article]. We contend that a significant number of developing country governments implemented "smart" regulations on foreign firms, which now prevent TNC activities from displaying their potentially negative impact on socio-economic development in each and every situation. Yet, two points deserve to be mentioned. First, it should be clear that this state-oriented interpretation of our findings is rather tentative and requires further exploration. We clearly need more knowledge on the specific possibilities, and limitations, of host country governments to convert the activities of foreign-controlled firms into equitable growth. This knowledge can only be gathered in detailed case studies and "small-N comparisons," which eventually result in policy variables to be used in future cross-national tests. Second, it should be pointed out that our analyses focus on medium-term effects, i.e., the consequences of TNC presence within a 10-year growth period. The absence of such medium-term growth effects for the 1980s and early 1990s does not preclude the existence of long-term effects as discovered by Kentor (1998, 2001). To disentangle these medium-term and long-term effects is thus an important task at the top of the research agenda. It can be accomplished by simultaneous consideration of past and present TNC activities in one empirical model.

Another interesting task for future research will be to theorize and investigate sector-specific differences. This becomes more and more critical, since TNCs from the service sector are nowadays playing a much more important role than two or three decades ago. Even in developing nations, TNC presence can no longer be equated with extractive activities or with industrial production for the host country's internal market. There are "new" types of TNC activities to be accounted for. Assuming that these new activities are more beneficial than the activities of traditional TNCs, this could serve as an additional explanation for the fact that our new results differ from older findings. Unfortunately, as mentioned in section 3 [of the original article], sectoral FDI data is very rare and thus unsuitable for broad cross-national studies.

Finally, we need to go on studying not only TNCs but also other factors that influence growth and income distribution. Only then can we disentangle the diverse sources of success and failure in overcoming the burden of underdevelopment. The better we can isolate TNC-related factors, the better our case for making TNCs accountable.

References

Beer, Linda/Boswell, Terry (2002). "The Resilience of Dependency Effects in Explaining Income Inequality in the Global Economy: A Cross-National Analysis, 1975–1995." *Journal of World-Systems Research* 8 (1):30–59. http://jwsr.ucr.edu/.

Blomström, Magnus/Kokko, Ari (1996). "The Impact of Foreign Investment on Host Countries: A Review of the Empirical Evidence." *NBER Working Paper No. 4639.* Cambridge: National Bureau of Economic Research.

Borensztein, Eduardo/De Gregorio, José/Lee, Jong-Wha (1995). "How Does Foreign Direct Investment Affect Economic Growth?" *NBER Working Paper 5057.* Cambridge: National Bureau of Economic Research.

Bornschier, Volker/Ballmer-Cao, Than Huyen (1979). "Income Inequality. A Cross-National Study of the Relationships between MNC Penetration, Dimensions of the Power Structure and Income Distribution." *American Sociological Review* 44 (3):487–506.

Bornschier, Volker/Chase-Dunn, Christopher (1985). *Transnational Corporations and Underdevelopment.* New York: Praeger.

De Soysa, Indra/Oneal, John R. (1999). "Boon or Bane?—Reassessing the Productivity of Foreign Direct Investment." *American Sociological Review* 64:766–782.

Dixon, William J./Boswell, Terry (1996a). "Dependency, Disarticulation, and Denominator Effects: Another Look at Foreign Capital Penetration." *American Journal of Sociology* 102 (2):543–562.

Dixon, William J./Boswell, Terry (1996b). "Differential Productivity, Negative Externalities, and Foreign Capital Dependency: Reply to Firebaugh." *American Journal of Sociology* 102 (2):576–584.

Firebaugh, Glen (1992). "Growth Effects of Foreign and Domestic Investment." *American Journal of Sociology* 98:105–130.

Herkenrath, Mark (1999). *Transnationale Konzerne und nachholende Entwicklung: ein empirisch-quantitativer Ländervergleich.* Soziologisches Institut der Universität Zürich: Lizentiatsarbeit.

Hübner, Kurt (1998). *Der Globalisierungskomplex: grenzenlose Oekonomie–grenzenlose Politik?* Berlin: Sigma.

Kentor, Jeffrey (2001). "The Long-Term Effects of Globalization on Income Inequality, Population Growth, and Economic Development." *Social Problems* 48 (4):435–455.

Kentor, Jeffrey (1998). "The Long-Term Effects of Foreign Investment Dependence on Economic Growth 1940–1990." *American Journal of Sociology* 103 (4):1024–1046.

Khor, Martin (2000). "Globalization and the South: Some Critical Issues." *UNCTAD* (United Nations Conference on Trade and Development) *Discussion Paper No. 147.*

Kiely, Ray (1996). "Transnational Companies, Global Capital and the Third World." In: Kiely, Ray/Marfleet, Phil (eds.): *Globalisation and the Third World.* London/New York: Routledge. Pp. 45–66.

UNCTAD (United Nations Conference on Trade and Development) (several issues): World Investment Report. New York/Geneva: United Nations.

PART 7

The Role of Institutions

25

Big Bills Left on the Sidewalk: Why Some Nations Are Rich, and Others Poor

MANCUR OLSON JR.

During his lifetime Mancur Olson Jr. was one of the most influential champions of rational choice theory. Here he dismisses many of the proposed causes of the gap between rich and poor countries offered throughout this volume—access to productive knowledge, access to capital markets, population stresses, lack of natural resources, quality of human capital, culture, and so on—declaring that the cause is the quality of institutions and economic policies. Olson argues that all governments and policies are not made equally and countries do not produce as much as their natural endowments permit, but rather strong institutions that get the policy right are the decisive factor in a country's economic performance. According to Olson, convergence theorists are not right about convergence because most poor countries, despite having a higher propensity to grow than richer countries, have poorer economic policies and institutions than richer countries. ∎

THERE IS ONE METAPHOR THAT NOT ONLY ILLUMINATES THE IDEA BEHIND MANY complex and seemingly disparate articles, but also helps to explain why many nations have remained poor while others have become rich. This metaphor grows out of debates about the "efficient markets hypothesis" that all pertinent publicly available information is taken into account in existing stock market prices, so that an investor can do as well by investing in randomly chosen stocks as by drawing on expert judgment. It is embodied in the familiar old joke about the assistant professor who, when walking with a full professor,

Reprinted with permission of the American Economic Association from the *Journal of Economic Perspectives*, vol. 10, no. 2 (1996): 3–24.

reaches down for the $100 bill he sees on the sidewalk. But he is held back by his senior colleague, who points out that if the $100 bill were real, it would have been picked up already. This story epitomizes many articles showing that the optimization of the participants in the market typically eliminates opportunities for supranormal returns: big bills aren't often dropped on the sidewalk, and if they are, they are picked up very quickly.

Many developments in economics in the last quarter century rest on the idea that any gains that can be obtained are in fact picked up. Though primitive early versions of Keynesian macroeconomics promised huge gains from activist fiscal and monetary policies, macroeconomics in the last quarter century has more often than not argued that rational individual behavior eliminates the problems that activist policies were supposed to solve. If a disequilibrium wage is creating involuntary unemployment, that would mean that workers had time to sell that was worth less to them than to prospective employers, so a mutually advantageous employment contract eliminates the involuntary unemployment. The market ensures that involuntarily unemployed labor is not left pacing the sidewalks.

Similarly, profit-maximizing firms have an incentive to enter exceptionally profitable industries, which reduces the social losses from monopoly power. Accordingly, a body of empirical research finds that the losses from monopoly in U.S. industry are slight: Harberger triangles are small. In the same spirit, many economists find that the social losses from protectionism and other inefficient government policies are only a minuscule percentage of the GDP [gross domestic product].

The literature growing out of the Coase theorem similarly suggests that even when there are externalities, bargaining among those involved can generate socially efficient outcomes. As long as transactions costs are not too high, voluntary bargaining internalizes externalities, so there is a Pareto-efficient outcome whatever the initial distribution of legal rights among the parties. Again, this is the idea that bargainers leave no money on the table.

Some of the more recent literature on Coaseian bargains emphasizes that transactions costs use up real resources and that the value of these resources must be taken into account in defining the Pareto frontier. It follows that, if the bargaining costs of internalizing an externality exceed the resulting gains, things should be left alone. The fact that rational parties won't leave any money on the table automatically insures that laissez faire generates Pareto efficiency.

More recently, Gary Becker (1983, 1985) has emphasized that government programs with deadweight losses must be at a political disadvantage. Some economists have gone on to treat governments as institutions that reduce transactions costs, and they have applied the Coase theorem to politics. They argue, in essence, that rational actors in the polity have an incentive to bargain politically until all mutual gains have been realized, so that democratic government, though it affects the distribution of income, normally produces socially efficient results (Stigler, 1971, 1992; Wittman, 1989, 1995; Thompson and Faith, 1981; Breton, 1993). This is true even when the policy chosen runs counter to the prescriptions of economists: if some alternative political bargain would have left the rational parties in the polity better off, they would have chosen it! Thus, the elemental idea that mutually advantageous bargaining will obtain all gains that are worth obtaining—that there are no bills left on the sidewalk—leads to the conclusion that, whether we observe laissez faire or rampant interventionism, we are already in the most efficient of all possible worlds.

The idea that the economies we observe are socially efficient, at least to an approximation, is not only espoused by economists who follow their logic as far as it will go, but is also a staple assumption behind much of the best-known empirical work. In the familiar aggregate production function or growth accounting empirical studies, it is assumed that economies are on the frontiers of their aggregate production functions. Profit-maximizing firms use capital and other factors of production up to the point where the value of the marginal product equals the price of the input, and it is assumed that the marginal private product of each factor equals its marginal social product. The econometrician can then calculate how much of the increase in social output is attributable to the accumulation of capital and other factors of production and treat any increases in output beyond this—"the residual"—as due to the advance of knowledge. This procedure assumes that output is as great as it can be, given the available resources and the level of technological knowledge.

If the ideas evoked here are largely true, then the rational parties in the economy and the polity ensure that the economy cannot be that far from its potential, and the policy advice of economists cannot be especially valuable. Of course, even if economic advice increased the GDP by just 1 percent, that would pay our salaries several times over. Still, the implication of the foregoing ideas and empirical assumptions is that economics cannot save the world, but at best can only improve it a little. In the language of Keynes' comparison of professions, we are no more important for the future of society than dentists.

The Boundaries of Wealth and Poverty

How can we find empirical evidence to test the idea that the rationality of individuals makes societies achieve their productive potential? This question seems empirically intractable. Yet there is one type of place where evidence abounds: the borders of countries. National borders delineate areas of different economic policies and institutions, and so—to the extent that variations in performance across countries cannot be explained by the differences in their endowments—they tell us something about the extent to which societies have attained their potentials.

Income levels differ dramatically across countries. According to the best available measures, per capita incomes in the richest countries are more than 20 times as high as in the poorest. Whatever the causes of high incomes may be, they are certainly present in some countries and absent in others. Though rich and poor countries do not usually share common borders, sometimes there are great differences in per capita income on opposite sides of a meandering river, like the Rio Grande, or where opposing armies happened to come to a stalemate, as between North and South Korea, or where arbitrary lines were drawn to divide a country, as not long ago in Germany.

At the highest level of aggregation, there are only two possible types of explanations of the great differences in per capita income across countries that can be taken seriously.

The first possibility is that, as the aggregate production function methodology and the foregoing theories suggest, national borders mark differences in the scarcity of productive resources per capita: the poor countries are poor because they are short of resources. They might be short of land and natural resources, or of human capital, or of equipment that embodies the latest technology, or of other types of resources. On this theory, the Coase theorem holds as much in poor societies as in rich ones: the rationality of individuals brings each society reasonably close to its potential, different as these potentials are. There are no big bills on the footpaths of the poor societies, either.

The second possibility is that national boundaries mark the borders of public policies and institutions that are not only different, but in some cases better and in other cases worse. Those countries with the best policies and institutions achieve most of their potential, while other countries achieve only a tiny fraction of their potential income. The individuals and firms in these societies may display rationality, and often great ingenuity and perseverance, in eking out a living in extraordinarily difficult conditions, but this individual achievement does not generate anything remotely resembling a socially efficient outcome. There are hundreds of billions or even trillions of dollars that could be—but are not—earned each year from the natural and human resources of these countries. On this theory, the poorer countries do not have a structure of incentives that brings forth the productive cooperation that would pick up the big bills, and the reason they don't have it is that such structures do not emerge automatically as a consequence of individual rationality. The structure of incentives depends not only on what economic policies are chosen in each period, but also on the long run or institutional arrangements: on the legal systems that enforce contracts and protect property rights and on political structures, constitutional provisions, and the extent of special-interest lobbies and cartels.

How important are each of the two foregoing possibilities in explaining economic performance? This question is extraordinarily important. The answer must not only help us judge the theories under discussion, but also tell us about the main sources of economic growth and development.

I will attempt to assess the two possibilities by aggregating the productive factors in the same way as in a conventional aggregate production function or growth-accounting study and then consider each of the aggregate factors in turn. That is, I consider separately the relative abundance or scarcity of "capital," of "land" (with land standing for all natural resources) and of "labor" (with labor including not only human capital in the form of skills and education, but also culture). I will also consider the level of technology separately, and I find some considerations and evidence that support the familiar assumption from growth-accounting studies and Solow-type growth theory that the same level of technological knowledge is given exogenously to all countries. With this conventional taxonomy and the assumption that societies are on frontiers of their aggregate neoclassical production functions, we can derive important findings with a few simple deductions from familiar facts.

The next section shows that there is strong support for the familiar assumption that the world's stock of knowledge is available at little or no cost to all the countries of the world. I next examine the degree to which the marginal productivity of labor changes with large migrations and evidence on population densities, and I show that diminishing returns to land and other natural resources cannot explain much of the huge international differences in income. After that, I borrow some calculations from Robert Lucas on the implications of the huge differences across countries in capital intensity—and relate them to facts on the direction and magnitude of capital flows—to show that it is quite impossible that the countries of the world are anywhere near the frontiers of aggregate neoclassical production functions. I then examine some strangely neglected natural experiments with migrants from poor to rich countries to estimate the size of the differences in endowments of human capital between the poor and rich countries, and I demonstrate that they are able to account for only a small part of the international differences in the marginal product of labor.

Since neither differences in endowments of any of the three classical aggregate factors of production nor differential access to technology explain much of the great variation in per capita incomes, we are left with the second of the two (admittedly highly aggregated) possibilities set out above: that much the most important explanation of the differences in income across countries is the difference in their economic policies and institutions. There will not be room here to set out many of the other types of evidence supporting this conclusion, nor to offer any detailed analysis of what particular institutions and policies best promote economic growth. Nonetheless, by referring to other studies—and by returning to something that the theories with which we began overlook—we shall obtain some sense of why variations in institutions and policies are surely the main determinants of international differences in per capita incomes. We shall also obtain a faint glimpse of the broadest features of the institutions and policies that nations need to achieve the highest possible income levels.

The Access to Productive Knowledge

Is the world's technological knowledge generally accessible at little or no cost to all countries? To the extent that productive knowledge takes the form of unpatentable laws of nature and advances in basic science, it is a non-excludable public good available to everyone without charge. Nonpurchasers can, however, be denied access to many discoveries (in countries where intellectual property rights are enforced) through patents or copyrights, or because the discoveries are embodied in machines or other marketable products. Perhaps most advances in basic science can be of use to a poor country only after they have been combined with or embodied in some product or process that must be purchased from firms in the rich countries. We must, therefore, ask whether most of the gains from using modern productive knowledge in a poor country are mainly captured by firms in the countries that discovered or developed this knowledge.

Since those third world countries that have been growing exceptionally rapidly must surely have been adopting modern technologies from the first world, I tried (with the help of Brendan Kennelly) to find out how much foreign technologies had cost some such countries. As it happens, there is a study with some striking data for South Korea for the years from 1973 to 1979 (Koo, 1982). In Korea during these years, royalties and all other payments for disembodied technology were minuscule—often less than one-thousandth of GDP. Even if we treat all profits on foreign direct investment as solely a payment for knowledge and add them to royalties, the total is still less than 1.5 percent of the *increase* in Korea's GDP over the period. Thus the foreign owners of productive knowledge obtained less than a fiftieth of the gains from Korea's rapid economic growth.

The South Korean case certainly supports the long-familiar assumption that the world's productive knowledge is, for the most part, available to poor countries, and even at a relatively modest cost. It would be very difficult to explain much of the differences in per capita incomes across countries in terms of differential access to the available stock of productive knowledge.

Overpopulation and Diminishing Returns to Labor

Countries with access to the same global stock of knowledge may nonetheless have different endowments, which in turn might explain most of the differences in per capita income across countries. Accordingly, many people have supposed that the poverty in the poor countries is due largely to overpopulation, that is, to a low ratio of land and other natural resources to population. Is this true?

There is some evidence that provides a surprisingly persuasive answer to this question. I came upon it when I learned through Bhagwati (1984) of Hamilton and Whalley's (1984) estimates about how much world income would change if more workers were shifted from low-income to high-income countries. The key is to examine how much migration from poorer to richer countries *changes* relative wages and the marginal productivities of labor.

For simplicity, suppose that the world is divided into only two regions: North and South, and stick with the conventional assumption that both are on the frontiers of their aggregate production functions. As we move left to right from the origin of Figure 25.1, we have an ever larger workforce in the North until, at the extreme right end of this axis, all of the world's labor force is there. Conversely, as we move right to left from the right-hand axis, we have an ever larger workforce in the South. The marginal product of labor or wage in the rich North is measured on the vertical axis at the left of Figure 25.1. The curve MPL_N gives the marginal product or wage of labor in the North, and, of course, because of diminishing returns, it slopes downward as we move to the right. The larger the labor force in the South, the lower the marginal product

Figure 25.1   Population Distribution and Relative Wages

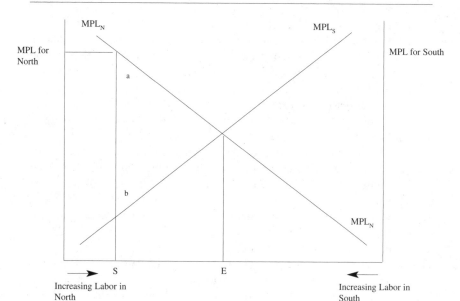

of labor in the South, so MPL_S, measured on the right-hand vertical axis, slopes down as we move to the left. Each point on the horizontal axis will specify a distribution of the world's population between the North and the South. A point like S represents the status quo. At S, there is relatively little labor and population in relation to resources in the North, and so the Northern marginal product and wage are high. The marginal product and wage in the overpopulated South will be low, and the marginal product of labor in the North exceeds that in the South by a substantial multiple.

This model tells us that when workers migrate from the low-wage South to the high-wage North, world income goes up by the difference between the wage the migrant worker receives in the rich country and what that worker earned in the poor country, or by amount ab. Clearly, the world as a whole is not on the frontier of its aggregate production, even if all of the countries in it are: some big bills have not been picked up on the routes that lead from poor to rich countries. Of course, the argument that has just been made is extremely simple, and international migration involves many other considerations. We can best come to understand these considerations—as well as other matters—by staying with this simple factor proportions story a while longer.

The Surprising Results of Large Migrations

This elementary model reminds us that, if it is diminishing returns to land and other natural resources that mainly explain international differences in per capita incomes, then large migrations from poorer to richer societies will, if other things (like the stocks of capital) remain equal, necessarily reduce income differentials. Such migration obviously raises the resource-to-population ratio in the country of emigration and reduces it in the country of immigration, and if carried far enough will continue until wages are equalized, as at point E in Figure 25.1.

Now consider Ireland, the country that has experienced much the highest proportion of outmigration in Europe, if not the world. In the census of 1821, Ireland had 5.4 million people, and Great Britain a population of 14.2 million. Though the Irish have experienced the same rates of natural population increase that have characterized other European peoples since 1821, in 1986, Ireland had only 3.5 million people. By this time, the population of Great Britain had reached 55.1 million. In 1821, the population density of Ireland was greater than that of Great Britain; by 1986, it was only about a fifth as great.

If the lack of "land" or overpopulation is decisive, Ireland ought to have enjoyed an exceptionally rapid growth of per capita income, at least in comparison with Great Britain, and the outmigration should eventually have ceased. Not so. Remarkably, the Irish level of per capita income is still only about five-eighths of the British level and less than half of the level in the United States, and the outmigration from Ireland is still continuing. As we shall see later, such large disparities in per capita income cannot normally be explained by differences in human capital. It is clear that in the United States, Britain and many other countries, immigrants from Ireland tend to earn as much as other peoples, and any differences in human capital could not explain the *increase* in wage that migrants receive when they go to a more productive country. Thus we can be sure that it is not the ratio of land to labor that has mainly determined per capita income in Ireland.

Now let us took at the huge European immigration to the United States between the closing of the U.S. frontier in about 1890 and the imposition of U.S. immigration restrictions in the early 1920s. If diminishing returns to labor were a substantial part of the story of economic growth, this vast migration should have caused a gradual reduction of the per capita income differential between the United States and Europe. In fact, the United States had a bigger lead in per capita income over several European countries in 1910 and 1920 than it had in the nineteenth century. Although many European countries did *not* narrow the gap in per capita incomes with the United States in the nineteenth century when they experienced a large outmigration to the United States, many of these same countries did nearly close that gap in the years after 1945, when they had relatively little emigration to the United States, and when their own incomes ought to have been lowered by a significant inflow of migrants and guest workers. Similarly, from the end of World War II until the construction of the Berlin wall, there was a considerable flow of population from East to West Germany, but this flow did not equalize income levels.

Consider also the irrepressible flow of documented and undocumented migration from Latin America to the United States. If diminishing returns to land and other natural resources were the main explanation of the difference in per capita incomes between Mexico and the United States, these differences should have diminished markedly at the times when this migration was greatest. They have not.

Several detailed empirical studies of relatively large immigration to isolated labor markets point to the same conclusion as the great migrations we have just considered. Card's (1990) study of the Mariel boatlift's effect on the wages of natives of Miami, Hunt's (1992) examination of the repatriation of Algerian French workers to Southern France, and Carrington and De Lima's (1996) account of the repatriates from Angola and Mozambique after Portugal lost its colonies all suggest that the substantial immigration did not depress the wages of natives.

Perhaps in some cases the curves in Figure 25.1 would cross when there was little population left in a poor country. Or maybe they would not cross at all: even that last person who turned the lights out as he left would obtain a higher wage after migrating.

Surprising Evidence on Density of Population

Let us now shift focus from changes in land/labor ratios due to migration to the cross-sectional evidence at given points in time on ratios of land to labor. Ideally, one should have a good index of the natural resource endowments of each country. Such an index should be adjusted to take account of changes in international prices, so that the value of a nation's resources index would change when the prices of the resources with which it was relatively well endowed went up or down. For lack of such an index, we must here simply examine density of population. Fortunately, the number of countries on which we have data on population and area is so large that population density alone tells us something.

Many of the most densely settled countries have high per capita incomes, and many poor countries are sparsely settled. Argentina, a country that fell from having one of the highest per capita incomes to third world status, has only 11 persons per square kilometer; Brazil, 16; Kenya, 25; and Zaire, 13. India, like most societies with a lot of irrigated agriculture, is more densely settled, with 233 people per square kilometer. But high-income West Germany, with 246 people per square kilometer, is more densely settled than India. Belgium and Japan have half again more population density than India, with 322 and 325 people per square kilometer, and Holland has still more density with 357. The population of Singapore is 4,185 per square kilometer; that of Hong Kong, over 5,000 persons per square kilometer (United Nations, 1986). These two densely settled little fragments of land also have per capita incomes 10 times as high as the poorest countries (and as of this writing they continue, like many other densely settled countries, to absorb migrants, at least when the migrants can sneak through the controls).

The foregoing cases could be exceptions, so we need to take all countries for which data are available into account and summarily describe the overall relationship between population density and per capita income. If we remember that the purpose is description and are careful to avoid drawing causal inferences, we can describe the available data with a univariate regression in which the natural log of real per capita income is the left-hand variable, and the natural log of population per square kilometer is the "explanatory" variable. Obviously, the per capita income of a country depends on many things, and any statistical test that does not take account of all important determinants is misspecified, and thus must be used only for descriptive and heuristic purposes. It is nonetheless interesting—and for most people surprising—to find that there is a positive and even a statistically significant relationship between these two variables: the greater the number of people per square kilometer the higher per capita income.

The law of diminishing returns is indisputably true: it would be absurd to suppose that a larger endowment of land makes a country poorer. This consideration by itself would, of course, call for a negative sign on population density. Thus, it is interesting to ask what might account for the "wrong" sign and to think of what statistical tests should ultimately be done. Clearly, there is a simultaneous two-way relationship between population density and per capita income: the level of per capita income affects population growth just as population, through diminishing returns to labor, affects per capita income.

The argument offered here suggests that perhaps countries with better economic policies and institutions come to have higher per capita incomes than countries with inferior policies and institutions, and that these higher incomes bring about a *higher population* growth through more immigration and lower death rates. In this way, the effect of better institutions and policies in raising per capita income swamps the tendency of diminishing returns to labor to reduce it. This hypothesis also may explain why many empirical studies have not been able to show a negative association between the rate of population growth and increases in per capita income.

One reason why the ratio of natural resources to population does not account for variations in per capita income is that most economic activity can now readily be separated from deposits of raw materials and arable land. Over time, transportation technologies have certainly improved, and products that have a high value in relation to their weight, such as most services and manufactured goods like computers and airplanes, may have become more important. The Silicon Valley is not important for the manufacture of computers because of deposits of silicon, and London and Zurich are not great banking centers because of fertile land. Even casual observation suggests that most modern manufacturing and service exports are not closely tied to natural resources. Western Europe does not now have a *high* ratio of natural resources to population, but it is very important in the export of manufactures and services. Japan has relatively little natural resources per capita, but it is a great exporter of manufactures. Certainly the striking successes in manufactures of Hong Kong and Singapore cannot be explained by their natural resources.

Diminishing Returns to Capital

We have seen that large migrations of labor do not change the marginal productivities of labor the way that they would if societies were at the frontiers of aggregate neoclassical production functions and that there is even evidence that labor is on average more *highly paid* where it is combined with less land. We shall now see that the allocation of capital across countries—and the patterns of investment and migration of capital across countries of *high and* low capital intensities—contradict the assumption that countries are on the frontiers of aggregate neoclassical production functions in an even more striking way.

This is immediately evident if we return to Figure 25.1 and relabel its co-ordinates and curves. If we replace the total world labor supply given along the horizontal axis of Figure 25.1 with the total world stock of capital and assume that the quantity of labor as well as natural resources in the North and South do not change, we can use Figure 25.1 to analyze diminishing returns to capital in the same way we used it to consider diminishing returns to labor.

As everyone knows, the countries with *high per* capita incomes have incomparably *higher capital* intensities of production than do those with low incomes. The countries of the third world use relatively little capital, and those of the first world are capital rich: most of the world's stock of capital is "crowded" into North America, western Europe and Japan.

If the countries of the world were on the frontiers of neoclassical production functions, the marginal product of capital would therefore be many times higher in the low-income than in the high-income countries. Robert Lucas (1990) has calculated, albeit in a somewhat different framework, the marginal product of capital that should be expected in the United States and in India. Lucas estimated that if an Indian worker and an American worker supplied the same quantity and quality of labor, the marginal product of capital in India should be 58 times as great as in the United States. Even when Lucas assumed that it took five Indian workers to supply as much labor as one U.S. worker, the predicted return to capital in India would still be a multiple of the return in the United States.

With portfolio managers and multinational corporations searching for more profitable investments for their capital, such gigantic differences in return should generate huge migrations of capital from the high-income to the low-income countries. Capital should be struggling at least as hard to get into the third world as labor is struggling to migrate into the high-wage countries. Indeed, since rational owners of capital allocate their investment funds across countries so that the risk-adjusted return at the margin is the same across countries, capital should be equally plentiful in all countries. (As we know from the Hecksher-Ohlin-Stolper-Samuelson discovery, if all countries operate on the same aggregate production functions, free trade alone is sometimes enough to equalize factor price ratios and thus factor intensities even in the absence of capital flows.)

Obviously, the dramatically uneven distribution of capital around the world contradicts the familiar assumption that all countries are on the frontiers of aggregate neoclassical production functions. A country could not be Pareto efficient and thus could not be on the frontier of its aggregate production unless it had equated the marginal product of capital in the country to the world price of capital. If it were not meeting this law-of-one-price condition, it would be passing up the gains that could come from borrowing capital abroad at the world rate of interest, investing it at home to obtain the higher marginal product of capital and pocketing the difference—it would be leaving large bills on the sidewalk. Accordingly, the strikingly unequal allocation of the world's stock of capital across nations proves that the poor countries cannot be any-where near the frontiers of their aggregate production functions.

Sometimes the shortcomings of the economic policies and institutions of the low-income countries keep capital in these countries from earning rates of return appropriate to its scarcity, as we may infer from Harberger's (1978) findings and other evidence. Sometimes the shortcomings of the economic policies and institutions of poor countries make foreign investors and foreign firms unwelcome, or provoke the flight of locally owned capital, or make lending to these countries exceedingly risky. Whether the institutional and pol-icy shortcomings of a country keep capital from having the productivity ap-propriate to its scarcity or discourage the investments and lending that would equalize the marginal product of capital across countries, they keep it from achieving its potential.

On top of all this, it is not rare for capital and labor to move *in the same direction:* both capital and labor are sometimes trying to move out of some countries and into some of the same countries. Of course, in a world where countries are on the frontiers of their aggregate production functions, capital and labor move in opposite directions.

Given the extraordinarily uneven allocation of capital across the countries of the world and the strong relationship between capital mobility and the eco-nomic policies and institutions of countries, the stock of capital cannot be taken to be exogenous in any reasonable theory of economic development.

Distinguishing Private Good and Public Good Human Capital

The adjustment of the amount of human capital per worker in Lucas's (1990) foregoing calculation for India and the United States raises a general issue: can the great differences in per capita income be mainly explained by differences in the third aggregate factor, labor, that is, by differences in the *human* capital per capita, broadly understood as including the cultural or other traits of dif-ferent peoples as well as their skills? The average level of human capital in the form of occupational skills or education in a society can obviously influence the level of its per capita income.

Many people also argue that the high incomes in the rich countries are due in part to cultural or racial traits that make the individuals in these countries adept at responding to economic opportunities: they have the "Protestant ethic" or other cultural or national traits that are supposed to make them hard workers, frugal savers and imaginative entrepreneurs. Poor countries are al-leged to be poor because they lack these traits. The cultural traits that perpet-uate poverty are, it is argued, the results of centuries of social accumulation and cannot be changed quickly.

Unfortunately, the argument that culture is important for economic development, though plausible, is also vague: the word "culture," even though it is widely used in diverse disciplines, has not been defined precisely or in a way that permits comparison with other variables in an aggregate production function. We can obtain conceptions of culture that are adequate for the present purpose by breaking culture down into two distinct types of human capital.

Some types of human capital are obviously marketable: if a person has more skill, or a propensity to work harder, or a predilection to save more, or a more entrepreneurial personality, this will normally increase that individual's money income. Let us call these skills, propensities, or cultural traits that affect the quality or the quantity of productive inputs that an individual can sell in the marketplace "marketable human capital" or, synonymously, "personal culture." Max Weber's analysis of what he called the Protestant ethic was about marketable human capital or personal culture.

The second type of culture or human capital is evident when we think of knowledge that individuals may have about how they should vote: about what public policies will be successful. If enough voters acquire more knowledge about what the real consequences of different public policies will be, public policies will improve and thereby increase real incomes in the society. But this better knowledge of public policy is usually not marketable: in a society with given economic policies and institutions, the acquisition of such knowledge would not in general have any affect on an individual's wage or income. Knowledge about what public policy should be is a public good rather than a private or marketable good. Thus this second kind of human capital is "public good human capital" or "civic culture." Whereas marketable human capital or personal culture increases an individual's market income under given institutions and public policies, public good human capital or civic culture is not normally marketable and only affects incomes by influencing public policies and institutions.

With the aid of the distinction between marketable and public good human capital, we can gain important truths from some natural experiments.

Migration as an Experiment

As it happens, migration from poor to rich countries provides researchers with a marvelous (and so far strangely neglected) natural experiment. Typically, the number of individuals who immigrate to a country in any generation is too small to bring about any significant change in the electorate or public policies of the host country. But the migrant who arrives as an adult comes with the marketable human capital or personal culture of the country of origin; the Latin American who swims the Rio Grande is not thereby instantly baptized with the Protestant ethic. Though the migrant may in time acquire the culture of the host country, the whole idea behind the theories that emphasize the cultural or other characteristics of peoples is that it takes time to erase generations of socialization: if the cultural or other traits of a people could be changed overnight, they could not be significant barriers to development. Newly arrived immigrants therefore have approximately the same marketable human capital or personal culture they had before they migrated, but the institutions and public policies that determine the opportunities that they confront are those of the host country. In the case of the migration to the United States, at least, the data about newly arrived migrants from poor countries are sufficient to permit some immediate conclusions.

Christopher Clague (1991), drawing on the work of Borjas (1987), has found that individuals who had just arrived in the United States from poor countries, in spite of the difficulties they must have had in adjusting to a new environment with a different language and conditions, earned about 55 percent as much as native Americans of the same age, sex and years of schooling. New immigrants from countries where per capita incomes are only a tenth or a fifth as large as in the United States have a wage more than half as large as comparable American workers. Profit-maximizing firms would not have hired these migrants if they did not have a marginal product at least as large as their wage. The migrant's labor is, of course, combined with more capital in the rich than in the poor country, but it is not an accident that the owners of capital chose to invest it where they did: as the foregoing argument showed, the capital-labor ratio in a country is mainly determined by its institutions and policies.

Migrants might be more productive than their compatriots who did not migrate, so it might be supposed that the foregoing observations on immigrants are driven by selection bias. In fact, no tendency for the more productive people in poor countries to be more likely to emigrate could explain the huge increases in wages and marginal products of the migrants themselves. The migrant earns and produces much more in the rich country than in the poor country, so no tendency for migrants to be more productive than those who did not migrate could explain the increase in the migrant's marginal product when he or she moves from the poor to the rich country. In any event, developing countries often have much more unequal income distributions than developed nations, and the incentive to migrate from these countries is greatest in the least successful half of their income distributions. In fact, migrants to the United States are often drawn from the lower portion of the income distribution of underdeveloped countries (Borjas, 1990).

It is also instructive to examine the differences in productivity of migrants from poor countries with migrants from rich countries and then to see how much of the difference in per capita incomes in the countries of origin is likely to be due to the differences in the marketable human capital or personal culture of their respective peoples. Compare, for example, migrants to the United States from Haiti, one of the world's least successful economies, with migrants from West Germany, one of the most successful. According to the 1980 U.S. Census, self-employed immigrants from Haiti earned $18,900 per year, while those from West Germany earned $27,300; salaried immigrants from Haiti earned $10,900, those from West Germany, $21,900. Since the average Haitian immigrants earned only two-thirds or half as much as their West German counterparts in the same American environment, we may suspect that the Haitians had, on average, less marketable human capital than the West Germans.

So now let us perform the thought experiment of asking how much West Germans would have produced if they had the same institutions and economic policies as Haiti, or conversely how much Haitians would have produced had they had the same institutions and economic policies as West Germany. If we infer from the experience of migrants to the United States that West Germans have twice as much marketable capital as the Haitians, we can then suppose that Haiti with its present institutions and economic policies, but with West German levels of marketable human capital, would have about twice the per capita income that it has. But the actual level of Haitian per capita income is only about a tenth of the West German level, so Haiti would still, under our thought experiment, have less than one-fifth of the West German per capita income. Of course, if one imagines Haitian levels of marketable human capital operating with West German institutions and economic policies, one comes up with about half of the West German per capita income, which is again many times larger than Haiti's actual per capita income.

Obviously, one of the reasons for the great disparity implied by these thought experiments is the different amounts of tangible capital per worker in the two countries. Before taking this as given exogenously, however, the reader should consider investing his or her own money in each of these two countries. It is also possible that different selection biases for immigrants from different countries help account for the results of the foregoing thought experiments. Yet roughly the same results hold when one undertakes similar comparisons from migrants from Switzerland and Egypt, Japan and Guatemala, Norway and the Philippines, Sweden and Greece, the Netherlands and Panama, and so on. If, in comparing the incomes of migrants to the United States from poor and rich countries, one supposes that selection bias leads to an underestimate of the differences in marketable human capital between the poor and rich countries, and then makes a larger estimate of this effect than anyone is likely to think plausible, one still ends up with the result that the rich countries have vastly larger leads over poor countries in per capita incomes than can possibly be explained by differences in the marketable human capital of their populations. Such differences in personal culture can explain only a small part of the huge differences in per capita income between the rich and the poor countries.

History has performed some other experiments that lead to the same conclusion. During most of the postwar period, China, Germany and Korea have been divided by the accidents of history, so that different parts of nations with about the same culture and group traits have had different institutions and economic policies. The economic performances of Hong Kong and Taiwan, of West Germany and of South Korea have been incomparably better than the performances of mainland China, East Germany and North Korea. Such great differences in economic performance in areas of very similar cultural characteristics could surely not be explained by differences in the marketable human capital of the populations at issue.

It is important to remember that the foregoing experiments involving migration do not tell us anything about popular attitudes or prejudices in different countries regarding what public policy should be. That is, they do not tell us anything about the public good human capital or civic cultures of different peoples. As we know, the migrants from poor to rich countries are normally tiny minorities in the countries to which they migrate, so they do not usually change the public policies or institutions of the host countries. The natural experiments that we have just considered do not tell us what would happen if the civic cultures of the poor countries were to come to dominate the rich countries. For example, if traditional Latin American or Middle Eastern beliefs about how societies should be organized came to dominate North America or western Europe, institutions and economic policies—and then presumably also economic performance—would change.

The Overwhelming Importance of Institutions and Economic Policies

If what has been said so far is correct, then the large differences in per capita income across countries cannot be explained by differences in access to the world's stock of productive knowledge or to its capital markets, by differences in the ratio of population to land or natural resources, or by differences in the quality of marketable human capital or personal culture. Albeit at a high level of aggregation, this eliminates each of the factors of production as possible explanations of most of the international differences in per capita income. The only remaining plausible explanation is that the great differences in the wealth of nations are mainly due to differences in the quality of their institutions and economic policies.

The evidence from the national borders that delineate different institutions and economic policies not only contradicts the view that societies produce as much as their resource endowments permit, but also directly suggests that a country's institutions and economic policies are decisive for its economic performance. The very fact that the differences in per capita incomes across countries—the units with the different policies and institutions—are so large in relation to the differences in incomes across regions of the same country supports my argument. So does the fact that national borders sometimes sharply divide areas of quite different per capita incomes.

Old Growth Theory, New Growth Theory and the Facts

The argument offered here also fits the relationships between levels of per capita income and rates of growth better than does either the old growth theory or the new. As has often been pointed out, the absence of any general tendency for the poor countries with their opportunities for catch-up growth to grow faster than the rich countries argues against the old growth theory. The new or endogenous growth models feature externalities that increase with investment or with stocks of human or tangible capital and can readily explain why countries with high per capita incomes can grow as fast or faster than low-income countries.

But neither the old nor the new growth theories predict the relationship that is actually observed: *the fast-growing countries are never the countries with the highest per capita incomes but always a subset of the lower-income countries.* At the same time that low-income countries as a whole fail to grow any faster than high-income countries, a subset of the lower-income countries grows far faster than *any* high-income country does. The argument offered here suggests that poor countries on average have poorer economic policies and institutions than rich countries, and, therefore, in spite of their opportunity for rapid catch-up growth, they need not grow faster on average than the rich countries.

But any poorer countries that adopt relatively good economic policies and institutions enjoy rapid catch-up growth: since they are far short of their potential, their per capita incomes can increase not only because of the technological and other advances that simultaneously bring growth to the richest countries, but also by narrowing the huge gap between their actual and potential income (Barro, 1991). Countries with the highest per capita incomes do not have the same opportunity.

Thus the argument here leads us to expect what is actually observed: no necessary connection between low per capita incomes and more rapid rates of growth, but much the highest rates of growth in a subset of low-income countries—the ones that adopt better economic policies and institutions. During the 1970s, for example, South Korea grew seven times as fast as the United States. During the 1970s, the four countries that (apart from the oil-exporting countries) had the fastest rates of growth of per capita income grew on average 6.9 percentage points faster per year than the United States—more than five times as fast. In the 1980s, the four fastest growers grew 5.3 percentage points faster per year than the United States—four times as fast. They outgrew the highest income countries as a class by similarly large multiples. All of the four of the fastest-growing countries in each decade were low-income countries.

In general, the endogenous growth models do not have anything in their structures that predicts that the most rapid growth will occur in a subset of low-income countries, and the old growth theory is contradicted by the absence of general convergence.

Note also that, as the gap in per capita incomes between the relatively poor and relatively rich countries has increased over time, poor countries have also fallen further behind their potential. Therefore, the argument offered here predicts that the maximum rate of growth that is possible for a poor country— and the rate at which it can gain on the highest per capita income countries— is increasing over time. This is also what has been observed. In the 1870s, the four continental European countries with the fastest growth of per capita incomes grew only 0.3 of 1 percent per annum faster than the United Kingdom. The top four such countries in the 1880s also had the same 0.3 percent gain over the United Kingdom. As we have seen, the top four countries in the 1970s grew 6.9 percentage points faster than the United States, and the top four in the 1980s, 5.3 percentage points faster. Thus, the lead of the top four in the 1970s was 23 times as great as the lead of the top four in the 1870s, and the lead of the top four in the 1980s was more than 17 times as great as the top four a century before.

Thus neither the old nor the new growth theory leads us to expect either the observed overall relationship between the levels and rates of growth of per capita incomes or the way this relationship has changed as the absolute gap in per capita incomes has increased over time. The present theory, by contrast, suggests that there should be patterns like those we observe.

Picking Up the Big Bills

The best thing a society can do to increase its prosperity is to wise up. This means, in turn, that it is very important indeed that economists, inside government and out, get things right. When we are wrong, we do a lot of harm. When we are right—and have the clarity needed to prevail against the special interests and the quacks—we make an extraordinary contribution to the amelioration of poverty and the progress of humanity. The sums lost because the poor countries obtain only a fraction of—and because even the richest countries do not reach—their economic potentials are measured in the trillions of dollars.

None of the familiar ideologies is sufficient to provide the needed wisdom. The familiar assumption that the quality of a nation's economic institutions and policies is given by the smallness, or the largeness, of its public sector—or by the size of its transfers to low-income people—does not fit the facts very well (Levine and Remit, 1992; Rubinson, 1977; Olson, 1986).

But the hypothesis that economic performance is determined mostly by the structure *of* incentives—and that it is mainly national borders that mark the boundaries of different structures of incentives—has far more evidence in its favor. This lecture has set out only one of the types of this evidence; there is also direct evidence of the linkage between better economic policies and institutions and better economic performance. Though it is not feasible to set out this direct evidence here, it is available in other writings (Clague, Keefer, Knack and Olson, 1995; Olson, 1982, 1987a, 1987b, 1990).

We can perhaps obtain a glimpse of another kind of logic and evidence in support of the argument here—and a hint about what kinds of institutions and economic policies generate better economic performance—by returning to the theories with which we began. These theories suggested that the rationality of the participants in an economy or the parties to a bargain implied that there would be no money left on the table. We know from the surprisingly good performance of migrants from poor countries in rich countries, as well as from other evidence, that there is a great deal of rationality, mother wit and energy among the masses of the poor countries: individuals in these societies can pick up the bills on the sidewalk about as quickly as we can.

The problem is that the really big sums cannot be picked up through uncoordinated individual actions. They can only be obtained through the efficient cooperation of many millions of specialized workers and other inputs: in other words, they can only be attained if a vast array of gains from specialization and trade are realized. Though the low-income societies obtain most of the gains from self-enforcing trades, they do not realize many of the largest gains from specialization and trade. They do not have the institutions that enforce contracts impartially, and so they lose most of the gains from those transactions (like those in the capital market) that require impartial third-party enforcement. They do not have institutions that make property rights secure over the long run, so they lose most of the gains from capital-intensive production. Production and trade in these societies is further handicapped by misguided economic policies and by private and public predation. The intricate social cooperation that emerges when there is a sophisticated array of markets requires far better institutions and economic policies than most countries have. The effective correction of market failures is even more difficult.

The spontaneous individual optimization that drives the theories with which I began is important, but it is not enough by itself. If spontaneous Coase-style bargains, whether through laissez faire or political bargaining and government, eliminated socially wasteful predation and obtained the institutions that are needed for a thriving market economy, then there would not be so many grossly inefficient and poverty stricken societies. The argument presented here shows that the bargains needed to create efficient societies are not, in fact, made. Though that is another story, I can show that in many cases such bargains are even logically inconsistent with rational individual behavior. Some important trends in economic thinking, useful as they are, should not blind us to a sad and all-too-general reality: as the literature on collective action demonstrates (Olson, 1965; Hardin, 1982; Sandler, 1992; and many others), individual rationality is very far indeed from being sufficient for social rationality.

References

Barro, Robert J., "Economic Growth in a Cross Section of Countries," *Quarterly Journal of Economics,* May 1991, 106.2, 407–43.

Becker, Gary, "A Theory of Competition Among Pressure Groups for Political Influence," *Quarterly Journal of Economics,* August 1983, 98, 371–400.

Becker, Gary, "Public Policies, Pressure Groups, and Dead Weight Costs," *Journal of Public Economics,* December 1985, 28:3, 329–47.

Bhagwati, Jagdish, "Incentives and Disincentives: International Migration," *Weltswirtschaftliches Archiv,* 1984, 120, 678–701.

Borjas, George, "Self-Selection and the Earnings of Immigrants," *American Economic Review,* September 1987, 77, 531–53.

Borjas, George, *Friends or Strangers: The Impact of Immigrants on the U.S. Economy.* New York: Basic Books, 1990.

Breton, A., "Toward a Presumption of Efficiency in Politics," *Public Choice,* September 1993, 77:1, 53–65.

Card, David, "The Impact of the Mariel Boatlift on the Miami Labor Market," *Industrial and Labor Relations Review,* January 1990, 43:2, 245–57.

Carrington, William J., and Pedro J. F. De Lima, "The Impact of 1970s Repatriates from Africa on the Portuguese Labor Market," *Industrial and Labor Relations Review,* January 1996, 49:2, 330–47.

Clague, Christopher, "Relative Efficiency, Self-Containment and Comparative Costs of Less Developed Countries," *Economic Development and Cultural Change,* April 1991, 39:3, 507–30.

Clague, Christopher, P. Keefer, S. Knack, and Mancur Olson, "Contract-Intensive Money: Contract Enforcement, Property Rights, and Economic Performance." IRIS Working Paper No. 151, University of Maryland, 1995.

Great Britain Central Statistical Office, *Annual Abstract of Statistics.* London: H.M.S.O., 1988.

Hamilton, Bob, and John Whalley, "Efficiency and Distributional Implications of Global Restrictions on Labour Mobility Calculations and Policy Implications," *Journal of Development Economics,* January/February 1984, 14, 61–75.

Harberger, Arnold, "Perspectives on Capital and Technology in Less Developed Countries." In Artis, M., and A. Nobay, eds., *Contemporary Economic Analysis.* London: Croom Helm, 1978, pp. 12–72.

Hardin, Russell, *Collective Action.* Baltimore: Johns Hopkins University Press, 1982.

Hunt, Jennifer, "The Impact of the 1962 Repatriates from Algeria on the French Labor Market," *Industrial and Labor Relations Review,* April 1992, 45.3, 556–72.

Ireland Central Statistics Office, *Statistical Abstract.* Dublin: Stationery Office, 1986.

Koo, Bohn-Young, "New Forms of Foreign Direct Investment in Korea." Korean Development Institute Working Paper No. 82-02, June 1982.

Krueger, Alan B., and Jörn-Steffen Pischke, "A Comparative Analysis of East and West German Labor Markets." In Freeman, Richard, and Lawrence Katz, eds., *Differences and Changes in Wage Structures.* Chicago: University of Chicago Press, 1995, pp. 405–45.

Landes, David, "Why Are We So Rich and They So Poor?," *American Economic Review,* May 1990, 80, 1–13.

Levine, Ross, and David Remit, "A Sensitivity Analysis of Cross-Country Growth Regressions," *American Economic Review,* September 1992, 82, 942–63.

Lucas, Robert, "'Why Doesn't Capital Flow from Rich to Poor Countries?," *American Economic Review,* May 1990, 80, 92–96.

Mitchell, Brian R., *Abstract of British Historical Statistics.* Cambridge, UK: Cambridge University Press, 1962.

Mitchell, Brian R., and H. G. Jones, *Second Abstract of British Historical Statistics.* Cambridge, UK: Cambridge University Press, 1971.

Mokyr, Joel, *My Ireland Starved: A Quantitative and Analytical History of the Irish 1800–1850.* London and Boston: Allen & Unwin, 1983.

Olson, Mancur, *The Logic of Collective Action.* Cambridge: Harvard University Press, 1965.

Olson, Mancur, *The Rise and Decline of Nations.* New Haven: Yale University Press, 1982.

Olson, Mancur, "Supply-Side Economics, Industrial Policy, and Rational Ignorance." In Barfield, Claude E., and William A. Schambra, eds., *The Politics of Industrial Policy.* Washington: American Enterprise Institute for Public Policy Research, 1986, pp. 245–69.

Olson, Mancur, "Diseconornies of Scale and Development," *The Cato Journal,* Spring/ Summer 1987a, 7:1, 77–97.

Olson, Mancur, "Economic Nationalism and Economic Progress, the Harry Johnson Memorial Lecture," *The World Economy,* September 1987b, 10:3, 241–64.

Olson, Mancur, "The IRIS Idea," IRIS, University of Maryland, 1990.

Olson, Mancur, "Transactions Costs and the Coase Theorem: Is This Most Efficient of All Possible Worlds?" working paper, 1995.

Rubinson, Richard, "Dependency, Government Revenue, and Economic Growth, 1955–1970," *Studies in Comparative Institutional Development,* Summer 1977, 12:2, 3–28.

Sandler, Todd, *Collective Action.* Ann Arbor: University of Michigan Press, 1992.

Stigler, George J., "The Theory of Economic Regulation," *Bell Journal of Economics and Management Science,* Spring 1971, 2, 3–21.

Stigler, George J., "Law or Economics?," *The Journal of Law and Economics,* October 1992, 35:2, 455–68.

Thompson, Earl, and Roger Faith, "A Pure Theory of Strategic Behavior and Social Institutions," *American Economic Review,* June 1981, 71:3, 366–80.

United Nations, *Demographic Yearbook.* New York: United Nations, 1986.

Wittman, Donald, "Why Democracies Produce Efficient Results," *Journal of Political Economy,* December 1989, 97:6, 1395–424.

Wittman, Donald, *The Myth of Democratic Failure. Why Political Institutions are Efficient.* University of Chicago Press, 1995.

26

Mauritius: A Case Study

ARVIND SUBRAMANIAN

Case study evidence of Mancur Olson's thesis from Chapter 25 is found here. In this chapter, Arvind Subramanian argues that Mauritius was able to achieve 5.9 percent economic growth between 1973 and 1999 due to the strength of its institutions and its economic policy. Robert Bates is well-known for highlighting the extreme corruption of marketing boards, but Subramanian argues that even though Mauritius has an export-processing zone, strong institutions allowed them to avoid the rent-seeking and corruption of other African countries. Like Olson, Subramanian points to institutions and policy as the keys to the economic success of Mauritius. ■

FEW SUB-SAHARAN AFRICAN COUNTRIES HAVE ACHIEVED HIGH STANDARDS OF LIVing. A notable exception has been Mauritius. Yet we had it on the highest possible authority—the economist and Nobel Prize winner James Meade, who prophesied in the early 1960s that Mauritius's development prospects were poor—that Mauritius was a strong candidate for failure, with its heavy economic dependence on one crop (sugar), vulnerability to terms of trade shocks, rapid population growth, and potential for ethnic tensions. History—or, rather, Mauritius—proved Meade's dire prognostication famously wrong.

Are Mauritius's achievements due to favorable initial conditions, good policies—especially openness to trade and foreign investment—sound domestic institutions, or other factors?

Reprinted with permission from *Finance and Development,* vol. 38, no. 4 (December 2001). Copyright © 2001 by the International Monetary Fund.

Achievements

Between 1973 and 1999, real GDP [gross domestic product] in Mauritius grew 5.9 percent a year, on average, compared with 2.4 percent for sub-Saharan Africa as a whole. Through the magic of compounding, the income of the average Mauritian more than tripled over a 40-year period, while that of the average African increased by only 32 percent.

Improvements in human development indicators have been equally impressive. Life expectancy at birth increased from 61 years in 1965 to 71 years in 1996; primary school enrollment increased from 93 to 107 per 100 children of school age between 1980 and 1996, while it decreased from 78 to 75 in the rest of Africa. (Enrollment rates may be higher than 100 percent because of repeaters, adults who are enrolled even though they are not in the age group being measured, and other discrepancies.) The income gap between the richest and the poorest Mauritians has narrowed considerably: the Gini coefficient (a measure of income inequality, with 0.0 representing total equality and 1.0 representing total inequality) declined from 0.5 in 1962 to 0.37 in 1986–87.

High growth rates have been achieved in a stable macroeconomic environment. Between 1973 and 2000, annual consumer price inflation averaged 7.8 percent in Mauritius, compared with more than 25 percent for sub-Saharan Africa as a whole. The unemployment rate declined from nearly 20 percent in 1983 to 3 percent in the late 1980s, although it has since edged up above 7 percent.

Social protection in Mauritius is similar to that seen in the industrial countries: a large and active presence for trade unions, which are able to engage in centralized wage bargaining, and generous social security benefits, particularly for the elderly and civil servants. Social protection is also afforded through price controls, especially on a number of socially sensitive items. In contrast with the member countries of the Organization for Economic Cooperation and Development, however, generous social programs in Mauritius have thus far not necessitated high taxes, reflecting both strong growth and favorable demographics, a large proportion of the population being of working age.

Initial Conditions

Did Mauritius grow fast because its inheritance was favorable? A retrospective answer can be provided based on the indicators that have been identified as important for long-term growth. On the one hand, a number of factors—especially the initial level of income, geography, and commodity dependence—have exerted a drag on long-term growth. For example, Mauritius is disadvantaged by being at least 25–30 percent more distant from world markets than the average African country. On the other hand, favorable demographic developments and very high initial levels of human capital have boosted growth. Formal analysis shows that on balance, however, the disadvantages outweigh the advantages: initial conditions have slowed growth by about 1 percentage point a year relative to the average African country and by nearly 2 percentage points relative to the fast-growing developing economies of East Asia.

Globalization Strategy

Perhaps the most interesting aspect of Mauritius's development has been its trade and development strategy. At one level, Mauritius can be seen as a case study proving that openness and an embrace of globalization are unambiguously beneficial. Since the mid-1980s, the volume of goods imported and exported by Mauritius has grown rapidly, at annual rates of 8.7 percent and 5.4 percent, respectively. Its openness ratio (the ratio of trade-in-goods to GDP) has increased from about 70 percent to 100 percent, while Africa's openness ratio has stagnated at around 45 percent. Particularly strong was the growth in manufacturing exports originating predominantly in Mauritius's export-processing zone.

There are three possible explanations for the impressive growth of trade: first, liberal trade policies; second, trade policies that, although interventionist, did not distort incentives in favor of the import-competing sector; third, openness to foreign direct investment.

The first explanation does not fit the facts. During the 1970s and 1980s, protection in Mauritius was high and dispersed throughout the economy. In 1980, the average tariff exceeded 100 percent, and it was still very high—65 percent—at the end of the 1980s. Moreover, until the 1980s, there were extensive quantitative restrictions in the form of import licensing, which covered nearly 60 percent of imports.

Clearly, by the usual measures, Mauritius had a highly restrictive import regime. But why did this not translate into an export tax and, hence, a tax on all trade? Not only was an effective institutional mechanism—the export-processing zone—in place but Mauritius's own domestic policies and the policies of its trading partners ensured very high returns to the export sector, effectively segmenting it from the rest of the economy and discouraging the diversion of domestic resources to the country's inefficient import-competing sector. First, all imported inputs entered the country duty free, ensuring that the export sector's competitiveness on world markets was not undermined by costly inputs. Second, a variety of tax incentives were provided to firms operating in the export-processing zone, which had the effect of subsidizing exports. Third, until the mid-to-late 1980s, labor market conditions in the export sector were different from those in the rest of the economy (in the import-competing sector, in particular): employers in the export-processing zone had greater flexibility to discharge workers, and the conditions of overtime work were more flexible. Most important, although the legal minimum wage was the same in the export-processing zone as in the rest of the economy, the minimum wage for women was lower than that for men. Because the export-processing zone employed a disproportionate number of women, their lower wages also implicitly subsidized exports, encouraging producers to concentrate on the export, rather than on the import-competing, sector.

However, these interventionist policies did not, on their own, fully offset the anti-export bias created by restrictive import policies. Preferential access provided by Mauritius's trading partners in the sugar, textile, and clothing sectors, which together accounted for about 90 percent of Mauritius's total exports, also implicitly subsidized the export sector and was responsible, to a large degree, for overcoming the anti-export bias of the import regime.

Since it gained its independence in 1968, Mauritius has been guaranteed a certain volume of sugar exports to the European Union (EU) at a price that was, on average, about 90 percent above the market price between 1977 and 2000. The resulting rents to Mauritius have amounted to a hefty 5.4 percent of GDP, on average, each year and as much as 13 percent in some years. From a macroeconomic perspective, these rents have played a crucial role in sustaining high levels of investment and explain why domestic, rather than foreign, savings have financed domestic investment during Mauritius's growth boom.

The preferential access given to textile and clothing exports from Mauritius has been equally important. The international regime known as the Multifiber Arrangement (MFA) was established by the United States and the European Union to limit imports of textiles and clothing by awarding country-specific quotas. As a result, imports were redistributed among the countries that produced these goods, to Mauritius's benefit.

The third explanation ascribes Mauritius's success to its openness to foreign direct investment, facilitated by the creation of the export-processing zone. The latter, a resounding success, has transformed the Mauritian economy. Since 1982, output has grown by 19 percent a year, on average, employment by 24 percent, and exports by 11 percent. The export-processing zone accounts for 26 percent of GDP, 36 percent of employment, 19 percent of capital stock, and 66 percent of exports. Moreover, a growth-accounting analysis demonstrates the exceptional productivity of the zone. During 1983–99, total factor productivity growth in the export-processing zone averaged about 3.5 percent a year, compared with 1.4 percent in the economy as a whole. In the 1990s, productivity growth in the export-processing zone was remarkable, averaging 5.4 percent a year.

But these explanations, although plausible, do not really get at the underlying causes of Mauritius's trade and growth performance. Other developing countries had similar preferential trade opportunities and also created export-processing zones. But many of them failed where Mauritius succeeded. Clearly, there were deeper reasons for Mauritius's success.

Institutions

To a considerable extent, strong domestic institutions have contributed to Mauritius's success. Two examples illustrate the role played by domestic institutions. Mauritius successfully overcame its macroeconomic imbalances in the early 1980s. Macroeconomic adjustment was, in fact, implemented by three different governments of divergent ideological persuasions: this presupposed consultation and a recognition of the need to develop a national consensus in favor of adjustment. Further, a culture of transparency and participatory politics ensured that early warning signals and feedback mechanisms were in place, allowing emerging economic problems to be tackled at an early stage. Second, the export-processing zones established by other African countries may have provided the same incentives for investors but, unlike the zone in Mauritius, they have been plagued by rent seeking, abuses, and leakages deriving from weak administration.

Special Factors

Formal analysis of Mauritius's growth performance shows, however, that even after accounting for the positive role played by institutions, there is a sizable unexplained component. It is plausible that some factors specific to Mauritius may also have played an important role. Foremost among these was the country's ethnic diversity and how it was managed.

First, some ethnic communities had important links with the rest of the world. The Chinese community, for example, attracted investment by Hong Kong entrepreneurs who sought overseas locations for their textile operations in an attempt to circumvent the textile quotas imposed on Hong Kong. Second, diversity, particularly the separation of economic and political power, helped ensure balance and prevented excessive taxation (by the politically powerful) of the sugar sector (owned by the economic elite), the country's cash cow. Third, diversity played an important role in the development of participatory institutions. Assuaging the misgivings of a large minority that had reservations about independence and were concerned about the possibility of domination by the majority made participatory politics in the post-independence era a necessity. These institutions ensured, in turn, the rule of law and respect for property rights that have made Mauritius attractive to investors. Perhaps, instilling confidence in the Mauritians in "their rights, their votes, the power of their opinions"—a major political achievement—was the key to Mauritius's economic success.

For further details, see Arvind Subramanian and Devesh Roy, 2001, "Who Can Explain the Mauritian Miracle: Meade, Romer, Sachs, or Rodrik?" IMF Working Paper 01/116 (Washington: International Monetary Fund), as well as their chapter in a forthcoming book, *Analytical Development Narratives,* ed. by Dani Rodrik, to be published by Princeton University Press. The challenges facing Mauritius in the period ahead are discussed in the IMF staff report for Mauritius's 2001 Article IV consultation (IMF Country Report No. 01/77).

27

Urban Bias and Inequality

MICHAEL LIPTON

Michael Lipton is the principal advocate of the thesis that the primary explanation for the internal gap between rich and poor is "urban bias." He argues that even though leaders of developing countries sympathize with the plight of the rural poor, they consistently concentrate scarce development resources in the urban sector. The result is that the urban sectors, which are already well-off in a comparative sense, get an increasing share of national income, which exacerbates the inequalities. In the book from which this chapter is drawn, Lipton tries to show that it is in the interests of the elites of developing countries to maintain this urban bias because they benefit directly from it. Critics of Lipton's thesis claim that historically there has been a rural bias in development and that much political power continues to reside in the hands of the rural elite. One might also ask if there is anything about the cultures found in developing nations that encourages policies favoring one sector over another; rural or urban biases (if they truly exist) might be a function of conditions estsablished by the international environment. ∎

THE MOST IMPORTANT CLASS CONFLICT IN THE POOR COUNTRIES OF THE WORLD today is not between labor and capital. Nor is it between foreign and national interests. It is between the rural classes and the urban classes. The rural sector contains most of the poverty, and most of the low-cost sources of potential advance; but the urban sector contains most of the articulateness, organization,

Reprinted with permission of Ashgate Publishing Limited from *Why Poor People Stay Poor: A Study of Urban Bias in World Development,* by Michael Lipton.

and power. So the urban classes have been able to "win" most of the rounds of the struggle with the countryside; but in so doing they have made the development process needlessly slow and unfair. Scarce land, which might grow millets and beansprouts for hungry villagers, instead produces a trickle of costly calories from meat and milk, which few except the urban rich (who have ample protein anyway) can afford. Scarce investment, instead of going into water-pumps to grow rice, is wasted on urban motorways. Scarce human skills design and administer, not village wells and agricultural extension services, but world boxing championships in showpiece stadia. Resource allocations, within the city and the village as well as between them, reflect urban priorities rather than equity or efficiency. The damage has been increased by misguided ideological imports, liberal and Marxian, and by the town's success in buying off part of the rural elite, thus transferring most of the costs of the process to the rural poor.

But is this urban bias really damaging? After all, since 1945 output per person in the poor countries has doubled; and this unprecedented growth has brought genuine development. Production has been made more scientific: in agriculture, by the irrigation of large areas, and more recently by the increasing adoption of fertilizers and of high-yield varieties of wheat and rice; in industry, by the replacement of fatiguing and repetitive effort by rising levels of technology, specialization and skills. Consumption has also developed, in ways that at once use and underpin the development of production; poor countries now consume enormously expanded provisions of health and education, roads and electricity, radios and bicycles. Why, then, are so many of those involved in the development of the Third World—politicians and administrators, planners and scholars—miserable about the past and gloomy about the future? Why is the United Nations' "Development Decade" of the 1960s, in which poor countries as a whole exceeded the growth target,[1] generally written off as a failure? Why is aid, which demonstrably contributes to a development effort apparently so promising in global terms, in accelerating decline and threatened by a "crisis of will" in donor countries?[2]

The reason is that since 1945 growth and development, in most countries, have done so little to raise the living standards of the poorest people. It is scant comfort that today's mass-consumption economies, in Europe and North America, also featured near-stagnant mass welfare in the early phases of their economic modernization. Unlike today's poor countries, they carried in their early development the seeds of mass consumption later on. They were massively installling extra capacity to supply their people with simple goods: bread, cloth, and coal, not just luxury housing, poultry, and airports. Also the nineteenth-century "developing countries," including Russia, were developing not just market requirements but class structures that practically guaranteed subsequent "trickling down" of benefits. The workers even proved able to raise their share of political power and economic welfare. The very preconditions of such trends are absent in most of today's developing countries. The sincere egalitarian rhetoric of, say, Mrs. Indira Gandhi or Julius Nyerere was—allowing for differences of style and ideology—closely paralleled in Europe during early industrial development: in Britain, for example, by Henry Brougham and Lord Durham in the 1830s.[3] But the rural masses of India and Tanzania, unlike the urban masses of Melbourne's Britain, lack the power to organize the pressure that alone turns such rhetoric into distributive action against the pressure of the elite.

Some rather surprising people have taken alarm at the persistently unequal nature of recent development. Aid donors are substantially motivated by foreign-policy concerns for the stability of recipient governments; development banks, by the need to repay depositors and hence to ensure a good return on the projects they support. Both concerns coalesce in the World Bank, which raises and distributes some £3,000 million of aid each year. As a bank it has advocated—and financed—mostly "bankable" (that is, commercially profitable) projects. As a channel for aid donors, it has concentrated on poor countries that are relatively "open" to investment, trade and economic advice from those donors. Yet the effect of stagnant mass welfare in poor countries, on the well-intentioned and perceptive people who administer World Bank aid, has gradually overborne these traditional biases. Since 1971 the president of the World Bank, Robert McNamara, has in a series of speeches focused attention on the stagnant or worsening lives of the bottom 40 percent of people in poor countries.[4] Recently this has begun to affect the World Bank's projects, though its incomplete engagement with the problem of urban bias restricts the impact. For instance, an urban-biased government will prepare rural projects less well than urban projects, will manipulate prices to render rural projects less apparently profitable (and hence less "bankable"), and will tend to cut down its own effort if donors step up theirs. Nevertheless, the World Bank's new concern with the "bottom 40 percent" is significant.

These people—between one-quarter and one-fifth of the people of the world—are overwhelmingly rural: landless laborers, or farmers with no more than an acre or two, who must supplement their incomes by wage labor. Most of these countryfolk rely, as hitherto, on agriculture lacking irrigation or fertilizers or even iron tools. Hence they are so badly fed that they cannot work efficiently, and in many cases are unable to feed their infants well enough to prevent physical stunting and perhaps even brain damage. Apart from the rote-learning of religious texts, few of them receive any schooling. One of four dies before the age of ten. The rest live the same overworked, underfed, ignorant, and disease-ridden lives as thirty, or three hundred, or three thousand years ago. Often they borrow (at 40 percent or more yearly interest) from the same moneylender families as their ancestors, and surrender half their crops to the same families of landlords. Yet the last thirty years have been the age of unprecedented, accelerating growth and development! Naturally men of goodwill are puzzled and alarmed.

How can accelerated growth and development, in an era of rapidly improving communications and of "mass politics," produce so little for poor people? It is too simple to blame familiar scapegoats—foreign exploiters and domestic capitalists. Poor countries where they are relatively unimportant have experienced the paradox just as much as others. Nor, apparently, do the poorest families cause their own difficulties, whether by rapid population growth or by lack of drive. Poor families do tend to have more children than rich families, but principally because their higher death rates require it, if the aging parents are to be reasonably sure that a son will grow up, to support them if need be. And it is the structure of rewards and opportunities within poor countries that extracts, as if by force, the young man of ability and energy from his chronically stagnant rural background and lures him to serve, or even to join, the booming urban elite.

The disparity between urban and rural welfare is much greater in poor countries now than it was in rich countries during their early development. This huge welfare gap is demonstrably inefficient, as well as inequitable. It persists mainly because less than 20 percent of investment for development has gone to the agricultural sector (the situation has not changed much since 1965), although over 65 percent of the people of less-developed countries (LDCs), and over 80 percent of the really poor who live on $1 per week each or less, depend for a living on agriculture. The proportion of skilled people who support development—doctors, bankers, engineers—going to rural areas has been lower still; and the rural-urban imbalances have in general been even greater than those between agriculture and industry. Moreover, in most LDCs, governments have taken numerous measures with the unhappy side-effect of accentuating rural-urban disparities: their own allocation of public expenditure and taxation; measures raising the price of industrial production relative to farm production, thus encouraging private rural saving to flow into industrial investment because the value of industrial output has been artificially boosted; and educational facilities encouraging bright villagers to train in cities for urban jobs.

Such processes have been extremely inefficient. For instance, the impact on output of $1 of carefully selected investment is in most countries two to three times as high in agriculture as elsewhere, yet public policy and private market power have combined to push domestic savings and foreign aid into nonagricultural uses. The process has also been inequitable. Agriculture starts with about one-third the income per head as the rest of the economy, so that the people who depend on it should in equity receive special attention not special mulcting. Finally, the misallocation between sectors has created a needless and acute conflict between efficiency and equity. In agriculture the poor farmer with little land is usually efficient in his use of both land and capital, whereas power, construction, and industry often do best in big, capital-intensive units; and rural income and power, while far from equal, are less unequal than in the cities. So concentration on urban development and neglect of agriculture have pushed resources away from activities where they can help growth and benefit the poor, *and* toward activities where they do either of these, if at all, at the expense of the other.

Urban bias also increases inefficiency and inequity within the sectors. Poor farmers have little land and much underused family labor. Hence they tend to complement any extra developmental resources received—pumpsets, fertilizers, virgin land—with much more extra labor than do large farmers. Poor farmers thus tend to get most output from such extra resources (as well as needing the extra income most). But rich farmers (because they sell their extra output to the cities instead of eating it themselves, and because they are likely to use much of their extra income to support urban investment) are naturally favored by urban-biased policies; it is they, not the efficient small farmers, who get the cheap loans and the fertilizer subsidies. The patterns of allocation and distribution within the cities are damaged too. Farm inputs are produced inefficiently, instead of imported, and the farmer has to pay, even if the price is nominally "subsidized." The processing of farm outputs, notably grain milling, is shifted into big urban units and the profits are no longer reinvested in agriculture. And equalization between classes inside the cities becomes more risky, because the investment-starved farm sector might prove unable to deliver the food that a better-off urban mass would seek to buy.

Moreover, income in poor countries is usually more equally distributed within the rural sector than within the urban sector.[5] Since income creates the power to distribute extra income, therefore, a policy that concentrates on raising income in the urban sector will worsen inequalities in two ways: by transferring not only from poor to rich, but also from more equal to less equal. Concentration on urban enrichment is triply inequitable: because countryfolk start poorer; because such concentration allots rural resources largely to the rural rich (who sell food to the cities); and because the great inequality of power *within* the towns renders urban resources especially likely to go to the resident elites.

But am I not hammering at an open door? Certainly the persiflage of allocation has changed recently, under the impact of patently damaging deficiencies in rural output. Development plans are nowadays full of "top priority for agriculture."[6] This is reminiscent of the pseudo-egalitarian school where, at mealtimes, Class B children get priority, while Class A children get food.[7] We can see that the new agricultural priority is dubious from the abuse of the "green revolution" and of the oil crisis (despite its much greater impact on *industrial* costs) as pretexts for lack of emphasis on agriculture: "We don't need it," and "We can't afford it," respectively. And the 60 to 80 percent of people dependent on agriculture are still allocated barely 20 percent of public resources; even these small shares are seldom achieved; and they have, if anything, tended to diminish. So long as the elite's interests, background and sympathies remain predominantly urban, the countryside may get the "priority" but the city will get the resources. The farm sector will continue to be squeezed, both by transfers of resources from it by prices that are turned against it. Bogus justifications of urban bias will continue to earn the sincere, prestige-conferring, but misguided support of visiting "experts" from industrialized countries and international agencies. And development will be needlessly painful, inequitable and slow.

Notes

1. The UN target was a 5 percent yearly rate of "real" growth (that is, allowing for inflation) of total output. The actual rate was slightly higher.

2. Net aid from the donor countries comprising the Development Assistance Committee (DAC) of the Organization for Economic Cooperation and Development (OECD) comprises over 95 percent of all net aid to less-developing countries (LDCs). It fell steadily from 0.54 percent of donors' GNP in 1961 to 0.30 percent in 1973. The real value of aid per person in recipient countries fell by over 20 percent over the period. M. Lipton, "Aid Allocation When Aid is Inadequate," in T. Byres, ed., *Foreign Resources and Economic Development,* Cass, 1972, p. 158; OECD (DAC), *Development Cooperation* (1974 Review), p. 116.

3. L. Cooper, *Radical Jack,* Cresset, 1969, esp. pp. 183–97; C. New, *Life of Henry Brougham to 1830,* Clarendon, 1961, Preface.

4. See the mounting emphasis in his *Addresses to the Board of Governors,* all published by the International Bank for Reconstruction and Development, Washington; at Copenhagen in 1970, p. 20; at Washington in 1971, pp. 6–19, and 1972, pp. 8–15; and at Nairobi in 1973, pp. 10–14, 19.

5. M. Ahluwalia, "The Dimensions of the Problem," in H. Chenery et al., *Redistribution with Growth,* Oxford, 1974.

6. See K. Rafferty, *Financial Times,* 10 April 1974, p. 35, col. 5; M. Lipton, "Urban Bias and Rural Planning," in P. Streeten and M. Lipton, eds., *The Crisis of Indian Planning,* Oxford, 1968, p. 85.

7. F. Muir and D. Norden, "Comonon Entrance," in P. Sellers, *Songs for Swinging Sellers,* Parlophone PMC 111, 1958.

28

Political Regimes and Economic Growth

Adam Przeworski and Fernando Limongi

In this chapter, Adam Przeworski and Fernando Limongi review the findings of eighteen articles that assess the relationship between regime type and economic growth. The authors show that the results have been inconclusive. According to Przeworski and Limongi, the confusion stems from the need for a more complex research design. Whereas the authors demonstrate that previous studies mistakenly attribute regime type as a cause of growth, they do not attempt to resolve the debate empirically. They state that ample evidence suggests that politics does affect growth, but they do not believe the debate over regime types captures the relevant differences between regimes that may be under investigation. ■

Arguments: How Democracy
Might Affect Growth

ARGUMENTS THAT RELATE REGIMES TO GROWTH FOCUS ON PROPERTY RIGHTS, PRESsures for immediate consumption, and the autonomy of dictators. While everyone seems to agree that secure property rights foster growth, it is controversial whether democracies or dictatorships better secure these rights. The main mechanism by which democracy is thought to hinder growth is pressures for immediate consumption, which reduce investment. Only states that are institutionally insulated from such pressures can resist them, and democratic states

Reprinted with permission of the American Economics Association from *Journal of Economic Perspective,* vol. 7, no. 3 (summer 1993).

are not. The main argument against dictatorships is that authoritarian rulers have no interest in maximizing total output. . . .

The Statistical Evidence

In one way, the critics and defenders of democracy talk past each other. The critics argue that dictatorships are better at mobilizing savings; the defenders that democracies are better at allocating investment. Both arguments can be true but, as we shall see, the statistical evidence is inconclusive and the studies that produced it are all seriously flawed.

Table 28.1 summarizes the 18 studies we examined. These generated 21 findings, since some distinguished areas or periods. Among them, eight found in favor of democracy, eight in favor of authoritarianism, and five discovered no difference. What is even more puzzling is that among the 11 results published before 1988, eight found that authoritarian regimes grew faster, while none of the nine results published after 1987 supported this finding. And since this difference does not seem attributable to samples or periods, one can only wonder about the relation between statistics and ideology.[1]

For reasons discussed below, we hesitate to attach much significance to these results one way or another. Hence, we still do not know what the facts are.

Inferences Based on
Standard Regression Models Are Invalid

The reason social scientists have little robust statistical knowledge about the impact of regimes on growth is that the research design required to generate such knowledge is complex. This complexity is due to three sources: simultaneity, attrition, and selection.

Following the seminal work of Lipset (1960), there is an enormous body of theoretical and statistical literature to the effect that democracy is a product of economic development. This literature suffers from ambiguities of its own. While the belief is widespread that democracy requires as a "prerequisite" some level of economic development, there is much less agreement which aspects of development matter and why. Some think that a certain level of development is required for a stable democracy because affluence reduces the intensity of distributional conflicts; others because development generates the education or the communication networks required to support democratic institutions; still others because it swells the ranks of the middle class, facilitates the formation of a competent bureaucracy, and so on. Statistical results are somewhat mixed (Lipset 1960; Cutright 1963; Neubauer 1967; Smith 1969;

Table 28.1   Studies of Democracy, Autocracy, Bureaucracy, and Growth

Author	Sample	Time Frame	Finding
Przeworksi (1966)	57 countries	1949–1963	dictatorships at medium development level grew fastest
Adelman and Morris (1967)	74 underdeveloped countries (including communist bloc)	1950–1968	authoritarianism helped less and medium developed countries
Dick (1974)	59 underdeveloped countries	1959–1968	democracies develop slightly faster
Huntington and Dominguez (1975)	35 poor nations	the 1950s	authoritarian grew faster
Marsh (1979)	98 countries	1955–1970	authoritarian grew faster
Weede (1983)	124 countries	1960–1974	authoritarian grew faster
Kormendi and Meguire (1985)	47 countries	1950–1977	democracies grew faster
Kohli (1986)	10 underdeveloped countries	1960–1982	no difference in 1960s; authoritarian slightly better in 1970s
Landau (1986)	65 countries	1960–1980	authoritarian grew faster
Sloan and Tedin (1987)	20 Latin American countries	1960–1979	bureaucratic-authoritarian regimes do better than democracy; traditional dictatorships do worse
Marsh (1988)	47 countries	1965–1984	no difference between regimes
Pourgerami (1988)	92 countries	1965–1984	democracies grew faster
Scully (1988, 1992)	115 countries	1960–1980	democracies grew faster
Barro (1989)	72 countries	1960–1985	democracies grew faster
Grier and Tullock (1989)	59 countries	1961–1980	democracy better in Africa and Latin America; no regime difference in Asia
Remmer (1990)	11 Latin American countries	1982–1988 1982 and 1988	democracy faster, but result statistically insignificant
Pourgerami (1991)	106 less developed countries	1986	democracies grow slower
Helliwell (1992)	90 countries	1960–1985	democracy has a negative, but statistically insignificant effect on growth

Hannan and Carroll 1981; Bollen and Jackman 1985; Soares 1987; Arat 1988; Helliwell 1992). They suggest that the level of development, measured by a variety of indicators, is positively related to the incidence of democratic regimes in the population of world countries, but not necessarily within particular regions. Moreover, the exact form of the relationship and its relation to regime stability are left open to debate. Yet the prima facie evidence in support of this hypothesis is overwhelming: all developed countries in the world constitute stable democracies while stable democracies in the less developed countries remain exceptional.

Attrition is a more complicated issue. Following Lipset again, everyone seems to believe that durability of any regime depends on its economic performance. Economic crises are a threat to democracies as well as to dictatorships. The probability that a regime survives a crisis need not be the same, however, for democracies and dictatorships: one reason is that under democracy it is easier to change a government without changing the regime, another is that democracies derive legitimacy from more than their economic performance. We also have the argument by Olson (1963; also Huntington 1968) that rapid growth is destabilizing for democracies but not for dictatorships.

This evidence suffices to render suspect any study that does not treat regimes as endogenous. If democratic regimes are more likely to occur at a higher level of development or if democracies and dictatorships have a different chance of survival under various economic conditions, then regimes are endogenously selected. Since this is the heart of the statistical difficulties, we spell out the nature of this problem in some detail. (The following discussion draws on Przeworski and Limongi 1992.)

We want to know the impact of regimes on growth. Observing Brazil in 1988, we discover that it was a democracy which declined at the rate of 2.06 percent. Would it have grown had it been a dictatorship? The information we have, the observation of Brazil in 1988, does not answer this question. But unless we know what would have been the growth of Brazil in 1988 had it been a dictatorship, how can we tell if it would have grown faster or slower than under democracy?

Had we observed in 1988 a Brazil that was simultaneously a democracy and a dictatorship, we would have the answer. But this is not possible. There is still a way out: if the fact that Brazil was a democracy in 1988 had nothing to do with economic growth, we could look for some country that was exactly like Brazil in all respects other than its regime and, perhaps, its rate of growth, and we could match this country with Brazil. But if the selection of regimes shares some determinants with economic growth, an observation that matches Brazil in all respects other than the regime and the rate of growth will be hard to find. And then the comparative inferences will be biased: Whenever observations are not generated randomly, quasi-experimental approaches yield inconsistent and biased estimates of the effect of being in a particular state on outcomes. Indeed, this much is now standard statistical wisdom, as evidenced in the vast literature reviewed by Heckman (1990), Maddala (1983), and Greene (1990). Yet the implications of this failure are profound: we can no longer use the standard regression models to make valid inferences from the observed to the unobserved cases. Hence, we cannot compare.

The pitfalls involved in the studies summarized above can be demonstrated as follows. Averaging the rates of growth of ten South American countries between 1946 and 1988, one discovers that authoritarian regimes grew at the average rate of 2.15 percent per annum while democratic regimes grew at 1.31

percent. Hence, one is inclined to conclude that authoritarianism is better for growth than democracy. But suppose that in fact regimes have no effect on growth. However, regimes do differ in their probabilities of surviving various economic conditions: authoritarian regimes are less likely than democracies to survive when they perform badly. In addition, suppose that the probability of survival of both regimes depends on the number of other democracies in the region at each moment. These probabilities jointly describe how regimes are selected: the dependence of survival on growth constitutes endogenous selection, the diffusion effect represents exogenous selection.

In Przeworski and Limongi (1992), we used the observed regime-specific conditional survival probabilities to generate 5,000 (500 per country) 43-year histories obeying these assumptions, each beginning with the level and the regime observed in 1945. As one would expect, authoritarian regimes grew faster than democracies—indeed, we reproduced exactly the observed difference in growth rates—despite the fact that these data were generated under the assumption that regimes have no effect on growth. It is the difference in the way regimes are selected—the probabilities of survival conditional on growth—that generate the observed difference in growth rates. Hence, this difference is due entirely to selection bias.[2]

If one applies ordinary least squares to data generated in this way, with a dummy variable set to 1 for Authoritarianism and 0 for Democracy, the regime coefficient turns out to be positive and highly significant. Thus standard regression fails the same way as the comparison of means, even with controls. To correct for the effect of selection, we followed the procedure developed by Heckman (1978) and Lee (1978). Once we corrected the effects of selection, we generated the unbiased means for the two regimes and these, not surprisingly, reproduced the assumptions under which the data were generated: no difference in growth between the two regimes.

These methodological comments should end with a warning. Selection models turn out to be exceedingly sensitive: minor modifications of the equation that specifies how regimes survive can affect the signs in the equations that explain growth. Standard regression techniques yield biased (and inconsistent) inferences, but selection models are not robust (Greene 1990, 750; Stolzenberg and Relles 1990). While reverting to simulation provides at least the assurance that one does not attribute to regimes the effects they do not have, it may still fail to capture the effects they do exert.

Conclusions

The simple answer to the question with which we began is that we do not know whether democracy fosters or hinders economic growth.[3] All we can offer at this moment are some educated guesses.

First, it is worth noting that we know little about determinants of growth in general. The standard neoclassical theory of growth was intuitively unpersuasive and it implied that levels of development should converge: a prediction not born by the facts. The endogenous growth models are intuitively more appealing but empirically difficult to test since the "engine of growth" in these models consists, in Romer's (1992, 100) own words, of "ephemeral externalities." Statistical studies of growth notoriously explain little variance and are very sensitive to specification (Levine and Renelt 1991). And without a good economic model of growth, it is not surprising that the partial effect of politics is difficult to assess.

Secondly, there are lots of bits and pieces of evidence to the effect that politics in general does affect growth. At least everyone, governments and international lending institutions included, believes that policies affect growth and, in turn, scholars tend to think that politics affect policies. Reynolds (1983), having reviewed the historical experience of several countries, concluded that spurts of growth are often associated with major political transformations. Studies examining the impact of government spending on growth tend to find that the size of government is negatively related to growth, but the increase of government expenditures has a positive effect (Ram 1986; Lindauer and Velenchik 1992). Studies comparing the Far East with Latin America argue that there is something about the political institutions of the Asian countries which makes them propitious for growth. But while suggestive stories abound, there is little hard evidence.

Our own hunch is that politics does matter, but "regimes" do not capture the relevant differences. Postwar economic miracles include countries that had parliaments, parties, unions, and competitive elections, as well as countries run by military dictatorships. In turn, while Latin American democracies suffered economic disasters during the 1980s, the world is replete with authoritarian regimes that are dismal failures from the economic point of view.[4] Hence, it does not seem to be democracy or authoritarianism per se that makes the difference but something else.

What that something else might be is far from clear. "State autonomy" is one candidate, if we think that the state can be autonomous under democracy as well as under authoritarianism, as do Bardhan (1988, 1990) and Rodrik (1992). But this solution meets the horns of a dilemma: an autonomous state must be both effective at what it wants to do and insulated from pressures to do what it does not want to do. The heart of the neo-liberal research program is to find institutions that enable the state to do what it should but disable it from doing what it should not.

In our view, there are no such institutions to be found. In a Walrasian economy, the state has no positive role to play, so that the constitutional rule is simple: the less state, the better. But if the state has something to do, we would need institutions which enable the state to respond optimally to all contingent states of nature and yet prevent it from exercising discretion in the face of group pressures. Moreover, as Cui (1992) has argued, if markets are incomplete and information imperfect, the economy can function only if the state insures investors (limited liability), firms (bankruptcy), and depositors (two-tier banking system). But this kind of state involvement inevitably induces a soft-budget constraint. The state cannot simultaneously insure private agents and not pay the claims, even if they result from moral hazard.

Even if optimal rules do exist, pre-commitment is not a logically coherent solution. The reason is that just any commitment is not good enough: it must be a commitment to an optimal program. And advocates of commitment (like Shepsle 1989) do not consider the political process by which such commitments are established. After all, the same forces that push the state to suboptimal discretionary interventions also push the state to a suboptimal commitment. Assume that the government wants to follow an optimal program and it self-commits itself. At the present it does not want to respond to private pressures but it knows that in the future it would want to do so; hence, it disables its capacity to do it. The model underlying this argument is Elster's (1979) Ulysses.[5] But the analogy does not hold since Ulysses makes his decision *before* he hears the Sirens. Suppose that he has already heard them: why does he not respond to their song now and is afraid that he would respond later? If governments do bind themselves, it is already in response to the song of the Sirens and their pre-commitment will not be optimal.

Clearly, the impact of political regimes on growth is wide open for reflection and research.

Notes

1. Indeed, it is sufficient to read Scully (1992, xiii–xiv) to stop wondering: "The Anglo-American paradigm of free men and free markets unleashed human potential to an extent unparalleled in history. . . . One needs evidence to persuade those who see promise in extensive government intervention in the economy. I have found such evidence, and the evidence is overwhelmingly in favor of the paradigm of classical liberalism." The evidence on the effect of democracy on growth consists of cross-sectional OLS regressions in which investment is controlled for, so that political effects measure efficiency but not the capacity to mobilize savings.

2. We could have gotten the same result in a different way. Suppose that (1) levels converge, that is, growth is a negative function of income, and (2) dictatorships occur at low levels while democracies are more frequent at high levels. Then we will observe fast growing dictatorships (at low levels) and slowly growing democracies (at high levels).

3. Note that we considered only indirect impacts of regimes on growth via investment and the size of the public sector, but we did not consider the impacts via income equality, technological change, human capital, or population growth.

4. As Sah (1991) has argued, authoritarian regimes exhibit a higher variance in economic performance than democracies: President Park of South Korea is now seen as a developmentalist leader, while President Mobutu of Zaire is seen as nothing but a thief (Evans 1989). But we have no theory that would tell us in advance which we are

going to get. We do know, in turn, that until the early 1980s the democratic regimes which had encompassing, centralized unions combined with left-wing partisan control performed better on most economic variables than systems with either decentralized unions or right-wing partisan dominance.

5. Note that Elster (1989, 196) himself argues against the analogy of individual and collective commitment.

References

Adelman, Irma, and Cynthia Morris. 1967. *Society, Politics and Economic Development.* Baltimore: Johns Hopkins University Press.

Alesina, Alberto, and Dani Rodrik. 1991. "Distributive Politics and Economic Growth," National Bureau of Economic Research, Working Paper No. 3668.

Amsden, Alice H. 1989. *Asia's Next Giant: South Korea and Late Industrialization.* New York: Oxford University Press.

Arat, Zehra F. 1988. "Democracy and Economic Development: Modernization Theory Revisited," *Comparative Politics,* October, 21:1, 21–36.

Bardhan, Pranab. 1988. "Comment on Gustav Ranis' and John C. H. Fei's 'Development Economics: What Next?'" In Ranis, Gustav, and T. Paul Schultz, eds., *The State of Development Economics: Progress and Perspectives.* Oxford: Basil Blackwell, pp. 137–38.

Bardhan, Pranab. 1990. "Symposium on the State and Economic Development." *Journal of Economic Perspectives,* Summer, 4:3, 3–9.

Barro, Robert J. 1989. "A Cross-country Study of Growth, Saving, and Government," NBER Working Paper No. 2855.

Barro, Robert J. 1990. "Government Spending in a Simple Model of Endogenous Growth," *Journal of Political Economy,* October, 98:5, S103–S125.

Becker, Gary S. 1983. "A Theory of Competition Among Pressure Groups for Political Influence," *Quarterly Journal of Economics,* August, 98:3, 371–400.

Bollen, K. A., and R. W. Jackman. 1985. "Economic and Noneconomic Determinants of Political Democracy in the 1960s," *Research in Political Sociology,* 1, 27–48.

Collini, Stefan, Donald Winch, and John Burrow. 1983. *That Noble Science of Politics.* Cambridge: Cambridge University Press.

Crain, W. Mark. 1977. "On the Structure and Stability of Political Markets." *Journal of Political Economy,* August, 85:4, 829–42.

Cui, Zhiyuan. 1992. "Incomplete Markets and Constitutional Democracy," manuscript, University of Chicago.

Cutright, Philips. 1963. "National Political Development: Measurement and Analysis," *American Sociological Review,* 28, 253–64.

de Schweinitz, Karl Jr. 1959. "Industrialization, Labor Controls and Democracy," *Economic Development and Cultural Change,* July, 385–404.

de Schweinitz, Karl Jr. 1964. *Industrialization and Democracy.* New York: Free Press.

Dick, William G. 1974. "Authoritarian Versus Nonauthoritarian Approaches to Economic Development," *Journal of Political Economy,* July/August, 82:4, 817–27.

Dore, Ronald. 1978. "Scholars and Preachers." *IDS Bulletin.* Sussex, U.K.: International Development Studies, June.

Downs, Anthony. 1957. *An Economic Theory of Democracy.* New York: Harper and Row.

Elster, Jon. 1979. *Ulysses and the Sirens: Studies in Rationality and Irrationality.* Cambridge: Cambridge University Press.

Elster, Jon. 1989. *Solomanic Judgements. Studies in the Limitations of Rationality.* Cambridge: Cambridge University Press.

Elster, Jon, and Karl Ove Moene, eds. 1989. "Introduction." In *Alternatives to Capitalism.* Cambridge: Cambridge University Press, 1–38.

Evans, Peter B. 1989. "Predatory, Developmental, and Other Apparatuses: A Comparative Political Economy Perspective on the Third World State." *Sociological Forum,* December, 4:4, 561–87.

Fernandez, Raquel, and Dani Rodrick. 1991, "Resistance to Reform; Status Quo Bias in the Presence of Individual-Specific Uncertainty," *American Economic Review,* December, 81:5, 1146–55.

Findlay, Ronald. 1990. "The New Political Economy: Its Explanatory Power for the LDCS," *Economics and Politics,* July, 2:2, 193–221.

Galenson, Walter. 1959. "Introduction" to Galenson, W., ed. *Labor and Economic Development.* New York: Wiley.

Galenson, Walter, and Harvey Leibenstein. 1955. "Investment Criteria, Productivity and Economic Development," *Quarterly Journal of Economics,* August, 69, 343–70.

Gereffi, Gary, and Donald L. Wyman, eds. 1990. *Manufacturing Miracles: Paths of Industrialization in Africa and East Asia.* Princeton: Princeton University Press.

Greene, William H. 1990. *Econometric Analysis.* New York: Macmillan.

Grier, Kevin B., and Gordon Tullock. 1989. "An Empirical Analysis of Cross-national Economic Growth, 1951–80," *Journal of Monetary Economics,* September 1989, 24:2, 259–76.

Haggard, Stephan. 1990. *Pathways from Periphery: The Politics of Growth in the Newly Industrializing Countries.* Ithaca: Cornell University Press.

Hannan, M. T., and G. R. Carroll. 1981. "Dynamics of Formal Political Structure: An Event-History Analysis," *American Sociological Review,* February, 46:1, 19–35.

Heckman, James J. 1978. "Dummy Endogenous Variables in a Simultaneous Equation System," *Econometrica,* July, 46:4, 931–59.

Heckman, James J. 1990. "Selection Bias and Self-selection." In Eatwell, John, Murray Milgate, and Peter Newman, eds., *The New Palgrave Econometrics.* New York: W. W. Norton, 287–97.

Helliwell, John F. 1992. "Empirical Linkages Between Democracy and Economic Growth," NBER Working Paper #4066. Cambridge: National Bureau of Economic Research.

Huntington, Samuel P. 1968. *Political Order in Changing Societies.* New Haven: Yale University Press.

Huntington, Samuel P., and Jorge I. Dominguez. 1975. "Political Development." In Greenstein, F. I., and N. W. Polsby, eds. *Handbook of Political Science,* 3. Reading: Addison-Wesley, 1–114.

Kaldor, Nicolas. 1956. "Alternative Theories of Distribution," *Review of Economic Studies,* 23:2, 83–100.

Kohli, Atul. 1986. "Democracy and Development." In Lewis, John P., and Valeriana Kallab, eds. *Development Strategies Reconsidered.* New Brunswick: Transaction Books, 153–82.

Kormendi, Roger C., and Philip G. Meguire. 1983. "Macroeconomic Determinants of Growth: Cross-Country Evidence," *Journal of Monetary Economics,* September, 162: 141–63.

Landau, Daniel. 1986. "Government and Economic Growth in the Less Developed Countries: An Empirical Study for 1960–1980," *Economic Development and Cultural Change,* October, 35:1, 35–75.

Lee, L. F. 1978. "Unionism and Wage Rates: A Simultaneous Equations Model with Qualitative and Limited Dependent Variables," *International Economic Review,* June, 19:2, 415–33.

Levine, Ross, and David Renelt. 1991. "A Sensitivity Analysis of Cross-country Growth Regressions," World Bank Working Paper WPS 609.

Lindauer, David L., and Ann D. Velenchik. 1992. "Government Spending in Developing Countries: Trends, Causes, and Consequences," *World Bank Research Observer,* January, 7:1. Washington, D.C.: The World Bank, 59–78.

Lipset, Seymour M. 1960. *Political Man.* Garden City: Doubleday, 1960.

Macaulay, Thomas B. 1900. *Complete Writings,* 17. Boston and New York: Houghton-Mifflin.

Maddala, G. S. 1983. *Limited-Dependent and Qualitative Variables in Econometrics.* Cambridge: Cambridge University Press.

Marsh, Robert M. 1979. "Does Democracy Hinder Economic Development in the Latecomer Developing Nations?" *Comparative Social Research,* 2:2, 215–48.

Marsh, Robert M. 1988. "Sociological Explanations of Economic Growth," *Studies in Comparative International Development,* Winter, 23:4, 41–76.

Marx, Karl. 1934. *The Eighteenth Brumaire of Louis Bonaparte.* Moscow: Progress Publishers.

Marx, Karl. 1952. *The Class Struggle in France, 1848 to 1850.* Moscow: Progress Publishers.

Marx, Karl. 1971. *Writings on the Paris Commune.* Edited by H. Draper. New York: International Publishers.

Neubauer, Deane E. 1967. "Some Conditions of Democracy," *American Political Science Review,* December, 61:4, 1002–9.

North, Douglass C. 1990. *Institutions, Institutional Change and Economic Performance.* Cambridge, U.K.: Cambridge University Press.

North, Douglass C., and Robert Paul Thomas. 1973. *The Rise of the Western World: A New Economic History.* Cambridge, U.K.: Cambridge University Press.

North, Douglass C., and Barry R. Weingast. 1989. "Constitutions and Commitment: The Evolution of Institutions Governing Public Choice in Seventeenth-Century England," *Journal of Economic History,* December, 49:4, 803–32.

O'Donnell, Guillermo. 1973. *Modernization and Bureaucratic-Authoritarianism.* Berkeley: UC Berkeley Press.

Olson, Mancur, Jr. 1963. "Rapid Growth as a Destabilizing Force," *Journal of Economic History,* December, 23, 529–52.

Olson, Mancur, Jr. 1991. "Autocracy, Democracy and Prosperity." In Zeckhauser, Richard J., ed., *Strategy and Choice.* Cambridge: MIT Press, 131–57.

Pasinetti, Luigi. 1961-62. "Rate of Profit and Income Distribution in Relation to the Race of Economic Growth," *Review of Economic Studies,* October, 29:81, 267–79.

Persson, Torsten, and Guido Tabellini. 19. "Is Inequality Harmful for Growth? Theory and Evidence." Working paper No. 91-155, Department of Economics, University of California, Berkeley, 1991.

Pourgerami, Abbas. 1988. "The Political Economy of Development: A Cross-national Causality Test of Development-Democracy-Growth Hypothesis," *Public Choice,* August, 58:2, 123–41.

Pourgerami, Abbas. 1991. "The Political Economy of Development: An Empirical Investigation of the Wealth Theory of Democracy," *Journal of Theoretical Politics,* April, 3:2, 189–211.

Przeworski, Adam. 1966. *Party Systems and Economic Development.* Ph.D. dissertation. Northwestern University.

Przeworski, Adam. 1990. *The State and the Economy Under Capitalism: Fundamentals of Pure and Applied Economics,* 40. Chur, Switzerland: Harwood Academic Publishers.

Przeworski, Adam, and Fernando Limongi. 1992. "Selection, Counterfactuals and Comparisons," manuscript, Department of Political Science, University of Chicago.

Przeworski, Adam, and Michael Wallerstein. 1988. "Structural Dependence of the State on Capital," *American Political Science Review,* March, 82:1, 11–29.

Ram, Rati. 1986. "Government Size and Economic Growth: A New Framework and Some Evidence from Cross-Section and Time-Series Data," *American Economic Review,* March, 76:1, 191–203.

Rao, Vaman. 1984. "Democracy and Economic Development," *Studies in Comparative International Development,* Winter 1984, 19:4, 67–81.

Remmer, Karen. 1990. "Democracy and Economic Crisis: The Latin American Experience," *World Politics,* April, 42:3, 315–35.

Reynolds, Lloyd G. 1983. "The Spread of Economic Growth to the Third World: 1850-1980," *Journal of Economic Literature,* September, 21:3, 941–80.

Rodrik, Dani. 1992. "Political Economy and Development Policy." *European Economic Review,* April, 36:2/3, 329–36.

Romer, Paul. 1992. "Increasing Returns and New Developments in the Theory of Growth." In Barnett, W. A., ed. Equilibrium Theory and Applications. New York: Cambridge University Press, 83–110.

Sah, Raaj K. 1991. "Fallibility in Human Organizations and Political Systems," *Journal of Economic Perspectives,* Spring 1991, 5:2, 67–88.

Schepsle, Kenneth. 1989. "Studying Institutions: Some Lessons from the Rational Choice Approach," *Journal of Theoretical Politics,* April, 1:2, 131–49.

Scully, Gerald W. 1988. "The Institutional Framework and Economic Development," *Journal of Political Economy,* June, 96:3, 652–62.

Scully, Gerald W. 1992. *Constitutional Environments and Economic Growth.* Princeton: Princeton University Press.

Sloan, John, and Kent L. Tedin. 1987. "The Consequences of Regimes Type for Public-Policy Outputs," *Comparative Political Studies,* April, 20:1, 98–124.

Smith, Arthur K. Jr. 1969. "Socio-economic Development and Political Democracy: A Causal Analysis," *Midwest Journal of Political Science,* 13: 95–125.

Soares, G. A. D. 1987. "Desenvolvimento Economico e Democracia na America Latina," *Dados,* 30:3, 253–74.

Stolzenberg, Ross M., and Daniel A. Relles. 1990. "Theory Testing in a World of Constrained Research Design," *Sociological Methods and Research,* May, 18:4, 395–415.

Wade, Robert. 1990. *Governing the Market: Economic Theory and the Role of Government in West Asian Industrialization.* Princeton: Princeton University Press, 1990.

Weede, Erich. 1983. "The Impact of Democracy on Economic Growth: Some Evidence from Cross-National Analysis," *Kyklos,* 36:1, 21–39.

Westphal, Larry E. 1990. "Industrial Policy in an Export-Propelled Economy: Lessons from South Korea's Experience," *Journal of Economic Perspectives,* Summer, 4:3, 41–60.

Wittman, Donald. 1989. "Why Democracies Produce Efficient Results," *Journal of Political Economy,* December, 97:6, 1395–1424.

World Bank. 1987. *World Development Report.* Washington, DC: The World Bank.

29

Inequality as a Constraint on Growth in Latin America

Nancy Birdsall and Richard Sabot

This chapter presents strong evidence that inequality and slow growth in the Third World are not inevitable but are the direct outcome of choices made by governments. The chapter contrasts Latin America, where growth has been slow and inequality high, with East Asia, where growth has been extremely rapid and inequality very low. The empirical research on which the chapter is based demonstrates that large investments in education in East Asia help to explain a "virtuous circle" that leads to both higher growth and greater equality, whereas the low and stagnating investment in education in Latin America creates an opposite "vicious circle." Human capital investment is what sets East Asia apart from Latin America, a lesson many developing countries need to learn. ■

THE CONVENTIONAL WISDOM HAS BEEN THAT THERE IS A TRADEOFF BETWEEN AUGmenting growth and reducing inequality, so that an unequal distribution of income is necessary for, or the likely consequence of, rapid economic growth. If this is so, however, why do we find in Latin America relatively low rates of economic growth and high inequality, and in East Asia low inequality and rapid growth? Figure 29.1 shows rates of GNP growth for the period 1965 to 1989 and levels of income inequality in the mid-1980s (measured by the ratio of the income shares of the top and bottom quintiles) for Latin American and East Asian countries. The difference between the two regions is striking: Latin American countries, concentrated in the southeast corner, experienced slow or

Reprinted from *Development Policy,* Inter-American Development Bank, vol. 3, no. 3 (September 1994): 1–5.

Figure 29.1   Income Inequality and Growth of GDP, 1965–1989

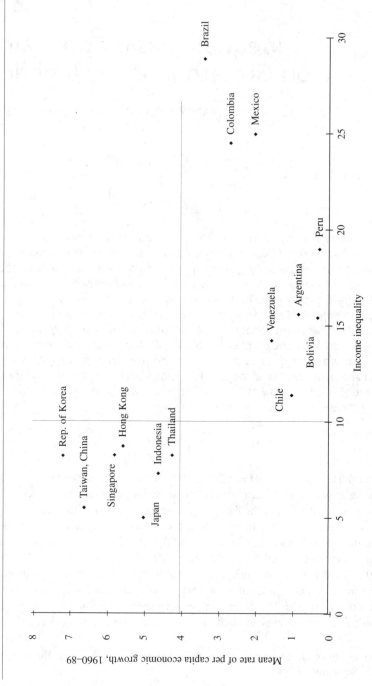

Source: World Bank, 1993. *The East Asian Miracle: Econmic Growth and Public Policy.*

negative growth with high inequality, while East Asian countries, concentrated in the northwest corner, achieved rapid growth with low inequality.

Differences in the political economy of the two regions may be part of the explanation. In the postwar period, governing elites in East Asia, their legitimacy threatened by domestic communist insurgents, sought to widen the base of their political support via policies such as land reform, public housing, investment in rural infrastructure, and, most common, widespread high-quality basic education. In Latin America governing elites appear to have believed they could thrive irrespective of what happened to those with the lowest incomes since tax, expenditure, and trade policies benefitted the poor relatively little. For example, East Asia's export oriented, labor-demanding development strategy contributed to rapid growth of output and, by increasing employment opportunities and wages, ensured that the benefits of that growth were widely shared. In contrast, Latin America's strategy tended to be biased against both agriculture and exports, resulting in relatively slow growth in the demand for labor. . . .

The association of slow growth and high inequality in Latin America could in part be due to the fact that high inequality itself may be a constraint on growth. Conversely, East Asia's low level of inequality may have been a significant stimulus to economic growth. If so, investment in education is a key to a sustained growth not only because it contributes directly through productivity effects, but also because it reduces income inequality.

Econometric Results

To assess the impact of the distribution of income on subsequent economic growth we regressed the growth rate of real per capita income of 74 developing countries over the period 1960–85 on determinants of growth such as per capita GDP and education enrollments at the start of the period and on a measure of income inequality, the ratio of the income shares of the top 40 percent and the bottom 20 percent. We found that inequality and growth are in fact inversely related: countries with higher inequality tend to have lower growth.

How big a constraint on growth is high inequality? It is substantial. The results suggest that ceteris paribus, after 25 years, GDP per capita would be 8.2 percent higher in a country with low inequality than in a country with inequality one standard deviation higher. How big was the constraint of high inequality in Latin America? The ratio of the income shares of the top 20 percent to the bottom 20 percent is 26 in Brazil and 8 in Korea. Simulations suggest that if, in 1960, Brazil had had Korea's lower level of inequality Brazil's predicted growth rate over the following 25 years would have been 0.66 percentage points higher each year. This implies that after 25 years GDP per capita in Brazil would have been 17.2 percent higher.

Poor Educational Performance, Slow Growth, and High Inequality in Latin America

Differences in educational performance help to explain why Latin America experienced relatively low rates of growth and high inequality while East Asia experienced high rates of growth and low inequality. Most countries in East Asia have significantly higher primary and secondary enrollment rates than predicted based on their per capita income; most Latin American countries have rates at or below those predicted. Moreover, where enrollment rates are low, as in Brazil and Guatemala, children of the poor are the least likely to be enrolled, perpetuating high income inequality.

Furthermore, in contrast to East Asia, where increases in quantity were associated with improvements in the quality of education, expansion of enrollments in many Latin American countries has resulted in the erosion of quality. In Brazil, the expansion of primary school coverage has been associated with declines in completion rates—probably a sign of failure to raise quality. By contrast, in East Asian countries, as quantity increased completion rates remained high. Declines in quality also tend to hurt the poor most, since they are least able to use private schools or change residence.

Education and Growth

Human capital theory says that education augments cognitive and other skills of individuals which, in turn, augment their productivity as workers. Our growth rate functions show that this accumulation of skills at the individual level translates into higher economic growth at the country level. Our statistical work also shows that increasing primary-school enrollments for girls, though they are less likely to become formal workers, is just as effective in stimulating growth as increasing primary enrollments for boys.

The reason: the economic payoff to educating girls is not confined to increases in the productivity of wage labor. It works through changes in behavior within households. For example, educated mothers have fewer children. Closing a virtuous circle, the fertility decline in East Asia that started in the mid-1960s resulted in a marked slowing of the growth of the school-age population in the 1970s. This made it easier to increase public expenditures on basic education per child, permitting rapid increases in the quantity of schooling as well as improvements in the quality of schools. . . .

Although fertility rates in Latin America have declined during the past two decades, they remain high relative to East Asian rates, particularly in the poorer countries. High fertility has placed added stress on already strained resources for education; per child spending on books, equipment, and teacher training in Latin America has declined. Declines in per-child spending in the region (from an estimated $164 per primary school child in 1980 to $118 in 1989) have probably contributed to declines in school quality and continued high repetition—the highest in the world—and high dropout rates. Between 1970 and 1990 expenditure on basic education per eligible child increased by 350 percent in Korea and 64 percent in Mexico. During the same period, the number of eligible children increased by 59 percent in Mexico, in Korea the number of eligible children actually declined by 27 percent. . . .

In addition, Latin America missed out on the positive feedback between rapid growth and household behavior with respect to human-capital accumulation. Investment in human capital by households is greater in East Asia than in Latin America in part because the demand for educated workers is greater, and consequently the returns to the household of investment in schooling are higher. In other words, stronger demand for educated workers elicits a greater supply. Furthermore, rapid economic growth in East Asia increased the numerator, while declining fertility reduced the denominator, of the ratio of public expenditures on basic education per school-age child. Neither in 1960 nor in 1989 was public expenditure on education as a percentage of GNP much higher in East Asia than in Latin America. However, it is obvious that the more rapid the growth of aggregate output, the more rapid the growth of the constant share of GDP that goes to education.

Education and Inequality

In Korea the proportion of high school and postsecondary graduates in the wage-labor force sharply increased between the mid-1970s and the mid-1980s, and the proportion of workers with elementary schooling or less declined to just 8 percent. As a consequence, the wage premium earned by educated workers in Korea declined. In Brazil the increment to the labor force of relatively well-educated workers was so small that it did not take much of an increase in the demand for educated workers to offset any wage compression effect of the increase in supply. As a result, the educational structure of wages barely changed in Brazil. What would the inequality of pay in Brazil have been had educational policy resulted in educational attainment comparable to that in Korea in the mid-1980s? Simulations indicate that Brazil would have had a log variance of wages in the mid-1980s some 17 percent lower than the actual. This 17 percent reduction represents over one-quarter of the gap between Brazil and Korea in the log variance of wages.

In Latin America there has also been a feedback effect, one that closed a vicious circle from high inequality to low enrollment rates. High income inequality limits household demand for education among the poor. Poor families may want to keep children in school, but they cannot afford to do so because they do not have money for school clothes or books or because they need children to work. Unable to borrow, poor households thus do not invest in their children's education even if they know that the benefits would be great. The pressing need to use income simply to subsist crowds out this high-return investment and reduces society's demand for education. High inequality makes this problem worse. For example, while the per capita income of Brazil (in 1983) slightly exceeded average income in Malaysia (in 1987) the bottom quintile received 4.6 percent of total income in Malaysia but only 2.4 percent of total income in Brazil. The per capita income of the poorest households in Brazil was thus only half the income of the poorest in Malaysia. Given an income elasticity of demand for basic education of 0.50 if the distribution of income were as equal in Brazil as in Malaysia, enrollments among poor Brazilian children would be more than 40 percent higher.

The Direct Effect of Inequality on Growth

Our results indicate that low inequality stimulates growth independent of its effects through education. However, using income transfers to reduce income inequality is unlikely to be good for growth: transfers often result in the diversion of scarce savings from investment to the subsidization of consumption; the targeted group is often not the one to benefit from transfers, reducing their effectiveness as a means of raising the standard of living, and hence the savings and investment rates, of the poor; transfers tend to distort incentives and reduce both allocative efficiency and X efficiency. But policies that increase the productivity and earning capacity of the poor may be quite a different matter.

Consider four ways in which low inequality can be a stimulus to growth:

- by inducing large increases in the savings and investments of the poor
- by contributing to political and macroeconomic stability—for example by reducing the tendency for fiscal prudence to be sacrificed to political expediency, by discouraging inappropriate exchange rate valuation, and by accelerating the adjustment to macroeconomic
- by increasing the "X-efficiency" of low-income workers, and
- by raising rural incomes, which limits intersectoral income gaps and the rent seeking associated with them, while increasing the domestic multiplier effects of a given increase in per capita income.

Conclusion

The contrasting experiences of Latin America and East Asia suggest that, contrary to conventional wisdom, inequalities in the distribution of both education and income may have a significant and negative impact on the rate of economic growth. The unequal distribution of education in Latin America, in terms of both quantity and quality, constrained economic growth in the region by forestalling opportunities to increase labor productivity and change household behavior. At the same time, the relatively small size of the educated labor force and high scarcity rents of the more educated contributed to high inequality in the distribution of income. Closing a vicious circle, slower growth and high income inequality, in turn, further limited the supply of, and demand for, education.

Education policy alone, however, does not explain the marked differences in equity and growth between Latin America and East Asia. Macroeconomic and sectoral policies in the former, which favored capital-intensive production and were biased against the agricultural sector, almost certainly exacerbated the inequality problem and have hindered growth as well. The East Asian development strategy promoted instead a dynamic agricultural sector and a labor-demanding, export-oriented growth path, thereby reducing inequality and stimulating growth. In East Asia low inequality not only contributes to growth indirectly, for example, by increasing investment in education, but appears to have had a direct positive effect on the growth rate.

The experience of the two regions is sufficient to reject the conventional wisdom of a necessary link between high income inequality and rapid growth. While our analysis has not been sufficient to confirm the opposite, we hope others will now seriously consider the hypothesis that high inequality, and policies that ignore or even exacerbate inequality, constrain growth in the long run. The challenge in Latin America is to find ways to reduce inequality, not by transfers, but by eliminating consumption subsidies for the rich and increasing the productivity of the poor.

PART 8

The Impact of Globalization

30

Globalisation

ANTHONY GIDDENS

Anthony Giddens, former director of the London School of Economics, was asked by the BBC to give a series of lectures on globalization. The following excerpt from the lecture titled "Globalisation" seeks to explain how the current wave of globalization is different from previous eras of globalization. Made a Life Peer in 2004, Lord Giddens has had a profound impact on sociology and politics. His advice has been sought by political leaders around the world. Here he describes the economic, social, and political ramifications of globalization. While he is a proponent of globalization, he notes that to some it looks much like global pillage; however, he asserts that increasingly, globalization is becoming "decentered," and the direction of influence that in the past has appeared to flow from the rich to the poor is reversing. ■

A FRIEND OF MINE STUDIES VILLAGE LIFE IN CENTRAL AFRICA. A FEW YEARS AGO, SHE paid her first visit to a remote area where she was to carry out her fieldwork. The day she arrived, she was invited to a local home for an evening's entertainment. She expected to find out about the traditional pastimes of this isolated community. Instead, the occasion turned out to be a viewing of *Basic Instinct* on video. The film at that point hadn't even reached the cinemas in London. . . .

Such vignettes reveal something about our world. And what they reveal isn't trivial. It isn't just a matter of people adding modern paraphernalia— videos, television sets, personal computers and so forth—to their existing ways of life. We live in a world of transformations, affecting almost every aspect of

Excerpted from *Runaway World: How Globalisation Is Reshaping Our Lives* (London: Taylor and Francis, 2003). Reprinted with permission of the author.

what we do. For better or worse, we are being propelled into a global order that no one fully understands, but which is making its effects felt upon all of us. . . .

Given its sudden popularity, we shouldn't be surprised that the meaning of the notion isn't always clear, or that an intellectual reaction has set in against it. Globalisation has something to do with the thesis that we now all live in one world—but in what ways exactly, and is the idea really valid? Different thinkers have taken almost completely opposite views about globalisation in debates that have sprung up over the past few years.

Some dispute the whole thing. I'll call them the skeptics. According to the skeptics, all the talk about globalisation is only that—just talk. Whatever its benefits, its trials and tribulations, the global economy isn't especially different from that which existed at previous periods. The world carries on much the same as it has done for many years.

Most countries, the skeptics argue, gain only a small amount of their income from external trade. Moreover, a good deal of economic exchange is between regions, rather than being truly world-wide. The countries of the European Union, for example, mostly trade among themselves. The same is true of the other main trading blocks such as those of Asia-Pacific or North America.

Others take a very direct position. I'll label them the radicals. The radicals argue that not only is globalisation very real, but that its consequences can be felt everywhere. The global market-place they say, is much more developed than even in the 1960s and 1970s and is indifferent to national borders. Nations have lost most of the sovereignty they once had and politicians have lost most of their capability to influence events. It isn't surprising that no one respects political leaders any more, or has much interest in what they have to say. The era of the nation-state is over. Nations, as the Japanese business writer Kenichi Ohmae puts it, have become mere 'fictions'. Authors such as Ohmae see the economic difficulties of the 1998 Asian crisis as demonstrating the reality of globalisation, albeit seen from its disruptive side.

The skeptics tend to be on the political left, especially the old left. For if all of this is essentially a myth, governments can still control economic life and the welfare states remain intact. The notion of globalisation, according to the skeptics, is an ideology put about by free-marketeers who wish to dismantle welfare systems and cut back on state expenditures. What has happened is at most a reversion to how the world was a century ago. In the late nineteenth century there was already an open global economy, with a great deal of trade, including trade in currencies.

Well, who is right in this debate? I think it is the radicals. The level of world trade today is much higher than it ever was before, and involves a much wider range of goods and services. But the biggest difference is in the level of finance and capital flows. Geared as it is to electronic money—money that exists only as digits in computers—the current world economy has no parallels in earlier times.

In the new global electronic economy, fund managers, banks, corporations, as well as millions of individual investors, can transfer vast amounts of capital from one side of the world to another at the click of a mouse. As they do so, they can destabilize what might have seemed rock-solid economies—as happened in the events in Asia.

The volume of world financial transactions is usually measured in US dollars. A million dollars is a lot of money for most people. Measured as a stack of hundred-dollar notes, it would be eight inches high. A billion dollars—in other words, a thousand million—would stand higher than St. Paul's Cathedral. A trillion dollars—a million million—would be over 130 miles high, 20 times higher than Mount Everest.

Yet far more than a trillion dollars is now turned over each day on global currency markets. This is a massive increase from only the late 1980s, let alone the more distant past. The value of whatever money we may have in our pockets, or our bank accounts, shifts from moment to moment according to fluctuations in such markets.

I would have no hesitation, therefore, in saying that globalisation as we are experiencing it is in many respects not only new, but also revolutionary. Yet I don't believe that either the skeptics or the radicals have properly understood either what it is or its implications for us. Both groups see the phenomenon almost solely in economic terms. This is a mistake. Globalisation is political, technological and cultural, as well as economic. It has been influenced above all by developments in systems of communication, dating back only to the late 1960s. . . .

Globalisation, of course, isn't developing in an even-handed way and is by no means wholly benign in its consequences. To many living outside Europe and North America, it looks uncomfortably like Westernisation—or, perhaps, Americanisation, since the US is now the sole superpower, with a dominant economic, cultural and military position in the global order. Many of the most visible cultural expressions of globalisation are American—Coca-Cola, McDonald's, CNN.

Most of the giant multinational companies are based in the US too. Those that aren't all come from the rich countries, not the poorer areas of the world. A pessimistic view of globalisation would consider it largely an affair of the industrial North, in which the developing societies of the South play little or no active part. It would see it as destroying local cultures, widening world inequalities and worsening the lot of the impoverished. Globalisation, some argue, creates a world of winners and losers, a few on the fast track to prosperity, the majority condemned to a life of misery and despair.

Indeed, the statistics are daunting. The share of the poorest fifth of the world's population in global income has dropped, from 2.3 per cent to 1.4 per cent between 1989 and 1998. The proportion taken by the richest fifth on the other hand has risen. In sub-Saharan Africa, 20 countries have lower incomes per head in real terms than they had in the late 1970s. In many less developed countries, safety and environmental regulations are low or virtually non-existent. Some transnational companies sell goods there that are controlled or banned in the industrial countries—poor-quality medical drugs, destructive pesticides or high tar and nicotine content cigarettes. Rather than a global village, one might say, this is more like global pillage.

Along with ecological risk, to which it is related, expanding inequality is the most serious problem facing world society. It will not do, however, merely to blame it on the wealthy. It is fundamental to my argument that globalisation today is only partly Westernisation. Of course the Western nations, and more generally the industrial countries, still have far more influence over world affairs than do the poorer states. But globalisation is becoming increasingly decentred—not under the control of any group of nations, and still less of the large corporations. Its effects are felt as much in Western countries as elsewhere.

This is true of the global financial system, and of changes affecting the nature of government itself. What one could call 'reverse colonization' is becoming more and more common. Reverse colonization means that non-Western countries influence developments in the West. Examples abound—such as the Latinizing of Los Angeles, the emergence of a globally oriented high-tech sector in India or the selling of Brazilian television programmes to Portugal.

Is globalisation a force promoting the general good? The question can't be answered in a simple way, given the complexity of the phenomenon. People who ask it, and who blame globalisation for deepening world inequalities, usually have in mind economic globalisation and, within that, free trade. Now, it is surely obvious that free trade is not an unalloyed benefit. This is especially so as concerns the less developed countries. Opening up a country, or regions within it, to free trade can undermine a local subsistence economy. An area that becomes dependent upon a few products sold on world markets is very vulnerable to shifts in prices as well as to technological change.

Trade always needs a framework of institutions, as do other forms of economic development. Markets cannot be created by purely economic means, and how far a given economy should be exposed to the world market-place must depend upon a range of criteria. Yet to oppose economic globalisation, and to opt for economic protectionism, would be a misplaced tactic for rich and poor nations alike. Protectionism may be a necessary strategy at some times and in some countries. In my view, for example, Malaysia was correct to introduce controls in 1998, to stem the flood of capital from the country. But more permanent forms of protectionism will not help the development of the poor countries, and among the rich would lead to warring trade blocs.

31

Globalization and Inequality

BRANKO MILANOVIC

In this chapter, World Bank expert Branko Milanovic explores three different measures of inequality: unweighted international inequality, international inequality weighted by population, and global inequality based on individuals' household income. Using the three different measures of global inequality, he begins the process of untangling the conflicting conclusions and prescriptions with regard to findings concerning the gap between rich and poor countries. In sum he argues that conclusions about inequality are often strongly influenced by specific cases, such as China, and that convergence of policy has not led to convergence of income. In the concluding sections of this chapter, Milanovic discusses how increased access to mass communications and cheap transportation (globalization) has impacted the debate over the gap and inequality. He suggests that this increased awareness of what others have and consume could lead to individuals around the world basing their satisfaction with their lot in life on the global community rather than the people around them. ∎

IN OUR EFFORTS TO UNDERSTAND THE STATE OF INEQUALITY TODAY, WE NEED FIRST to define the key concepts and terms. Most crucially, we need to distinguish between international and global inequality in order to avoid terminological confusion. I explore these two concepts throughout the essay. Here it suffices

Excerpted from David Held and Ayse Kaya, eds., *Global Inequality: Patterns and Explanations* (Cambridge, UK: Polity Press, 2007). Reprinted with the permission of the author.

to say that international inequality denotes the inequality between nations, more exactly between mean incomes of nations. Global inequality (also known as 'world inequality'), on the other hand, is an inequality between individuals in the world regardless of their nation, regardless of where they live. In other words when measuring global inequality, we see the entire world as if it were one country.

In this essay I will utilize three concepts of inequality in order to explore the patterns of *international* and *global* inequality and map out changes in inequality over time. I will call these three different ways of assessing inequality Concept 1, Concept 2 and Concept 3.

Concept 1 Inequality

Concept 1 measures *unweighted international inequality*. As previously explained, international inequality measures the inequality between mean incomes of different nations. This sort of inequality is captured in statements like 'the mean income in the United States is higher than the mean income in Pakistan'. In measuring this inequality, we generally rely on national accounts, that is Gross Domestic Income (GDI) of the countries. We compare the GDIs of countries to each other to grasp Concept 1 inequality. Because populations of countries are left out, Concept 1 is unweighted international inequality. Notice also that inequality *within* countries is ignored.

Concept 2 Inequality

Concept 2 inequality is similar to Concept 1. Like Concept 1, Concept 2 measures international inequality by relying on the representative income of a country: GDI per capita. Differently from Concept 1, however, Concept 2 takes into consideration the population of countries. In these calculations China's weight is approximately 20 per cent of the world rather than, as in Concept 1, having the same weight as any other country. Consequently, when calculating the inequality of Concept 2, the role of China and India would be very important. To make the difference clear, note that Concept 1 inequality is akin to the UN General Assembly: there is one ambassador for each country and each country is represented by its GDI per capita. In contrast with Concept 1, here we have 6 billion ambassadors (the world's population) and all the ambassadors from, say, China display the mean income of China, all ambassadors from India display the mean income of India and so forth. Hence with Concept 2, each country would be represented in accordance with its population but it would be still represented by ambassadors having *representative* incomes of their nations—not actual incomes of people who live there. Thus Concept 2 also ignores differences in incomes within countries.

Concept 3 Inequality

The final type of measurement we will rely on to explore inequality in this chapter is Concept 3 inequality. Concept 3 denotes *world inequality* or *global inequality*. Differently from international inequality, this concept captures inequality between individuals. To use the previous metaphor, we dispense with ambassadors: every individual enters into the calculations with his/her actual income. The only source of data from which we learn about people's incomes is household surveys. Ideally, we should have a world household survey to find out what is world income distribution. But short of that we have to use individual countries' household surveys, collate them and derive a world distribution of income across individuals. This further differentiates Concept 3 from the other two Concepts: it relies on an entirely different source of data, income distribution data obtained from household surveys. Thus the data requirements are much more formidable than they are for Concepts 1 and 2 where we need respectively only one variable (GDI per capita) or two (GDI per capita and population). This huge jump in the data requirement makes the move from Concept 2 to Concept 3 even more problematic because of the difference between disposable income from household surveys (our welfare aggregate in Concept 3 calculations) and national accounts data from which we get our GDIs per capita. The largest part of the difference is definitional: household disposable income is after-tax income and it excludes publicly provided health, education and other government services and goods. The latter are, of course, included in Gross Domestic Income. Another part of the discrepancy comes from the under survey of rich people and their income sources (mostly property income I in household surveys. These sources are better captured by national accounts simply because rich people are loath to fully reveal their actual income to survey enumerators. These points will be discussed further.

Patterns of Inequality

Let us now see how Concepts 1, 2 and 3 have moved over time in order to explain the changing patterns of inequality. 1 will start with a historical perspective before discussing the contemporary patterns of inequality. This historical perspective applies primarily to Concepts 1 and 2. We do not know much about how Concept 3 has moved over time simply because we lack the relevant data on household surveys. Since incomes or expenditures from household surveys are not available for a historical period, we shall focus on a briefer period, 1988–98.

Historical Perspective

Figure 31.1 displays the historical movement of Concept 1 inequality. This figure, based on Maddison (2004) GDI per capita data which are the only source of long-run historical income statistics, shows that between 1820 and 1870 international inequality was on the rise. The increase is present whether measured by the Gini coefficient or Theil Index. Inequality also ascended during 1870–1913, although it declined or stabilized during the inter-war period of 'deglobalization', 1913–38. Following this period, we witness a sharp increase in Concept 1 inequality between 1938 and 1952. This is related to the Second World War and the fact that some of the rich countries (United States, Australia, New Zealand and Argentina) did very well while most of the rest of the world lost out. From roughly 1952 to 1978, Concept 1 inequality remains at the same level as measured by the Gini and declines rather substantially as measured by the Theil Index. For the less developed countries, this was the period associated with decolonization and application of import substitution policies including a strong role of the state. For the rich world that was the pe-

Figure 31.1   Concept 1 Inequality, 1820–2000

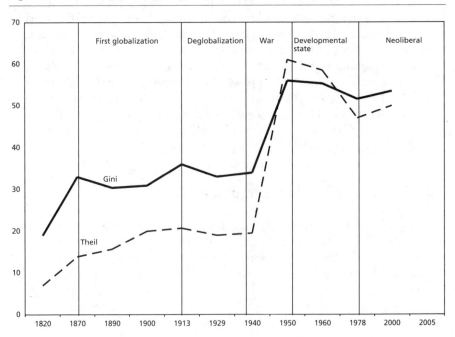

riod of unmatched growth that became known as the 'Golden Age'. But despite the rich world's fast growth, there was clearly, on average, a catch up of poor and middle-income countries or income convergence; it proved short-lived. Starting from around 1978, the beginning of the 'neoliberal regime', there is a sharp turnaround and Concept 1 inequality rises whether measured by the Gini or Theil.

Figure 31.1 demonstrates that Concept 1 inequality has generally been on an upward trend from 1820 up to today. This finding tells us that differences between mean incomes of countries are much greater today than they were some 200 years ago. It is also true that our sample size has gone up because originally in Maddison's data we had approximately only 35 or 40 countries, but over time the number of countries has increased to 50, 60 or 80. Today we have more than 150 nations in the sample. Thus a *part* of the increase in Concept 1 inequality can be explained by the increase in the sample size (that is, in the number of independent states in the world). But, it is important to emphasize that only a part of the change can be attributed to this factor. If we were to take only the countries for which we have data over the entire period 1820–2000, we would still find that international inequality of this sort has been on the rise. When we use Concept 2 inequality, we observe a different picture. Here, I use the same data as I did for Concept 1 inequality above, viz, the same GDP per capita data from Maddison (2004) and the same countries, but this time around the data are weighted by population. I will discuss later some pitfalls of the data on China but let us assume here that these data are reliable. Figure 31.2 demonstrates the historical journey of Concept 2 inequality. As this figure shows, during the period from 1850, which is the first year in the figure, to about 1950, which represents a peak, there is a clear upward trend. From the mid-1950s to today Concept 2 inequality remains broadly stable (or just slightly decreasing). This finding is confirmed by Bourguignon and Morrisson (2002).

Contemporary Patterns of Inequality

Now let us move from this very brief historical sketch to a focus on what inequality is today analyzing the period 1950–2000. To paraphrase a well-known dictator, Figure 31.3 illustrates the 'mother of all inequality disputes'. The essence of the dispute is about what happened to inequality roughly between 1950 and 2000.

Figure 31.3 examines inequality during this period using the three Concepts of inequality. As we see from the figure, unweighted international inequality—the Concept 1 inequality—has gone up. Of particular importance to note is that it has been going up over the last 20 years. Moreover, we see that the 'watershed years' 1978–80—the term coined by Paul Bairoch (1997)—characterized by rising oil prices and real interest rates, the onset of the debt

Figure 31.2 Concept 2 Inequality (Gini Coefficient), 1850–2000

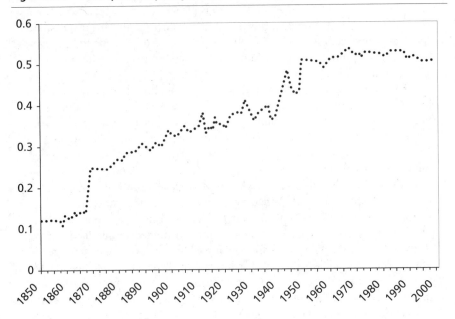

Figure 31.3 Concepts of Inequality, 1950–2000

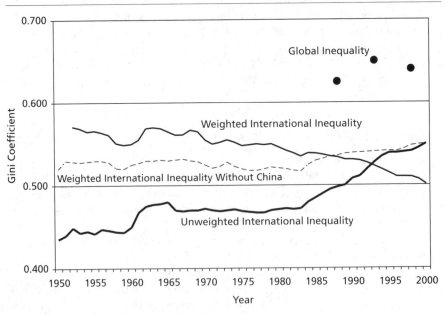

Source: Calculated using World Bank WDI data.

crisis and the beginning of the Thatcher and Reagan rule in Great Britain and the United States, were at the origin of this unmistakable upward trend which has persisted ever since.

Concept 2 inequality charts a very different course. As Figure 31.3 shows, Concept 2 inequality has declined over precisely the same time during which Concept 1 inequality rose. Moreover Concept 2 inequality begins its downward trend exactly around 1978–80. The decline is driven by the fact that China has grown very fast ever since 1978 when the responsibility system was introduced in the countryside and communes were dismantled by the Deng Xiaoping regime. China was a very poor country with a huge population and as people in China have become richer overall inequality in the world has tended to go down. The role of China is crucial, as it becomes clear when we calculate Concept 2 inequality without China: we see that inequality of this sort has been stable or even rising (see the dotted line in Figure 31.3). In sum, *inequalities between countries have been rising since around 1978, although population-weighted inequality between countries has been decreasing since 1978 thanks to growth in China and more recently in India.*

Let us now look at global inequality, Concept 3. Based on my own calculations, Figure 31.3 displays three years—1988, 1993 and 1998—that capture global inequality. These three dots are based on household survey data. There are some important points to highlight here. To begin with, we cannot really extract similar data for the past because we do not have household surveys for many important parts of the world (China, the Soviet Union, most of Africa) for any years before the early 1980s. As we see in Figure 31.3, these three years do not follow a pattern: there is first a strong increase in inequality followed by a more modest decline. The gap between global inequality (the three dots) and weighted international inequality is explained by inequality within nations. We can write it out as,

(1) Global inequality = Concept 2 inequality (or between-country inequality) + within-country inequality

Overall, the three dots inform us that *inequality among people in the world today* is *extremely high, though its direction of change is unclear.* The Gini Index of inequality between people in the world lies between 62 and 66. A Gini of 62, which is a very high number, is a higher level of inequality than what is found in any individual country: for instance, Brazil's inequality is in the upper 50s level; South Africa is in the low 60s. This level of inequality is perhaps unparalleled in world history. If such extreme inequality existed in smaller communities or in a nation-state, governing authorities would find it too destabilizing to leave it alone, or revolutions or riots might break out. The fact that such extreme levels of inequality exist on the global level perhaps causes us to react against it relatively less severely.

A number of different forces impact upon global inequality, causing a very complicated pattern to emerge. First, fast economic growth in China and India—populous nations that were very poor and are still relatively poor—pushes world inequality down. Second, the relative decline of many poor and middle-income countries has the opposite effect: it contributes to global inequality. Third, higher inequality within large nations, such as the United States, China, India, and Russia, adds to global inequality, pushing the dots in Figure 31.3 further upwards from the line that captures Concept 2 inequality. Thus as one force reduces global inequality, the other one or two increase it.

Regionally, the last 20 to 25 years have been characterized by the following basic trends: China and India pulled ahead, Latin America and Eastern Europe—the middle-income countries—declined, and Africa's position became even worse. The rich world (Western Europe, North America and Oceania) grew relatively fast. As for within-nation inequalities, they increased almost everywhere. We *are witnessing the Africanization of poverty,* since most of the African nations are now extremely poor and many of them are actually poorer than they were in 1960. The correlation between being poor and being African is probably stronger than ever in recorded history. Another interesting fact is that, for the first time since the early nineteenth century, all Latin American nations are poorer in per capita terms than the poorest West European country (Portugal).

The complicated way in which different forces impact upon global inequality should encourage us to avoid broad generalizations. The difficulty of saying what happens to global inequality stems, in part, from the fact that it is hard to calculate because it requires access to detailed household survey data from most countries in the world. While there is no dispute that global inequality is extremely high today, there remains a debate on the direction of change in global inequality as well as on the significance and meaning of this putative change. We would also like to draw some sort of causal link between globalization and global inequality. This is exceedingly difficult because globalization affects differently the growth rates of GDIs per capita of poor and rich nations, within-nation inequalities in poor and rich countries, and may influence differently the populous and small nations. Sometimes these effects may work in the same direction, for example if greater openness helps accelerate growth of poor countries and reduces within-nation inequalities, and sometimes they may offset each other, for example if openness helps poor countries but widens their internal income distributions.

Why Inequality Between Countries Matters

Before we explore the relationship between the three concepts of inequality and how they are related to globalization, let us briefly address one question that the debate on inequality raises: why does inequality between countries matter? The convergence hypothesis, grounded in growth economics, posits that poor countries should grow faster than rich countries, whether controlling for other factors (so called beta convergence) or even unconditionally (so called sigma convergences). The latter is no different to our Concept 1 inequality which as we have seen, *pace* economic theory, has rapidly increased during the last two decades, Since we expect from economic theory that convergence should take place, the question becomes why it did not. Some authors claim that it did not because some countries were not really 'globalizing' so only those countries that follow 'globalization friendly' policies should be considered and they are, these authors claim, converging (Sachs and Warner 1997; World Bank 2002; Dollar and Kraay 2001). Evidence disproves these claims: economic policies (including those that can be included under the heading of 'globalization friendly') are much more similar today than they were 20 or 30 years ago.

The pertinent question then becomes why there is a divergence of outcomes while economic policies converge. I believe that the currently available studies do not allow us to come up with a definitive answer to the question. There are several possible explanations however. According to one explanation (Mukand and Rodrik 2002), divergence of outcomes may coexist with convergence of policies if the same set of policies (basically, of the Washington Consensus type) is applied in different institutional settings. Since efficiency of policies is not independent of the environment where they are applied, the same policies will produce inferior outcomes in countries that are institutionally very different from the advanced market economies. According to Mukand and Rodrik, some poor countries would have been better off had they followed a 'heterodox' mix of policies, that is policies not identical to the ones contained in the Washington Consensus package. This is because a heterodox mix might have been more appropriate for their conditions. This is how Mukand and Rodrik explain China's and India's success since neither country followed the dominant paradigm *à la lettre*. Another explanation is that recent technological progress has been characterized by economies of scale. In such a world, diminishing marginal productivity of capital, on which the convergence hypothesis rests, no longer holds. On the contrary, marginal productivity of capital may be greater in more capital-rich countries—which then of course implies divergence.

Beyond its potential implications for the convergence theory, inequality between countries matters for other reasons too. Inequality between nations is important for migration issues, for instance. Concept 1 inequality may matter also if countries represent distinct cultures and modes of life. If we believe that cultures have some intrinsic value in themselves, then we might feel discomforted by the idea that there are huge differences in income or unbridgeable differences of wealth between nations so that the nations that are in decline might over time disappear. However, a social Darwinist view of the world might refute the importance of this argument. The point is that inequality between countries does not only matter in terms of assessing the efficacy of our current set of development policies, it may also have important social repercussions.

The Future of Global Inequality

Where is global inequality heading? Lucas (1998) and Firebaugh (2003) argue that we are likely to experience 'inequality transition' and that global inequality has peaked so that we can actually expect a decline. This will happen because the effects of the industrial and technological revolutions will spread gradually across the globe evening out incomes. The repercussions of the industrial revolution, which originated in England and later encompassed Western Europe before broadening to Northern America and elsewhere, are today felt in China and India. Lucas and Firebaugh essentially argue that because Concept 2 inequality drove global inequality since the Industrial Revolution and since this type of inequality has been on the decline for the last 30 years, then Concept 3 inequality should follow the same trajectory.

I find the Lucas and Firebaugh argumentation problematic for several reasons. First, as already discussed, policy convergence has not led to income convergence and the 20 years of recent history demonstrate this point. Second, the authors present a static view of technological progress. There have been many technological revolutions since the Industrial Revolution, most recently the computer revolution. Thus we might have poor countries catching up in some areas while rich countries carry on with further technological innovations in others and the gap between the two increases rather than narrows. Third, the expectation Lucas and Firebaugh set out depends on the decline in Concept 2 inequality. Yet as I have suggested, the downward slide in Concept 2 inequality hinges on one set of numbers for one country, China. These numbers themselves can be questioned, and more importantly the future evolution of the Chinese economy (particularly since the country still needs—one would expect—to democratize) remains a matter of speculation, not a certainty.

Although we have gained some understanding of inequality today, we have not yet addressed the most important question: does global inequality matter?

Does Global Inequality Matter?

Some commentators put forward that global inequality really does not matter because it is too abstract an idea and the world lacks a government, an entity that should, in principle, be 'in charge' of inequality. It even lacks a 'global polity' that would, through political pressure or persuasion, raise the issues and effect change. But the situation in which we find ourselves today is not much different from the situation in which people found themselves prior to the creation of nation states. As long as there were disparate groups of individuals who hardly interacted at all, living in small hamlets and villages, there was no concept of a nation. Without this mental concept, inequality does not matter because there are only very few people (those from the village) to be compared against. It is only once a mental concept of what constitutes a nation is born (or created), and there is a government that governs that nation, that people may begin to compare themselves to others from the same nation. Similarly, as the world becomes more globalized, the concept of one world will become much more acceptable. As we increase our awareness of the globe as a whole, poverty and inequality elsewhere will affect many more of us than they do today. In this regard, global inequality matters, not the least because the globalization process itself increases people's awareness of each other and highlights income differences.

So much for the change in mutual awareness and creation of a global polity. But one could still argue that inequality does not matter because people are only interested in their own welfare and not in the welfare of those who are better off. So what is the correct utility function then? Asked in another way, are we interested only in our own consumption or income, or does relative consumption/income matter too? Two different quotes capture the opposing answers to this question. On the one hand, Anne Krueger (2002) remarks that: 'Poor people are desperate enough to improve their material conditions in absolute terms rather than to march up the income distribution. Hence it seems far better to focus on impoverishment than on inequality.' Krueger claims the only thing which matters is one's own income and incomes of others are immaterial. The implication here, drawn explicitly by Feldstein (1999), is that people who take into account other people's incomes are full of envy and their preferences should not concern us. On the other hand, we have a quote from Simon Kuznets (1965) that advocates a position that opposes Krueger's. He contends that 'one could argue that the reduction of physical misery associated with low income and consumption levels . . . permits an increase rather than a diminution of political tensions.' Kuznets goes on to explain that these 'political tensions' stem from 'the *political misery* of the poor, the tension created by the observation of the much greater wealth of other communities'. Long before the days of the current globalization, Kuznets captured that people are social animals. Although we are concerned about our absolute income first because we have essential needs, such as food, clothing and shelter, that have to be satisfied, we are also concerned about our own income compared to that of others. Recent empirical studies confirm this concern with one's relative position as soon as the essential needs are satisfied (see Graham and Felton 2005; Frank 2005). Whether we believe that this concern with other people's income is grounded in the desire for fairness or in envy, the *key* and the only relevant point is that we are not indifferent to other people's incomes. This is where globalization comes in. If, as hypothesized, globalization increases awareness of what other people are receiving, then to a person living in a poor country, the income with which he or she would normally be satisfied may no longer seem enough. The very process of globalization might influence our perception and our satisfaction with a given level of income. This is a crucial point: as the process of globalization enfolds how much will it influence our perception of our own position in it? If it does, maintaining large inter-country income differences becomes more and more difficult. But in the face of greater mutual interaction between people and declining travel costs, the rich world will have to become a fortress in order to keep the poor people out; but this is almost impossible.

References

Bairoch, Paul 1997. *Victoires et déboires: Histoire économique et sociale du monde du XVIe siècle a nos jours,* vol. 2. Paris: Folio Histoire Galliard.

Banerji, Abhijit and Piketty, Thomas 2005. 'Top Indian Incomes, 1956–2000.' *World Bank Economic Review* 19 (1): 1–20.

Bhalla, Surjit 2002. *Imagine There's No Country*. Washington, DC: Institute for International Economics.

Bourguignon, François, and Morrisson, Christian 2002. 'The Size Distribution of Income Among World Citizens. 1820–1990.' *American Economic Review*, September: 727–44.

Dollar, David and Kraay, Aart 2001. 'Trade, Growth, and Poverty.' *Policy Research Working Paper,* no. 2615. Washington, DC: World Bank.

Feldstein, Martin 1999. 'Reducing Poverty not Inequality.' *Public Interest*, Fall 1999.

Firebaugh, Glenn 2003. *The New Geography of Global Income Inequality*. Cambridge, Mass.: Harvard University Press.

Frank, Robert H. 2005. 'Positional Externalities Cause Large and Preventable Welfare Losses.' *American Economic Review*, Papers and Proceedings 95 (2): 137–51.

Graham, Carol, and Felton, Andrew 2005. *Does Inequality Matter to Individual Welfare? An Exploration Based on Happiness Surveys from Latin America.* Center on Social and Economic Dynamics Working Paper, no. 38. Washington, DC: Brookings Institution.

Krueger, Anne O. 2002. 'Supporting globalization.' Remarks at the 2002 Eisenhower National Security Conference on 'National Security for the 21st Century: Anticipating Challenges, Seizing Opportunities, Building Capabilities', 26 September 2002. At www.imf.org/external/np/speeches/2002/092602a.htm.

Kuznets, Simon 1965. *Economic Growth and Structure: Selected Essays*. New Delhi: Oxford & IBH Publishing Company.

Lucas, Robert 1998. *'The Industrial Revolution: Past and Future.'* Mimeo: University of Chicago.

Maddison, Angus 1998. *Chinese Economic Performance in the Long Run*. Paris: OECD, Development Centre.

Maddison, Angus 2004. 'World population, GDP and GDP per capita, 1–2000 AD.' At http://www.ggdc.netrrnaddison.

Milanovic, Branko 2002. 'The Ricardian Vice: Why Sala-i-Martiri's Calculations of World Income Inequality are Wrong.' At SSRN: http://ssrn.com/abstract= 403020.

Milanovic, Branko 2005. *Worlds Apart: Global and International Inequality 1950–2000*. Princeton, NJ: Princeton University Press.

Mukand, Sharun and Rodrik, Dani 2002. "In Search of the Holy Grail: Policy Convergence, Experimentation, and Economic Performance." At http://ksghome.harvard.edui-drodrikjpapers.html.

Sachs, Jeffrey D. and Warner, Andrew M. 1997. "Fundamental Sources of Long-Run Growth." *American Economic Review*, Papers and Proceedings 87 (2), May 1997: 184–8.

Sala-i-Martin, Xavier 2002. 'The Disturbing "Rise" of Global Income Inequality." NBER Working Paper, no. 8904, April. At http://www.nber.orgtpapersjwssu-t.

World Bank 2002. *Globalization, Growth and Poverty: Building an Inclusive World Economy*. Policy Research Report. Washington, DC, and New York: World Bank and Oxford University Press.

32

The New Wave
of Globalization and
Its Economic Effects

A WORLD BANK POLICY RESEARCH REPORT

The following excerpt was taken from a World Bank Policy Research Report titled Globalization, Growth, and Poverty, *in which a report team describes three eras of globalization and their economic impact. The authors examine each era and try to determine what motivated globalization and which countries benefited and which did not. Like Giddens (Chapter 30), the World Bank report argues that the current round of globalization is distinct from the previous two rounds. It goes on to report that the third wave of globalization, which began around 1980, is more thorough and intrusive than the previous rounds.* ■

MOST DEVELOPING COUNTRIES HAVE TWO POTENTIAL SOURCES OF COMPARATIVE AD-vantage in international markets: abundant labor and abundant land. Before about 1870 neither of these potentials was realized and international trade was negligible.

The First Wave of Globalization: 1870–1914

The first wave of global integration, from 1870 to 1914, was triggered by a combination of falling transport costs, such as the switch from sail to steamships, and reductions in tariff barriers, pioneered by an Anglo-French

Excerpted from the World Bank Policy Research Report, *Globalization, Growth, and Poverty: Building an Inclusive World Economy* ((New York: World Bank and Oxford University Press, 2002). Reprinted with the permission of the World Bank.

agreement. Cheaper transport and the lifting of man-made barriers opened up the possibility of using abundant land. New technologies such as railways created huge opportunities for land-intensive commodity exports. The resulting pattern of trade was that land-intensive primary commodities were exchanged for manufactures. Exports as a share of world income nearly doubled to about 8 percent (Maddison 2001).

The production of primary commodities required people. Sixty million migrated from Europe to North America and Australia to work on newly available land. Because land was abundant in the newly settled areas, incomes were high and fairly equal, while the labor exodus from Europe lightened labor markets and raised wages both absolutely and relative to the returns on land. South-South labor flows were also extensive (though less well documented). Lindert and Williamson (2001b) speculate that the flows from densely populated China and India to less densely populated Sri Lanka, Burma, Thailand, the Philippines, and Vietnam were of the same order of magnitude as the movements from Europe to the Americas. That would make the total labor flows during the first wave of globalization nearly 10 percent of the world's population.

The production of primary commodities for export required not just labor but large amounts of capital. As of 1870 the foreign capital stock in developing countries was only about 9 percent of their income. However, institutions needed for financial markets were copied. These instructions, combined with the improvements in information permitted by the telegraph, enabled governments in developing countries to tap into the major capital markets. Indeed, during this period around half of all British savings were channeled abroad. By 1914 the foreign capital stock of developing countries had risen to 32 percent of their income.

Globally growth accelerated sharply. Per capita incomes, which had risen by 0.5 percent per year in the previous 50 years, rose by an annual average of 1.3 percent. Did this lead to more or less equality? The countries that participated in it often took off economically, both the exporters of manufactures, people and capital, and the importers. Argentina, Australia, New Zealand, and the United States became among the richest countries in the world by exporting primary commodities while importing people, institutions, and capital. All these countries left the rest of the world behind.

Between the globalizing countries themselves there was convergence. Mass migration was a major force equalizing incomes between them. Emigration is estimated to have raised Irish wages by 32 percent, Italian by 28 percent, and Norwegian by 10 percent. Immigration is estimated to have lowered Argentine wages by 22 percent, Australian by 15 percent, Canadian by 16 percent, and American by 8 percent. Indeed, migration was probably more important than either trade or capital movements (Lindert and Williamson 2001b).

The impact of globalization on inequality within countries depended in part on the ownership of land. Exports from developing countries were land-intensive primary commodities. Within developing countries this benefited predominantly the people who owned the land. Since most were colonies, landownership itself was subject to the power imbalance inherent in the colonial relationship. Where land ownership was concentrated, as in Latin America, increased trade could be associated with increased inequality. Where land was more equally owned, as in West Africa, the benefits of trade were spread more widely. Conversely in Europe, the region importing land-intensive goods, globalization ruined landowners.

For example, Cannadine (1990) describes the spectacular economic collapse of the English aristocracy between 1880 and 1914. In Europe the first wave of globalization also coincided with the establishment for the first time in history of the great legislative pillars of social protection-free mass education, worker insurance, and pensions (Gray 1998).

Ever since 1820—50 years before globalization—world income inequality as measured by the mean log deviation had started to increase drastically. This continued during the first wave of globalization. Despite widening world inequality, the unprecedented increase in growth reduced poverty as never before. In the 50 years before 1870, the incidence of poverty had been virtually constant, falling at the rate of just 0.3 percent per year. During the first globalization wave, the rate of decline more than doubled to 0.8 percent. Even this was insufficient to offset the increase in population growth, so that the absolute number of poor people increased.

The Retreat into Nationalism: 1914–1945

Technology continued to reduce transport costs: during the inter-war years sea freight costs fell by a third. However, trade policy went into reverse. As Mundell (2000) puts it: "The twentieth century began with a highly efficient international monetary system that was destroyed in World War 1, and its bungled re-creation in the inter-war period brought on the great depression." In turn, governments responded to depression by protectionism—a vain attempt to divert demand into their domestic markets. The United States led the way into the abyss: the Smoot-Hawley tariff, which led to retaliation abroad, was the first: between 1929 and 1933 U.S. imports fell by 30 percent and, significantly, exports fell even more, by almost 40 percent.

Globally, rising protectionism drove international trade back down. By 1950 exports as a share of world income were down to around 5 percent—roughly back to where it had been in 1870. Protectionism had undone 80 years of technical progress in transport.

During the retreat into nationalism capital markers fared even worse than merchandise markets. Most high-income countries imposed controls preventing the export of capital, and many developing countries defaulted on their liabilities. By 1950 the foreign capital stock of developing countries was reduced to just 4 percent of income—far below even the modest level of 1870.

Unsurprisingly, the retreat into nationalism produced anti-immigrant sentiment and governments imposed drastic restrictions on newcomers. For example, immigration to the United States declined from 15 million during 1870–1914 to 6 million between 1914 and 1950.

The massive retreat from globalization did not reverse the trend to greater world inequality. By 1950 the world was far less equal than it had been in 1914. Average incomes were, however, substantially lower than had the previous trend been maintained: the world rate of growth fell by about a third. The world's experiment with reversing globalization showed that it was entirely possible but not attractive. The economic historian Angus Maddison summarizes it thus: "Between 1913 and 1950 the world economy grew much more slowly than in 1870–1913, world trade grew much less than world income, and the degree of inequality between regions increased substantially" (Maddison 2001, p. 22).

The combination of a slowdown in growth and a continued increase in inequality sharply reduced the decline in the incidence of poverty—approximately back to what it had been in the period from 1820 to 1870. The decline in the incidence was now well below the rate of population growth, so that the absolute number of poor people increased by about 25 percent. Despite the rise in poverty viewed in terms of income, this was the great period of advances in life expectancy due to the global spread of improvements in public health. Poverty is multi-dimensional, and not all its aspects are determined by economic performance.

The Second Wave of Globalization: 1945–1980

The horrors of the retreat into nationalism gave an impetus to internationalism. The same sentiments that led to the founding of the United Nations persuaded governments to cooperate to reduce the trade barriers they had previously erected. However, trade liberalization was selective both in terms of which countries participated and which products were included. Broadly, by 1980 trade between developed countries in manufactured goods had been substantially freed of barriers, but barriers facing developing countries had been substantially removed only for those primary commodities that did not compete with agriculture in the developed countries. For agriculture and manufactures, developing countries faced severe barriers. Further, most developing countries erected barriers against each other and against developed countries.

The partial reduction in trade barriers was reinforced by continued reductions in transport costs: between 1950 and the late 1970s sea freight charges again fell by a third. Overall, trade doubled relative to world income, approximately recovering the level it had reached during the first wave of globalization. However, the resulting liberalization was very lopsided. For developing countries it restored the North-South pattern of trade—the exchange of manufactures for land-intensive primary commodities—but did not restore the international movements of capital and labor.

By contrast, for rich countries the second wave of globalization was spectacular. The lifting of barriers between them greatly expanded the exchange of manufactures. For the first time international specialization within manufacturing became important, allowing agglomeration and scale economies to be realized. This helped to drive up the incomes of the rich countries relative to the rest.

Economies of Agglomeration

The second wave introduced a new type of trade: rich country specialization in manufacturing niches that gained productivity from agglomerated clusters. Most trade between developed countries became determined not by comparative advantage based on differences in factor endowments but by cost savings from agglomeration and scale. Because such cost savings are quite specific to each activity, although each individual industry became more and more concentrated geographically industry as a whole remained very widely dispersed to avoid costs of congestion.

Firms cluster together, some producing the same thing and others connected by vertical linkages (Fujita, Krugman, and Venables 1999). Japanese auto companies, for example, are well known for wanting certain of their parts suppliers to locate within a short distance of the main assembly plant. As Sutton (2000) describes it: "Two-thirds of manufacturing output consists of intermediate goods, sold by one firm to another. The presence of a rich network of manufacturing firms provides a positive externality to each firm in the system, allowing it to acquire inputs locally, thus reducing the costs of transport, of coordination, of monitoring and of contracting."

Clustering enables greater specialization and thus raises productivity. In turn, it depends upon the ability to trade internationally at low cost. The classic statement of this was indeed Adam Smith's: "The division of labor is limited only by the extent of the market" (*The Wealth of Nations*). Smith argued that a larger market permits a finer division of labor, which in turn facilitates innovation. For example, Sokoloff (1988) shows that as the Erie Canal progressed westward in the first half of the 19th century, patent registrations rose county by county as the canal reached them. This pattern suggests that ideas that were already in people's heads became economically viable through access to a larger market.

However, while agglomeration economies are good news for those in the clusters, they are bad news for those left out. A region may be uncompetitive simply because not enough firms have chosen to locate there. As a result "a 'divided world' may emerge, in which a network of manufacturing firms is clustered in some 'high wage' region, while wages in the remaining regions stay low" (Sutton 2000).

Firms will not shift to a new location until the gap in production costs becomes wide enough to compensate for the loss of agglomeration economies. Yet once firms start to relocate, the movement becomes a cascade: as firms rebase to the new location, it starts to benefit from agglomeration economies.

During the second globalization wave most developing countries did not participate in the growth of global manufacturing and services trade.

The combination of persistent trade barriers in developed countries, and poor investment climates and anti-trade policies in developing countries, confined them to dependence on primary commodities. Even by 1980 only 25 percent of the merchandise exports of developing countries were manufactured goods.

Cascades of relocation did occur during the second wave but they were to low-wage areas within developed countries. For example, until 1950 the U.S. textile industry was clustered in the high-wage Northeast. The cost pressure for it to relocate built up gradually as northern wages rose and as institutions and infrastructure improved in southern states. Within a short period in the 1950s the whole industry relocated to the Carolinas.

The Effect on Inequality and Poverty

During globalization's second wave there were effectively two trading systems: the old North-South system, and the new intra-North system. The intra-North system was quite powerfully equalizing: lower-income industrial countries caught up with higher-income ones. Figure 32.1 shows this pattern of long-term convergence among OECD economies.

Second-wave globalization coincided with the growth of policies for redistribution and social protection within developed societies. Not only did inequalities reduce between countries—probably an effect of globalization—but inequality was reduced within countries, probably as a result of these social programs. [Figure 1.5 in the original text] shows the dramatic reduction both in between-country and within-country inequality that occurred in developed countries during the period. The second wave of globalization was thus spectacularly successful in reducing poverty within the OECD countries. Rapid growth coincided with greater equity, both to an extent without precedent. For the industrial world it is often referred to as the "golden age."

Second-wave globalization was not golden for developing countries. Although per capita income growth recovered from the inter-war slowdown, it was substantially slower than in the rich economies. The number of poor peo-

Figure 32.1   Long-Term Convergence Among OECD Countries

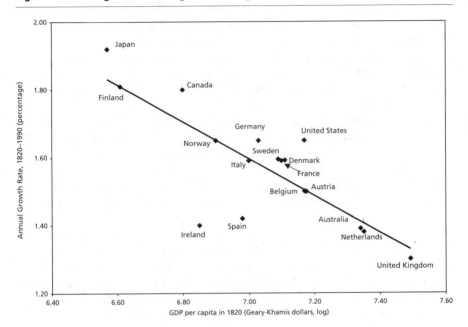

ple continued to rise. Non-income dimensions of poverty improved—notably rising life expectancy and rising school enrollments. In terms of equity, within developing countries in aggregate there was little change either between countries or within them. As a group, developing countries were being left behind by developed countries.

World inequality was thus the sum of three components: greater equity within developed countries, greater inequality between developed and developing countries, and little net change in developing countries. The net effect of these three very different components was broadly no change. World inequality was about the same in the late 1970s as it had been a quarter of a century earlier.

What Have Been the Effects of Third-Wave Globalization on Income Distribution and Poverty?

The breakthrough of developing countries into global markets for manufactures and services, and the re-emergence of migration and capital flows, have affected poverty and the distribution of income between and within countries. Domestic policy choices unrelated to globalization also affect income distribution.

Among developed countries globalization has continued to generate the convergence of the first and second waves. By 1995 inequality between countries was less than half what it had been in 1960 and substantially less than it had been in 1980. However, as Figure 32.2 shows, there was a serious offsetting increase in inequality within individual countries, reversing the trend seen during the second wave. A part of this may have been due to immigration. However, it may also have been due to policy changes on taxation and social spending unconnected to globalization. Global economic integration is consistent with wide differences in domestic distributional policies: inequality differs massively between equally globalized economies. For the OECD economies taken as a whole, localization has probably been equalizing as inequality between countries has radically decreased.

Among the new globalizers the same pattern of convergence has been evident as has occurred among the OECD economies over a longer period. Sachs and Warner (1995) find that this is indeed a general phenomenon among open economies. Treating the OECD and the new globalizers as a common group of integrated economies, overall inequality has declined.

As in the OECD countries, within-country inequality has increased in the new globalizers. However, this is entirely due to the rise in inequality in China, which alone accounts for one-third of the population of the new globalizers. China started its modernization with an extremely equal distribution of income

Figure 32.2   Household Inequality in the Developing World, 1960–1980

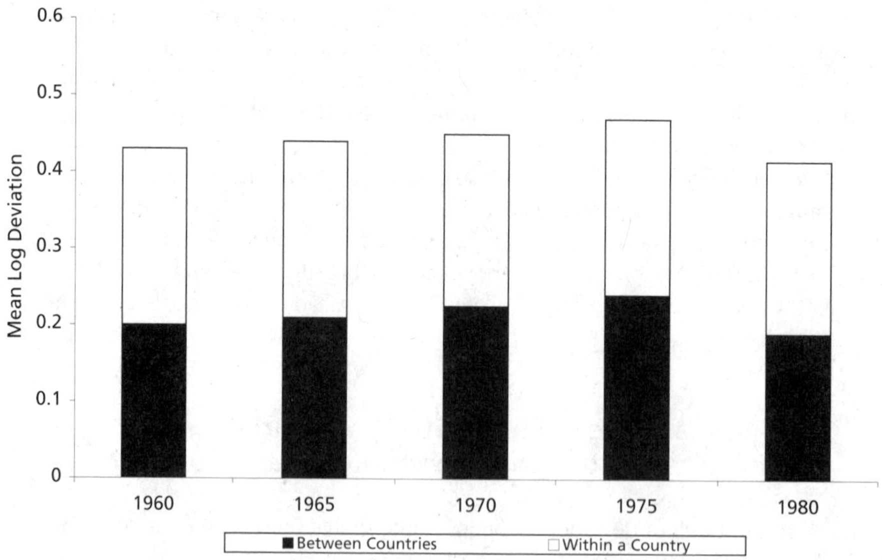

Source: Clark, Dollar, and Kraay (2001).

and extremely high poverty. Intra-rural inequality in China has actually decreased. The big growth in inequality has been between the rural areas and the rising urban agglomerations, and between those provinces with agglomerations and those without them.

A closer investigation of the changes in inequality within countries is provided in Dollar and Kraay (2001a) and Ravallion (forthcoming). There are substantial difficulties in comparing income distribution data across countries. Countries differ in the concept measured (income versus consumption), the measure of income (gross versus net), the unit of observation (individuals versus households), and the coverage of the survey (national versus subnational). Dollar and Kraay restrict attention to distribution data based on nationally representative sources identified as high-quality by Deininger and Squire (1996), and perform some simple adjustments to control for differences in the types of surveys. These data cover a total of 137 countries. They focus on what has happened to the income of the poorest 20 percent of the population. They find that on average there is a one-to-one relationship between the growth rate of income of the poor and the growth rate of average income in society. However, there is much variation around that average relationship. They then investigate whether changes in trade account for any of this variation. They find no relationship between changes in openness and changes in inequality, whether openness is measured by the share of trade in income, the Sachs-Warner measure of openness, average tariff rates, or capital controls. Ravallion qualifies this result. He finds that although on average openness does not affect inequality, in low-income countries it is associated with greater inequality. Regardless of its net effect, there are winners and losers from trade policies.

The combination of rapid growth with no systematic change in inequality has dramatically reduced absolute poverty in the new globalizing countries. Between 1993 and 1998 (the most recent period for which we have data) the number of people in absolute poverty declined by 14 percent to 762 million. For them, the third wave of globalization is indeed the golden age. Poverty is predominantly rural. As the new globalizers have broken into world markets their pace of industrialization and urbanization has increased. People have taken the opportunity to migrate from risky and impoverished rural livelihoods to less vulnerable and better paid jobs in towns and cities. Not only has poverty declined viewed in terms of income, but other dimensions of poverty have rapidly improved. Both average years of schooling and life expectancy have improved to levels close or equal to levels reached by the rich countries in 1960. Vietnam illustrates this experience. As it has integrated into the world economy, it has had a large increase in per capita income and no significant change in inequality. The income of the poor has risen dramatically, and the level of absolute poverty has dropped sharply from 75 percent of the population in 1988 to 37 percent in 1998. Poverty was cut in half in only 10 years. We can be unusually confident of this information because a representative household survey was conducted early in the reform process (1992–93), and the same 5,000 households were visited again six years later. Of the poorest 5 percent of households in 1992, 98 percent had higher incomes six years later. Vietnam was unusually successful in entering global markets for labor-intensive products such as footwear, and the increased employment might be expected to benefit poor households. Uganda had a similar experience: dramatic poverty reduction and no increase in inequality.

While the more globalized economies grew and converged, the less globalized developing economies declined and diverged. Their growth experience was worse than during the second wave, but their divergence has been long-standing. Ades and Glaeser (1999) find that at least since 1960, less globalized developing countries, defined by the share of trade in income, have tended to diverge. Decline and divergence had severe consequences for poverty in its various dimensions. Between 1993 and 1998 the number of people in absolute poverty in the less globalized developing countries rose by 4 percent to 437 million. Not only were per capita incomes falling, but in many countries life expectancy and school enrollments declined.

During the second wave of globalization the rich countries diverged from the poor countries, a trend that had persisted for a century. During the third wave the new globalizers have started to catch up with the rich countries, while the weak globalizers are falling further behind.

The changes in the overall distribution of world income and the number of poor people are thus the net outcomes of offsetting effects. Among rich countries there has been convergence: the less rich countries have caught up with the richest, while within some rich countries there has been rising inequality. Among the new globalizers there has also been convergence and falling poverty. Within China there has also been rising inequality, but not on average elsewhere. Between the rich countries and the new globalizers there has been convergence. Between all these groups and the weak globalizers there has been divergence. The net effect is that the long trend of rising global inequality and rising numbers of people in absolute poverty has been halted and even reversed. Bourguignon and Morrisson (2001) estimate that the number of people in absolute poverty fell by about 100 million between 1980 and 1992 (the endpoint of their analysis). Chen and Ravallion (2001) estimate that there was a further fall of about 100 million between 1993 (the closest date for comparison) and 1998. Thus, globalization clearly can be a force for poverty reduction.

References

Ades, A., and E. Glaeser. 1999. "Evidence on Growth, Increasing Returns, and the Extent of the Market." *Quarterly Journal of Economics* 114(3): 1025–46.

Bourguignon, F., and C. Morrisson. 2001. "Inequality Among World Citizens: 1820–1992." Working Paper 2001-25, DELTA, Paris.

Cannadine, David. 1990. *The Decline and Fall of the British Aristocracy.* New Haven, CT: Yale University Press.

Clark, X., D. Dollar, and A. Kraay. 2001. "Decomposing Global Inequality, 1960–1999." World Bank, Washington, D.C.

Deininger, K., and L. Squire. 1996. "A New Data Set Measuring Income Inequality." *The World Bank Economic Review* 10(3): 565–91.

Fujita, M. P. Krugman, and A. J. Venables. 1999. *The Spatial Economy: Cities, Regions, and International Trade.* Cambridge, MA: MIT Press.

Gray, J. 1998. *False Dawn: The Delusions of Global Capitalism.* London, Great Britain: Granta Books.

Kraay, A. 1999. "Exports and Economic Performance: Evidence from a Panel of Chinese Enterprises." *Revue d'Economie du Développement* (1–2): 183–207.

Lindert, P., and J. Williamson. 2001a. "Does Globalization Make the World More Unequal?" National Bureau of Economic Research Working Paper No. 8228, National Bureau of Economic Research, Cambridge, MA.

———. 2001b. "Globalization: A Long History." Paper prepared for the Annual Bank Conference on Development and Economics–Europe Conference. World Bank, Europe–Barcelona. June 25–27.

Maddison, Angus. 2001. *The World Economy: A Millennial Perspective.* Paris: Organization for Economic Co-operation and Development.

Mundell, R. 2000. "A Reconsideration of the Twentieth Century." *American Economic Review* 90(3): 327–40.

Ravallion, M. Forthcoming. "Growth, Inequality, and Poverty: Looking Beyond Averages." *World Development.*

Sachs, J. D., and A. Warner. 1995. "Economic Reform and the Process of Global Integration." *Brookings Papers on Economic Activity* 1(96): 1–118.

Sokoloff, K. 1988. "Inventive Activity in Early Industrial America: Evidence from Patent Records." *Journal of Economic History* XLVIII (4): 813–50.

Sutton, J. 2000. "Rich Trade, Scarce Capabilities: Industrial Development Revisited." Discussion Paper No. EI/28 (Sept.), London School of Economics and Political Science, London, United Kingdom.

PART 9

Conclusion

33

Inequality in a Global Perspective: Directions for Further Research

Mitchell A. Seligson

Where do we go from here? The reader of this volume now clearly knows that there is a vast gap between the world's rich and its poor. While the debates are far from concluded, almost fifty years of research has given us some clear answers to the causes and trends in the gaps between rich and poor. Indeed, it can be said that research in this area represents one of the best illustrations of a cumulative social science continually deepening its understanding of a complex problem. In this concluding chapter I suggest some directions for future research so that continued rapid progress can be made in our understanding of the problem.

Evolution of Research on the Gaps

With each passing day, there is growing evidence that inequality in income, both within and between countries, is failing to disappear or even diminish. Whereas classical economic theory predicted that all countries would evolve, in stages, toward universal prosperity, we know that this has not happened. Hundreds of millions of people live in abject poverty, while the number of the world's multibillionaires seems to grow each passing day. Some of the best research in the field—included in this volume—has provided some very clear explanations for the trend.

Early thinking focused on the cultural distinctiveness of the Third World. The observation that these cultures were indeed different from those found in the First World of industrial capitalist development was enough to convince a generation of social scientists to view cultural barriers as the principal explanation for underdevelopment. Many of these explanations were extraordinarily intriguing, showed creative scholarship, and, moreover, seemed to make a good deal of sense. As research proceeded, however, disenchantment with this perspective began to grow. The more that was known about the Third World, the less cultural factors seemed to be able to explain its underdevelopment. Many researchers found the explanation ethnocentric at best and insulting at worst. Studies also revealed many instances of a single "underdeveloped culture" producing vastly different developmental outcomes; wide variation was observed within supposedly monolithic cultures. In addition, people proved highly capable of tailoring their cultures to conform to more "modern" ways of doing things. Cultures proved to be far more malleable and responsive than had been originally believed. Finally, despite putative cultural limitations, some Third World nations made rapid strides in economic growth; some middle-income countries, for example, have been able to achieve higher growth rates in recent years than many industrialized countries. Yet, in recent years the debate on the impact of culture on development has become quite lively, and the empirical research reported in this volume in Chapter 20 shows that values might matter. This entire paradigm of thinking is reflected by Francis Fukuyama (1995a, 1995b), who has argued for the importance of trust in development. More recently, Lawrence Harrison and Samuel P. Huntington have edited a book called *Culture Matters: How Values Shape Human Progress* (Harrison and Huntington 2002) that collects a great deal of scholarship on this point. The debate has become more technical as a series of quantitative studies have attempted to reinvigorate the study of culture (Inglehart 1988, 1990) and other studies that have challenged this approach (Booth and Seligson 1984; Seligson and Booth 1993). One of the most recent empirical studies on the subject is included in this volume in Chapter 20. That article by Ronald Inglehart and his collaborators was strongly refuted, however, by Robert Jackman and Ross Miller (Jackman and Miller 1996a, 1996b) in an article on the subject, and I have criticized the entire approach elsewhere (Seligson 2002). Most recently, as shown by Gregory Clark (Chapter 10), certain cultural values related to education and hard work may be concentrated in certain populations and not others. According to Clark the Industrial Revolution is the outcome, a revolution that dramatically widened the gap between rich and poor nations.

Whatever their explanatory power, cultural explanations no longer dominate the field, and as a result, other theories have emerged. Increasingly, thinking about development has become "globalized." The very nature of the gap problem probably forced such thinking to emerge. After all, in order to study the gap, one must first specify the frame of reference in some sort of comparative perspective. Studies can focus on the absolute or relative gap, but these terms have no meaning unless they are situated within a comparative framework; poor people are poor only with respect to rich people.

In this book extensive consideration has been given to the "inverted U curve" of development. In global terms, according to Kuznets (Chapter 11) and other proponents of this thesis, developing nations are likely to experience a widening internal gap before they see the gap narrow in the later phases of industrialization. Dependency and world-system thinkers agree that the gaps are widening but do not believe that they will ultimately narrow as industrialization matures because both the widening internal and the widening external gaps between rich and poor are seen as a function of the world capitalist economic system.

The studies by John Passé-Smith (Chapters 2 and 5) suggest strongly that the gaps are very wide and continue to widen with each passing decade. Yet, the controversy presented in Part 4 of this book—between those who argue that the economies of the world are on a path toward convergence and those who argue that the gaps are widening—shows that the issue has still not been resolved.

This disagreement has led some to examine more closely key cases of dependency and development. Heather-Jo Hammer and John Gartrell (Chapter 22) show that dependency is not confined to poor nations but seems to affect Canada as well, and Denis O'Hearn (Chapter 23) shows that it has an impact on Ireland. Yet, the masterful analysis by Glenn Firebaugh (Chapter 4) shows that much of the slowed growth reportedly caused by dependency (as argued by Andre Gunder Frank, Chapter 21) comes from a serious misreading of the data. Like the culture paradigm before it, dependency and world-systems thinking no longer seem to offer *the* explanation for the gaps between rich and poor.

The current attention is focused on the role of institutions, policies, and the state, and some of the key thinking in that area is contained in the contributions in Part 7 of this volume. Mancur Olson's careful comparison (Chapter 25) of cases such as North Korea versus South Korea, in which culture, history, and resources are largely held constant and what varies are the political system and the policies they make, presents a strong case that countries are not prisoners of their pasts or their environments but can make good or bad choices. Some states choose a capitalist route but then engage in "rent-seeking" behavior that enables privileged groups to benefit from state policies while producing an overall negative impact on the national level of economic development. The contribution by Michael Lipton (Chapter 27) shows how rent-seeking has a pernicious impact on development. Rent-seeking states, therefore, seem bad for economic growth. At the same time, however, the democratic versus authoritarian nature of the state seems to make little difference in growth. For a long time it was thought that dictatorships do better than democracies, and that allowed such highly regarded scholars as Samuel P. Huntington to suggest that in order to get development, one needs to pass through a protected period of strongman rule. Yet, as Adam Przeworski and Fernando Limongi show in Chapter 28, dictatorships seem no better at stimulating economic development than do democracies. Indeed, in other work by this team, it has been shown that democracies do better on a per capita basis than dictatorships, and Erich Weede has found that democracies produce more stable growth than do dictatorships (Weede and Tiefenbach 1981). What does seem to be true, however, is that investment in human capital in the form of education and health really does spur growth and stem inequality (see Nancy Birdsall and Richard Sabot, Chapter 29).

Considerable data have been brought to bear on the various theories seeking to explain these dual gaps. It is in the analysis and interpretation of these data that we see the clearest example of cumulative social science in the making. This book presents some of the best examples of rigorous testing of theory with data. While it is too early to predict a definitive resolution of the debates, and it may be even too early to say which side seems to have the edge, it is possible to look ahead and suggest some directions for future research. A pessimistic interpretation of the present state of the debate is that each side is locked into its own respective position and that future research will be stalemated. The vital importance of the problem, not only to the world's poor but to those responsible for helping to secure peace, requires that such a stalemate be avoided. It is therefore appropriate at this juncture to assess where research has taken us and where it ought to go. The contributions in this volume trace the intellectual history of the debate over the gaps; the remainder of this chapter is devoted to outlining the directions in which fruitful further research might proceed.

The International Gap

By the early 1980s, in GNP per capita terms, a small group of oil-exporting nations enjoyed incomes higher than the average income found among industrial market economies. In 1981 Saudi Arabia had a GNP per capita of $12,600; Kuwait, $20,900; and the United Arab Emirates, $24,660; while the mean income of the industrial market economies was $11,120. None of the industrialized countries even came close to exceeding the income of Kuwait and the United Arab Emirates; Switzerland had $17,430, the highest GNP per capita of the industrial countries. The United States, traditionally the world's GNP per capita leader, was far behind at $12,820. Oil-rich Libya was moving up rapidly, with its per capita GNP reaching $8,450, only slightly behind that of the United Kingdom ($9,110).

Yet, we now know that much of the dramatic increase in the GNP of the oil states was a short-term phenomenon owing to the sharp price rises of petroleum in the 1970s. By 2001 the World Bank (2003, 234–235) was reporting that Saudi Arabia had income per capita of only $7,230, compared to the United States, with $34,870. Kuwait, still recovering from the Gulf War, had declined to a GNP of $18,030.

The rapid growth and equally rapid decline of the oil states, however, are the exception to the rule. As John Passé-Smith has shown in Chapter 2 of this volume, there is very little movement over the long term, from rich to poor and vice versa. While South Korea, Taiwan, and Malaysia, for example, have been rapidly growing, they have incomes that are only a fraction of those found in the industrialized countries. Consider China, which has had very strong growth for over ten years: the per capita income was only $2,010 in 2007, versus the United States at $44,970. In GNP per capita terms, it seems clear, there is a near-universal widening gap between rich and poor.

This conclusion, however, is based on a single indicator, namely GNP per capita, recently renamed by the World Bank as gross national income (GNI). The use of a single indicator of any social phenomenon has long fallen into disrepute in the social sciences. Why then base conclusions about such an important subject entirely on per capita income data? The response to this query from those who use it in their research as a sole indicator of income is that it is by far the most widely accepted indicator. The principal problem emerges not because of the unreliability of data collected on each nation but because of validity problems associated with converting local currency values into dollars using exchange rates, the standard currency normally employed by those who compare such data.

In order to convert the multitude of currencies used around the world into a single standard, it has long been common practice to use the exchange rate of the foreign currency in US dollars. The exchange rate appeared for a long time to be the only reasonable way to compare the value of different currencies. In fact, however, it is now known that such comparisons introduce considerable distortion in the data. The exchange-rate comparisons do not accurately measure differences in the relative domestic purchasing power of currencies. The net result is that the exchange-rate GNP measures can greatly exaggerate the gap between rich and poor countries. This exaggeration occurs in part because international exchange rates are susceptible to fluctuations from equilibrium value. In addition, according to the "law of one price," the cost of goods and services that are traded (among countries) tends to equalize. For a developing country in which most of the production does not enter the world trade market, the exchange-rate-converted GNP figures will be an underestimate of true income.

In order to correct for this bias, the United Nations has undertaken the International Comparisons Project, which has provided some revealing findings. Using purchasing power figures (called PPP) rather than exchange rates, Passé-Smith (Chapter 5) finds that the gap is less expansive than it is when measured with exchange-rate-converted GNPs, but it is still considerable. For some countries the change was large; for example, a country like Sri Lanka exhibits a gap nearly four times as large when the traditional measure is used as when the new purchasing power index is computed. Countries such as Colombia and Mexico also reveal considerable differences, although these differences are not as great as in the case of Sri Lanka. Because of these shifts, the appendix of this book provides PPP figures as well as GNI figures.

It would seem appropriate to suggest that future research on the international gap employ the purchasing power index rather than the exchange-rate-based comparison in order to obtain a truer picture of income comparisons. This is what Firebaugh does in Chapter 4 of this volume. When measured with purchasing-power-converted GNPs, the gap remains, though it is slightly smaller overall. Hence, despite the dramatic narrowing of the international gap in the case of Sri Lanka, as noted previously, even when using the purchasing power index, that country's income per capita in 2006 was only 8 percent of that of the United States. Kenya, in which the GNP per capita is more than quadrupled with the new index, still confronts income levels that are only 3.3 percent of those of the United States, according to the World Bank. The revised measure, therefore, does not eliminate the gap between rich and poor. It does, however, provide what appears to be a more appropriate standard of comparison. The mere fact that the gap narrows through the use of the new index does not necessarily imply that there is an overall trend toward a narrowing of the international gap. Fortunately, the World Bank now annually reports these purchasing power parity measures online.

Another way of looking at the gap question is to shift the focus away from per capita income measures and to look at human needs and human development instead. Using this criterion, one obtains a rather different perspective on the international gap question. According to studies conducted by the World Bank (1980, 32–45), major strides have been made in the reduction of absolute poverty since the close of World War II. These studies have found that the proportion of people around the world living in absolute poverty has declined. In addition, there has been a worldwide increase in literacy levels such that over the past thirty years, literacy in low-income countries has increased from 30 percent to 63 percent of the population. Even more dramatic improvements have been experienced in the area of health. Infant mortality rates have dropped considerably, and life expectancy has been extended. For example, citizens of low-income countries in 1950 had a life expectancy of only 35.2 years, whereas by 2005 that had risen to 59 years.

Research on the international gap more consciously directed at these indicators of basic human needs may provide a clearer picture of the impact of the gap than that presented by income figures alone. But before one leaps to the conclusion that the human needs approach can demonstrate that the gap is narrowing, some additional context needs to be added to the discussion. While it is true that the *proportion* of people who are experiencing improved education, health, and life expectancy has increased, the absolute number of poor people in the world has increased dramatically because of high birthrates in the developing world. Hence, the World Bank (1980, 35) estimated that despite the increases in the levels of literacy, the number of illiterate people had grown by some 100 million since 1950. And by 1995, in the low-income countries of the world alone, the number of illiterate adults had grown to 1.1 billion compared to 800 million in 1980 (World Bank 1980, 110; 1995, 214). Moreover, there is increasing evidence that the quality of education in much of the developing world outside of East Asia lags far behind that found in the industrialized countries. The quality gap is especially acute in secondary and higher education, where technical advances are so very rapid and the cost of obtaining modern training equipment is ever more expensive. It is increasingly difficult for developing countries to adequately train their young people for the skills they need to compete in the high-technology world of today.

The education gap has two particularly pernicious implications. First, the increasing frustration that the brightest youngsters face in developing countries as a result of antiquated equipment and poorly prepared teachers results in an increasing tendency for them to migrate to the industrialized nations. Hence, the problem of the "brain-drain" is a growing one, one that promises to continue to adversely affect the ability of poor nations to develop as they steadily lose that sector of their population with the greatest intellectual potential. Second, the high-technology nature of contemporary society seems to be creating a higher and more impenetrable barrier between rich and poor countries. The efficiency of modern manufacturing techniques along with the requirement of exceptional precision in manufacturing makes it more and more difficult for developing nations to compete with the industrialized nations. The price advantage that developing nations have as a result of their considerably lower labor costs remains an advantage only for those items that require relatively low technical inputs. Hence, the proliferation of in-bond industries (i.e., maquiladoras) in Latin America, where consumer goods are assembled for re-export, only highlights the gap in technology since nearly all of the machinery and a good deal of the managerial skill used in those factories are imported from the industrialized nations. Even without tariff barriers the Third World faces a growing gap in technology that is serving to reinforce the income gap.

In sum, the use of improved income measures and basic needs data provides important avenues of research for those who wish to study the international income gap. A look at some of these data gives reason for optimism that conditions in poor countries are improving. At the same time, however, there is little reason to believe that the international income gap is narrowing. In fact, it would appear that each passing day finds the world inhabited by a larger *number* of people who live in absolute poverty, even though the *proportion* of the world's population in absolute poverty may be declining. This gap, then, seems to remain the single most serious problem confronting the family of nations, and it cries out for the attention of policymakers.

The Internal Gap

However problematical the reliability, validity, and availability of data on the international gap, they present an even more formidable barrier to the study of the internal gap. The empirical testing of dependency/world-system explanations for the internal gap has produced widely varying results. Any reader of the major social science journals today would be rightly confused by the varied findings reported in the frequently appearing articles on this subject. In reviewing this growing body of research, Edward N. Muller (1993) has pointed out a number of the weaknesses of those articles and goes a long way toward correcting many of them. Nonetheless, there are at least four chronic problems that beset macrolevel empirical tests of internal gap theories and that may ultimately lead down a blind alley of inconclusive findings even after the "best" methodology has been applied.

The first difficulty plaguing these macroanalytical investigations concerns sample skewing. Inequality data are difficult to obtain because many nations do not collect them (or at least do not publicly acknowledge that they do), a problem noted in several of the chapters included in this volume. In spite of the availability problem, researchers have proceeded with the data that are available, following the time-honored tradition in the social sciences of making do with what one finds rather than postponing research indefinitely. While such a procedure is often justifiable in many research situations, one wonders if it is justifiable in this one. The principal reason for expressing this cautionary note is that it is probably not the case that the countries reporting income distribution data are a random sample of all nations. Rather, one suspects that there are at least two factors that tend to skew the sample. First, the poorest, least developed nations often do not have the resources (financial and technical) to conduct such studies, and indeed there may not even arise the need for such data to be collected in some of these nations. Second, nations in which the income distributions are very badly skewed are probably reluctant to authorize the collection of such data, and even if the data are collected, governments may not make them publicly available. Hence, the data we do have may reflect a sample that has fewer cases of the poorest nations and fewer cases of highly unequal distribution than one might expect if the sample were random.

The second major problem with macroanalytical investigations is a direct outgrowth of the first. I call this problem the "Mauritania effect," that is, the dramatic differences in regression results that are produced from the inclusion or exclusion of as few as one or two countries. In one investigation, for example, the inclusion of Mauritania, with a population of only 2.8 million people, had a major impact on the results of a key regression equation. The findings, therefore, tend not to be robust when minor variations in sample design occur; one's confidence in the results, therefore, is shaken. An unusually frank comment by a proponent of macroanalytical investigations of this type is contained in an article coauthored by Erich Weede: "it seems impossible to predict with any confidence what would happen if inequality data on all or about twice as many countries were to become available" (Weede and Tiefenbach 1981).

The third problem concerns the general lack of cross-time data. However limited the sample of countries may be for the present period, even less reliable information exists on developing countries for the pre–World War II period. This is a particularly serious problem since both dependency/world-system analysis and the traditional developmental approach propose longitudinal hypotheses, whereas data limitations generally impose cross-sectional designs. While such cross-sectional designs can sometimes be a useful surrogate for longitudinal studies, the problem of skewed samples reduces the value of these studies.

One serious manifestation of the lack of longitudinal data emerges in studies that include Latin American cases. As a region, Latin America is more developed than most Third World nations and not surprisingly has somewhat more income distribution data available than other Third World regions. It is also the case that Latin American nations have been found to exhibit comparatively high levels of both dependency and income inequality. One might leap to the conclusion, as some have, that this proves that inequality is a function of dependency. However, there is another equally appealing thesis: that inequality in Latin America is part of a corporatist bureaucratic/authoritarian political culture considered to be characteristic of the region. One does not know, therefore, if Latin America's comparatively high level of inequality is a function of its intermediate level of development (as Kuznets, Chapter 11, would suggest), or its dependency (as the dependency/world-system proponents would suggest; see Part 6), or its culture (Part 5). To determine which of these hypotheses is correct would require longitudinal data to explore the dynamics of dependency, development, and inequality.

A final difficulty with the macroanalytical research is that there is no meeting of the minds as to suitable standards of verifiability. For example, there is a wide gulf separating many dependency/world-system theorists on the one hand, and those researchers who seek to test their hypotheses with quantitative data on the other. F. Cardoso and E. Faletto (1979), whose book on dependency theory is among the most influential and highly respected works on the subject (see Packenham 1982, 131–132), argue that empirical tests of dependency theory have largely missed the target. Cardoso (1977, 23 n12) explains that this is so because the tests have been "ahistorical." In addition, although not rejecting empirical verification as useful, he questions the validity of many of these studies, even those sustaining the dependency approach. Finally, in the preface to the English edition of their book, Cardoso and Faletto argue that "statistical information and demonstrations are useful and necessary. But the crucial questions for demonstration are of a different nature" (Cardoso and Faletto 1979, xiii). The thrust of the demonstrations proposed are ones heavily grounded in historical detail and therefore highlight all the more the problem of the lack of longitudinal income distribution data.

In the coming years, it is likely that many more macroanalytical empirical investigations will be published and will continue to add to our understanding. However, it is difficult to imagine how the four major problems enumerated previously will be overcome entirely. Given the difficulties apparently inherent (to a greater or lesser degree) in the macroanalytical studies conducted to date, more attention needs to be paid to methodologies that will examine from a microanalytic perspective the question of the origin of domestic inequality. In concluding an extensive review of the dependency/world-system literature, G. Palma (1981, 413) argues for micro-studies of "specific situations in concrete terms." And the study by V. Bornschier, C. Chase-Dunn, and R. Rubinson (1978) concludes by arguing for microsociological studies that would "clarify the specific mechanisms by which these processes operate."

Problems of data availability need not cause the abandonment of future studies of the internal gap. Rather, a series of microanalytical studies would seem like a promising alternative. Such investigations would make it possible to trace the ways in which inequality is stimulated in developing countries. The emphasis needs to be placed on drawing the explicit links, if they exist, between income distribution and factors such as culture, dependency, rent-seeking, urban bias, and so on. Indeed, it can be argued that even if the data problems were not as serious as they in fact are, and if macroanalytical empirical research were to demonstrate unequivocally the existence of a connection between, for example, culture and domestic inequality, one would still need to understand *how* one affects the other, something that cannot be known from the macro-studies. Without knowing how the process works, it is not possible to recommend policy "cures."

Some research has already been published that opens the door to this type of analysis. Studies of transnational corporations in Colombia (Chudnowsky 1974) and Brazil (Evans 1979; Newfarmer 1980) reveal much about the internal dynamics of dependency. A more recent micro-study, however, has demonstrated that imperialist penetration in one African state, Yorubaland, at the end of the nineteenth century produced a "vibrant and creative" reaction on the part of Yoruba traders in response to new opportunities in the international market (Laitin 1982, 702).

These microanalytical studies, helpful though they are in beginning to penetrate the "black box," reflect weaknesses that would need to be overcome by those seeking to test the various explanations of income inequality proposed in this volume. First, these detailed case studies, while providing a wealth of rich, descriptive material, betray all of the limitations of generalizability inherent in the case study method. It is to be hoped, of course, that the accumulation of these various cases ultimately will lead to a synthesis; but given the widely divergent methods, time periods, and databases employed in these studies, it is unclear at this juncture if such optimism is warranted. What is clear is that if a cumulative social science is to continue to emerge in this field, future research will need to be not only microanalytical but self-consciously comparative as well. Only by applying the comparative method at the outset of a study of the internal causes of inequality will the data generated allow immediate comparisons and subsequent theory testing.

Recently, as discussed by the authors of Part 7 of this volume, policies and institutions have seemed to be crucial factors in explaining the gap. Over the long term, "good" institutions seem to powerfully explain high growth in some countries, while "bad" institutions explain slow growth in other countries. Among the key institutions that seem to matter are private property rights. States that guarantee such rights have citizens who invest for the long term. When those rights are in doubt, quick profits and a lack of investment for the long term are the outcome. But, how do such institutions come into being, and why are some resilient while others disappear? These are the questions that require micro-level analysis.

In sum, an appropriate study ought to be (1) microanalytical, (2) comparative, and (3) capable of testing the relative merits of competing paradigms. That certainly is a tall order for any researcher, but one way to achieve this goal and still plan a project of manageable proportions is to focus on key institutions through which dependency mechanisms are thought to operate. In an effort to accomplish this task, one study analyzed exchange-rate policies as the "linch-pin" that helps "uncover the mechanisms through which these various [dependency] effects occur" (Moon 1982, 716). A major advance of this study over previous work is the explicit linking of dependency effects to particular policies of Third World governments. Hence, the analysis goes far beyond most dependency literature, which typically makes frequent reference to the so-called internal colonialist *comprador* elite without revealing precisely how such elites affect income distribution. Studies such as B. E. Moon's, which examine the impact of other such crucial linchpins through which dependency is thought to operate, are to be encouraged.

Two efforts, therefore, need to be made if one is to hope for the advancement of the debate beyond its present state. First, historians need to assist those working in this field to develop measures of income distribution for prior epochs. Creative use of historical records (e.g., tax roles, property registers, census data, etc.) might permit the reconstruction of such information. This, in turn, would provide the longitudinal data that are so sadly lacking at this time. John H. Coatsworth (1993) has already done precisely this for Latin America, and the payoffs of his approach are evident since he seems to have been able to refute dependency theory and make a case for the role of institutions on development and underdevelopment. William Glade (1996) has recently extended this argument. Second, once the historical data have been gathered, social scientists need to direct their attention to the various linchpins of the causes of growth and inequality and study them in a comparative context. Perhaps with these two efforts under way, significant advances are possible in a relatively short period of time.

Conclusions

The research presented in this volume was not written in a vacuum. Investigators study problems such as the gap between rich and poor because they are concerned, and the great majority of them hope that their findings ultimately will be translated into public policy. Even though definitive findings are still far from our grasp, as has been made clear by the debate presented in this volume, many world leaders already have sought to implement policies to correct the problem.

As the gaps between rich and poor grow wider throughout the world, the debate grows more heated. Discussions in international fora today are characterized by increasing intolerance, and terrorism has become a way of life in many parts of the world. It is hoped that this collection of studies along with the suggestions made in this concluding chapter will help, in some small way, to moderate tempers and guide thinking and research toward more productive answers to the important question of the causes and consequences of the gap between the rich and poor.

References

Booth, J. A., and M. A. Seligson. 1984. "The Political Culture of Authoritarianism in Mexico: A Reexamination." *Latin American Research Review* 1: 106–124.

Bornschier, V., C. Chase-Dunn, and R. Rubinson. 1978. "Cross-National Evidence of the Effects of Foreign Investment and Aid on Economic Growth and Inequality: A Survey of Findings and a Reanalysis." *American Journal of Sociology* 84 (November).

Cardoso, F. H. 1977. "The Consumption of Dependency Theory in the United States." *Latin American Research Review* 12, 3: 7–24.

Cardoso, F. H., and E. Faletto. 1979. *Dependency and Development in Latin America*. Berkeley: University of California Press.

Chudnowsky, D. 1974. *Empresas multinacionales y ganancias monopolicias en una economía latinoamericana*. Buenos Aires: Siglo XXI Editores.

Coatsworth, John H. 1993. "Notes on the Comparative Economic History of Latin America and the United States." In Walther L. Bernecker and Hans Werner Tobler, *Development and Underdevelopment in America: Contrasts of Economic Growth in North and Latin America in Historical Perspective*. Berlin: Walter de Gruyter.

Collier, D., ed. 1979. *The New Authoritarianism in Latin America*. Princeton, NJ: Princeton University Press.

Evans, P. 1979. *Dependent Development: The Alliance of Multinational, State, and Local Capital in Brazil*. Princeton, NJ: Princeton University Press.

Fukuyama, Francis. 1995a. "Social Capital and the Global Economy." *Foreign Affairs* 74 (September/October): 89–103.

———. 1995b. *Trust: The Social Virtues and the Creation of Prosperity*. New York: Free Press.

Glade, William. 1996. "Institutions and Inequality in Latin America: Text and Subtext." *Journal of Interamerican Studies and World Affairs* 38 (Summer/Fall): 159–179.

Harrison, Larry E., and Samuel P. Huntington. *Culture Matters: How Values Shape Human Progress*. New York: Basic, 2002.

Inglehart, R. 1990. *Culture Shift in Advanced Industrial Societies*. Princeton, NJ: Princeton University Press.

———. 1988. "The Renaissance of Political Culture." *American Political Science Review* 82 (December): 1203–1230.

Jackman, Robert W. 1982. "Dependency on Foreign Investment and Economic Growth in the Third World." *World Politics* 34 (January): 175–197.

Jackman, R. W., and R. A. Miller. 1996a. "The Poverty of Political Culture." *American Journal of Political Science* 40 (August): 697–717.

———. 1996b. "A Renaissance of Political Culture?" *American Journal of Political Science* 40, 3: 632–659.

Kravis, I., et al. 1982. *World Product and Income: International Comparisons of Real GDP*. Baltimore: Johns Hopkins University Press.

———. 1975. *A System of International Comparisons of Gross Product and Purchasing Power*. Baltimore: Johns Hopkins University Press.

Laitin, David D. 1982. "Capitalism and Hegemony: Yorubaland and the International Economy." *International Organization* 36 (Autumn): 687–714.

Moon, B. E. 1982. "Exchange Rate System, Policy Distortions, and the Maintenance of Trade Dependence." *International Organization* 36 (Autumn): 715–740.

Muller, Edward N. 1993. "Financial Dependence in the Capitalist World Economy and the Distribution of Income Within States." In Mitchell A. Seligson and John T Passé-Smith, *Development and Underdevelopment: The Political Economy of Inequality*. Boulder, CO: Lynne Rienner.

Newfarmer, Richard. 1980. *Transnational Conglomerates and the Economics of Dependent Development: A Case Study of the International Electrical Oligopoly and Brazil's Electrical Industry*. Greenwich, CT: JAI.

O'Donnell, Guillermo. 1973. *Modernization and Bureaucratic Authoritarianism: Studies in South American Politics*. Berkeley: Institute of International Studies of the University of California, Politics of Modernization Series No. 9.

Packenham, R. A. 1982. "Plus ça change . . . The English Edition of Cardoso and Faletto's Dependencia y Desarrollo en América Latina." *Latin American Research Review* 17, 1: 131–151.

Palma, G. 1981. "Dependency: A Formal Theory of Underdevelopment or a Methodology for the Analysis of Concrete Situations." In Paul Streetin and Richard Jolly, eds., *Recent Issues in World Development*. New York: Pergamon.

Ray, James L., and T. Webster. 1978. "Dependency and Economic Growth in Latin America." *International Studies Quarterly* 22 (September): 409–434.

Seligson, Mitchell A. "The Renaissance of Political Culture or the Renaissance of Ecological Fallacy." *Comparative Politics* 34 (2002): 273–292.

Seligson, Mitchell A., and J. A. Booth. 1993. "Political Culture and Regime Type: Evidence from Nicaragua and Costa Rica." *Journal of Politics* 55 (August): 777–792.

Weede, Erich, and H. Tiefenbach. 1981. "Some Recent Explanations of Income Inequality." *International Studies Quarterly* 25 (June): 255–282.

World Bank. 2003. *World Development Report, 2003*. New York: Oxford University Press.

———. 1995. *World Development Report, 1995*. New York: Oxford University Press.

———. 1980. *World Development Report, 1980*. New York: Oxford University Press.

APPENDIX:
BASIC INDICATORS OF THE
GAPS BETWEEN RICH
AND POOR COUNTRIES

	Gross National Income (GNI)[a] $ per Capita, 2005	PPP Gross National Income (GNI)[b] $ per Capita, 2005	Gross Domestic Product per Capita % Growth 2004–2005	Life Expectancy at Birth Male Years 2004	Life Expectancy at Birth Female Years 2004	Adult Literacy Rate (% ages 15 and older) 2000–2004	Survey Year for Income Inequality	Inequality Measures Refer to Distribution of Consumption Expenditures (c) or Incomes (y)*	Gini Index	90th/10th Percentile Ratio
Afghanistan	—j	—	—	—	—	28	—	—	—	—
Albania	2,580	5,420	4.9	71	77	99	2002	c	0.31	3.95
Algeria	2,730	6,770c	3.7	70	73	70	1995	c	0.35	—
American Samoa	—k	—	—	—	—	—	—	—	—	—
Andorra	—l	—	—	—	—	—	—	—	—	—
Angola	1,350	2,210c	11.5	40	43	67	—	—	—	—
Antigua and Barbuda	10,920	11,700	2.6	—	—	—	—	—	—	—
Argentina	4,470	13,920	8.2	71	79	97	2001	y	0.51	13.7
Armenia	1,470	5,060	14.4	68	75	99	2003	c	0.26	13.17
Aruba	—l	—	—	—	—	97	—	—	—	—
Australia	32,220	30,610	1.5	77	83	—	1994	y	0.32	4.88
Austria	36,980	33,140	1.4	76	82	—	1997	y	0.28	3.58
Azerbaijan	1,240	4,890	25.0	70	75	99	2001	c	0.36	4.62
Bahamas	—l	—	—	67	74	—	—	—	—	—
Bahrain	14,370	21,290	5.3	73	76	87	—	—	—	—
Bangladesh	470	2,090	3.5	63	64	—	2000	c	0.31	3.85
Barbados	—k	—	—	73	78	—	—	—	—	—
Belarus	2,760	7,890	9.8	63	74	100	2000	c	0.30	—
Belgium	35,700	32,640	0.7	76	82	—	2000	y	0.26	3.22
Belize	3,500	6,740	-0.2	69	74	—	—	—	—	—
Benin	510	1,110	0.7	54	55	35	2003	c	0.36	4.93
Bermuda	—l	—	—	—	—	—	—	—	—	—
Bhutan	870	—	3.3	36	65	—	—	—	—	—
Bolivia	1,010	2,740	2.1	62	67	87	2002	y	0.58	29.65

Bosnia and Herzegovina	2,440	7,790	5.4	72	77	97	1993	c	0.63	—
Botswana	5,180	10,250	4.0	62	35	81	2001	c	0.25	3.25
Brazil	3,460	8,230	0.9	67	75	89	2001	y	0.59	16.25
Brunei	—i	—	—	75	79	93	—		—	—
Bulgaria	3,450	8,630	5.8	69	76	98	2003	c	0.28	3.56
Burkina Faso	400	1,220c	1.6	47	49	22	2003	c	0.38	4.91
Burundi	100	640c	-2.6	43	45	59	1998	c	0.42	6.49
Cambodia	380	2,490c	5.0	53	60	74	1997	c	0.40	4.80
Cameroon	1,010	2,150	0.8	45	47	68	2001	c	0.45	—
Canada	32,600	32,220	2.0	77	83	—	2000	y	0.33	4.52
Cape Verde	1,870	6,000g	3.0	67	74	—	—		—	—
Cayman Islands	—i	—	—	—	—	—	—		—	—
Central African Republic	350	1,140c	0.9	39	40	49	1993	c	0.61	—
Chad	400	1,470	2.3	43	45	26	—		—	—
Channel Islands	—i	—	—	76	83	—	—		—	—
Chile	5,870	11,470	5.2	75	81	96	2000	y	0.51	10.72
China	1,740	6,600d	9.2	70	73	91	2001	c	0.45	—
Colombia	2,290	7,420c	3.6	70	76	93	1999	y	0.54	15.00
Comoros	640	2,000g	0.7	61	65	—	—		—	—
Congo, Dem. Rep.	120	720c	3.5	43	45	67	—		—	—
Congo, Rep.	950	810	6.0	51	54	—	—		—	—
Costa Rica	4,590	9,680c	2.3	76	81	95	2000	y	0.46	9.65
Côte d'Ivoire	840	1,490	-1.9	45	47	49	2002	c	0.45	6.75
Croatia	8,060	12,750	4.2	72	79	98	2001	c	0.29	—
Cuba	—n	—	—	75	79	100	—		—	—
Cyprus	16,510	22,230g	—	77	81	97	—		—	—
Czech Republic	10,710	20,140	6.2	73	79	—	1996	y	0.25	—
Denmark	47,390	33,570	2.8	75	80	—	1997	y	0.27	—
Djibouti	1,020	2,240g	1.4	52	54	—	—		—	—
Dominica	3,790	5,560	2.3	—	—	—	—		—	—
Dominican Republic	2,370	7,150c	3.0	64	71	87	1997	y	0.47	9.17
Ecuador	2,630	4,070	2.5	72	78	91	1998	y	0.54	16.09
Egypt, Arab Rep.	1,250	4,440	2.9	68	73	71	2000	c	0.34	—

continues

Appendix   continued

	Gross National Income (GNI)[a] $ per Capita, 2005	PPP Gross National Income (GNI)[b] $ per Capita, 2005	Gross Domestic Product per Capita % Growth 2004–2005	Life Expectancy at Birth Male Years 2004	Life Expectancy at Birth Female Years 2004	Adult Literacy Rate (% ages 15 and older) 2000–2004	Survey Year for Income Inequality	Inequality Measures Refer to Distribution of Consumption Expenditures (c) or Incomes (y)	Gini Index	90th/10th Percentile Ratio
El Salvador	2,450	5,120[c]	1.0	68	74	—	2002	y	0.50	15.88
Equatorial Guinea	—[k]	7,580[g]	—	42	43	87	—	—	—	—
Eritrea	220	1,010[c]	0.8	53	56	—	—	—	—	—
Estonia	9,100	15,420	10.1	66	77	100	1998	c	0.32	4.73
Ethiopia	160	1,000[c]	6.8	42	43	—	2000	c	0.30	3.34
Faeroe Islands	—[i]	—	—	—	—	—	—	—	—	—
Fiji	3,280	5,960	0.9	66	70	—	—	—	—	—
Finland	37,460	31,170	1.8	75	82	—	2000	y	0.25	3.12
France	34,810[e]	30,540	0.9	77	84	—	1994	y	0.31	—
French Polynesia	—[i]	—	—	71	76	—	—	—	—	—
Gabon	5,010	5,890	0.6	54	55	—	1998	c	0.48	6.11
Gambia	290	1,920[g]	2.2	55	58	—	2002	c	0.38	3.58
Georgia	1,350	3,270[e]	10.4	67	75	—	2000	y	0.28	7.30
Germany	34,580	29,210	0.9	76	81	—	1999	c	0.41	—
Ghana	450	2,370[c]	3.7	57	58	58	1998	c	0.36	—
Greece	19,670	23,620	3.4	77	81	96				
Greenland	—[i]	—	—	—	—	—	—	—	—	—
Grenada	3,920	7,260	0.2	—	—	—	—	—	—	—
Guam	—[i]	—	—	73	77	—	—	—	—	—
Guatemala	2,400	4,410[c]	0.8	64	71	69	2000	y	0.58	16.81
Guinea	370	2,240	0.8	54	54	29	2003	c	0.39	5.09

Guinea-Bissau	180	700	0.5	44	46	—	1993	c	0.40	—
Guyana	1,010	4,230ᵍ	-2.9	61	67	—	1998	y	0.45	—
Haiti	450	1,840ᶜ	0.5	51	53	—	2001	y	0.68	45.43
Honduras	1,190	2,900ᶜ	2.3	66	70	80	1999	y	0.52	11.72
Hong Kong, China	27,670	34,670	6.3	79	85	—	—	—	—	—
Hungary	10,030	16,940	4.3	69	77	—	2002	c	0.24	2.96
Iceland	46,320	34,760	4.5	78	82	—	—	—	—	—
India	720	3,460ᶜ	7.1	63	64	61	1999/2000	c	0.33	—
Indonesia	1,280	3,720	4.2	66	69	90	2000	c	0.34	—
Iran, Islamic Rep.	2,770	8,050	4.9	69	72	77	1998	c	0.43	—
Iraq	—ⁿ	—	—	—	—	74	—	—	—	—
Ireland	40,150	34,720	2.6	76	81	—	2000	y	0.31	4.27
Isle of Man	27,770	—	—	—	—	—	—	—	—	—
Israel	18,620	25,280	3.5	77	81	97	2001	c	0.35	4.90
Italy	30,010	28,840	0.2	77	83	98	2000	c	0.31	4.26
Jamaica	3,400	4,110	1.3	69	73	80	2001	c	0.42	5.90
Japan	38,980	31,410	2.6	78	85	—	1993	y	0.25	—
Jordan	2,500	5,280	4.5	70	73	90	2002	c	0.39	5.46
Kazakhstan	2,930	7,730	8.4	60	71	100	2003	c	0.30	3.88
Kenya	530	1,170	0.4	49	48	74	1997	c	0.44	6.56
Kiribati	1,390	—	-0.9	—	—	—	—	—	—	—
Korea, Dem. Rep.	—ʲ	—	—	61	67	—	—	—	—	—
Korea, Rep.	15,830	21,850	3.5	74	81	—	1998	y	0.32	—
Kuwait	24,040	24,010ᶜ	5.3	75	80	93	—	—	—	—
Kyrgyz Republic	440	1,870	-1.8	64	72	99	2002	c	0.29	3.63
Lao PDR	440	2,020	4.6	54	57	69	1997/1998	c	0.35	4.10
Latvia	6,760	13,480	10.8	66	78	100	1998	c	0.34	—
Lebanon	6,180	5,740	-0.0	70	75	—	—	—	—	—
Lesotho	960	3,410	1.4	35	37	82	1995	c	0.63	—
Liberia	130	—	3.9	42	43	—	—	—	—	—
Libya	5,530	—	1.5	72	77	—	—	—	—	—
Liechtenstein	—ˡ	—	—	—	—	—	—	—	—	—
Lithuania	7,050	14,220	8.0	66	78	100	2000	c	0.29	3.94

continues

Appendix continued

	Gross National Income (GNI)[a] $ per Capita, 2005	PPP Gross National Income (GNI)[b] $ per Capita, 2005	Gross Domestic Product per Capita % Growth 2004–2005	Life Expectancy at Birth Male Years 2004	Life Expectancy at Birth Female Years 2004	Adult Literacy Rate (% ages 15 and older) 2000–2004	Survey Year for Income Inequality	Inequality Measures Refer to Distribution of Consumption Expenditures (c) or Incomes (y)	Gini Index	90th/10th Percentile Ratio
Luxembourg	65,630	65,340	3.2	75	81	—	2000	y	0.29	3.92
Macao, China	—[i]	—	—	78	82	91	—	—	—	—
Macedonia, FYR	2,830	7,080	3.8	71	76	96	2003	c	0.36	5.60
Madagascar	290	880	1.8	54	57	71	2001	c	0.46	8.05
Malawi	160	650	0.4	40	40	64	1997/1998	c	0.50	—
Malaysia	4,960	10,320	3.4	71	76	89	1997	y	0.49	—
Maldives	2,390	—	-6.0	68	67	96	—	—	—	—
Mali	380	1,000	2.3	48	49	19	2001	c	0.39	5.81
Malta	13,590	18,960	1.8	77	81	88	—	—	—	—
Marshall Islands	2,930	—	0.2	—	—	—	—	—	—	—
Mauritania	560	2,150[c]	2.3	52	55	51	2000	c	0.38	5.92
Mauritius	5,260	12,450	3.4	69	76	84	—	—	—	—
Mayotte	—[k]	—	—	—	—	—	—	—	—	—
Mexico	7,310	10,030	1.9	73	78	91	2002	y	0.49	11.87
Micronesia, Fed. Sts.	2,300	—	-0.4	67	69	—	—	—	—	—
Moldova	880[f]	2,150	7.3	65	72	98	2001	c	0.36	—
Monaco	—[i]	—	—	—	—	—	—	—	—	—
Mongolia	690	2,190	4.6	62	68	98	1998	c	0.30	—
Morocco	1,730	4,360	0.4	68	72	52	1998	c	0.38	5.33
Mozambique	310	1,270[c]	5.7	41	42	90	1996/1997	c	39.60	—
Myanmar	—[j]	—	—	58	64	—	—	—	—	—
Namibia	2,990	7,910[c]	2.4	47	48	85	1993	c	70.70	—

Country										
Nepal	270	1,530	0.3	62	63	49	1996	c	0.36	4.54
Netherlands	36,620	32,480	0.8	76	81	—	1999	y	0.29	3.87
Netherlands Antilles	—	—	—	73	79	—	—	—	—	—
New Caledonia	—[l]	—	—	72	78	96	—	—	—	—
New Zealand	25,960	23,030	0.7	77	82	77	1997	y	0.37	—
Nicaragua	910	3,650	1.9	68	73	29	2001	c	0.40	6.52
Niger	240	800[c]	1.1	45	45	—	1995	c	0.51	—
Nigeria	560	1,040[c]	4.7	43	44	—	2003	c	0.41	7.26
Northern Mariana Islands	—[k]	—	—	—	—	—	—	—	—	—
Norway	59,590	40,420	1.7	78	82	—	2000	y	0.27	2.95
Oman	9,070	14,680	—	73	76	81	—	—	—	—
Pakistan	690	2,350	5.2	64	66	50	2001	c	0.27	3.09
Palau	7,630	—	4.5	—	—	—	—	—	—	—
Panama	4,630	7,310[c]	4.5	73	78	92	2000	c	0.55	18.65
Papua New Guinea	660	2,370[c]	1.0	55	57	57	—	—	—	—
Paraguay	1,280	4,970[c]	0.4	69	74	—	2001	y	0.55	18.26
Peru	2,610	5,830	5.1	68	73	88	2000	c	0.48	14.60
Philippines	1,300	5,300	3.3	69	73	93	2000	c	0.46	—
Poland	7,110	13,490	3.3	70	79	—	2002	c	0.31	4.03
Portugal	16,170	19,730	-0.2	74	81	—	1997	y	0.39	—
Puerto Rico	—[l]	—	—	74	—	—	—	—	—	—
Qatar	—[l]	—	—	72	76	89	—	—	—	—
Romania	3,830	8,940	4.4	68	75	97	2002	c	0.28	3.63
Russian Federation	4,460	10,640	6.9	59	72	99	2002	c	0.32	4.67
Rwanda	230	1,320	—	—	—	—	—	—	—	—
80[g]	4.8	67	73	—	—	—	—	—	—	—
San Marino	—[l]	—	—	—	—	—	—	—	—	—
São Tomé and Principe	390	—	0.7	62	64	79	—	—	—	—
Saudi Arabia	11,770	14,740[c]	3.9	70	74	39	—	—	—	—
Senegal	710	1,770[c]	3.7	55	57	96	1995	c	0.40	5.18
Serbia and Montenegro	3,280[g]	—	5.7	71	76	92	2003	c	0.28	3.60
Seychelles	8,290	15,940[g]	-3.3	—	—	—	—	—	—	—
Sierra Leone	220	780	3.8	40	43	35	—	—	—	—

continues

Appendix continued

	Gross National Income (GNI)[a] $ per Capita, 2005	PPP Gross National Income (GNI)[b] $ per Capita, 2005	Gross Domestic Product per Capita % Growth 2004–2005	Life Expectancy at Birth Male Years 2004	Life Expectancy at Birth Female Years 2004	Adult Literacy Rate (% ages 15 and older) 2000–2004	Survey Year for Income Inequality	Inequality Measures Refer to Distribution of Consumption Expenditures (c) or Incomes (y)	Gini Index	90th/10th Percentile Ratio
Singapore	27,490	29,780	3.7	77	81	93	—	—	—	—
Slovak Republic	7,950	15,760	5.9	70	78	100	1998	y	0.43	—
Slovenia	17,350	22,160	3.8	73	81	—	1996	y	0.26	—
Solomon Islands	590	1,880	1.8	62	63	—	—	—	—	—
Somalia	—j	—	—	46	48	—	—	—	—	—
South Africa	4,960	12,120c	5.6	44	45	82	1998	c	0.28	16.91
Spain	25,360	25,820	1.7	77	84	—	2000	c	0.58	4.74
Sri Lanka	1,160	4,520	4.4	72	77	91	2000	y	0.35	—
St. Kitts and Nevis	8,210	12,500	2.7	—	—	—	—	—	—	—
St. Lucia	4,800	5,980	3.9	72	75	—	2002	c	0.38	4.98
St. Vincent and the Grenadines	3,590	6,460	4.4	69	74	—	—	—	—	—
Sudan	640	2,000	5.9	55	58	61	1995	c	0.44	9.38
Suriname	2,540	—	4.5	66	73	90	—	—	—	—
Swaziland	2,280	5,190	0.8	43	42	80	—	—	—	—
Sweden	41,060	31,420	2.3	78	83	—	—	—	—	—
Switzerland	54,930	37,080	1.2	79	84	—	2000	y	0.25	3.18
Syrian Arab Republic	1,380	3,740	1.7	72	75	80	1992	y	0.31	—
Tajikistan	330	1,260	6.2	61	67	99	2000	c	0.24	2.86
Tanzania	340h	730	5.0	46	47	69	2003	c	0.32	4.08
Thailand	2,750	8,440	3.6	67	74	93	2001	c	0.35	4.89

Togo	350	1,550^c	0.2	53	57	53	2002	c	0.40	5.56
Tonga	2,190	8,040^g	2.0	71	74	99	—	—	—	—
Trinidad and Tobago	10,440	13,170	6.4	67	73	—	1992	c	0.39	6.24
Tunisia	2,890	7,900	3.3	71	75	74	2000	c	0.40	—
Turkey	4,710	8,420	6.0	69	71	87	2002	c	0.37	5.73
Turkmenistan	—^i	—	—	59	67	99	1998	c	0.41	—
Uganda	280	1,500^c	1.9	48	50	67	—	—	—	—
Ukraine	1,520	6,720	3.3	63	74	99	—	—	—	—
United Arab Emirates	23,770	24,090	—	77	81	—	—	—	—	—
United Kingdom	37,600	32,690	1.2	76	81	—	1999	y	0.29	—
United States	43,740	41,950	2.5	75	80	—	1999	y	0.34	5.00
Uruguay	4,360	9,810	5.8	72	79	—	2000	y	0.38	6.30
Uzbekistan	510	2,020	5.5	64	70	—	2000	y	0.43	7.73
Vanuatu	1,600	3,170^g	4.8	67	71	74	—	—	—	—
Venezuela, RB	4,810	6,440	7.5	71	77	93	2000	c	0.27	—
Vietnam	620	3,010	7.4	68	73	90	2000	y	0.42	7.94
Virgin Islands (U.S.)	—^i	—	—	76	81	—	—	—	—	—
West Bank and Gaza	1,120	—	—	71	75	92	2002	c	0.35	4.73
Yemen, Rep.	600	920	1.0	60	63	68	—	—	—	—
Zambia	490	950	3.4	39	38	—	1998	c	0.33	4.56
Zimbabwe	340	1,940	-7.6	38	37	—	1998	c	0.53	—
World	6,987	9,420	2.4	65	69	80	—	—	—	—
Low-income	580	2,486	5.6	58	60	62	—	—	—	—
Middle-income	2,640	7,195	5.4	68	73	90	—	—	—	—
Lower-middle-income	1,918	6,313	5.9	68	73	89	—	—	—	—
Upper-middle-income	5,625	10,924	5.0	66	73	94	—	—	—	—
Low- and middle-income	1,746	5,151	5.2	63	67	80	—	—	—	—
East Asia and Pacific	1,627	5,914	7.8	68	72	91	—	—	—	—
Europe and Central Asia	4,113	9,142	5.9	64	73	97	—	—	—	—
Latin America and Caribbean	4,008	8,111	3.1	69	75	90	—	—	—	—
Middle East and North Africa	2,241	6,076	2.8	68	71	72	—	—	—	—
South Asia	684	3,142	6.4	63	64	60	—	—	—	—

continues

Appendix continued

	Gross National Income (GNI)[a] $ per Capita, 2005	PPP Gross National Income (GNI)[b] $ per Capita, 2005	Gross Domestic Product per Capita % Growth 2004–2005	Life Expectancy at Birth		Adult Literacy Rate (% ages 15 and older) 2000–2004	Survey Year for Income Inequality	Inequality Measures Refer to Distribution of Consumption Expenditures (c) or Incomes (y)	Gini Index	90th/10th Percentile Ratio
				Male Years 2004	Female Years 2004					
Sub-Saharan Africa	745	1,981	3.1	46	47	—	—	—	—	—
High-income	35,131	32,524	2.1	76	82	—	—	—	—	—

Sources: World Bank, *World Development Report, 2007* (Washington, DC: World Bank, 2007), table 1, pp. 288, 289, 298; and *World Development Report, 2006* (Washington, DC: World Bank, 2006), table A2, pp. 281, 282.

Notes: Figures in italics are for years other than those specified.

— denotes no data.

c in this column indicates that the inequality measures refer to a distribution of consumption expenditures; *y* indicates that the inequality measures refer to a distribution of incomes.

a. Calculated using the World Bank Atlas method.

b. PPP is purchasing power parity.

c. The estimate is based on regression; others are extrapolated from the latest International Comparison Program benchmark estimates.

d. Based on a 1986 bilateral comparison of China and the United States employing a different methodology than that used for other countries. See Ren Ruoen and Chen Kai, "China's GDP in US Dollars Based on Purchasing Power Parities," *Policy Research Working Paper 1415* (Washington, DC: World Bank, 1995).

e. GNI and GNI per capita estimates include the French overseas departments of French Guiana, Guadeloupe, Martinique, and Réunion.

f. Excludes data for Transnistria.

g. Excludes data for Kosovo.

h. Data refer to mainland Tanzania only.

i. Estimated to be lower-middle-income ($876–$3,465).

j. Estimated to be low-income ($875 or less).

k. Estimated to be upper-middle-income ($3,466–$10,725).

l. Estimated to be high-income ($10,726 or more).

m. The estimate is based on regression; others are extrapolated from the latest International Comparison Program benchmark estimates.

n. Estimated to be lower-middle-income ($876–$3,465).

INDEX

ABOUT THE BOOK

THIS NEW EDITION OF *DEVELOPMENT AND UNDERDEVELOPMENT* RETAINS THE strongest contributions of the previous three editions but includes twelve new chapters that reflect the many seminal contributions made to the field in recent years. There are also two new sections: one addressing the historical origins of the gap between rich and poor countries, and another focusing on how globalization has affected the gap between countries and between the rich and poor within countries.

The editors' short introductions to each selection, highlighting its significance, remain a key feature of the book.

Mitchell A. Seligson is Centennial Professor of political science at Vanderbilt University. **John T Passé-Smith** is professor of political science at the University of Central Arkansas.